Union Learning

Canadian Labour Education in the Twentieth Century

Dedication

This book is dedicated, with love, to
Ursule, Nissa, Elise and Colin.

UNION LEARNING

Canadian Labour Education in the Twentieth Century

Jeffery Taylor

Athabasca University

TEP

THOMPSON EDUCATIONAL PUBLISHING, INC.

Toronto

Information on how to obtain copies of this book may be obtained from:

Web site: www.thompsonbooks.com
E-mail: publisher@thompsonbooks.com
Telephone: (416) 766-2763
Fax: (416) 766-0398

Canadian Cataloguing in Publication Data

Taylor, Jeffery M., 1953-

Union learning : Canadian labour education in the twentieth century

Includes bibliographical references and index.

ISBN 1-55077-117-5

1. Labor unions and education – Canada – History – 20th century.
2. Working class – Education – Canada – History – 20th century.
I. Title.

LC5054.T39 2001   374'.971   C00-932447-X

Copy Editing: Elizabeth Phinney
Cover Design: Elan Designs
Text Design: Danielle Baum

Every reasonable effort has been made to acquire permission for copyrighted materials used in this book and to acknowledge such permissions accurately. Any errors or omissions called to the publisher's attention will be corrected in future printings.

We acknowledge the support of the Government of Canada through the Book Publishing Industry Development Program for our publishing activities.

Printed in Canada.
1 2 3 4 5   06 05 04 03 02 01

Table of Contents

Acknowledgements

The research on which this book is based was supported by a standard research grant from the Social Sciences and Humanities Research Council of Canada. Research on telelearning, reported in chapter 6, is supported by the Telelearning NCE, which is part of the Network of Centres of Excellence programme funded by the Natural Sciences and Engineering Research Council of Canada, the Social Sciences and Humanities Research Council of Canada, the Canadian Institutes of Health Research and Industry Canada. The preparation of the final manuscript was aided by a President's Award for Research and Scholarly Excellence from Athabasca University.

Many archivists across the country assisted me in my quest for materials related to labour education. David Fraser at the National Archives of Canada was particularly helpful. And I am grateful to Keith Thompson and Elizabeth Phinney at Thompson Educational Publishing for their help in turning the manuscript into a book.

I have been fortunate to meet and work with a number of talented trade unionists over the past few years who have either provided support or aided me in crystallizing my ideas about labour education and training. These include Ursule Critoph, Winston Gereluk, Janet Dassinger, Gord Falconer, D'Arcy Martin and, at the Canadian Labour Congress, Lynn Carlile and Michael MacIsaac. And my old comrade Zenon Gawron provided both research assistance and advice throughout this project. Zenon also developed the multimedia content on the history of Canadian labour education that can be found at http:// unionlearning.athabascau.ca. I am, however, solely responsible for any errors of fact or interpretation.

List of Abbreviations

ACCL	All-Canadian Congress of Labour
ACWA	Amalgamated Clothing Workers of America
ADC	Atlantic Development Council
AERC	University of British Columbia's Adult Education Research Centre
AFL	American Federation of Labor
AFL-CIO	American Federation of Labor-Congress of Industrial Organizations
ADC	Atlantic Development Council
AIFLD	American Institute for Free Labor Development
AO	Archives of Ontario
ARLEC	Atlantic Region Labour Education Centre
BCFL	British Columbia Federation of Labour
BEST	Basic Education and Skills Training
Boilermakers	Boilermakers and Iron Shipbuilders Union
CAAE	Canadian Association for Adult Education
CAIMAW	Canadian Association of Industrial, Mechanical and Allied Workers
CANDLE	Canadian Network for Democratic Learning
CAW	Canadian Auto Workers
CBC	Canadian Broadcasting Corporation
CBRE	Canadian Brotherhood of Railway Employees & Other Transport Workers (called the CBRT after 1958)
CBRT	Canadian Brotherhood of Railway, Transport and General Workers (called the CBRE before 1958)
CCCL	Canadian and Catholic Confederation of Labour
CCF	Co-operative Commonwealth Federation
CCL	Canadian Congress of Labour
CCU	Confederation of Canadian Unions
CDAC	Curriculum Development Advisory Committee
CIDA	Canadian International Development Agency
CEP	Communication, Energy and Paperworkers Union
CIO	Committee for Industrial Organization (1935-38); Congress of Industrial Organizations (1938-1955)

CLC	Canadian Labour Congress
CLERA	Canadian Labour Education and Research Association
CNTU	Confederation of National Trade Unions
CPC	Communist Party of Canada
CRWS	Centre for Research on Work and Society
CSU	Canadian Seamen's Union
CUPE	Canadian Union of Public Employees
CUPW	Canadian Union of Postal Workers
CWA	Communication Workers of America
IAM	International Association of Machinists and Aerospace Workers
IATSE	International Alliance of Technical Stage Employees
IBEW	International Brotherhood of Electrical Workers
ICFTU	International Confederation of Free Trade Unions
ILGWU	International Ladies Garment Workers' Union
ILO	International Labour Organization
IUE	International Union of Electrical Workers
IWA	International Woodworkers of America
JLC	Jewish Labour Committee
LCC	Labour College of Canada
LESC	Labour Education and Studies Centre
LPP	Labour Progressive Party
LUDL	Local Union Discussion Leader
MFL	Manitoba Federation of Labour
Mine-Mill	International Union of Mine, Mill, and Smelter Workers
MLEC	Metro Toronto Labour Education Centre
MLI	Manitoba Labor Institute
NAC	National Archives of Canada
NEAC	National Education Advisory Committee (Canadian Labour Congress)
NFB	National Film Board
NDP	New Democratic Party
NLS	National Literacy Secretariat
NTP	National Training Programme
NUL	New Union Leader
NUPGE	National Union of Provincial Government Employees (to 1993)
	National Union of Public and General Employees (from 1993)
OBU	One Big Union
OFL	Ontario Federation of Labour
OISE	Ontario Institute for Studies in Education

PEL	Paid Educational Leave
PI	Programmed Instruction
PLAR	Prior Learning Assessment and Recognition
PSAC	Public Service Alliance of Canada
PWA	Provincial Workmen's Association
QFL	Quebec Federation of Labour
StFX	St. Francis Xavier University
SFU	Simon Fraser University
Steelworkers	United Steelworkers of America
SWOC	Steel Workers Organizing Committee
TLC	Trades and Labor Congress of Canada
TUC	Trades Union Congress
TWUA	Textile Workers Union of America
UAW	United Automobile Workers
UBC	University of British Columbia
UBCJA	United Brotherhood of Carpenters and Joiners of America
UE	United Electrical, Radio and Machine Workers
UFAW	United Fishermen and Allied Workers
UFCW	United Food and Commercial Workers
UMWA	United Mine Workers of America
UNITE	Union of Needletrades, Industrial and Textile Employees
UPWA	United Packinghouse Workers of America
URWA	United Rubber Workers of America
VDLC	Vancouver and District Labour Council
WEA	Workers' Educational Association
WEB	Workers' Education Bureau of America
WEST	Workers' Education for Skills Training
WIB	Wartime Information Board
WTS	Workplace Training Strategy (Canadian Labour Congress)
WUL	Workers Unity League

CHAPTER 1

Introduction

At the beginning of the twentieth-first century, over one hundred thousand Canadian workers participate annually in educational programmes conducted by their union or the broader labour organizations to which their unions belong. It is estimated that union-based education is the most significant non-vocational education available to working people. Walk into a unionized hotel with conference facilities anywhere in Canada on a Saturday or a Sunday and there's a reasonable chance that you will find labour education on the day's activity board. If you step into one of the workshops taking place in that hotel, or if you visit one of the labour movement's own educational facilities, such as the Canadian Auto Workers' Port Elgin Family Education Centre, you will witness a special type of adult education in which participants are engaged in learning primarily in order to contribute to the greater good of their union and the broader labour movement. Participants in a union education class are there for various reasons. They may be there as a result of having accepted a voluntary position, such as that of shop steward (workplace representative for their union); because of their membership on a union committee; because, as experienced union activists, they seek to deepen their understanding of labour issues, such as labour history or workplace harassment; or because they are learning to be peer instructors who will later teach and/or facilitate their own courses. Furthermore, you will see that the learning taking place in these sessions starts with the experiences of the participants and proceeds through active interaction between those experiences and the course material. If you accompanied these people back to their workplaces, you would observe the extent to which their one-to-five days of labour education has deepened their personal understanding of the relevant issues and, more importantly, has contributed to the welfare of their fellow workers.

People involved in labour education—whether they are course participants, course leaders, programme planners or elected union leaders who provide overall programme direction—know little about the history of this crucial area of union practice, however. Those most interested in the subject, such as the members of the Canadian Labour Congress's National Education Advisory Committee, might know bits and pieces of the history as a result of conversations with movement elders such as Larry Wagg, but they would be disappointed if they went searching for a written overview. Furthermore, most Canadians with an interest in adult learning don't know much about labour education, don't care about it, or just ignore it. But in the heyday of liberal adult education in the 1940s and 1950s, labour educators were among the leading adult educators and most adult educators recognized that labour education was an integral part of the adult education movement of the day. However, in the intervening years, beginning in the 1950s, adult education in general became more professionalized and individualized while labour education continued to keep alive the spirit of socially engaged education that was the dominant feature of the mid-century movement.

This volume seeks to uncover the heritage of Canadian labour education, to provide interested readers with a basic narrative of the subject and to offer an interpretation of its development. Little has been written about this aspect of Canada's history; labour historians have ignored education, while educational historians have ignored labour-related learning. Previous accounts have focused on the experience of the Workers' Educational Association (WEA), but other topics, such as the internal development of union education or the origins and growth of post-secondary labour studies programmes, have been left uninvestigated. What follows is a general history of labour education in English Canada from the WEA's founding in 1918 to the turn of the twenty-first century, with an emphasis on the years after 1940.

Given the dearth of literature in this area, this volume cannot offer a comprehensive history. There are gaps, and many topics are given only cursory treatment. Most notably, the focus is on Canada outside of Quebec, although the discussion touches on Quebec to some degree. As with other areas of Canadian history (including the closely related area of adult education), the Quebec experience is sufficiently different to merit a separate treatment. Others, I hope, will pursue further research in the area and expand, enhance and contradict what is written here.

The balance of this chapter is devoted to a discussion of basic concepts in labour education and to a brief historical overview of Canadian workers' education prior to 1918.

Chapters 2 and 3 cover the years from 1918 to 1956, chronicling the rise and decline of the WEA, describing the nature and range of union education prior to the formation of the Canadian Labour Congress (CLC) and illustrating the sporadic involvement of universities in labour education. While labour education was slow to develop during the first twenty years of this period, the growth of new industrial unions and increasing government involvement in industrial relations from the late 1930s onward meant that there was a need for trained union leaders and activists. The WEA initially provided much of this education, but its efforts were eclipsed by the development of internal union programmes beginning in the 1940s.

Chapter 4 traces the development of labour education from 1956 to 1972, including the programmes of individual unions, the CLC system of week-long and weekend schools and the Labour College of Canada. The permanent educational structures established by labour organizations during this period corresponded to a relatively stable period of capitalist development, marked by economic growth, low unemployment and a firm collective bargaining system in which labour had a legitimate legal standing. Although some links were made between labour organizations and universities, post-secondary educational institutions remained largely aloof from the labour movement until the 1970s.

Chapter 5 chronicles the impact on labour education of certain shifts that occurred during the 1970s and early 1980s. After 1972, governments and employers responded to international economic changes by pursuing policies and practices that eroded workers' incomes and attacked the limited workplace rights that had been won over the previous three decades. In addition, the face of labour changed, as women, public-sector workers and others made their presence felt within the movement. In addition, this chapter surveys the early years of the CLC's Labour Education and Studies Centre, which was financed with an unprecedented federal government grant. This chapter also charts the emergence of labour studies programmes in universities and community colleges, and the uneasy relationship that continued between trade unionists and the academy.

Chapter 6 covers the last fifteen years of the century, during which union educators began to rebuild a labour education movement that placed as much emphasis on organizing and mobilizing workers as on training activists for steward and leadership responsibilities. The scope of labour education also broadened as unions became more directly involved in workplace training. A number of collaborative initiatives with colleges and universities during the 1990s suggested that the historic divide between unions and post-secondary educational institutions might finally be closing.

Basic Concepts

Union education, labour studies, labour education and *workers' education* are terms that are used in North America to refer to various types of informal, non-formal and formal educational activity among members of the adult working class. The terms are often used interchangeably, leading to some confusion. Union education refers to educational programmes conducted by labour organizations (unions, federations, labour councils, congresses) for their members. Labour studies refers to post-secondary courses and programmes that focus on labour and the working class and includes subjects such as labour history, labour law and the sociology of work. Labour education encompasses union education, labour studies and other non-vocational courses and programmes offered for trade unionists by educational and other social institutions. Finally, the term workers' education includes non-vocational education for all workers, whether or not they are union members.

Informal, non-formal and *formal education,* meanwhile, are different forms of adult education. Informal education is the everyday learning that we all engage in from time to time. In the case of workers' education, for example, participating in collective bargaining or a strike (either as participant or observer) or simply experiencing a workplace as a waged or salaried worker can result in informal learning if, in the process, one acquires and retains some knowledge about the process or event. Or, alternatively, a group of workers talking about labour or workplace issues in an unstructured fashion is an example of informal workers' education. Narrower forms of adult education are what students of education call non-formal and formal education. The former refers to non-accredited education, such as short courses or lectures offered by various organizations. The structured programmes offered by labour organizations fall into this category as do non-credit labour courses and programmes offered by colleges and universities. The latter, meanwhile, refers to credit programmes offered by accredited educational institutions. Within workers' education, these are accredited labour studies programmes at colleges and universities.

Historically, workers' education encompassed all of the structured or semi-structured non-vocational learning that adult workers undertook. The term originated in the United Kingdom, where it can be traced back to the efforts of reform-spirited employers and professionals (lawyers, medical doctors and clergy, for example) to teach workers basic literacy and numeracy in the early years of industrial capitalism at the turn of the nineteenth century. By the early twentieth century, there was a workers' education movement in the United Kingdom providing liberal, non-vocational education (humanities, social science and cultural subjects) for members of the working class. The leadership of the movement was provided by a mix of employers, professionals and skilled workers who were motivated by the desire to ensure that workers improved their understanding of politics, society and economics. It was hoped that the workers would, as a result, exercise their civic responsibilities in a responsible way (which meant, at least in part, supporting electoral rather than revolutionary politics). The (British) Workers' Educational Association was formed in 1903 to organize the provision of this education through collaboration with universities. Dissidents in the movement, who supported "independent working class" education with a socialist perspective, eventually split from the WEA to form the Plebs League and the National Council of Labour Colleges. These organizations were completely under working-class control and free of employer and professional influence, including university collaboration.[1]

The workers' education movement in the United States dates from the Socialist Party's 1906 formation of the Rand School for Social Science in New York. In the spirit of the British Plebs League and the National Council of Labour Colleges, the Rand School was designed to provide workers with a critical liberal education that would equip them with the skills to build a new socialist society. The Rand School also provided educational services for the International Ladies Garment Workers' Union and the Amalgamated Clothing Workers of America until these unions established their own pioneering educational departments late in the 1910s. By the 1920s there was a flourishing workers' education movement in the United States, with a network of independent labour colleges operating across the country. The Affiliated Summer Schools of Women Workers in Industry and the Women's Trade Union Educational League attended to the specific educational needs of women workers, the Workers' Education Bureau of America ((WEB; formed in 1921) coordinated union-centred educational activities and a number of university extension services added workers' education to their programmes. All of the participants in the American workers' education movement of the early twentieth century agreed that the purpose of their endeavours was to contribute in some way to social action. University-based educators were closer to the British WEA in arguing that an objective assessment of subjects in the classroom would lead worker-participants to some type of undefined social activity, while those in the labour colleges and the unions maintained that the purpose of workers' education was to contribute to the creation of a new democratic, egalitarian and worker-friendly society.

The term *labor education* began to displace *workers' education* in the United States in the 1930s. In 1929 the American Federation of Labor (AFL) exerted its control over the WEB to ensure that trade union educational endeavours supported collective bargaining rather than attempts to change society. Moreover, the industrial organizing that flowed from the New Deal labour legislation created new mass labour organizations composed of members with no experience or understanding of the labour movement. The leaders, staff and rank-and-file activists in these new unions had to learn how to make their unions work and they had to understand the new legal environment in which they existed. Even though many of the leaders of the new industrial unions—in contrast to the AFL leadership—shared with the older workers' education movement a commitment to creating a new social order, their immediate educational need in the 1930s and 1940s was to get their unions up and running for the benefit of the union memberships. As a result, the dominant emphasis in the education of American workers shifted from a general workers' education to a union-centred labour education by the end of the Second World War.[2]

Canada had been influenced by the British example earlier in its history and by the American experience beginning in the 1930s. As will be documented in greater detail in the next chapter, the Canadian WEA (formed in 1918) began as a workers' education organization in the British mould and shifted by the 1940s to a hybrid of the British association (continuing the university connection), the American labour colleges and the emerging labour education of the new industrial unions. As the Canadian WEA's influence waned after 1950, education for Canadian workers followed the American pattern and shifted to union-centred education. Canada differed from the American example, however, in the extent to which unions relied on universities and colleges for their union education; Canadian unions were less likely to use the services of post-secondary institutions than were their American counterparts. In both countries, however, labour studies programmes grew from the late 1960s and early 1970s onward.

They were much more prolific south of the border, however, because of the more amiable relations there between the academy and the union hall.

This book is a history of Canadian labour education as understood by these definitions and by this brief history of the concept. While it is more accurate to use the term *workers' education* when writing about the early years of this history (prior to the early 1940s), I use the term *labour education* throughout for the sake of clarity and simplicity. With these definitions and this history in mind, let's look more closely at what labour education is about.

Union education and labour studies, though closely allied, have slightly different purposes that may occasionally conflict. Union education is concerned with educating union members to perform union functions and to support the goals and objectives of the union. The primary objectives of union education, however, may vary depending on the conditions facing the union. A union that is struggling to win collective bargaining rights in a tenuous legal environment—such as a North American industrial union of the 1930s or a black South African union of the 1970s and 1980s—may be most concerned with developing a group of activists committed to organizing workplaces in the face of hostile employers and governments. In these cases, education is mostly informal rather than non-formal, is geared to the basic needs of organizing, and is often linked, at least in a rudimentary way, to broader political questions. For a union that has won the legal right to bargain for a group of workers, and has therefore secured standing as a legitimate social organization in the eyes of the law—such as a North American industrial union of the 1940s or a South African union of the 1990s—the main educational objective is to train enough union activists to allow the union to function effectively in its collective bargaining role. At this point the union begins to establish some form of educational programme, with an emphasis on courses dealing with the various aspects of collective bargaining (shop steward training, bargaining, arbitration, labour law) and with establishing an effective union (parliamentary procedure, union administration, effective union committees). These *tools courses* are supplemented by *issues courses* such as labour history, economics and political action as the union becomes more established. tools & issues courses may work hand in hand

This distinction, while useful in identifying some important differences between these types of courses, may tend to suggest that mere training is happening in the tools courses while a more substantial education is taking place in the issues courses. In fact, most tools courses—historically and currently—contain significant treatment and discussion of a variety of issues related to the subject matter. Furthermore, the nature of the union will determine the degree to which broader issues are discussed in courses and the nature of those discussions. A union that is concerned only with servicing its membership through effective collective bargaining will focus on the nuts-and-bolts of bargaining and contract administration in all of its courses, while a union that has a broader social vision—perhaps, but not necessarily, related to support for a political party—will connect workplace issues to broader social, economic and political forces. A communist-led union, for example, might have an educational programme based on Marxist social analysis, while a union with a leadership professing political neutrality might limit its education to the techniques of collective bargaining and union administration, supplemented by some discussion of broader issues based on liberal social science.

All union education, regardless of its political orientation, is characterized by a commitment to the development and furthering of the union's organizational goals and the objectives of the labour movement. These may range from ensuring that collective agreements are negotiated and enforced to supporting the labour movement's wider political and social agenda, which may mean supporting a moderate political party, supporting a revolutionary party or working with other social groups to pursue a common agenda. Whatever the objectives and goals, union activity is determined from the outset by the subordinate position that workers and their unions occupy in workplaces and society. This means that union activity—including union educational activity—is about challenging the dominant power of employers and their supporters on the one hand, and building worker and union capacity on the other.

Within this context, there may be some room for instructors and participants to openly debate questions, but ultimately the educational programme and the course content are determined by the internal political dynamics of the union or other labour organization that is sponsoring the programme. Formally, most unions are democratically controlled, which means that union education is determined ultimately by the policies established by the duly constituted policy-making bodies of the organization. Informally, union education is subject to the rough-and-tumble politics that characterizes the labour movement. A union educator has to keep in mind the various political currents in the union, the immediate political context of a particular course or programme and, most important, the views of the union leadership who determine whether or not the educator has a job. Furthermore, the participants in union education programmes are not simply members of an organization being trained for better organizational effectiveness (though they are partly that), but are workers and union activists (or potential activists) with their own views and experiences. Historical and union context and the course facilitator determine the degree to which these are honoured and incorporated into the courses. As Australian educator Michael Newman has noted, union education consists of three contracts or relationships: one between the union and the educator, one between the union and the participant and one between the educator and the participant.[3]

Labour studies—labour education conducted in post-secondary educational institutions—differs from union education in that community colleges and universities exist to deliver a range of educational goods to people and, especially in the case of universities, to conduct basic research in the pursuit of knowledge. Furthermore, labour studies in these institutions is committed formally to impartial, open and critical education about labour in society while union education, in contrast, is explicitly committed to pursuing the specific goals of unions and the more general goals of the labour movement. Community colleges, with a more applied mandate than universities, may offer labour studies programmes because they view the labour movement as one constituency among many that they should serve or because unions are viewed as a potential market for the educational services that they offer. There are in fact two audiences for post-secondary labour studies. One is organized workers, who may enrol as individual students or as a result of a formal arrangement between their labour organization and a university or college. The other is composed of students who are not union members but who enrol in labour studies purely as a result of interest.

Needless to say, conflicts may arise between unions and post-secondary institutions over the purposes of labour education. Canadian unions, in comparison with unions in the United States and the United Kingdom, for example, have made little use of post-secondary institutions to deliver their basic union education, largely because of a desire to ensure that control of the content and delivery remains in union hands. There has been more cooperation with respect to issues-type courses, such as labour history and labour law, which are similar in subject matter to the courses found in university- and college-based labour studies programmes. And many labour studies programmes have advisory committees composed of trade union representatives, who provide input into the nature and scope of the offerings. Regardless of the type of relationship that exists between unions and post-secondary institutions, conflicts arise over issues of control. Labour studies academics are normally committed to the labour movement and its values in a general way, and therefore these conflicts usually do not involve fundamental questions about the legitimacy or place of unions in workplaces and society (whereas in some other post-secondary programmes, such as industrial relations, students are more likely to encounter instructors and course materials that are hostile to trade unionism). Unions may want a particular point of view taught in a course or programme, however, whereas the labour-friendly academic staff may want the freedom to teach the material in an open and critical way without favouring one point of view over another in order to develop the critical capacity of the participants. For example, in teaching about workplace reorganization, the labour studies academic may want to introduce the participants to employer perspectives, the views of unions that are willing to participate with employers in workplace reorganization schemes and the perspective of unions that resist all employer-initiated reorganizations. The advisory committee member from the more militant union may object to one aspect of the course, whereas the advisory committee member from the less militant union may object to another part of the course.[4]

There are other types of non-formal education that are very close to labour education. Left-wing or labour-friendly political parties have historically conducted their own educational programmes that contain elements of labour or workers' education in that they focus on the place of labour and the working class in society. As important as these activities are, they are not labour education in this definition, although this book contains occasional references to political education of this type. Furthermore, there are a number of institutions that support labour education for a variety of reasons. Governments, for example, may have programmes from time to time to support the educational activities of unions and kindred organizations. Publicly funded broadcasters and film companies may also support labour education, as may voluntary organizations in the field of education, especially adult education. But to reiterate, labour education is education undertaken by labour organizations and educational institutions about labour and the working class, and the most important and substantial part of labour education consists of the efforts of labour organizations to acquaint their members with issues that affect them as trade unionists and workers.

Historical Background to 1918

Informal workers' education has been part of the Canadian labour movement since the first significant stirrings of union organization in the early nineteenth century. Canada's first unions were local, city-based initiatives on the part of skilled and established journeymen craftworkers to protect their particular crafts against changes—such as wage reductions or apprenticeship erosion—that employers were beginning to introduce. These unions were organized around individual crafts. Carpenters, shoemakers and other trades each had their own union and membership was open only to skilled workers of the craft. By the 1830s and 1840s, local unions in a range of trades were a feature of cities and towns across British North America. Some of these early unions—notably the printers—used their collective strength to challenge employers. However, for the most part they served, first, as benefit societies to assist members through difficulties such as illness or unemployment and, second, to defend and extol the glories and traditions of their particular craft. Craftworkers took tremendous pride in their work, which was reflected in the craft banners carried in parades and in the banquets and other celebrations that were held in honour of stonemasons, cabinetmakers and other trades. Union-based education originated in these social activities. As workers spent time with other workers reflecting on their crafts and the value of their work, the idea of workers organizing in pursuit of their interests began to take hold.

The most significant organizations in the early nineteenth century with a mandate to deliver workers' education were the mechanics' institutes, which developed outside of the emerging labour movement. The institutes were born in the United Kingdom during the early years of the Industrial Revolution and were imported to British North America during the 1830s. By 1895 there were 311 institutes in Ontario alone, with others in the Maritimes, Quebec and British Columbia. Though designed to provide skilled workers with scientific and technical background for their crafts, the institutes were founded and administered by employers and professionals who wanted to ensure that workers accepted rather than resisted the power relationships of the new industrial order. Workers were minority participants in the mechanics' institutes and resisted using them for the purposes intended by their founders. Nonetheless, it appears that some workers made use of the libraries, the course offerings and the lectures for their own purposes, and were critical at times of the employer and professional management of the institutes. By the end of the nineteenth century, the institute movement had subsided and many of the institute buildings became local libraries.

Canadian labour organizations expanded as Canada's industrial revolution took off after 1850, marked by the expansion of factory production and an increase in the number of wage workers. In the process, employers reorganized work in order to control job processes more effectively and to increase their profits. Workers responded to these employer incursions by revitalizing old unions and forming new ones. Older craft organizations, such as printers and carpenters, were joined by new occupations, such as machinists and locomotive engineers. What remained constant across these various unions was the notion that each craft should have its own union to defend its interests. All craftworkers were faced with dramatic changes in their livelihoods as employers attacked the very basis of their crafts by diluting apprenticeship requirements through the recruitment of untrained workers, lowering of wages and undermining the skill requirements for the craft by introducing new technology or by subdividing the work. Besides providing a mechanism to counter these employer offensives, unions offered craftworkers a means to retain a degree of dignity and respectability in an uncertain world. Indeed, craft unions used informal educational methods to cultivate alternative collective values to counter the individualist values that were promoted by employers and their supporters. National and international unions facilitated the exchange of information about craft conditions in various locales. Craftworkers, such as shoemakers in the Knights of St. Crispin, employed people to read or lecture to them while they worked. Some craft unions and trade assemblies (city- or town-based groupings of unions) organized lectures and lending libraries, with one printers' union having a thousand titles in its lending library in the 1860s and 1870s. And the first significant labour newspaper, the *Ontario Workman*, was launched in 1872.[5]

During the 1880s the Canadian working class produced its most significant mobilization of the nineteenth century. The Knights of Labor, born in Philadelphia in 1869, differed from craft unions in that it welcomed into its ranks all workers, regardless of skill, gender or ethnicity. The basic unit of organization was the assembly, and workers could join either a trade assembly (based on a specific craft) or a mixed assembly (including all workers in a given workplace or community). In 1886 there were about two hundred assemblies in Canada and between the 1880s and the 1900s a total of twice that many assemblies were formed in the country. While the earlier history of the labour movement in Canada had been characterized by craft-based organizations meant to defend specific groups of workers, the Knights were a social movement governed by a central ethos or ideology. They were concerned with protecting and enhancing the nobility of human labour in the face of the growing inequality and poverty that seemed to be features of the new industrial capitalist society. They countered these developments with a workers' vision in which human labour was respected through a system based on democracy and cooperation.

As a social movement the Knights placed particular emphasis on educating workers about the organization and its purposes. Assemblies sponsored guest lecturers and established reading rooms. Furthermore, a network of labour newspapers—with names like *Palladium of Labor*, *Trade Union Advocate*, and *Industrial News*—developed to spread the word about the "labor reform" that the Knights represented. Self-taught working-class "brainworkers" and labour journalists contributed pieces to these publications that criticized the idle rich who benefited from nineteenth-century society at the expense of the toiling masses and proposed how workers could right these wrongs by electing worker representatives to parliament and legislatures.

While the Knights of Labor was a feature of working-class life west of the Maritimes in the 1880s, its Nova Scotia counterpart was the Provincial Workmen's Association (PWA), founded in 1879. Primarily a miners' organization, with some members in other occupations, local PWA miners' branches struggled to retain worker control over coal-mining activity. The organization was also successful in pressuring the provincial government to improve the mine-inspection system, extend the vote to those living in company housing and require the certification of miners. Educationally, the PWA conducted schools for miners seeking competency certificates as managers or engineers. By the early twentieth century the majority of those holding these positions in Nova Scotia mines had received their training at PWA schools and, when a new system of technical education was introduced in 1907, the schools were integrated into it.

While the labour movement grew slowly and incrementally throughout the nineteenth century, the rapid demise of the Knights of Labor in the 1890s convinced many craftworkers that it was foolish to try to represent all workers, regardless of skill, and that they should concentrate on bread-and-butter issues rather than mounting a wide-ranging critique of industrial capitalism. Meanwhile, other workers, especially those in resource industries such as mining, sharpened the Knights' critique into an analysis of the place of workers in the economy and society that focused more closely on the role of the employing class and its control of government.

At the turn of the century Canadian craftworkers were able to take advantage of a new brand of unionism proffered by the AFL, founded in 1886. The AFL employed full-time organizers, including one in Canada, and built trade-based unions to match the power of the new corporate employers. These new organizations featured higher dues than previously, full-time officers and staff representatives, and greater central control over union resources such as strike funds. Furthermore, the purpose of these unions was to use the workplace power of skilled workers to establish long-term collective bargaining relationships with employers through written, legally binding contracts. Between 1899 and 1903, thousands of Canadian workers joined AFL unions as part of a massive organizing drive, and in 1902, AFL unions expelled from the Trades and Labor Congress (TLC; formed in 1886) all unions and locals that were not affiliated with international AFL craft unions. AFL unionism, while based on a craft exclusivism that ignored the mass of so-called unskilled and semi-skilled workers, did establish labour organizations as a permanent presence in Canadian society. The TLC met annually and provincial federations of labour were formed in Ontario in 1902, in British Columbia in 1910 and in Alberta in 1912. Community based labour councils were the sites of most inter-union activity as local activists met regularly to address a range of issues, including support for strikes and for labour political candidates. And these councils were the most likely venues for education among craft unionists in this period, notably in the form of weekly labour newspapers and through cultural and educational activities held at council-built labour temples. James Simpson, a Toronto labour politician, joined with other trade unionists in 1903 to launch the Labour Educational Association in support of their political activities. The association was then converted into an actual electoral vehicle to contest the 1917 federal election.

While craftworkers responded to the demise of the Knights by building better and more permanent craft unions, non-craftworkers in the resource and other industries where large groups of workers were concentrated embraced industrial unionism. The Industrial Workers of the World (IWW), formed in 1905, was the most significant industrial union prior to the First World War. The Wobblies, as they were known, believed in organizing all workers for the ultimate goal of toppling capitalism through a general strike and building a new democratic and egalitarian society. They rejected the AFL practice of signing collective agreements, arguing instead that workers always had the right to withdraw their labour. The typical Wobbly was a transient unskilled or semi-skilled worker in a general labouring job, such as construction, logging or farm work. The IWW developed a rich and extensive system of informal education, no doubt as a result of its commitment to a specific ideological position. Its literature was printed in several languages and informal courses in Marxist education were conducted in construction camps and union halls. Furthermore, Wobbly artists were noted for their creative use of cartoons and music to get their point across, often taking popular songs or cartoon strips of the day and changing them to contain a worker-friendly message (or, in their words, "to make more sense").[6]

At the same time that the Wobblies were using a variety of educational means to build independent working-class consciousness and organization among these groups of workers, Frontier College began its literacy and cultural-uplift work with the same constituency. Formed in 1901 as the Reading Camp Association, Frontier College was an employer and professional initiative to educate immigrant and working-class labourers in Canadian citizenship. Alfred Fitzpatrick, the college's founder and a proponent of the Protestant "social gospel" attempt to soften the edges of industrial capitalism, represented the compassionate and socially conscious side of Canada's professional class. He had a genuine interest in using education to improve the lot of itinerant workers building Canadian railways and toiling in logging camps. But Fitzpatrick and the other college leaders countered the socialist education provided by groups like the Wobblies with the message that these workers should integrate into Canadian society and accept reforms proposed by social gospellers that would ameliorate the worst features of industrial capitalism. In pursuing its mission, Frontier College established a system of labourer-teachers, who were normally male university students who lived and worked in the camps and conducted classes during available non-work time. The college claimed that as many as 50 percent of the workers in the more stable lumber camps attended classes, with participation falling to between 2 and 10 percent in the railway camps. At the peak of college activity in 1913, seventy-one teachers were working in camps. By 1919, more than six hundred male (and some female) teachers had gone through the Frontier College system.[7]

Outside of formal trade unions, but closer to them than institutions such as Frontier College, socialist parties carried on their own educational activities through informal means similar to those of the IWW. The Socialist Party of Canada (SPC), the most significant socialist group prior to 1911, embraced a Marxist analysis to explain that capitalist exploitation was the source of workers' ills, that the concentration of capitalist ownership was leading inevitably to class polarization and that a socialist future was inevitable. This analysis led SPC leaders to argue that unions were detrimental to the interests of workers in that they helped ameliorate the worst effects of capitalism and hence delayed the inevitable arrival of socialism. Other socialists, who eventually left the SPC in 1911 to form the Social Democratic Party of Canada (SDP), agreed that capitalism was the source of what was wrong with Canadian society, but they argued that reforms—including union activity—were possible without jeopardizing the long-term goal of socialism. Both the SDP and the SPC sponsored lectures, held indoor and outdoor meetings, distributed socialist literature and published party newspapers in a variety of languages.[8]

At the other end of the political spectrum, the Catholic Church began to take an interest in labour matters and the condition of the working class following Pope Leo XIII's 1891 encyclical, which held that workers in industrial societies had certain rights and that capital had certain responsibilities towards labour. The church in Quebec used this encyclical to intervene in industrial relations in the province, notably to counter the presumed socialist and materialist influence of the broader North American labour movement. Educationally, from 1900 onward, the archbishop of Montreal hosted an annual labour festival at Notre Dame cathedral so that Catholic workers could hear the Church's views on labour issues. A more systematic system of Catholic workers' education began in 1908 with the organization of workers' study circles, which by 1911 had become L'Ecole Social Populaire. L'Ecole was eclipsed in 1918 by the birth of the Cercle Leo XIII, another workers' education centre, which established a programme of studies to acquaint workers with the Church's position on contemporary labour problems and to deter Catholics from joining international unions. This and other activity in the first two decades of the twentieth century laid the groundwork for the 1921 founding of the Canadian and Catholic Confederation of Labour.[9]

At the end of the First World War the church in Quebec was beginning to establish some non-formal programmes for educating workers, but there was little comparable activity in English Canada. During the workers' revolt of 1919, there was scattered talk of creating labour colleges, but there is no evidence to suggest that anything developed from these ideas.[10] Rather, between the earliest stirrings of union activity in the early nineteenth century and the latter part of the second decade of the twentieth century, labour education was primarily informal and was conducted as part of wider labour activities, such as meetings, lectures and publications. In some cases, such as in the IWW, unions conducted sporadic short courses on specific topics, but these too were embedded in broader labour cultural activities. Non-working-class adult education institutions such as Frontier College developed more systematic programmes from the turn of the century, but there were no structured activities in unions or activities directed at trade unionists. This would change with the arrival in Canada of the Workers' Educational Association in 1918.

Notes

1. Brian Simon, "The Struggle for Hegemony," in Brian Simon, ed., *The Search for Enlightenment: The Working Class and Adult Education in the Twentieth Century* (London: Lawrence and Wishart, 1990), 15-70.

2. Richard E. Dwyer, *Introduction to Labor Education in the U.S.: An Annotated Bibliography* (Metuchen, N.J. & London: The Scarecrow Press, 1977); Stanley Aronowitz, "The New Labor Education: A Return to Ideology," in Steven H. London, Elvira R. Tarr, and Joseph F. Wilson, *The Re-education of the American Working Class* (Westport, Conn.: Greenwood Press, 1990), 21-34.

3. Michael Newman, *The Third Contract: Theory and Practice in Trade Union Training* (Sydney, Australia: Stewart Victor Publishing, 1993); D'Arcy Martin, *Thinking Union: Activism and Education in Canada's Labour Movement* (Toronto: Between the Lines, 1995); Bruce Spencer, "Workers' Education for the Twenty-First Century," in Sue M. Scott, Bruce Spencer, and Alan M. Thomas, eds., *Learning for Life: Canadian Readings in Adult Education* (Toronto: Thompson Educational Publishing Inc., 1998), 164-175; Linda Cooper, "From 'Rolling Mass Action' to 'RPL': the changing discourse of experience and learning in the South African labour movement," *Studies in Continuing Education* 20 (2): 143-157 (1998).

4. Bruce Spencer and Jeff Taylor, "Labour Education in Canada: a SoliNet Conference," *Labour/Le Travail* 34 (fall 1994): 217-237; Helmut J. Golatz, "Labor Studies: New Kid on Campus," *Labor Studies Journal* 2 (spring 1977).

5. Craig Heron, *The Canadian Labour Movement: A Short History,* 2d ed. (Toronto: James Lorimer and Company, 1996), 2-7, 11-14; Desmond Morton, *Working People: An Illustrated History of the Canadian Labour Movement,* 4th ed. (Montreal: McGill-Queen's University Press, 1998), 12-16, 19; Bryan Palmer, *Working Class Experience: Rethinking the History of Canadian Labour, 1800-1991,* 2d ed. (Toronto: McClelland and Stewart, 1992), 56-60; Harold Logan, *The History of Trade-Union Organization in Canada* (Chicago: University of Chicago Press, 1928), 7-14, 19; Nora Robins, "'Useful Education for the Workingman': The Montreal Mechanics' Institute, 1828-70," in Michael Welton, ed., *Knowledge for the People* (Toronto: OISE Press, 1987), 20-34; Ellen L. Ramsay, "Art and Industrial Society: The Role of the Toronto Mechanic's Institute in the Promotion of Art, 1831-1883," *Labour/Le Travail* 43 (spring 1999): 71-103; Bryan D. Palmer, *A Culture in Conflict: Skilled Workers and Industrial Capitalism in Hamilton, Ontario, 1860-1914* (Montreal: McGill-Queen's University Press, 1979), 49-52.

6. Heron, *The Canadian Labour Movement,* 23, 31-42; Morton, *Working People,* 40, 95-96; Palmer, *Working-Class Experience,* 111, 127-135, 187-188; Logan, *The History of Trade-Union Organization,* 113; Salvatore Salerno, *Red November, Black November: Culture and Community in the Industrial Workers of the World* (Albany: State University of New York Press, 1989).

7. George L. Cook, "Educational Justice for the Campmen: Alfred Fitzpatrick and the Foundation of Frontier College, 1899-1922," in Michael R. Welton, ed., *Knowledge for the People* (Toronto: OISE Press, 1987), 35-51; Bruce Spencer, *The Purpose of Adult Education: A Guide for Students* (Toronto: Thompson Educational Publishing, 1998), 31-32, 38.

8. Heron, *The Canadian Labour Movement,* 44-45; Palmer, *Working-Class Experience,* 180-186.

9. Logan, *The History of Trade-Union Organization,* 321-328.

10. "A 'Labour College' Project in Vancouver," in Gregory S. Kealey and Reg Whitaker, eds., *RCMP Security Bulletins: The Early Years, 1919-1929* (St. John's Nfld.: Canadian Committee on Labour History, 1994), 126-127.

CHAPTER 2

Building a Movement: 1918-1946

Canadian labour education grew from what was primarily a small group of university-based educators and trade union leaders in Toronto offering university-level evening classes in the 1920s to a wide range of educational activities, centred in the Workers' Educational Association (WEA), by 1946. During the 1930s, the WEA slowly expanded from its Toronto base to become a fledgling national organization. Some unions established minimal internal educational services and some university extension departments began to take labour education seriously. It was during the Second World War, however, that organized labour education became firmly established in Canada. The WEA played a central strategic and coordinating role, but the impetus was provided by the expansion of the labour movement. By the end of the war, a shaky and haphazard network of evening classes, study groups, weekend institutes, summer schools and visual education was in place, organized primarily by the WEA. The Canadian Congress of Labour (CCL) and individual unions, however, began to think seriously in this period about developing their own internal educational capacity, separate from the WEA, with significant implications for the future.

Context

Beginning in 1916, Canadian workers engaged in unprecedented organizing and resistance, culminating in the Winnipeg General Strike and other strikes during 1918-19. Across the country new groups of industrial, service-sector, minority-group and women workers were brought into labour's fold, and all workers pressed employers for wage gains and bargaining rights. With the crushing of the revolt in Winnipeg in 1919 and other actions over the next few years, however, employers and governments (and craft unions in some cases) collaborated to repress this new militancy. High levels of unemployment and underemployment in the two decades prior to 1940, and especially during the 1930s, ensured that employers continued to have the upper hand in deterring any signs of renewed worker resistance.

Nonetheless, there were four broad Canadian labour organizations (or labour centrals) by 1930. The first and largest was the craft-dominated Trades and Labor Congress (TLC). Second was the All-Canadian Congress of Labour (ACCL), founded in 1927 and composed of Canadian-based, nationalist unions of which the most important was the Canadian Brotherhood of Railway

Employees (CBRE). Third was the Quebec-based Canadian and Catholic Confederation of Labour (CCCL), formed in 1921 by the Catholic Church to provide Quebec workers with a Catholic alternative to American-based international unions. And fourth was the communist Workers' Unity League (WUL), founded in 1929 and dedicated to militant industrial unionism and socialist revolution. Besides these labour centrals that grouped together a number of unions, the numerous railway brotherhoods other than the CBRE remained aloof from any labour central until much later and there was a handful of One Big Union (OBU) locals in Winnipeg, which were formed during the workers' revolt of 1918-19 and survived the subsequent repression.

While a minority current in the Canadian labour movement, the WUL accounted for the most significant organizing and strike activity in the country during the early 1930s. Militant and dedicated activists organized new unions among miners, longshoremen, garment workers, loggers and others. In 1935, however, in response to a policy change on the part of the international communist movement, the WUL was disbanded and its activities were transferred back into existing labour organizations. Whereas for five years communists around the world had been instructed to build independent revolutionary organizations, they were now told by the Soviet-controlled Communist International to forge popular fronts in alliance with progressive individuals and organizations as part of the global struggle against a rising fascism. In the Canadian labour context, this meant dissolving independent communist unions and merging them with existing TLC unions.

Also in 1935, and more significant for the future of Canadian labour, American labour leaders such as John L. Lewis of the United Mine Workers of America (UMWA), who were impatient with the craft conservatism prevalent in the American Federation of Labor (AFL), formed the Committee for Industrial Organization (CIO) within the AFL to organize the legions of workers in mass production industries, such as auto, steel and rubber. Canadian supporters of industrial unionism, primarily communists who had been previously active in the WUL but were now stymied by a similar craft conservatism in the TLC, asked the CIO to extend its organizing efforts into Canada. As the Americans were too preoccupied with their own organizing to be of much assistance, the Canadian activists simply adopted the CIO name and began organizing industrial unions under the CIO banner. Canadian workers, with easy access to American media, were well aware of CIO organizing triumphs in such places as Flint, Michigan, (autoworkers) and Akron, Ohio (rubber workers). The first Canadian successes occurred in 1937 among autoworkers in Oshawa (despite strong opposition from the company and the provincial government), steelworkers in Sydney (where the formerly independent union joined the Steel Workers Organizing Committee), and garment workers in Montreal.

Even so, substantial organizing among industrial workers would have to wait until the economic revival that accompanied the Second World War, in contrast to the experience south of the border. The difference between American and

Canadian organizing successes was partly the result of the respective legal environments. After 1935 American workers and unions enjoyed the legal right to bargain collectively and to have their unions recognized and certified. In Canada, by comparison, some provinces introduced legislation during the late 1930s to encourage collective bargaining, but employers were not compelled to bargain with their employees so the legislation was worth little to real workers in real jobs.

AFL leaders had been reluctant participants in the formation of the CIO in 1935 and continued to believe in the craft organization of workers. As a result, in 1937 the American labour central expelled the CIO, which immediately re-established itself as the Congress of Industrial Organizations (CIO). Two years later, in the face of threats from its AFL big brother to the south, the craft-dominated TLC followed suit and expelled its industrial unions. In 1940 the CIO unions in Canada (Canadian locals of the United Autoworkers, United Steelworkers, United Electrical Workers and so on) merged with the thirteen-year-old ACCL to form the CCL as a labour central to rival the TLC.

Military recruitment and war-related production resulted in the virtual elimination of unemployment during the Second World War, and, in fact, labour shortages caused employers and governments to recruit new workers from the ranks of women and farmers. The government also introduced widespread economic planning to coordinate the war effort, including wage and price controls and the extension of the Industrial Disputes Investigation Act to all essential workers, which, among other things, made strike votes compulsory. Canadian workers took advantage of the tight labour market and the limited bargaining rights they enjoyed to push for union recognition and improvements to their wages and working conditions. In 1943 one in three union members were on strike, exceeding the number out in 1919. But Canadian employers continued to enjoy a labour-law environment in which governments merely "encouraged" them to bargain with their employees.

In 1944, however, increasing worker resistance coupled with the threat of rising political support for the social democratic and communist parties forced the federal government to pass order-in-council PC 1003 to incorporate the principle of compulsory collective bargaining in federal labour legislation. (In contrast to the situation during peacetime, during the war most Canadian workplaces were governed by federal labour-relations legislation under the federal government's emergency powers.) A labour relations board was established, which could certify a union as representing a given group of workers if it could prove it had majority support, compelling the employer to bargain with them. Union recognition strikes became a thing of the past and the new legal term *unfair labour practices* entered the trade union vocabulary. The conciliation process from the older *Industrial Disputes Investigation Act* was incorporated in the new legislation. Canadian workers now had a legal framework to pursue their workplace rights, and in the final years of the war they took advantage of it to win a number of first contracts with employers.

There were continuing and new problems inside the labour movement as well. The war-generated economic activity had some effect in dissolving the old barriers between craft and industrial unions, although significant divisions continued to exist along this faultline in places such as British Columbia. Craft unions, such as the International Association of Machinists and Aerospace Workers (IAM), the United Brotherhood of Carpenters and Joiners (UBCJA) and the International Brotherhood of Electrical Workers (IBEW), allowed some factory-based semi-skilled workers into their ranks while the still craft-dominated TLC included the industrial International Ladies Garment Workers' Union (ILGWU) and Canadian Seamen's Union (CSU) among its affiliates. The CCL's mix of American-based international unions, such as the United Steelworkers of America (Steelworkers), and Canadian nationalist unions such as the CBRE, meanwhile, produced some new frictions around issues of Canadian autonomy.

More important, however, was the tension between communists and social democrats in the CCL (this did not become a significant issue in the TLC until about 1950). Unions such as the Steelworkers (the Steel Workers Organizing Committee until 1942), the United Packinghouse Workers of America (UPWA) and the CBRE had a leadership that generally favoured a reformist agenda focusing on stable collective bargaining and (after 1943) electoral support for the Co-operative Commonwealth Federation (CCF). Unions such as the United Electrical, Radio and Machine Workers (UE), the International Woodworkers of America (IWA) and the International Union of Mine, Mill, and Smelter Workers (Mine-Mill), in contrast, were led by communists or by people with close ties to the (communist) Labour Progressive Party (LPP). And the leadership of the United Automobile Workers (UAW) tended to move with the dominant political winds in the union, which meant being closer to the communists than the social democrats until 1947. These political differences, which became increasingly significant in the latter years of the 1940s, were subdued during the war by common struggles for union recognition and first contracts and by a more-or-less general commitment to the war effort.[1]

Adult education, meanwhile, evolved from a range of discrete activities in the early twentieth century to a fledgling social movement under progressive leadership in the 1930s and 1940s. In the early decades of the century, adult education was conducted primarily through governmental or para-governmental institutions, such as school boards and universities; commercial colleges operating as businesses; organized religion, through Protestant denominations and the Catholic Church; voluntary religious, ethnic and other organizations; and the women's, farm and other movements.

Governments became increasingly involved in education from the mid-nineteenth century, first in elementary and secondary education and later in post-secondary and adult education. Faced with the perceived problems of crime and poverty, ethnic diversity through immigration, promoting "useful knowledge," unruly youthful behaviour and training future workers in the rhythms of factory work, the dominant business and professional groups in Canadian society fashioned public and compulsory educational systems for children and youth during the nineteenth century. By the early twentieth century some school boards in urban areas were providing evening classes primarily for white-collar and professional male adults. With funds provided under the federal *Technical Education Act* of 1919, technical schools were built and school-based evening and distance education courses were expanded. Commercial establishments offering education for a fee were a feature of Canadian society throughout the nineteenth century. Prior to the introduction of public, compulsory schooling for children and youth, they offered a range of educational services, but in the twentieth century they were limited to adult students.

Some universities, meanwhile, notably those with an agricultural mandate such as the provincial universities in western Canada, developed extension programmes beginning in the teens. In Manitoba, for example, agricultural societies and farmers' institutes were publicly funded voluntary organizations dating from the nineteenth century in which agricultural experts and successful farmers lectured farm men on proper agricultural technique. When the Manitoba Agricultural College opened in 1905, farmers' institutes were integrated into its system of rural extension, and women's institutes were added in 1911 as a means of providing home-economics training for farm women. Beginning in 1915 district representatives and home-demonstration agents—university-trained agricultural scientists and home economists—were employed to provide professional training and advice to farm women and men. This special educational focus on rural Canada revealed anxiety on the part of the dominant business and professional groups about the place of farm people in the social order. There were more rural than urban Canadians until 1921 and the various farm protest movements of the late nineteenth and early twentieth centuries suggested that farmers could be an unruly lot. Furthermore, since farmers were dispersed in thousands of production units across thousands of miles (in contrast to workers, the other group causing unease among the dominant groups in this period, who were concentrated to a large degree in industrial and other complexes), governments and universities were given special responsibilities to ensure that the farm population contributed maximum wealth to the economy (and those who controlled it) and, as much as possible, identified their interests with the business class rather than with the working class. Agricultural education was the most important element of university extension until after the Second World War.[2]

The Antigonish Movement, which has achieved the level of romantic myth in the history of Canadian adult education, was born in the extension department of St. Francis Xavier University (StFX) and should be understood as part of this larger history of agricultural extension. What marked the StFX experience as different, particularly in contrast to the secular universities of western Canada, was its Catholic orientation and especially the influence of Pope Leo XIII's 1891 encyclical asserting that capital should respect the dignity of human labour.

Within that context the StFX extension department staff organized cooperatives and attempted to empower farmers and fishers, as long as they did not use their newly found power to pose a serious or fundamental challenge to the institutions of capitalist society.[3] While university extension departments were born to serve an agricultural population, they slowly added other courses to their programmes. By the 1940s, extension departments such as those at the University of British Columbia and the University of Toronto were offering a variety of general interest and vocational courses for urban Canadians.

Churches were early providers of adult education in Canada, opening libraries and reading rooms, offering lectures and organizing cultural activities. The YMCA and YWCA—church-related voluntary organizations—were particularly active in adult education in the late nineteenth and early twentieth centuries, providing vocational training and general interest evening courses at their facilities across the country. Meanwhile, organizations formed to advance the interests of particular groups—such as women and farm organizations— included educational components in their broader activities. The farm women's movements, for example, conducted lectures, meetings and short courses as part of their campaign to improve the conditions of rural women in the context of the broader farm movement to challenge corporate control of the farm economy.[4]

In 1935 the Canadian Association for Adult Education (CAAE) was formed as the first umbrella group to attempt to coordinate the diverse activity in this field. The CAAE became increasingly activist during the Second World War, promoting a progressive agenda in which adult education was used to pursue goals of social justice and equality. This leftish direction on the part of the CAAE was partly a result of the organization's leadership, which made some conservative adult educators anxious, but it was also a reflection of the times in that the war effort resulted in a more activist government in a variety of areas, including radio and film, which adult educators were beginning to use.

Filmmaker John Grierson was recruited from the United Kingdom by the federal Liberal government in 1938 to survey Canada's film needs; a year later he was hired to run the new National Film Board (NFB). Grierson believed that documentary film, which he invented, could be used to educate workers and farmers about the social and economic forces shaping their lives and to motivate them to take collective action. He was willing to use the NFB's facilities to work with adult education groups who shared his interest in education for social action. The federal government recognized Grierson's skills as a filmmaker and as a potential wartime propagandist when they hired him to run the NFB and when they added the directorship of the Wartime Information Board (WIB) to his duties four years later.

The WIB and the NFB worked together to produce and distribute films to bolster support for the war among Canadians. One avenue was 35-millimetre feature films, such as the *Canada Carries On* series, which were distributed and shown commercially in movie theatres. Another medium was 16-millimetre shorts meant to be distributed and shown outside of theatres in social and community groups as part of educational programmes. Three main film circuits were organized during the war as part of this strategy. In 1942 rural circuits began to operate across the country to distribute these low-budget, non-commercial films in the countryside and to teach farmers and farm workers that their participation in the war effort was vital. These circuits had limited success as educational vehicles because they were eventually transformed by audience demand into sources of family and community entertainment. A year later industrial circuits were established to serve production workers in industrial areas. These circuits were linked directly with the government's efforts to increase war production through labour-management cooperation. Films were shown in workplaces with the cooperation and under the eye of employers. The third circuit was organized by the WEA for the Canadian labour movement, and will be discussed in greater detail later in this chapter.[5]

Meanwhile, the CAAE cooperated with the Canadian Broadcasting Corporation (CBC) during the war years to launch two innovative radio-based educational initiatives. National Farm Radio Forum began operation in 1940 and was designed to help rural Canadians discuss and debate a variety of political, social and economic issues. The forum worked as follows: Participants received a pamphlet by post on a specific topic. A week or so later a predetermined discussion group would gather in a home to listen to a CBC broadcast that was designed to raise questions and provoke discussion on the topic at hand. The group would then discuss the topic and the results of their deliberations would be recorded by a secretary and submitted to a provincial coordinating office. The submissions from the various groups were summarized at the beginning of the next forum broadcast. National Farm Radio Forum operated for twenty-five years, and at its peak in 1949-50 had 1,600 groups with 30,000 members participating across the country. Citizens' Forum operated on the same principle, but was designed for city and town dwellers. It was less popular than its country cousin, but nonetheless was on the air from 1943 to 1967.[6]

By the end of the Second World War it was possible to speak of a Canadian adult education movement. Its left-liberal and social democratic leaders believed that the various mechanisms of adult education could be used to build better communities and a better society through citizenship education. Labour educators, just beginning to become a coherent group themselves in this period, were able to cooperate with and take advantage of this movement to pursue their own objectives.

The WEA and Other Activity in the 1920s and 1930s

The WEA was established in 1918 in Toronto as a voluntary association governed by trade unionists, university professors and members of the public. Modelled on the parent British body formed in 1903, its purpose was to provide university-level education (notably in the humanities and social sciences) to working people. Albert Mansbridge, founder of the British WEA, believed that workers required education in order to be better citizens and for democracy to function properly. Founders of the Canadian WEA, such as Upper Canada College principal W.L. Grant and University of Toronto president Robert Falconer, endorsed this view and contributed their energies to the WEA in large part out of a belief that the working class required educational guidance to act responsibly. In the immediate aftermath of the First World War, with heightened labour militancy, responsible working-class behaviour for these people meant moderate union demands and a reform politics that did not fundamentally challenge the prevailing system.

Grant and other professional educators interested in establishing the WEA in Canada enlisted the help of trade unionists from the Toronto and District Labour Council. Alfred McGowan, in particular, a member of the International Typographical Union, was a WEA member and activist who promoted the organization among Toronto trade unionists during the 1920s. While trade unionists such as McGowan shared with Grant and others a belief in workers' education for citizenship, they also hoped that the WEA would provide workers with access to educational opportunities that were otherwise not available to them and that WEA courses would stress issues of social justice as well as issues of democracy.

The WEA model, inherited from the British parent and established in Ontario during the 1920s, involved collaboration between a local association and a university to provide non-credit, inexpensive evening classes to a working-class constituency. The local association was expected to raise funds, solicit individual memberships and union affiliations, establish an annual or semi-annual programme of courses, determine course fees, organize class venues, recruit students and generally do whatever administrative work was required to mount a successful programme of courses. The university collaborator, usually using government money granted to support the WEA, was expected to supply and reimburse tutors from among its academic staff. The tutors were chosen on the basis of their subject-matter expertise and their ability to present an objective account of their topic. In practice, however, WEA tutoring attracted academic staff with some sympathy for workers and unions. Instruction was at a university standard, including reading and written work, although the WEA model differed from the didactic university practice of the period in that association tutors were expected to divide their class time evenly between lecture and discussion. Nonetheless, the instructional model was that of the authoritative university expert dispensing knowledge to worker-students, albeit tempered by workers' perspectives in the discussion portion of the course.

The Toronto WEA was the only Canadian association until 1929. The University of Toronto provided tutors, who were paid initially out of a university grant and, after 1923, from an Ontario government grant held by the university and administered by its department of extension. During this period classes were held in Toronto and Hamilton on topics such as finance, civics, public speaking, english, literature, labour problems and industrial psychology. Throughout the 1920s the association struggled to increase memberships, particularly working-class and trade union memberships. By 1926 there were eight hundred class members enrolled, but only fifty of these were trade unionists.[7]

In an attempt to increase trade union participation, the association changed its policies in 1927 to allow local unions to affiliate with it and thereby have a direct voice in its affairs. Local unions would then be encouraged to canvass their members for class participants and to support those members with class scholarships. A further change in 1927 limited participation in WEA classes to manual workers. This change was initiated by W.J. Dunlop, the University of Toronto's Director of Extension, who resented the fact that many professional and other middle-class people were taking WEA classes rather than the more expensive, regular university extension classes. Dunlop's proposal was obviously self-serving, and it had a short-term negative effect on WEA enrolments. However, it was accepted by a majority of the Toronto WEA executive, either because they believed in principle that the WEA should serve a working-class constituency or they did not want a political battle with Dunlop, since he controlled the government grant that paid for WEA tutors.

As a result of a difference of opinion with Dunlop over this and other issues, Alfred McGowan resigned as district secretary of the Toronto WEA in 1927. McGowan was replaced by Drummond Wren, who had been active in the association for a number of years. A native of Scotland and a veteran of the First World War, Wren was employed by a business-press clipping service when he began taking WEA classes in the early 1920s. In his new position, Wren concentrated on expanding trade union participation in the WEA and on extending the association's work beyond the Toronto and Hamilton areas. By 1930, when the WEA of Ontario was formed, there were ten local associations in Ontario, including Windsor, London and Hamilton, as well as Toronto. By 1932 there were forty-five labour organizations affiliated with local associations, including eight trades and labour councils, and in that year the WEA was invited for the first time in its history to participate in a TLC convention.[8]

Wren's ability to do organizing work during the 1930s was aided substantially by a series of grants from the Carnegie Corporation of New York. The first grant, for $5,000 in 1930, was used primarily to hire Wren as full-time general secretary during the year. The association received a further $5,000 for 1931. In 1932, however, the Carnegie Corporation suspended its grants for workers' education in the British Dominions pending a report on the subject by C.O.G. Douie from the United Kingdom. Douie surveyed the situation in Australia, New Zealand, South Africa and Canada, and concluded that workers' education was prospering in Ontario. As a result, in 1934 the WEA received a further $12,500 in Carnegie money, which was sufficient to cover Wren's salary for four more years.[9] With this temporary financial security, Wren strengthened the Ontario network and, at mid-decade, began organizing outside of the province.

The centrepiece of the WEA system in the 1930s was the district association's organizing of evening classes (and occasionally afternoon classes for shift workers) in collaboration with universities. By the end of the 1930s there were forty-two district associations in Ontario, Nova Scotia, Quebec, Manitoba, Alberta and British Columbia. Toronto and Hamilton remained the most active centres. Toronto offered as many as twenty courses a season and, from 1935, experimented with a three-year programme of evening classes in economics. In 1938 there were a total of 1,851 enrolments in fifty-nine regular tutorial classes across the country, and about one-third of these class enrolments were female. In Ontario, most tutors were from the University of Toronto, although professors from Queen's University in Kingston, the University of Western Ontario in London and McMaster University in Hamilton also served as tutors. Outside of Ontario, tutorial arrangements were made with Dalhousie University in Nova Scotia, McGill University in Quebec, the University of Manitoba and the University of Alberta.[10]

This model worked reasonably well in a city such as Toronto, which had a comparatively large pool of professors to draw upon, but in smaller centres it was less successful. In some cases, and with mixed results, local associations hired non-university tutors because of a lack of suitable university-based candidates. Moreover, in many areas there were not enough prospective students to justify hiring a tutor. In these situations, study circles were formed in which a small group of people met under the direction of a local voluntary group leader to study and discuss materials made available by the WEA. During the 1930s these materials usually came from *The Link*. This association periodical contained articles by academic supporters of the British WEA, such as G.D.H. Cole and R.H. Tawney, as well as contributions from Canadian writers.[11]

Study circles developed out of radio broadcasts and agricultural study clubs in the first half of the 1930s. To meet a demand from Ontario farmers for educational services, Wren organized "Agricola Study Clubs" in various parts of the province and supplied them with written bulletins to discuss and debate. This was supplemented, from 1934, by fifteen-minute, weekly WEA radio broadcasts from Toronto, which Agricola members could listen to and incorporate into their club discussions. The Agricola and radio broadcast experiences, coupled with the growing belief that there were circumstances where regular classes were not feasible, led Wren and others to reflect on how the study circle method might enhance their educational work. They knew about Scandinavian experiences with study circles and the British WEA's and National Council of Labour College's use of postal courses, and became convinced that similar techniques were well suited to Canadian conditions.

The study circle system took shape in the latter half of the decade. A booklet on the history and practice of trade unionism was developed specifically for study circle use and was supplemented by a series of bulletins on various topics including cooperation, economics and psychology. In 1938 there were about seven hundred people enrolled in study circles in seven provinces. Furthermore, the CBC provided the WEA with national-network facilities for a series of labour-related programmes from 1937 to 1939, which were aligned with study circles as much as possible. These weekly, half-hour programmes were more sophisticated educationally than the earlier Ontario-only series, in part because of the greater amount of national broadcast time available for each subject. Each week there was a fifteen-minute talk by one speaker, followed by another speaker who served as a discussion leader for three or four other discussants on the broadcast. This group of six or so was trained by the WEA in discussion techniques. Each broadcast also included an audience of about twenty members who were allowed to interject questions and comments.

The association also organized a women's auxiliary and classes for the unemployed during the 1930s. Tuition was waived for the unemployed, and for those lacking basic literacy and numeracy skills, the Unemployed Educational Association was formed in 1931. Besides organizing and providing domestic support for social events, members of the WEA Women's Auxiliary were addressed by speakers on issues of particular concern to women and raised money to send women trade unionists to the Bryn-Mawr (women's) Summer School in the United States.[12]

Study circles, radio broadcasts, unemployed work and summer schools marked a series of modifications to the tutorial method, which remained the centrepiece of the WEA system. These changes were motivated in large part by the need to develop teaching techniques that were appropriate for adult and working-class learners. While the tutorial method had a significant place in the system, it was clear that other pieces had to be in place as well. Broader changes in the labour movement during the 1930s were also important in changing the orientation of the WEA. The Canadian and United States labour movements were transformed during the 1930s and 1940s with the unionization of mass production industries, such as auto, rubber, electrical and steel. By the late 1930s, WEA overtures to unions to affiliate and use the facilities of the association were met by requests from new industrial unions for assistance in educating their newly organized memberships. In 1938, for example, the association conducted a series of weekend schools on group leadership for the United Rubber Workers of America (URWA; twenty-eight men and three women); a week-long labour history and sociology course for the UAW (fifty-nine men and six women); and English, public-speaking and labour-problems courses for the older ILGWU (eighty members). The new organizing provided opportunities for the WEA, but it was also a potential source of tension between the view that the primary purpose of the association was to provide workers with objective knowledge at a university standard and the desire to serve the educational interests of workers and unions in general.

The following is a quote from the 1932 report of the St. Francis Xavier University Extension Department:

The Extension Department began its work in September 1930. 179 study clubs were organized in the past two years. A start was made last winter in the mining centres of eastern Nova Scotia. Owing to the depression it was thought wise to go slowly in this field. 11 study groups were organized in the Glace Bay area. Many people in this area had been indoctrinated with the revolutionary philosophy of Russia and this fact makes the work of the Extension Department all the more difficult. The work of the department would be a great antidote to this extreme radicalism.... The department has already succeeded in enlisting the co-operation of men who at one time were avowed communists but who have lately returned to a saner way of thinking.

Source: St. Francis Xavier University Archives, *St. Francis Xavier University Extension Department Papers*, "1932, Report of the Work of the St. Francis Xavier University Extension Department."

Virtually all university participation in labour education during the 1930s was in collaboration with the WEA. The one exception to this pattern was StFX in Antigonish, Nova Scotia. During the 1920s, StFX's Catholic management was concerned about the depth of commitment that Cape Breton's Catholic industrial workers showed to the local communist leadership of the UMWA. Following the 1928 establishment of StFX's extension department, which was designed primarily to serve the educational needs of Catholic farmers and fishers in eastern Nova Scotia, a branch office of the department was opened in Glace Bay during 1932 specifically to do educational work among the region's industrial working class. Using funds from the Carnegie Corporation, as well as its own internal resources, the university established eleven study clubs in 1932 for coal miners and steelworkers in labour economics, consumer cooperation and other subjects. Over the following few years, about two hundred men were taught labour economics in tutorial classes. The extension department was also instrumental in organizing credit unions, cooperatives, housing groups and other community projects among industrial workers on Cape Breton Island during the decade. In this varied activity the Antigonish Movement's study group method of adult education, which was developed and refined at StFX during the 1920s and 1930s, was used to deliver anti-communist Catholic messages about the place of labour in capitalist society in an attempt to win workers back to, and keep them in, the fold of the church.[13]

Undoubtedly the most important organized labour education in Canada during the 1930s was provided or facilitated by the WEA. Some unions, however, were beginning to develop their own internal educational capacity. The most important of these was the ILGWU. This union was a pioneer in North American labour education, establishing an international education department in 1917. During the 1920s and 1930s the union developed an impressive educational programme in the United States, stressing language instruction and recreational activities as well as tools training and worker-centred liberal education. The ILGWU's activity in Canada was less extensive than in the United States, but during the 1930s, the union's locals in Montreal had an educational and recreational director on staff who ran a programme that was strong on recreation with some educational content. The union also cooperated with the WEA to offer courses in both Toronto and Montreal.[14]

Some of the new industrial unions began to create educational capacity soon after they were formed. The UAW, for example, at its founding convention in 1936, established an international education fund as suggested by Tucker Smith, Merlin Bishop and Roy Reuther. Smith was the director of Brookwood Labor College, a full-time residential workers' college that existed from 1921 until 1937. Brookwood was the leading institution in the flourishing autonomous labour education movement in the United States during this period. Many labour activists and educators who were involved in organizing and staffing the new industrial unions of the 1930s and 1940s were alumni of Brookwood or other labour colleges. Bishop and Reuther were Brookwood graduates who, in 1936, were working among Michigan autoworkers for the Works Progress Administration's workers' education programme. Smith and the UAW agreed that Brookwood would pay half the salary of the union's education director, providing that the candidate was acceptable to Brookwood as well as to the UAW. Bishop became the first UAW education director in 1936, but lost his job a year later when Homer Martin became UAW president. In 1938, meanwhile, the Canadian region of the UAW signalled its intention to use the WEA for its educational services.[15]

WEA-Centred Labour Education: 1939-1946

During the Second World War the WEA reached the pinnacle of its educational endeavours. It continued to organize tutorial classes, but for a variety of reasons, the association's focus shifted to other areas. Radio and film were added to its activities through alliances with the CBC and the NFB. Its research capacity was deepened to serve the expanding needs of the labour movement for assistance in dealing with the new wartime industrial relations machinery. And association activists came to realize that, in order to meet the educational needs of newly organized workers, a mass education strategy that included visual education, short training institutes, radio, film, discussion groups and study circles, as well as university-level classes, had to be implemented. As systematic as this strategy appears in hindsight, in practice it was stitched together piece by piece, and was subject to the vagaries of various funders and the shifting political and institutional currents in the labour movement. Nevertheless, by the end of the war an impressive, if shaky, WEA system of labour education was in place.

WEA funding in this period was cobbled together from a variety of sources. The $12,500 Carnegie Corporation grant the association received in 1934 to support Wren was renewed at $9,000 in 1938 and at $5,000 in 1942. This was

revenue for WEA

sufficient to pay Wren until the beginning of 1944, at which time he became education director of the UAW's Canadian region and shifted to the voluntary general secretaryship of the WEA. Additional Carnegie grants were received in 1939 for visual education ($6,000) and in 1942 for research ($900 annually for at least two years). Five thousand dollars from the federal government in 1940 allowed Wren to do some national organizing. A raffle for a house raised $20,000, money raised by a community committee for the war effort which was not needed for that purpose yielded $6,000, and donations from four industrialists added $4,000 to the association's coffers during the war years. Affiliation fees were another source of income. Union locals were encouraged to affiliate with the association for a variety of services, including evening classes, visual education and research bulletins and periodicals. An annual per capita fee of five cents allowed a local to purchase association materials at a reduced cost. Wren claimed in 1946 that 75,000 of the 200,000 trade unionists in Ontario were affiliated with the WEA. Furthermore, provincial and university grants supported classroom teaching, while film and radio budgets supported those endeavours. Finally, there were incidental receipts from literature sales, film rentals and the like.[16]

There were three formal levels in the WEA during this period: the national, Ontario and local associations. The national organization was responsible for pan-Canadian organizing, the visual education programme and research initiatives, which had impacts beyond the reaches of (southern) Ontario. The Ontario organization looked after such things as establishing local associations to conduct evening classes, conducting weekend or longer labour institutes and establishing and running the summer schools. The local association activities varied depending upon locale. Most associations concentrated on organizing evening classes, liasing with the local university and soliciting union affiliations. Local associations outside of Ontario, such as the one in Winnipeg, also liased with the provincial government regarding funding. And the Vancouver association, located as it was in the area with the most significant and concentrated union activity outside of southern Ontario, did a little bit of everything. In practice, too, the activities of the national, Ontario and Toronto organizations overlapped and were indistinct as they were all run out of the same downtown Toronto office.

The WEA had used some of the Carnegie money in the 1930s to establish a fledgling research and legal-service infrastructure to complement the direct teaching that it was doing. An Industrial Law Research Council, composed of academics, lawyers and trade unionists, was formed in Toronto in 1935 to provide legal research and seminars for trade unionists.[17] After 1939 this research capacity was deepened. Unions were confronted with various pieces of wartime labour legislation and they required assistance in understanding the legislation and using the regulatory machinery that accompanied it. Following the passage of order-in-council PC 2685, for example, the association prepared materials explaining the purpose of the legislation and clarifying how it provided labour with the legal right to organize. Bora Laskin, a University of Toronto law professor and later Chief Justice of the Supreme Court of Canada, prepared a pamphlet on union security for the association that was used by unions across the country in preparing maintenance-of-membership cases before the new Boards of Conciliation that accompanied the new labour legislation. Wren found himself doing research and serving on conciliation boards for various unions, beginning with the New Glasgow, Nova Scotia, local of the Steel Workers Organizing Committee. From 1940 the association issued *Labour News* every two weeks to provide labour with interpretations of relevant legislation and to convey information on economic and industrial relations problems. It also published research bulletins from time to time and, in 1944, began circulating the more popularly oriented *Labour Briefs* on a monthly basis. Wren claimed in 1944 that over two thousand copies of *Labour News* were distributed and that, since it was sent primarily to labour officials and a few others, it was reaching a large portion of the two thousand union locals in Canada. Meanwhile, 45,000 copies of the first issue of *Labour Briefs* were distributed during the same year. Idele Wilson, who was hired as a researcher with the Carnegie money, edited *Labour News* and did much of the research. She was aided in her work by a voluntary committee of university academic staff and other intellectuals.[18]

The research activity was linked directly to teaching with the development of visual education. At the end of the 1930s, Wren and the association reviewed the effectiveness of the tutorial and study circle methods for labour education. During an organizing trip to the Maritimes in 1940, for example, Wren noted that classes in the region were limited to the Halifax area and that study circles in industrial Cape Breton depended on the availability of able group leaders, who were in short supply. He was also aware of how Mark Starr, international education director of the ILGWU, was using film strips in union education. Wren therefore experimented during the trip with film strips as part of regular union meetings and concluded that the technique had potential for awakening in working people a desire to pursue knowledge relevant to them.

A film strip was a roll of 35-millimetre film on which was printed a number of still pictures and text. These were projected on a screen one at a time. The purpose was to facilitate teaching and to motivate further study. The visual or graphical material was meant to illustrate ideas, events and operations of direct importance to the subject. The text was written with one eye on word economy and the other on the particular photograph or cartoon it accompanied. Film strips were meant to be a medium unto themselves, complementing, not competing with, films.

As a result, the association applied for and received $6,000 from the Carnegie Foundation to develop film strips. The grant was used to purchase a projector, to acquire film strips where available and suitable and to produce new strips dealing with Canadian issues. Harold Beveridge was hired as a researcher on the project. Before he left the WEA in 1942, Beveridge researched and wrote bulletins on specific topics, which were used for the film strips and other purposes. He was aided by a research committee consisting of university professors such as Bora Laskin and Lorne Morgan, who helped with basic information. Beveridge's job, assisted by a visual education committee, was to produce material on the advice and with the assistance of the research committee. He then worked with the former committee to make the material more accessible to a working-class audience.

Film strips of fifteen to thirty-five frames were produced on a variety of issues, including Canadian social history, parliamentary procedure, and labour organization in Canada, for use at union and other meetings. Artists provided volunteer labour or worked at low cost to prepare visual material; photographers then made negatives from the work completed by the artists. These were then transferred to the film strips. Written material in the form of bulletins was produced to accompany the film strips, and distributed with the projector and the strip. After the strip was shown, a true-or-false questionnaire was presented to encourage discussion. Both questions and the film were based on the bulletin. The educational strategy assumed that workers would develop an interest in the bulletin material after viewing the film strips, and then study the bulletins as individuals or form study circles to discuss the bulletins. Then, it was hoped, they would move on to tutorial classes. However, even if participants in film strip discussions did not follow this progression, at least they were exposed to some labour education that they would not have otherwise received.

By 1942 ten unions in twenty-four centres were receiving and using film strips through the WEA's visual education service. Seventy-two hundred workers were served in this way during that year, and it was projected that 15,000 workers would participate in the service during 1943. Film strip circuits were organized in cooperation with local trades and labour councils in cities such as Moose Jaw, Regina and Vancouver; the Steelworkers and the UMWA also cooperated with the association to provide film strip services to their members in Nova Scotia. Film strips apparently had the desired effect of making education more accessible to working people. As a Vancouver journalist put it, the "amazing success of the program elsewhere is due to the fact that the sponsors have actually made education fun. They impart knowledge in the guise of entertainment."[19]

Film strips had become an important part of the WEA's educational programme by the early 1940s, but during this period motion-picture film was overtaking other media as the educational technology of choice among adult educators. The association was interested in the early 1940s in expanding its visual education service to include film, but it did not have the resources to mount a film programme on its own. Film strips were relatively inexpensive to produce, and the projector was relatively inexpensive, but motion-picture film production and film projectors were beyond its budgetary means. With an eye on the rapid organization of the rural film circuits during 1942, Wren approached John Grierson and the NFB with a proposal that the board produce films of interest to labour and make its projectors and films available to labour organizations and trade unionists. Wren wanted to use film as an educational tool to provide workers with the critical skills necessary to analyze the society in which they lived. Grierson shared this interest, but his immediate concern was to aid the war effort through film. Thus a limited and conditional space was made available for the labour education movement to use the publicly funded film board for its purposes.

An arrangement was negotiated in 1942 between the board, the CCL, the TLC and the WEA whereby the NFB provided the necessary projectors and equipment, a monthly programme of films and $125 monthly for a Trade Union Film Circuit. The two congresses each agreed to contribute $250 annually, while the WEA provided office space and expenses valued at $500 annually. The Trade Union Film Circuit was managed by the National Trade Union Film Committee. This committee, consisting of representatives from the four organizations, oversaw the development of the film circuits and chose the films to be shown, but it was Wren and the WEA who did the programme planning and, indeed, did the political work of putting this committee and initiative together.

By the end of 1942 five circuits were operating, four in Ontario and one in Montreal, and it was estimated that several thousand workers saw government and documentary films from the WEA and NFB libraries. Early in 1943 the agreement among the four organizations was renewed and expanded to become a national programme (not just Ontario and Montreal) and to include the use of projectionists, paid by the NFB but recruited by and acceptable to the WEA. By 1945 circuits were operating from September to May with an average of 450 shows a month to a total audience of over 40,000 trade unionists. The films shown on the circuits were a combination of NFB films made specifically for the Trade Union Film Circuit, other NFB-produced films and British and American films. *Labour Looks Ahead*, for example, was produced for the November 1945 circuit and featured Canadian trade unionists participating in a variety of activities, including education. *Our Northern Neighbour*, meanwhile, was an NFB documentary about the Soviet Union produced for general distribution in support of the war effort, and *Partners in Production* was a British-made film promoting the virtues of labour-management production committees in war industries. Supplementary educational materials, produced by the WEA, accompanied the film programme, and labour summer schools trained union educators to use the films for discussion purposes and to integrate film into their organizations' educational programmes.[20]

The projectionists on the Trade Union Film Circuit, who were drawn from the labour movement, worked as organizers as well as technicians. Besides making the rounds to show their monthly films, they organized the circuits and tried to ensure that the films were being used as much as possible as part of an educational programme. Normally, the films would be shown at the end of a local union business meeting or as part of a special film and/or educational evening. A busy projectionist, such as Claude Donald, might hold thirty screenings a month. Donald, a member of the Boilermakers and Iron Shipbuilders Union, began working as an NFB projectionist in British Columbia in 1943. He was also a WEA activist and a member of the (communist) LPP. Donald eventually resigned from the NFB to become the WEA organizer in British Columbia, but his activities changed little (although he was no longer responsible for the circuits) as he always tried to integrate film into labour education.

The International Woodworkers of America hired the WEA to provide education during a 1946 strike in British Columbia. The following excerpt is from letters Claude Donald wrote to Drummond Wren describing how visual education was integrated into a general education programme for the striking workers:

We have conducted three schools for the IWA pickets, shown innumerable films and record programs (union songs), sent groups of entertainers on a 24 hour basis to the picket lines, put on shows of union films at mass rallies, not to mention film showings at the main centres on the Island. We even had to get generators for the films on the picket lines. We have also put on quizz programs in Stanley Park on the 23rd and 24th of May, as well as two 2-hour musical programs, so you can see we have not been idle. The job of organising the equipment, most of it on a very temporary basis was a job in itself, as well as training discussion leaders to operate the machines, and manipulating transportation on a voluntary basis.... On top of this, organizing discussion groups on the picket lines day and night. To assist with this, the IWA have asked us to hire Watson Thomson and Bruce Yorke full-time as educational directors. One is education and the other is Research. Bruce is loaned from the Trade Union Research Bureau. The IWA are paying the salaries through us, and give us $25 to boot for expenses. Not much, but they are fearful of a long struggle and have already had many calls on their funds from needy strikers. The education programme was as follows: Discussion groups were held with the aid of films, filmstrips, and educational materials; these were done on the picket lines (nearly 100 of them) with the aid of generators, where necessary, and voluntary operators. There were several schools, both weekend and thru the week, to train discussion leaders, and people to circulate and look after reading materials on the lines, to operate projectors, and set up and edit wall newspapers. We even operated singers and musicians on a 24 hour basis touring every line in the Greater Vancouver Area, as well as going to the Island for a tour.... Lastly we took part in the trek to Victoria, assisting with sound equipment and movies and wall news. We also took a movie of the trek which you will likely be seeing before too long. Since none of us were experienced in the use of movie cameras, the film is only 50-50 good. However, we feel that there is enough to make a 15 or 20 minute movie, if they are willing to spend some dough to make it good.

Source: Archives of Ontario, *WEA Papers*, MU 3997, File "Vancouver, BC," Claude Donald to Drummond Wren, 6 June 1946 and 25 June 1946.

Discussion trailers were an educational enhancement developed for the Trade Union Film Circuit. They were produced for *Partners in Production, Our Northern Neighbour* and a number of other films that were shown on the circuits. The purposes of the trailers were to show the audience how discussions could be conducted and to raise points for discussion from the film. The trailers' designers wanted to use this medium to bridge the gap between the subject of the film and the experiences of the audience. Actual trade unionists were used in the trailers and the points raised for discussion were precise, simple and concrete. In preparing the trailer for *Veterans in Industry*, for example, NFB producer Stanley Rands and members of the production staff held preliminary meetings with Winnipeg trade unionists to discuss issues surrounding the reintegration of war veterans into the workforce. Rands then prepared a script for the trailer in which he made the general points of the film as relevant as possible to a trade union audience, and checked it with the trade unionists. Later these same trade unionists, many "acting" for the first time, were assembled to shoot the discussion trailer. Eleven hours of filming at Windsor Hall in St. Vital yielded the five- to six-minute final product.[21]

The Trade Union Film Circuit lasted until 1946. A number of factors led to its demise, including tensions within the labour movement and NFB policy changes for the post-war period. First, a conflict developed between the International Alliance of Technical Stage Employees (IATSE) and the NFB regarding the showing of 16-millimetre films. Wren negotiated a protocol agreement with IATSE's leadership on behalf of the board and the National Trade Union Film Committee whereby non-IATSE projectionists could be used to show educational films to local unions without charge, but if admission were charged for any film, an IATSE projectionist would be used. The IATSE membership in Canada rejected the agreement, prompting the NFB to reconsider its commitment to the Trade Union Film Circuit. Second, the leadership of the Steelworkers, the UPWA and the URWA urged the NFB to deal directly with unions in determining the board's labour film programme. The Steelworkers' Charles Millard, in particular, did not want the WEA involved in a significant way with any labour education, including government-sponsored film programmes. Meanwhile, Eugene Forsey, research director at the CCL, was telling his employer that the WEA was promoting a (communist) LPP line in the print material it distributed with the films for the Trade Union Film Circuit. Both Millard and Forsey were strong supporters of the social democratic CCF.[22]

Furthermore, at war's end the NFB expanded the Volunteer Projection Services, which had developed during the war as a means of showing NFB films to Canadians who were neither workers nor farmers, into a Community Film Service. The Volunteer Projection Services was a distribution and projectionist-training system that worked in cooperation with business groups, such as boards of trade and chambers of commerce. The Community Film Service, which absorbed the Trade Union Film Circuit, made films available to film groups organized on the basis of geography rather than other forms of community. In this system the labour movement was no longer served as a distinct national community, with broad-based identifiable interests, but became one interest group among many in a given city or town. This change was part of a more fundamental rightward shift at the NFB as progressive voices, including Grierson's, were purged.[23]

The WEA's wartime experience with radio was similar to that in film. Wren approached the CBC in the fall of 1941 to ask the corporation to again make its airwaves available for labour-issue broadcasts. CBC executives reluctantly allowed the WEA to produce and deliver a series called *Labour Forum* in the 1942 spring season (Wren's suggested title, *Union Grill*, was rejected by the CBC). The corporation retained the right to examine all scripts before broadcast. *Labour Forum* was expanded and reorganized in the fall of 1942 with the addition of a National Advisory Council, regional committees composed of members from each of the union centrals and a national executive committee with representation from the WEA, the CBC, the CCL and the TLC. The CBC provided broadcasting facilities and $40 per show for Wren's organizing and hosting time, paid for a scriptwriter and the mimeographing of scripts and covered all the incidental costs associated with putting the programmes on the air. In the fall of 1942 the WEA produced a print document called *Labour Facts* for each broadcast. It was distributed to local unions, listening groups and interested individuals across the country using funds contributed by various unions. For a short time there were sufficient resources to send this publication twice a month to all of the TLC and CCL affiliates in the country.

The *Labour Forum* programmes featured actual workers reading WEA-prepared scripts that explored various problems and issues, including the effect of new government programmes on workers and their role in war production. Each programme dealt with a specific region of the country, industrial sector, government programme or issue. The themes of profit gouging, poor planning and ineffective management were a feature of most of the broadcasts. The ideas of a national minimum wage and wage parity between women and men were promoted as well. Dramatization was sometimes used to convey a worker point of view. One broadcast, for example, used a sketch of an industrial accident in a shipyard to contrast the workers' intricate knowledge of production and its problems with employers' callous and often negligent regard for workplace safety. In another programme, CCL president Aaron Mosher and TLC president Percy Bengough appeared together for the first time. They both criticized the pro-employer orientation of federal government labour legislation and it was something of a coup for Wren and the WEA to get them both in the same room at the same time.

Labour Forum was received enthusiastically by working-class audiences. The CBC and the WEA received letters from a variety of Canadian workers—including union and non-union, communist and social democrat, and male and female—expressing appreciation for the labour point of view that was being presented in these broadcasts. Furthermore, a May 1942 telephone survey revealed that 70 percent of the total radio audience in western Canadian cities was tuned to *Labour Forum* and that an overwhelming majority of listeners agreed with the points made by the worker participants. While worker response to the series was favourable throughout 1942, by the fall employers were becoming increasingly critical of it and the government began to show signs of apprehension about these pro-union voices on its airwaves. In November C.D. Howe, the powerful Minister of Munitions and Supply, complained to the CBC about one particular programme. During the broadcast in question a letter was read aloud revealing irregularities in the management of a munitions plant under Howe's control. The correspondent, as it was later verified, was a worker in the plant and a member of the communist-led UE.

Given Howe's power and influence, the CBC felt compelled to bring *Labour Forum* under tighter control as a result of this incident. The CCL and TLC leadership defended and promoted *Labour Forum*, but they were not prepared to offer unconditional support for the WEA's organization and direction of the series, in large part because many in the labour movement were becoming concerned about the association's autonomy and its willingness to work with everyone in the labour movement, including communists. The CBC took advantage of this rupture between the WEA and the trade union leadership to tame *Labour Forum* by sacrificing Wren and the association while retaining the support of the CCL and the TLC. Wren was eased out of the general secretaryship of the series early in 1943 and was replaced by Sid Simpson from the CBRE. Brock King, the scriptwriter who had been recruited by Wren, was dismissed. The WIB then assumed responsibility for the direction and control of the broadcasts. *Labour Forum* thereby became integrated into the government's propaganda machine and began promoting labour-management cooperation. The form and tone of the broadcasts changed as well, with professional actors, government spokespeople and academics replacing the workers who were featured in the earlier WEA-produced programmes. Many trade union listeners disliked this sanitization and professionalization of *Labour Forum* and made their feelings known both to the CBC and to their unions. Both the TLC and the CCL, feeling pressure from below, had withdrawn their support from *Labour Forum* by the summer of 1943 without, it appears, reflecting on their own participation in its decline. The series went through a couple of other incarnations in the fall of 1943 and the winter of 1944, and then disappeared.[24]

This experiment in labour broadcasting resulted from a combination of the WEA's recognition that, in the 1940s, a variety of unconventional tools were available for labour education, the CBC's willingness to include challenging commentary on its airwaves, and a culture of wartime emergency that allowed workers, as crucial participants in the war effort, to have a legitimate voice and point of view in public discussions. Howe's complaint marked the limits of governmental and employer tolerance for these voices, and the autonomy and critical edge of the broadcasts were contained. Unfortunately, the labour movement's internal battles made it easier for the dominant forces in this drama to succeed.

Through the use of film strips, film and radio, Wren and the WEA were attempting to develop what they called mass education, which meant using popular media and new communication technologies to make knowledge and education more accessible to workers. Their experiments with film strips were most successful because the arms-length nature of the Carnegie money allowed for some strategic planning about what part the medium would play in their larger educational project. Film and radio, while ideally offering more potential because of their popularity and diffusion and because they were public resources, were less reliable because of the class forces at play within and around the public institutions that controlled access to filmmaking and broadcast facilities. The Trade Union Film Circuit and *Labour Forum* were exciting experiments, and the WEA attempted through discussion trailers and listening groups to integrate the media into structured educational activity, but they remained experiments because government was unwilling to make a sustained commitment of public resources to labour education.

While these experiments in alternative educational delivery proceeded, various forms of face-to-face interaction remained the WEA's main activity between 1939 and 1946. Evening classes were offered across the country, with local universities and provincial governments providing uneven support. Weekend institutes and summer schools were developed, often in collaboration with trade unions that increasingly used the WEA to satisfy their educational requirements.

Evening classes in Ontario were supported financially by the provincial government's workers' education grant, which was administered by the University of Toronto. This funding dated from 1923, when the United Farmers of Ontario government began providing $1,500 per year for WEA courses as a result of lobbying by association supporters. By 1939 this annual grant was $8,000. Wren and the association had a long-standing difference of opinion with W.J. Dunlop, director of Extension at the university, over the control of this money. Tension flared in 1937 when Wren attempted to have the provincial grant paid directly to the WEA. Dunlop, who had little sympathy for labour education, responded by attempting to exert greater control over Wren and the association. Two years later, when the university's grant from the province was cut by 10 percent, Dunlop took the opportunity to cut the WEA grant from $8,000 to $2,000. Association lobbying added an extra $900 for tutors and $1,000 for secretarial support to this figure, but the cut was still substantial. Then, in 1942, Dunlop cut the grant completely, although in this case it appears Dunlop and university president H.J. Cody were reacting to pressure from members of Toronto's employer class, who did not like the WEA's profile and message. By building support among the labour movement and exploiting their contacts in the Liberal provincial government, Wren and the association were able to have the grant reinstated and paid directly to the WEA. The $4,000 annual grant was paid to the WEA until the late 1940s, when other difficulties arose.

These financial difficulties had a direct impact on the health and existence of local associations and their evening classes. In 1938-39 when the grant was $8,000, for example, there were nineteen Ontario associations conducting a total of forty-five classes; by 1941-42, when the grant for tutors was $2,900, there were only five associations conducting twenty-four classes. By 1946 classes were limited to the Toronto, Hamilton, St. Catharines and Sarnia districts, while important industrial centres such as Windsor, Oshawa and Sudbury did not have local workers' educational associations. In any year about half of the classes were in Toronto. At the end of the 1930s in Toronto there were three-year programmes in psychology and economics and two-year programmes in public speaking. Across the province courses were taught in economics, history, philosophy and sociology, as well as in art and music appreciation, literature and other cultural subjects. These offerings were scaled back in the 1940s as a result of the smaller tutorial grants, with the multi-year programmes being the most significant casualties. University academic staff tutored most of these courses.[25]

With less money for traditional classes in Ontario during the 1940s, the WEA cultivated other areas of educational endeavour. The research, film and radio work were part of this broadening of activity, but it also included labour institutes and the summer labour college. The explosion of union organizing in the 1940s coupled with the heightened wartime regulation of industrial relations meant that active trade unionists needed information and education about the theory and practice of labour law and labour organizations. The association therefore began holding day or weekend institutes on new labour legislation and specific economic or industrial problems, and to train union stewards in grievance handling and contract negotiations. Between 1940 and 1946 institutes were held in Toronto, Kingston, Niagara Falls, Hamilton and Windsor. These events drew hundreds of activists from affiliates of both labour congresses. Speakers included trade union leaders such as Tom Moore of the TLC and Pat Conroy of the CCL, and academics such as political economist Harold Logan and lawyer Bora Laskin from the University of Toronto. Institute topics included the *Industrial Disputes Investigation Act*, P.C 1003 and other orders in council, union security and wages and prices.[26]

During the 1930s the WEA had rented accommodation at Gravenhurst, Pickering and some other sites for one- and two-week summer schools featuring University of Toronto professors, such as political economist H.A. Innis and scientist Sir Frederick Banting. The association established the first Canadian labour-owned workers' residential college in 1942 when it purchased the former Ontario College of Art summer-school property at Port Hope, Ontario. This beautiful old millhouse on a river's edge became the vacation destination of many trade unionists and association members over the following decade or so. The summer labour college programmes consisted of dedicated WEA courses in some weeks or on weekends and collaborative sessions between the association and individual unions in others. The WEA's own activities were a mix of academic courses, instruction about new government legislation and industrial relations training. The sessions with individual unions tended to be the same, but without the academic courses. The UAW was the most consistent supporter of the Port Hope facility during the war years; other supporters included the UE and the URWA.

The inaugural session in 1942 illustrates the range of activity that took place at the Port Hope facility. It opened in July with a weekend institute featuring the federal director of the National Selective Service, and was attended by eighty-one delegates from forty-five different union locals. This was followed by the WEA's own summer school for seventeen days, accommodating ninety-four persons for various lengths of time. Then the UAW's De Haviland local held a weekend institute on union principles and practices for twenty-nine members. After a break of five days, the second WEA school was held over sixteen days for eighty-five participants. The season concluded with separate weekend schools for the URWA and the UAW. The UAW school, organized jointly by the WEA and the union's international education department, attracted forty participants from both sides of the Canadian-American border. Throughout the summer, voluntary committees of participants handled the discipline and direction of the school and the educational programmme.[27]

Vancouver had the most active WEA outside of Ontario. Wren had made a western organizing trip in the fall of 1938. Between 1939 and 1941 there was a fledgling organization in Vancouver, with a total of five night classes held during the winters of 1939 and 1940 and a total enrolment of about 150. During this time there were only eleven local union affiliations out of over eighty locals contacted. Wren claimed that the local district secretary, Gordon Maxwell, was responsible for difficulties between differing groups in the Vancouver labour movement. It appears that Maxwell was unable to bridge the gap between TLC and CCL unions in the city. Those unions that did affiliate were TLC unions. Wren attempted via correspondence to generate some activity in Victoria in the year or so following his 1938 visit. As in Vancouver, however, differences between the TLC and CCL unions, combined with a general apathy towards labour education, meant that nothing got off the ground.

Wren was convinced, however, that British Columbia was fertile territory for labour education, despite the initial setbacks. In the fall of 1941 he made a two-week tour of British Columbia, organized by the IWA. Using the IWA's contacts with CCL-affiliated unions to supplement the TLC contacts that had been made earlier, Wren hoped to reinvigorate the moribund Vancouver WEA. In this he was assisted by Claude Donald, a WEA activist from Toronto who moved to Vancouver in 1941. Donald sparked the rebirth of the WEA in Vancouver, becoming district secretary in 1943 and a paid organizer (on a leave of absence from the NFB) in the fall of 1944. Donald let his LPP membership lapse when he became a WEA employee. While critical of LPP dogmatism, Donald was also impatient with the sectarianism he encountered among CCF supporters (or "see see iffers," as he called them) in the labour movement.

From 1943 to 1948, Donald and a group of other WEA activists attempted to build a labour education movement in British Columbia. During the 1940s the province was fertile ground for such an endeavour, with about 84,000 union members representing 30 percent of the labour force in 1945. It was also a labour movement deeply divided between craft and industrial unionists and between communists and social democrats. Drummond Wren concluded in 1941 that it was probably not possible to bring the AFL and CCL unions together in Vancouver and wondered if two workers' educational organizations should be established to conduct separate classes for each group. Throughout this period, however, Donald remained mostly optimistic about the prospect of building a broad-based, non-sectarian educational movement. The most consistent support for the association came from communist-led industrial unions in both labour centrals. The Boilermakers and Iron Shipbuilders Union (Boilermakers), the IWA, Mine-Mill, the Dock and Shipyard Workers, and the United Fishermen and Allied Workers (UFAW) provided support. Left-wing union leaders such as Gerry Culhane (Boilermakers), Nigel Morgan (IWA) and Harvey Murphy (Mine-Mill) taught WEA courses. Individual locals of traditional craft unions, such as the Street Railwaymen, Firefighters, Plumbers and Steamfitters, and the IAM, were among those affiliated to the WEA during this period. Nonetheless, the Vancouver TLC would not affiliate with the association until 1946 because of TLC-CCL labour wars in the city. And because of internal labour divisions, Donald was never able to establish a sustainable organization in Victoria.

Donald and the association encountered political sectarianism from both communists and social democrats, but mostly from the latter. An LPP organizer for the Boilermakers took exception to a perceived slight of the WUL in a WEA publication, for example, and refused to distribute it. And at one summer school, the organizers "had a talk privately to a few enthusiasts for the USSR and ask them to soft pedal that angle and concentrate on the Canadian scene." Both the LPP and the CCF conducted their own west-coast labour colleges, meanwhile, which competed with WEA courses. Donald was able to arrange with the LPP that the courses did not conflict, but he had less success with the CCF, although rank-and-file CCF supporters attended WEA winter courses and summer schools. Some CCF partisans, however, opposed any education other than CCF political training and used whatever means they could to discredit the WEA. Unions with CCF leadership, such as the Steelworkers and the UPWA, had little or nothing to do with the WEA in BC.[28]

The following are excerpts from letters written by Claude Donald to Drummond Wren describing the effects on WEA activity of political sectarianism in the British Columbia labour movement:

I ran into a snag today. The organiser of the Dock and Ship [McNeil] took exception to the reference to the Workers' Unity League, and 'boring from within.' [p. 28] He wanted to return a hundred copies of the Trade Union Handbook. I may get him to forget it. (8 March 1944) The TU Handbook is in the doghouse here now on account of the reference to 'boring from within.' I shall push it to the AFL unions, but if you need any, I can let you have a few. (19 April 1944) We got off to a good start on the WEA setup locally. It has a few CCF-ers who think that a Labour College would only be a duplication of their Labor College. However we have enough of the others to do the required pushing. (14 April 1944) I have been asked to go to Victoria and arrange classes for the unions there. It is a real problem, owing to the prevailing CCF attitude there, with its accompanying desire for union control and the substitution of CCF propoganda for education of any kind. Their education appears to consist of preaching the vanity of war, the inevitability of chaos after, and the logical and only way out—vote. I don't think you have quite the same degree of bitterness down east. (13 March 1945) We haven't yet included any of the actual CCF-dominated unions, such as Steelworkers, although we do have a Packing-House Union. While they, the CCF, do not really support us, they are not against us, and come to our classes and summer schools. (30 July 1945) There is a mean group of CCF partisans who disapprove any education other than CCF propaganda, and who class us with the rather lofty WEA in England. They peddle PLEBS booklets that tend to make WEA seem like stooges for Capitalism, and link us with the British WEA in a derogatory manner. One local of the IWA, #1-217 has the most active and cunning group of this sort. Of course, and thank goodness, they also contain our chairman and some of our warmest supporters. (10 May 1946)

Source: Archives of Ontario, *WEA Papers*, MU 3996 and MU 3997, various files labelled "Vancouver," various letters from Claude Donald to Drummond Wren.

Following the guidelines laid down by the WEA national constitution, and the historical practice in Ontario and Britain, the Vancouver WEA concentrated its initial efforts on establishing an ongoing programme of evening classes. Over the four winters in this period, evening classes were offered in subjects ranging from trade unionism and labour history to literature, philosophy and psychology. The Shop Steward, an applied course taught by Gerry Culhane, Tom Parkin and other trade unionists, combined practical issues and everyday problems for stewards with a broader treatment of labour issues. Several hundred workers took this course in the winter of 1945, with the shipyard unions requiring their stewards to attend the course and aircraft unions and the IWA encouraging attendance. The more academic courses were taught by labour-friendly academics or independent radical intellectuals. G.G. Sedgewick of the University of British Columbia (UBC) taught Social Changes in Modern Novels,

Kathleen Gorrie and Marjorie Smith of UBC taught Child Psychology, and J.I. Macdougall taught Psychology, emphasizing how workers might cope with wartime issues of speed-up, propaganda and fears of uncertainty and insecurity. These classes, according to Donald, were very different than traditional university classes. The atmosphere was more akin to that of a workers' group, where discipline was self-imposed and where a democratic and critical exchange of opinion took place between student and tutor. The local association also assembled distance education packages, based on the courses given in Vancouver, for local study or discussion groups in remote areas. The local association's class committee edited the courses for clarity.[29]

There was less contact between the university and the WEA in Vancouver than was the case in Toronto. Beginning in 1939, the provincial government provided a modest annual grant of $300 to UBC to support the WEA in British Columbia. This money was administered through the university's extension department, under the direction of Gordon Shrum. Shrum appears to have been as interested in the WEA and labour education as was necessary for his own political purposes. At times he was supportive and at other times he was distant. When he returned from the CAAE meetings in 1947, for example, where he heard the WEA criticized by some union leaders, he was unwilling to offer the local association any money. Generally speaking, though, during these years Shrum and UBC paid for tutor costs, following the Ontario model. Shrum was unwilling to pay for all tutors, however, and initially paid only for UBC staff members. This was later expanded to include UBC graduates. If the WEA employed an independent or trade union educator, their stipend had to found somewhere else or they taught for free.[30]

In the four summers from 1944 to 1947, week-long schools of up to three weeks per season were held at a variety of holiday camps in the Vancouver area. The 1944 Vancouver summer school, for example, included courses such as Growth and Development of Unions in Canada, Trade Union Techniques, Women in Industry, Writing for the Trade Unionist and Bookkeeping for the Trade Unionist. Gerry Culhane of the British Columbia Shipyard Federation ran a session on steward training and Leonard Chatwin of the NFB conducted a course on the Importance of Visual Education. Nigel Morgan, Harold Pritchett (IWA) and Harvey Murphy also taught during the week. A highlight of the 1944 British Columbia school was a course by Dr. Ralph Grundlach of the University of Washington, entitled Psychology of Leadership for Democracy. Grundlach's main point was that the essential factor in democratic organizations was the selection and training of new people to become leaders. He argued that democracy could be learned by a process of voluntary and responsible participation. Trade unions, he maintained, must select and train their own members in democratic participation and leadership. An internal educational programme was crucial in selecting and developing shop stewards and top leadership, he concluded. Following Grundlach's course, the theme of the 1945 school was "The Development of Democratic Leadership," and subjects included steward training, labour history, organizing, leadership psychology, union accounting (by Eric Bee of the Pacific Coast Labour Bureau), women and unions, parent education and film forums. Academics and trade unionists came north from Seattle for the school, including James Walsh from the University of Washington, who conducted workshops on Creative Workers Theatre.[31]

The following year's summer school featured Leo Huberman of New York. Huberman and Gerry Culhane co-taught a course on trade unionism, with Huberman handling the theoretical aspects of the topic and Culhane covering the practical problems of union organization. Huberman used his *The Truth About Unions* for the course, with each participant receiving a copy of the book. The material he presented was discussed thoroughly by the class. He also devoted considerable time to techniques for union educational committees and training in basic educational methods, with a view to ensuring that workers had the tools to teach themselves and each other. Culhane, coached by Huberman in educational technique, posed a series of scenarios for discussion and debate. In one scenario a worker is hired in a union plant employing several hundred workers, but conditions are poor and none of the workers know much about the union. Culhane suggests that this state of affairs means that the union is dormant with no shop steward movement and, if there are stewards, they probably confine themselves to collecting dues. What should the worker do? The suggested approach, open for class discussion, is as follows: The worker should join the union, go to meetings, talk to the other workers and find the union-conscious among them. If there is no shop steward movement, the worker should agitate for one and ensure that elections are held for stewards. If the union is bureaucratic, the worker should move to democratize it by raising issues that affect workers on the job and by attempting to get action on workers' basic problems.[32]

Other centres, including Edmonton, Calgary, Saskatoon, Montreal and Halifax, followed traditional evening-class programmes. Winnipeg's experience was typical and more substantial than most. Activists in the Manitoba capital enjoyed some early success at building union affiliations and mounting evening classes, but were not successful at expanding into other areas. Activity began in 1937-38 with six evening classes and total enrolments of 141. In each of the following four seasons, six classes were offered, with total enrolments fluctuating between a high of 172 in both 1938-39 and 1939-40 and a low of 129 in 1941-42. Women accounted for slightly over one-fifth of these enrolments. In 1942-43 four classes were offered initially, with one being cancelled for lack of interest. Total enrolments had declined to 105 by this year, completely due to declining male registrations, as the number of female students remained constant at about forty. Over the following three seasons, three classes were held each year, while in 1946-47 a fourth was added. Following a dip to seventy-eight in 1943-44, enrolments remained constant at about 100 per year.

The Winnipeg WEA enjoyed some comparative success at soliciting union affiliations, beginning well and then entering a decline. There were twenty-one affiliations in the association's first year, a high of twenty-three in 1939-40 and then a decline to thirteen in 1945-46. The affiliation lists suggest that the association had some success in drawing support from across the Winnipeg labour movement, with various One Big Union (remnants from 1918-19 organizing in Winnipeg), TLC and railway brotherhood union locals joining the association. The Winnipeg WEA had as many union affiliations as did the Toronto association, which had a much larger labour movement from which to draw support, but Winnipeg activists were nonetheless unhappy with their efforts. In 1940, for example, when they had as many affiliations as they ever would, the association officers noted that they had only fourteen of the seventy-nine international union locals in the city affiliated, with thirty-nine members from those locals enrolled in courses. This amounted to one-third of 1 percent of the 13,000 or so international union members in Winnipeg, they lamented. This was contrasted with the CBRE experience, in which nine of eleven city locals were affiliated and were contributing forty-seven of the students.

The University of Manitoba and the Manitoba Department of Education were consistent supporters of the local WEA, ensuring ongoing financial assistance prior to and during the Second World War. Sidney Smith, university president until 1944, supported adult education generally and labour education in particular. Throughout this period the tutor costs of $150 per each fifteen-week class were financed on the basis of a formula in which the province provided five-ninths of the budget, the university contributed slightly less than three-ninths of the budget and the WEA covered the rest. This peculiar arrangement was the brainchild of Ivan Schultz, Minister of Education until 1944. It is not clear how Schultz arrived at a provincial contribution of five-ninths, but his general principle was that individuals or organizations benefiting from government-funded instruction should make some contribution to the cost, however modest that contribution might be. He insisted that the WEA bear some of the tutorial cost. Wren had no choice but to accept this arrangement if he wanted the money, although he protested to no avail that the association contributed monies for course promotion, recruitment and other overhead costs (which were paid for by tuition fees). Nonetheless the Winnipeg association, in contrast to other local associations, was blessed with stable provincial and university funding throughout this period.

As a result of this support, a regular annual programme was offered. Courses included Public Speaking (three out of six classes in some years), Psychology, Economics, History, International Affairs, Political Science, and even Everyday Chemistry. All tutors were university academic staff and the courses paralleled, for the most part, traditional university disciplines. Nonetheless, attempts were made to make the subject matter more relevant to an adult, working-class audience. Public Speaking was a recast English course, taught by English professors. Psychology addressed questions about raising children. Historians covered industrial history and social history rather than the political history that was the normal fare in regular university courses. A variety of economics courses were offered, from Fundamental Principles of Economics to The Economist in the Witness Stand, which was an economic history course framed as an examination of the origins of twentieth-century economic ideas with an "opportunity to refute the witnesses and to introduce any relevant, or irrelevant, evidence you may desire."[33]

Overall, the Winnipeg association offered a traditional WEA programme of tutorial classes taught by university academic staff. They enjoyed the support of the university president and the provincial minister of education in their endeavours. The various members of the local association executive were trade unionists with good connections to the local labour movement. However, they were never able to expand beyond evening classes, a move which the national organization had discovered was necessary to make labour education more relevant to union women and men. This was no doubt partly because of the strength of the university and provincial connection; the association received good service from these bodies and could count on a programme of classes every year. Association activists, however, were aware in the 1940s that their efforts were stalled, and they wondered what to do about it. They noted, for example, that the university extension department's regular evening institute attracted more students, at a higher cost, than did the WEA courses. They also knew that declining enrolments in their evening classes were to a large degree a result of workers joining the war effort and the staggered shifts in war industries. Association members supported national initiatives such as *Labour Forum* and the Film Circuits, but they never developed a local mass education programme integrated with the evening courses. Such a programme would have recaptured some of those shift workers, but more importantly it would have made education more meaningful to more workers. In the end, it was a small minority of workers who were interested in university-level instruction in the absence of a programme to prepare them for it.

This history suggests that there were a variety of WEA educational practices across the country during the Second World War, with attempts at the national level to piece together a coordinated strategy that connected mass education, trade union training and university-level instruction. This practice continued to be guided by the liberal education principles that had been association hallmarks in the 1920s and 1930s. The fundamental purpose of WEA labour education was still "to teach *how* to think, not *what* to think," but in the war years, this neutral-sounding principle was grounded more firmly in working-class experience. The association was home to a variety of perspectives in the labour movement, including craft and industrial unionists, and social democrats and communists. Although its core of support came from left-leaning industrial unions such as the UAW in Ontario and the IWA in British Columbia, it was firm in its resolve that it not propagate a particular ideology or philosophy. This did not mean that the association accepted the status quo. Rather, as a workers' organization, it felt that it had an obligation to analyze critically the place of workers in society and to emphasize the social nature of education. Labour education, in this view, served social rather than individual purposes. The application of critical judgement to social and economic problems would lead eventually to the elimination of injustice. The WEA stood with the workers and helped them to acquire skills of critical judgement, then, but it was the responsibility of other bodies to organize and to mobilize workers for industrial and political action.

This philosophy of critical, supportive and semi-autonomous engagement became more difficult to sustain as the relationship with unions became closer and as trade unionists increasingly requested practical training in negotiations, arbitrations and so forth. There was some difference of opinion in the association as to how far it should proceed in this area. Some Toronto academic members, in particular, felt that to take on direct educational responsibilities for unions was to abandon the WEA's traditional commitment to objective education. In Vancouver, meanwhile, where the university link was virtually non-existent, the association provided a direct educational service for a portion of the local labour movement. Eventually, the dominant view was that the association had a crucial role to play in training union members in organizing, writing contracts, bargaining, conducting meetings and doing arbitration hearings. WEA trade union training, in other words, had to have a critical edge as part of a broader liberal labour education.[34]

Union-Centred and University-Centred Labour Education: 1939-1946

The CCL and many of its affiliates worked with the WEA in *Labour Forum*, the Trade Union Film Circuits, and the Port Hope labour college, but the most sustained support came from the UAW and the communist-led unions. The social democratic CCL leadership was cool to the WEA. Despite its occasional cooperation with the association, the congress began to develop its own education programme from about 1944. Many TLC locals affiliated with the WEA and used the association's services, but with the exception of the ILGWU, there was little internal education in TLC affiliates before the 1950s. The TLC itself did not develop an internal educational structure until a few years prior to its merger with the CCL in 1956. Most university-centred labour education during the war years was connected with the WEA. Exceptions to this pattern were Dalhousie University's Maritime Labour Institute and StFX's organized educational campaign against communist influence among the Cape Breton working class.

CCL educational initiatives were determined in part by developments in the CIO unions. American labour education underwent a shift in the 1930s and 1940s, from an older "workers' education" that stressed education for social change, was open to unorganized and organized workers and was organized primarily outside of trade unions, to a newer "labor education" that focused on training trade unionists to participate in collective bargaining. The labour college movement and summer institutes, which had been centrepieces of the older system, faded in the 1930s and were replaced by union-centred educational programmes in the new CIO unions. By 1946, ten CIO unions had educational departments, including the UAW, Steelworkers, UPWA, URWA and Textile Workers of America (TWUA).[35]

The impetus for a CCL educational strategy came from two sources: a memorandum on workers' education for local chartered unions produced in 1943 under Secretary-Treasurer Pat Conroy's name and a resolution on education submitted to the 1944 congress convention by the Education and Recreation Committee of the Montreal Labor Council. Conroy argued that the congress should initiate its own educational programme to assimilate new members, raise the cultural level of the membership and develop and train new leaders. The problem facing the congress in its infancy, he maintained, was a rapidly expanding membership with little understanding and less experience with trade unions. New locals were organized and then left in the hands of executives with no leadership experience. Furthermore, the general educational level of most workers was low, which left them ill-equipped to understand the society in which they lived or to respond to the anti-worker and anti-labour propaganda they faced from business, the media and the business-supported political parties. An extensive prospective educational programme was outlined, including study classes, handbooks or correspondence courses on the function of trade unions for new members; recreational facilities including drama groups, study classes and distance education courses on a variety of general subjects of interest to workers; union libraries to stimulate reading; and leadership training via handbooks, classes and institutes.

Conroy anticipated that some would suggest that the congress should act through the WEA to provide education for members of its chartered unions. He rejected this option primarily because the congress had endorsed the CCF and, since the WEA was "ostensibly non-partisan in its views," it could not carry its teachings to the logical conclusion of political action. Beyond this, if the congress developed its own programme, it could concentrate on its own priorities, work directly with local unions and service locals in those areas where the WEA did not have branches.[36]

The Montreal committee, chaired by Bert Hepworth (who later became CLC education director), was working at the time with the local YMCA to offer classes and was encouraging union locals to affiliate with the WEA. The resolution was referred to the executive and then forwarded for action to Eugene Forsey, the CCL's new research director. Forsey circulated a questionnaire to affiliates asking what they wanted in an educational programme. With the questionnaire results and other material, Forsey produced a document in the spring of 1945 for the CCL's new education committee, which he chaired. In the document Forsey proposed a modest programme for the 1945-46 season, including evening classes in two or three selected cities, distance education subjects, the formation of local education committees and the production of a handbook for the local committees. Suggested evening and distance education courses included public speaking and parliamentary procedure, trade unionism, the worker as consumer, labour history, and a special course for shop stewards. Evening courses were to be four to six weeks long. As it turned out, this programme was too ambitious. During the 1945-46 season, the congress ran two courses in Ottawa: one was a steward training course, taught by Jim McGuire of the CBRE, and the other was a film discussion forum organized by Roby Kidd from the local YMCA.

During the same year, Andy Andras, who was Forsey's assistant and who took over educational responsibilities at the CCL in 1945, produced another blueprint for congress educational activities. Andras based his document on two American trips he took during that year. The first, in the summer, was to the School for Workers at the University of Wisconsin. Andras was impressed with what he described as the progressive nature of the school, notably its stress on the cooperative movement and labour political action as well as collective bargaining, and the fact that it catered to workers alone. Later in the year Andras and Bert Hepworth travelled to New York to meet with labour educators Mark Starr of the ILGWU and Larry Rogin of the TWUA, among others. Andras argued in his document, without a single reference to the WEA, that there was a need for workers' education in Canada and that perhaps the Carnegie Corporation should be approached for assistance. He continued by stating that the field of workers' education in Canada was insufficiently developed, with many organized workers, who were never reached by evening classes or university extension departments, forming a potential student body. He concluded by proposing that the congress devote $50,000 over three years for salaries, promotion and travel to provide an educational programme.[37]

There was limited activity among CCL affiliates and most had some connection with the WEA. The UE, for example, conducted an annual two-week summer school at Port Hope beginning in 1944. The schools had two general purposes. The first was to consolidate the local UE unions through membership mobilization and organization, steward training and leadership development. The second purpose was to develop labour's political capacity. Here the programme ranged from an investigation of the creation of the United Nations at war's end to labour's role in the transition to a post-war economy and issues of independent political action. From 1945, education in UE's Canadian district was under the direction of John Wigdor, former assistant general secretary of the national WEA. The CBRE's education programme dates from 1942, when it first offered a public speaking course in Montreal. These classes, which expanded over later years as resources permitted, were really study groups to introduce potential leaders to a range of subjects, including the history of trade unionism and the need for labour education.[38]

The UAW experience was unique and the most extensive in Canada during this period as a result of its close and ongoing association with the WEA. There was sporadic collaboration during 1939 and 1940. In the fall of 1939, for example, the WEA showed a programme of labour films to UAW locals in Canada. In arranging this programme with Wren, George Burt (Canadian director) expressed his dissatisfaction with the service he was receiving from the international union's education department and hinted he would like to enter into a more formal arrangement with the WEA for educational services. Burt's room to move was limited, however, by the fact that at the time the position of Canadian educational director was an elected one and that person worked directly with the international education department. In the spring of 1940, Wren outlined his visual education programme to Burt, noting that he planned to link background research and film strips to discussion groups, film and radio, He further noted that selected union activists should receive group leadership training to carry on these educational activities successfully. In the fall of 1940, the organization of education in the UAW changed again, with responsibility shifting to a staff position in the regional office under Burt's control. Burt quickly arranged for the international union to give $50 per month for Canadian education, providing that the local unions in the region contributed an equal amount for the same purpose. This $1200 or so a year was then paid to the WEA for educational services. Burt recognized that he was not capable of taking on this responsibility himself and that the international education department was handicapped because of the differences between Canada and the United States.[39]

Wren suggested the following programme to Jim Wishart, international education director. First, a series of institutes in St. Catharines, Windsor and Oshawa would address the problems confronting stewards and committeemen. Second, group discussions using visual aids, charts, film strips and motion pictures would focus on the purposes and functions of trade unions, on the auto industry and the economy generally and on health and consumer issues. He also suggested to Burt that there should be a regional education committee, which would include Burt, to plan and oversee the educational programme. The committee would receive proposals from the WEA, which, when endorsed by the committee, the association would be responsible for implementing. Wren concluded that "the union members should be made to feel that the WEA is a labour educational movement which is theirs."[40]

Although the district council in Canada established an education committee in the fall of 1940, arrangements for educational programmes were negotiated initially between the WEA and local unions. Local 222 in Oshawa and Local 199 in St. Catharines established minimal programmes during 1941, but others, notably the Windsor locals, were less able or willing to initiate activities. Local 200 at Ford, in particular, needed some assistance, Burt noted in 1942, as there were fifty stewards and fourteen committeemen dealing with junior supervisors, and it was a challenge to make the industrial relations machinery work. Indeed, Burt suggested to Wren that the first order of business should be to give management some collective bargaining education and then turn attention to the UAW members. In Oshawa, meanwhile, Local 222's educational programme began at a 20 November 1940 meeting at which an educational motion picture was shown for fifteen minutes, followed by a fifteen-minute talk by Harold Beveridge from the WEA on Trade Unions and Democracy. The programme concluded with fifteen minutes of community singing of labour songs. The local established an ongoing programme for the following winter, which included instruction at stewards' meetings; women's auxiliary discussions of the WEA's *Cost of Living*, *Public Speaking*, and *Parliamentary Procedure* brochures; viewing and discussion by girls of a film strip on biological reproduction; gymnasium instruction for boys; discussion of hospitalization and credit unions; monthly meetings with movies, educational talks, questionnaires and discussions; and a drama club. The WEA also developed short bulletins on Chrysler, Ford and General Motors, as well as a brief on the *Early Beginnings and the Basic Economic Facts of the Automobile Industry* for the UAW, to supplement the general educational material that the association produced.[41]

The UAW became a consistent supporter of the Port Hope labour college after it opened in 1942. The 1943 week-long school, for example, organized jointly by the WEA and the UAW's international education department, included sessions on labour legislation and collective bargaining, local union educational problems, equal pay and discrimination, price control and rationing and the motion picture. Speakers and discussion leaders included George Burt, William Levitt (international education director) and Donald Montgomery (staff) from the UAW; Bora Laskin from the University of Toronto; Gordon Adamson from the NFB; and Drummond Wren and Idele Wilson from the WEA. UAW summer schools were held annually at Port Hope until 1947.[42]

In the fall of 1943 Willam Levitt invited Wren to become education director of the Canadian region of the UAW. Wren's initial inclination was to decline the offer, but he eventually accepted on the understanding that he would resign from the payroll of the WEA but would continue as voluntary general secretary. The Canadian UAW education director's office was established in Toronto in the WEA office. Wren doubled as WEA general secretary and UAW regional education director until he was fired from the UAW by Walter Reuther in 1947.[43]

There was no educational activity in the central TLC (nor in the parent AFL) organization during this period. The ILGWU had the most active programme among TLC unions. In Montreal, for example, a series of female education directors served a largely female membership with courses in French, English, dancing, singing, dramatics, painting, public speaking and first aid. Grace Wales, educational director in Montreal during 1939 and 1940, used a WEA filmstrip on reproduction in one of her courses. The presentation of the filmstrip combined a talk on physiology, stressing how the human body is a united and coordinated combination of millions of cells, with a lesson in effective trade unionism, where many workers unite for the common good. Other TLC unions, such as the United Hat, Cap and Millinery Workers' Union, offered individual courses from time to time, usually in conjunction with regular union meetings.[44]

Participants relaxing after an outdoor class at the Workers' Educational Association summer school at Port Hope, Ontario, in the 1940s. *Archives of Ontario, Workers' Educational Association Papers, AO 3914.*

Participants in an outdoor class at a Workers' Educational Association summer school at Port Hope, Ontario, in the 1940s. *Archives of Ontario, Canadian Association for Adult Education Papers, AO 3947.*

Drummond Wren, General Secretary of the Workers' Educational Association, welcoming participants to a WEA summer school at Port Hope, Ontario, circa 1945. Pat Sullivan of the Canadian Seamen's Union is seated behind Wren. *Archives of Ontario, Workers' Educational Association Papers, AO 3911.*

University involvement in labour education during these years was primarily in conjunction with the WEA. The Nova Scotia universities of Dalhousie and StFX were the exceptions to this pattern. With the participation of the Halifax TLC and CCL district councils, Dalhousie began in 1944 to offer educational services through its Maritime Labour Institute. In 1945, for example, the institute offered a three-day course attended by sixty union delegates from Nova Scotia and New Brunswick; weekend conferences for mineworkers, steelworkers and pulp-and-paper workers; discussion groups in various industrial districts using the CBC/CAAE *Citizen's Forum*; and short courses in Halifax to train labour leaders in union administration. The institute also maintained a library service for affiliated unions and published *Labour and Learning*, a monthly bulletin.[45]

It was at StFX, however, that the most extensive university labour education programme in Canada outside of the WEA developed in this period. The programme to counter communist support among the Cape Breton working class that had begun in the early 1930s was re-established in 1939. Catholic trade unionists were urged to register for one of the eight classes offered that year in order to ensure that their unions did not fall into "the hands of ... a group imbued with a desire to destroy everything that is Christian in our social order." StFX educators and Cape Breton mine managers agreed that the militant activity in the region resulted from the fact that the UMWA could not control its membership. Trade unionists had to learn, they argued, that it was selfish for them to place their interests above the interests of society as a whole. Hence it was imperative that the university proceed with an educational programme among Cape Breton workers. This was especially necessary to counter the influence of the WEA and its "materialist" message among some trade unionists in the region.[46]

StFX developed a programme that identified problems affecting labour, such as long hours, low wages and unemployment, and suggested that these could be solved "within the labour-capital family." Furthermore, the university taught that, while government had a temporary responsibility to govern the labour-capital relationship, ultimately labour and capital should settle their problems cooperatively. More specifically, workers were taught that, while unions could play a limited role in assisting workers to receive higher wages from employers, they would gain greater control over their purchasing power by organizing consumer cooperatives. There was a place for industrial organizing, but as part of a broader programme of producer and consumer organizing. This message was conveyed through short courses and radio broadcasts. Labour School of the Air began broadcasting from StFX's CJFX in 1943. The first season's "Radio Course in Labor Problems" was a series of ten broadcasts in which listening groups, under the direction of local group leaders, used print material from the university to guide their listening and discussion of issues. The group members interacted among themselves through discussion and with the course leaders in Antigonish through questions and comments sent in by post. In 1945, meanwhile, StFX began a five-year "Education of Urban Adults" programme in Cape Breton to train union leaders who could serve as a counterweight to the continuing communist appeal in the region. These classes, combining lecture and discussion, often included businessmen as well as trade unionists among their membership. There were 150 participants in this programme in 1945-46.[47]

While beyond the realm of labour education as it is defined here, the education programmes of the main left-wing political parties in the period contained some material that was similar to that offered in union programmes. Both the Communist Party of Canada (CPC; formed in 1921) and the CCF (born in 1932) conducted programmes designed to train party activists and to convey their respective messages to interested non-members. The CPC programme, which was the most developed of the two, contained three elements. The first was club educationals focusing on practical matters related to party purpose and mass political work. The second was labour colleges, which were more theoretical than club educationals and were designed for party members as well as non-members. And the third was party schools, which offered specialized theoretical education for those party members identified for higher-level training. A system of labour colleges was in place by the mid-1920s. These one-week or two-week day schools and twelve-week evening schools teaching Marxist social science were offered at various places across the country, but most often in Ontario and British Columbia locations. Courses included Introduction to Marxism, Political Economy,

Political Theory, Canadian History, Trade Unionism, and English as a Second Language. At the end of the 1930s the party's Toronto Labor College was conducting a regular programme of ten or so twelve-week evening courses once or twice a year. The range of courses in 1939 included Trade Unionism, taught by Joe Salsberg and Fred Collins; Journalism, taught by John Boyd and Jack Smaller; and Canadian Politics Today, taught by Harry Binder and Stewart Smith. According to CPC educators, working-class emancipation required workers to have a scientific understanding of capitalism and the purpose of party education was to provide this understanding in a general way for party cadres and workers who were not party members and to provide more systematic and theoretical training for those party members chosen for leadership positions.

Education was a central element of CCF practice as well. Party leaders believed that Canadians—notably those in subordinated social groups such as workers and farmers—could be convinced through education to support the CCF in its crusade to transform society. As a result, beginning in the mid-1930s the party established study groups, ran summer institutes, provided study guides for socialist books, and ran distance education courses. British Columbia and Saskatchewan operated summer camps combining recreation and education; during the 1940s the British Columbia camp operated over four weeks on Gabriola Island between the mainland and Vancouver Island. The Saskatchewan party also held regular winter schools in January covering topics such as Socialist Theory and Duties of Poll Captains. At one time the party published six newspapers across the country simultaneously and ran a Co-operative Press Association to provide material for them.

Education for and about the labour movement was part of the CCF's broader educational programme, although the party did not develop a systematic educational strategy for trade unionists. Courses such as History of Canadian Trade Unions were a feature of the party's face-to-face and distance education offerings in the 1940s, but these courses were open to all party members. Following the CCL's endorsement of the CCF as labour's political arm in 1943, the congress established a political action committee (PAC) which was dominated by CCF-supporting labour leaders but which was unable to endorse the CCF explicitly because of continued opposition among some CCL affiliates to such a plan. Nonetheless, it fell to the PAC to pursue political organizing and educational strategies within the labour movement. CCF-supporting labour leaders cooperated with leading party strategists such as David Lewis in these endeavours.

Sources: Thomas Fisher Rare Book Library, University of Toronto, *Robert S. Kenny Collection*, Box 18, File 5, "Communist Party Educational Material. Study plans, handbooks, general policy statements, etc." *A Handbook of Communist Party Education*, typescript, no date, and Box 20, File 11, "Toronto Labor College," "Seven Day Labor College, 26 July to 2 August, 1925," Beatrice Brigden, General Secretary, People's Forum Speakers' Bureau, Brandon, Manitoba, "Ten Days' Labor College," no date, and "Toronto Labor College,

Announcement of Courses, 9 January to 5 April 1939"; Dean E.
McHenry, *The Third Force in Canada: The Cooperative Commonwealth
Federation, 1932-1948* (Westport, Conn.: Greenwood Press, 1976), 96-
97; Walter D. Young, *The Anatomy of a Party: The National CCF, 1932-
1961* (Toronto: University of Toronto Press, 1969), 50-53, 76-90, 120-
122, 125.

Conclusion

Between 1918 and 1946 Canadian labour education grew from a limited
number of evening classes to a broad-based movement encompassing university-
level courses, weekend institutes, summer schools and visual education in a
variety of institutional settings, with the WEA playing a major strategic role. The
WEA was transformed in the process from an organization coordinating
university-level instruction for workers to the central player in a national labour
education movement involving a range of activities. What was most significant
about the association's role was its many attempts and partial ability to function
as a non-sectarian, autonomous, dedicated labour education organization in a
broader labour movement suffering from divisions around a variety of issues.
Although the communist-led unions and the UAW were the most likely to work
with the WEA, the association genuinely attempted to be a service for the whole
labour movement. This meant ensuring as much as possible that workers had the
critical skills and the knowledge to participate fully in society as citizens, trade
unionists and workers. What type of unionism worker-students chose to pursue
or what political party they supported was not part of the association's agenda.

For some trade unionists and others, this autonomous, non-sectarian labour
education was a threat, was naïve, was actually sectarian (communist) or was
simply unsuited to the contemporary requirements of trade unions to train their
members in the machinery of the new industrial relations order. Unions with
social democratic leadership and university educators such as those at StFX, in
particular, were beginning during this period to develop a different kind of
labour education that would become dominant in Canada after 1946.

Notes

1. Craig Heron, *The Canadian Labour Movement: A Short History*, 2d ed. (Toronto: James Lorimer and Company, 1996), 46-75.

2. Jeffery Taylor, *Fashioning Farmers: Ideology, Agricultural Knowledge and the Manitoba Farm Movement, 1890-1925* (Regina: Canadian Plains Research Center/University of Regina, 1994), 18-20, 41-44; Gordon Selman, "The Invisible Giant: A History of Adult Education in British Columbia," in *Adult Education in Canada: Historical Essays* (Toronto: Thompson Educational Publishing, 1995), 265-324; Gordon Selman, "Stages in the Development of Canadian Adult Education," in *Adult Education in Canada*, 63-72 .

3. A recent treatment of the Antigonish Movement is contained in Jim Lotz and Michael Welton, *Father Jimmy: Life and Times of Jimmy Tompkins* (Wreck Cove, N.S.: Breton Books, 1997).

4. Selman, "Stages in the Development of Canadian Adult Education," 63-71; Taylor, *Fashioning Farmers*, 24-26, 108-116.

5. Michael Welton, "'On the Eve of a Great Mass Movement': Reflections on the Origins of the CAAE," in Frank Cassidy and Ron Faris, eds., *Choosing Our Future: Adult Education and Public Policy in Canada* (Toronto: OISE Press, 1987), 12-35; Juliet Pollard, "Propaganda for Democracy: John Grierson and Adult Education During the Second World War," in Michael R. Welton, ed., *Knowledge for the People: The Struggle for Adult Learning in English-Speaking Canada, 1828-1973* (Toronto: OISE Press, 1987), 129-150; Leonard Chatwin, "The Documentary Film in Adult Education," in J.R. Kidd, ed., *Adult Education in Canada* (Toronto: Canadian Association for Adult Education, 1950), 188-191.

6. Gordon Selman, "The Imaginative Training for Citizenship," in Sue M. Scott, Bruce Spencer and Alan M. Thomas, eds., *Learning for Life: Canadian Readings in Adult Education* (Toronto: Thompson Educational Publishing, 1998), 28-29.

7. Archives of Ontario (AO), *Workers Educational Association (WEA) Papers*, MU 3990, File "Toronto WEA Records, 1923-1932," Seventh Annual Report, 1924-25, and Annual Report, 1929-30.

8. Drummond Wren, "Address to the President and Board Members of the WEA of Canada," presented 31 March 1951, "Education and Labour File, 1951-1971," Industrial Relations Centre Library, University of Toronto (Wren's Address, 1951), 6-7; AO, *WEA Papers*, MU 3990, File "Annual Report—WEA, 1932."

9. Wren's Address, 1951, 28-32; AO, *WEA Papers*, MU 4039, File "Seventh Annual Report—1936, WEA," C.O.G. Douie, "Adult Education in the Dominions."

10. Wren's Address, 1951, 6-7; Ian Radforth and Joan Sangster, "A Link Between Labour and Learning: The Workers Educational Association in Ontario, 1917-1951," *Labour/Le Travail* 8/9 (autumn 1981-82): 41-78; AO, *WEA Papers*, MU 4039, "Annual Report—WEA, 1938."

11. AO, *WEA Papers*, MU 3990, File "Minutes: WEA of Canada," Annual Report, 1942.

12. AO, *WEA Papers*, MU 4039, files "Eighth Annual Report—WEA, 1937" and "Annual Report—WEA, 1938."

13. St. Francis Xavier (StFX) University Archives, *Extension Department Records*, RG 30-3, "1932, Report of the Work of the St. Francis Xavier University Extension Department" and "Statement of an Educational.Program addressed to The Carnegie Corporation of New York by St. Francis Xavier University, Antigonish, Nova Scotia," no date; Jim Lotz and Michael R. Welton, "'Knowledge for the People': The Origins and Development of the Antigonish Movement," in Welton, ed., *Knowledge for the People*, 97-111; Lotz and Welton, *Father Jimmy*.

14. AO, *WEA Papers*, MU 4006, File "10.3 International Ladies Garment Workers Union"; Susan Stone Wong, "From Soul to Strawberries: The International Ladies Garment Workers' Union and Workers' Education, 1914-1950," in Joyce L. Kornbluh and Mary Frederickson, eds., *Sisterhood and Solidarity: Workers' Education for Women, 1914-1984* (Philadelphia: Temple University Press, 1984), 39-56; Elvira R. Tarr, "Union-based Labor Education: Lessons from the ILGWU," in Steven H. Landon, Elvira R. Tarr, and Joseph F. Wilson, *The Re-Education of the American Working Class* (New York: Greenwood Press, 1990), 63-70.

15. Thomas E. Linton, *An Historical Examination of the Purposes and Practices of the Education Program of the United Automobile Workers of America, 1936-1959* (Ann Arbor: School of Education, University of Michigan, 1965), 33-39; Richard J. Altenbaugh, *Education for Struggle: The American Labor Colleges of the 1920s and 1930s* (Philadelphia: Temple University Press, 1990); Daniel Benedict, "Good-bye to Homer Martin," *Labour/Le Travail* 29 (spring 1992): 142; Charlotte Yates, *From Plant to Politics: the Autoworkers Union in Postwar Canada* (Philadelphia: Temple University Press, 1993), 28. Go to http://unionlearning.athabascau.ca to see a video clip from *Building Industrial Unionism* (Detroit: United Autoworkers, 1943) showing UAW summer-school education.

16. AO, *WEA Papers*, MU 4029, File "Carnegie Corporation of New York," various letters from Wren to the Carnegie Corporation, 1940 to 1944; National Archives of Canada (NAC), *Canadian Labour Congress (CLC) Papers*, MG 28 I 103, Volume 242, File "General Correspondence, Workers Educational Association, 1946-1954," Brief Submitted to the Royal Commission on Education by the Workers' Educational Association, November 1946.

17. AO, *WEA Papers*, MU 3990, black binder, Minutes: WEA of Canada, "Annual Report, 1942."

18. AO, *WEA Papers*, MU 4029, File "Carnegie Corporation of New York," various letters from Wren to the Carnegie Corporation, 1940 to 1944, especially Wren to Robert Lester, 25 January 1944; Wren, 1951, 35-39.

19. AO, *WEA Papers*, MU 3997, File "Vancouver, B.C. (5)," clipping from the *Vancouver News Herald*, 1 February 1943, and MU 3990, black binder, "Minutes: WEA of Canada," Annual Report, 1942, 5, and MU 4029, File "Carnegie Corporation of New York," Drummond Wren to Charles Dollard, 3 February 1940 and 14 May 1942, and MU 3990, File "Minutes: WEA of Canada."

20. Wren's Address, 1951, 19-20; AO, *WEA Papers*, MU 3990, File "Minutes: WEA of Canada," Minutes of Board of Directors Meeting, 13 December 1942; NAC, *CLC Papers*, MG 28 I 103, Volume 242, File 14, Drummond Wren to Aaron Mosher, 14 April 1943.

21. *Labour's Film Forum* 2 (8): (May 1945); AO, *WEA Papers*, MU 3990, File "Minutes: WEA of Canada," various references from 1942 to 1945, and MU 3996, File "Vancouver, BC," various letters from Claude Donald to Drummond Wren, 1942-1945; NAC, *CLC Papers*, MG 28 I 103, Volume 188, File 25, Isabel Jordan, Information Section, NFB, to Norman Dowd, CCL, 10 December 1945; NAC, *CLC Papers*, MG 28 I 103, Volume 231, File 6, *Labour Film Handbook* (Ottawa: NFB, 1946). Go to http://unionlearning.athabascau.ca to see a video clip from the discussion trailer of *Partners in Production* (Ottawa: National Film Board, 1945).

22. Wren's Address, 1951, 21; NAC, *CLC Papers*, MG 28 I 103, Volume 128, File 25, C.H. Millard, National Director, USWA, to Ross MacLean, Deputy Commissioner, National Film Board, 4 April 1945, and Volume 242, File 11, Eugene Forsey to Pat Conroy, no date (but spring 1945).

23. NAC, *CLC Papers*, MG 28 I 103, Volume 231, File 6, Andy Andras to Pat Conroy, 17 April 1946; Pollard, "Propaganda for Democracy," 143-144; Chatwin, "The Documentary Film in Adult Education," 187-194; Reg Whitaker and Gary Marcuse, *Cold War Canada: The Making and Unmaking of a National Security State, 1945-1957* (Toronto: University of Toronto Press, 1994), chapter 10.

24. Marcus Klee, "'Hands-off Labour Forum': The Making and Unmaking of National Working-Class Radio Broadcasting in Canada, 1935-1944," *Labour/Le Travail* 35 (spring 1995): 107-132; Wren's Address, 1951, 16-18; AO, *WEA Papers*, MU 3990, File "Minutes: WEA of Canada," Annual Report, 1942.

25. Wren's Address, 1951, 24-27, 32-34; Radforth and Sangster, "'A Link between Labour and Learning'," 53, 69-71; AO, *WEA Papers*, MU 3990, File "Minutes: WEA of Canada," Annual Report, 1942; NAC, *CLC Papers*, MG 28 I 103, Volume 242, File "General Correspondence, Workers Educational Association, 1946-1954," Brief Submitted to the Royal Commission on Education by the Workers' Educational Association, November 1946, 13-14.

26. Wren's Address, 1951, 35-37.

27. Wren's Address, 1951, 10-13; AO, *WEA Papers*, MU 4029, File "Carnegie Corporation of New York," Drummond Wren to Charles Dollard, 19 May 1942, and MU 3990, File "Minutes: WEA Canada," Annual Report, 1942. Go to http://unionlearning.athabascau.ca to see a video clip of the Port Hope school from *Labour Looks Ahead* (Ottawa: National Film Board, 1945).

28. Paul Phillips, *No Power Greater: A Century of Labour in British Columbia* (Vancouver: B.C. Federation of Labour, 1967), 127; AO, *WEA Papers*, MU 3990, File "Minutes: WEA of Canada," Minutes of Board of Directors meeting, 18 May 1941; AO, *WEA Papers*, MU 3996, File "Vancouver, BC (2)," Claude Donald to Drummond Wren, 5 July 1945; AO, *WEA Papers*, MU 3996, files "Vancouver, BC (2)," "Vancouver, BC (3)," and "Vancouver, BC (4)," various documents; AO, *WEA Papers*, MU 3997, File "Vancouver, BC," various documents.

29. AO, *WEA Papers*, MU 3996, File "Vancouver, BC (2)," various documents, File "Vancouver, BC (3)," Claude Donald to Drummond Wren, 20 December 1944 and Claude Donald to Drummond Wren, 2 January 1945, and File "Vancouver, BC (4)," "WEA Offers New Study Courses to Out-of-town Unions," *BC District Union News* 10 January 1945.

30. AO, *WEA Papers*, MU 3997, File "Vancouver, BC (5)," Drummond Wren to Gordon Maxwell, 3 August 1939; and MU 3996, File "Vancouver, BC (4)," various documents.

31. AO, *WEA Papers*, MU 3996, File "Vancouver, B.C (3)," various documents.

32. Leo Huberman, *The Truth About Unions* (New York: Reynal & Hitchcock Inc., 1946); AO, *WEA Papers*, MU 3996, File "Vancouver, B.C.," Claude Donald to Drummond Wren, 17 September 1946; University of British Columbia (UBC) Library, Special Collections, *International Woodworkers of America Records*, Roll 2, "WEA Summer School 1946, G.S. Culhane, Problems of Union Organization."

33. AO, *WEA Papers*, MU 3997, File "Winnipeg, Man." and File "Winnipeg WEA: Annual Returns"; University of Manitoba, Department of Archives and Special Collections, *University of Manitoba Continuing Education Division Papers*, Box 34, File 7, various documents, Box 49, File 9, various documents, Box 60, File 11, various documents, Box 69, File 5, various documents, Box 77, File 23, various documents, and Box 86, File 18, various documents.

34. AO, *WEA Papers*, MU 3996, File "Vancouver, BC (3)," Address by Drummond Wren to annual convention of WEA BC, no date; NAC, *CLC Papers*, MG 28 I 103, Volume 242, File "General Correspondence, Workers Educational Association, 1946-1954," Brief Submitted to the Royal Commission on Education by the Workers' Educational Association, November 1946; Wren's Address, 1951.

35. Richard E. Dwyer, *Labor Education in the U.S.: An Annotated Bibliography* (Metuchen, N.J. and London: The Scarecrow Press, Inc., 1977), 1-16; Mark Starr, *Labor Looks at Education*, The Inglis Lecture, 1946 (Cambridge: Harvard University Press, 1947), 23-24.

36. NAC, *CLC Papers*, MG 28 I 103, Volume 122, File 21, Pat Conroy to A.R. Mosher, 29 November 1943, Memorandum on Workers' Education for Local Chartered Unions.

37. NAC, *CLC Papers*, MG 28 I 103, Volume 267, File 3, Bert Hepworth, Chair, Education and Recreation Committee, Montreal Labour Council, CCL, to Eugene Forsey, Director of Research, CCL, 10 November 1944, and Volume 122, File 21, Proposals for Educational Activities by the Canadian Congress of Labour during 1945-46, no date, The Canadian Congress of Labour, Committee on Education, Dr. E.A. Forsey, Chairman, no date, A. Andras, Report of Attendance as Student at the University of Wisconsin School for Workers, Madison, July 23rd to August 4th, 1945, A. Andras and Bert Hepworth, Report on Trip to New York, October 15-20, 1945, and A. Andras, A Proposal regarding the Promotion of Workers' Education by the Congress, no date.

38. NAC, *Clarence Jackson Papers*, MG 31 B 54, Volume 2, File 25 "UE education programme, 1944," and Volume 3, File 13, "UE education programme, no date, 1945-1953," UE-CIO Labor College, 21-28 July 1945, Port Hope, A Trade Union School for Local Leaders; NAC, *Lincoln Bishop Papers*, MG 31 B 18, Volume 8, File 4, Public Speaking and Leadership Training, Suggested Topics and Reading References, Grand Division, CBRE and OTW, Ottawa, 1946.

39. AO, *WEA Papers*, MU 4005, File 10.1.2[2], "United Automobile Workers Regional Office for Canada," Drummond Wren to George Burt, 30 August 1939; Burt to Wren, 26 October 1939; Wren to Burt, 15 May 1940; Burt to Wren, 24 September 1940.

40. AO, *WEA Papers*, MU 4005, File 10.1.2[2], "United Automobile Workers Regional Office for Canada," Drummond Wren to George Burt, 27 September 1940.

41. AO, *WEA Papers*, MU 4005, File 10.1.2[2], "United Automobile Workers Regional Office for Canada," George Burt to Drummond Wren, 12 February 1942, and Wren to Burt, 18 November 1940, and MU 4006, File 10.1.8, "United Automobile Workers Local 222 (Oshawa)," notes on educational meeting, local 222, 9 January 1941, and Educational Committee Meeting, local 222, 24 January 1941, and MU 4005, File 10.1.3, "United Automobile Workers District Council 26," Drummond Wren to Fred Joyce, Secretary-Treasurer, 4 March 1941.

42. AO, *WEA Papers*, MU 4005, File 10.1, "United Automobile Workers of America," UAW-CIO Canadian Summer School in cooperation with the Workers' Educational Association at the WEA Labour College, Port Hope, 7-14 August 1943.

43. AO, *WEA Papers*, MU 4005, File 10.1.2, "United Automobile Workers Regional Office for Canada," Drummond Wren to George Burt, 4 December 1943.

44. AO, *WEA Papers*, MU 4006, File 10.3, "International Ladies Garment Workers Union," various documents; Max Swerdlow, *Brother Max: Labour Organizer and Educator* (St. John's Nfld.: Committee on Canadian Labour History, 1990), 10-13.

45. NAC, *CLC Papers*, MG 28 I 103, Volume 218, File 9, "Dalhousie University, 1943-45," Trade Union Advisory Committee, Minutes of Meeting, Dalhousie University, 7 February 1944 and circular letter from L. Richter, Director, Maritime Labour Institute, 1 November 1945. Go to http://unionlearning.athabascau.ca to see a video clip of the Maritime Labour Institute from *Labour Looks Ahead* (Ottawa: National Film Board, 1945).

46. StFX University Archives, *Extension Department Records*, RG 30-3, "Announcement of Labor Classes, 1939," and "Action on Part of Locals Scored," *The Maritime Cooperator*, 8 November 1939, and "Labor Editorial," *The Maritime Cooperator*, 1 February 1940.

47. StFX University Archives, *Extension Department Records*, "Labor Unions Grow Strong," *The Maritime Cooperator*, 1 December 1941, and "Educational Program for Labor Leaders," *The Maritime Cooperator*, 1 March 1946, and "1943 Labour School of the Air, Radio Course in Labor Problems" and "The Program, by Rev. Joseph A. Macdonald."

CHAPTER 3

From a Movement to a System: 1947-1955

The decade after the Second World War was transitional in the history of Canadian labour education. The Workers' Educational Association (WEA) lost its central place in organization and provision, while individual unions and congresses developed more substantial internal educational capacity. The anti-communist hysteria that was a fundamental feature of North American society during these years permeated the labour movement. In this atmosphere, the WEA, as a non-sectarian organization that worked with non-communist- and communist-led unions, became identified and denounced as communist because of the company it sometimes kept. Furthermore, as unions settled into patterns of relative security and permanency in the post-war era, they devoted more attention and resources to their own union education. Unions turned inward and concentrated on survival and expansion, which meant that there was less need for groups such as the WEA that spanned the whole labour movement and delivered educational services designed as much to develop critical working-class thinkers as to train union officers and stewards. Furthermore, social democratic union leaders and staff wanted a political education that focused on support for the Co-operative Commonwealth Federation (CCF) rather than on broader public-policy issues. This shift was accompanied by a change in how the labour movement related to adult and post-secondary educators. In earlier years the WEA had mediated most of the interaction between labour and educational organizations. With the removal of the association as a significant player in labour education, congresses and their affiliates cultivated direct relations with universities, the Canadian Association for Adult Education (CAAE) and similar bodies. These new constellations created a Canadian labour education that was very different in 1956 than it had been in 1946.

Context

With war's end, and based on a trade union membership that had doubled during the war, workers were determined to gain pay raises after wartime wage controls. During 1946 and 1947, there were four hundred strikes across the resource and manufacturing sectors of the economy, involving about 175,000 workers. And, for the most part, these strikes were successful. Average wages increased from about seventy cents to ninety cents per hour and the average work week fell from forty-four to forty-two hours a week between 1945 and 1948. In the latter year the federal government passed the *Industrial Relations and Disputes*

Investigation Act to replace P.C. 1003 and establish a permanent industrial relations framework in Canada. The provinces followed suit and had passed their own legislation by the 1950s. This meant that employers were compelled to negotiate collective agreements with unions that had majority support in a workplace. In return, employers insisted on and received "management rights" clauses, giving them exclusive control over work organization and the overall direction of the firm; negotiations were restricted to salaries, benefits, and the ways in which management pursued its rights. Disputes over the agreement, once it was signed, were dealt with through a grievance system with a series of steps, ending with an independent arbitrator. Union stewards were responsible for representing members in this system and playing a role in administering the agreements. Strikes (and employer lockouts) were restricted to the period during which a new collective agreement was being negotiated. Union recognition strikes were no longer necessary because of the legal system now in place for establishing union representation in a workplace. More importantly, strikes were illegal during the life of the contract, which meant that any and all issues that arose in the workplace had to be dealt with through the grievance procedure (if they were covered by the agreement) or placed on the agenda for the next round of bargaining. Gone were the days of the short workplace action to resolve a specific issue. When these did take place, and they did occasionally, the union had a responsibility to police its membership to protect its legal interests. Unions, with these new responsibilities, grew in size and stature, but concentrated more of their energies on negotiating and administering collective agreements and less on mobilizing their memberships and engaging in broad-based political action.

In fact, the labour movement was engaged in internal political battles in the post-war period that shaped the future of the movement. Between 1948 and 1950, the Canadian Congress of Labour (CCL), under social democratic leadership, expelled the International Union of Mine, Mill, and Smelter Workers (Mine-Mill), the United Electrical, Radio and Machine Workers (UE), the International Woodworkers of America (IWA) and the International Leather and Fur Workers because their memberships continued to elect and support communist leaders. The Trades and Labor Congress of Canada (TLC) leadership, meanwhile, which tended to be Liberal or non-partisan, was slower to respond to the anti-communist hysteria of the time, but it too eventually expelled the Canadian Seamen's Union (CSU) and the United Fishermen and Allied Workers (UFAW) because of their communist leaders. Nothing was gained from these purges and much was lost. While a handful of communist trade unionists were dogmatically loyal to the Soviet Union, which raised questions about their ability to represent their members, the vast majority of Communist Party members and sympathizers in the labour movement were, first and foremost, militant activists who believed in organization, mobilization and industrial and political action. The silencing or chastening of these voices at a time when unions were moving towards a more institutionalized and bureaucratic role in industrial relations meant that unions were in danger of becoming, first and foremost, service organizations for their members.

In 1956, when the Canadian Labour Congress (CLC) was born from the merger of the TLC and the CCL, the typical union member was a skilled or semi-skilled male, working in the resource, manufacturing, transportation or construction industries. There were few white-collar or women workers in the movement. A major drive between 1948 and 1952 to organize Eaton's department stores was unsuccessful and government employees outside of Saskatchewan were excluded from the new collective bargaining legislation. Furthermore, the leadership of the movement at the time of the merger accepted the new industrial relations regime and expected employers—who often did their best to undermine the union-friendly aspects of collective-bargaining legislation—to do the same. Especially after their unions won automatic dues checkoffs, these leaders built and presided over substantial organizations legally empowered to negotiate and enforce collective agreements, and staffed by servicing, communications, research, education, support staff and other personnel.

By 1956 the labour movement was accepted by the mainstream of Canadian opinion as a legitimate, if tenuous, part of the social landscape. And labour leaders, while they championed social reform initiatives such as pensions, health care and expanded educational opportunities, accepted the right of private employers to own and manage their enterprises as they saw fit. What they sought for their members was a share of the economic wealth that was being generated in this period and a welfare system that would provide for them when they needed it.[1]

In adult education, the decade after the end of the Second World War was a period of experimentation, investigation and consolidation. Saskatchewan's CCF government established a Division of Adult Education shortly after it was elected in 1944, while Ontario addressed adult education issues as part of its 1945 Royal Commission on Education and Manitoba established a royal commission exclusively on adult education in the same year. At the national level, the federal government investigated adult education vicariously through the 1949 Royal Commission on Arts, Letters and Science, which led to increased support and funding for federal cultural institutions such as the Canadian Broadcasting Corporation (CBC) and the National Film Board (NFB). These governmental incursions into adult education reflected both an increased awareness of its potential for shaping citizens and an apprehensiveness on the part of some conservative elements that the field was dominated by leftists. Watson Thomson, the first director of Saskatchewan's Division of Adult Education, was labelled a radical by business people and was forced by his social democratic bosses to quit his job, while John Grierson resigned from the Manitoba royal commission because he was labelled a communist. The adult education field was not immune from the general purging of progressive voices that was a feature of the late 1940s and early 1950s.

The CAAE achieved some success after the war in coordinating adult education activity across the country, but it also lost much of the radical edge that had been reflected in the 1944 manifesto. From 1946 the Joint Planning

Commission, a CAAE committee representing a diverse range of adult educators from across the country, established an annual agenda around a single theme for participating organizations (about one hundred during the 1950s). The CAAE then provided print and audio-visual library resources to support the year's study topic, which might be intercultural relations, retraining and employment, broadcasting policy, industrial relations or some other area of public-policy interest.[2]

The Marginalization of the WEA

During the war, as was shown in Chapter 2, some social democratic labour leaders distanced themselves from the WEA because of its willingness to cooperate with all trade unionists, including communists. In the Cold War hysteria of the post-war period, this distance became greater and attacks on the association increased. A series of incidents between 1944 and 1951 resulted in the decline of WEA influence in the field of Canadian labour education.

Staff problems was one area of difficulty. In 1944 the association chose to sever its relationship with two staff members, one communist and the other social democrat, because neither seemed able to act in the non-sectarian style required of WEA employees. John Wigdor, a Labour Progressive Party (LPP) member, was hired in January 1944 as assistant general secretary when Wren became educational director for the United Automobile Workers' (UAW) Canadian district. Wigdor had established the Vancouver office of the San Francisco-based Pacific Coast Labor Bureau (which later became the Trade Union Research Bureau) in 1939 and was active in the Vancouver WEA and the Boilermakers and Iron Shipbuilders Union (Boilermakers). Wren was confident, when hiring Wigdor, that his new employee would be non-sectarian because, when the Vancouver association was formed, Wigdor told his party comrades that "this is the WEA and there will be no orders from Moscow." Unfortunately, however, after moving to Toronto to work for the national association, Wigdor included too much politics in his WEA messages for Wren's and the executive board's liking. Furthermore, according to the board, Wigdor did not appreciate that association work required advanced classroom activity as well as mass education. His interest was in the latter rather than the former. By Wren's account, Wigdor was well suited for internal union educational work, but not for WEA duties. With some persuading from Wren, UE hired Wigdor as its educational director and he resigned from the WEA in November 1944. Idele Wilson, who had been WEA research director since 1939, resigned in 1945 to work for UE as well.

While wrestling with the Wigdor issue, the national board was also trying to decide what to do about Harvey Ladd. Hired as an office assistant, Ladd was too much of a CCF partisan for Wren and the board. For example, he went to the 1943 CCL convention and was one of the most vocal supporters of CCF affiliation even though the understanding between Wren and Ladd before the convention was that he would not take part in any congress policy discussions. At the same convention, Ladd was offered a job as Mine-Mill's Canadian education director and newspaper editor. Bob Carlin, Mine-Mill's eastern Canadian director, reported incorrectly to his union brothers and sisters that Ladd was recommended by the WEA. This led others in the union, including western Canadian director Harvey Murphy, to believe that Ladd's appointment was non-partisan. Nigel Morgan, Murphy's comrade in the British Columbia LPP, "hit the roof" when he heard of the appointment, because he knew Ladd and considered him to be a CCF sectarian. The offer was withdrawn. Early in 1945, however, Ladd was hired by Mine-Mill's eastern region to edit its newspaper and he resigned from the WEA.

As it discussed the Wigdor and Ladd cases in late 1944, the WEA board was conscious of the political repercussions that would flow from the termination of one or both of these appointments. When rumours began to circulate that Wigdor would be fired, and that "serious political consequences" would follow, Wren met with LPP leader Tim Buck to determine what that party's attitude was towards the WEA. Buck responded that the party had no interest in controlling the WEA, but that there would be repercussions if Wigdor were fired and Ladd were retained. Meanwhile, it was clear that if Ladd were fired he would turn to Charlie Millard to mobilize the CCF forces in the labour movement in support of his cause. Wren suggested that a WEA delegation should visit Millard to explain the problems they had with Ladd. Millard subsequently cooperated with the association to find Ladd another position.[3]

While there was significant antipathy between communists and social democrats in the labour movement during 1944-45, and the WEA had to play a delicate game of maintaining its non-sectarian position in this context, it was possible to deal with these two staffing problems by ensuring that both groups were treated the same. After the war, however, as social democrats took advantage of the general anti-communist hysteria of the time to defeat their communist opponents in the labour movement, the WEA was less able to sustain its non-sectarian balancing act.

In 1947 another staffing issue arose that was more troublesome and was used by social democrats to label the association as communist. This case involved Harold Beveridge. Beveridge worked for the WEA from 1939 to 1942, primarily as a researcher on the film strip project but also doing educational work for the UAW and others. From 1942 to 1944 he worked for the federal government's Wartime Prices and Trade Board as an economist, and from 1944 to 1946 he was at the NFB as a production assistant, learning the various aspects of film production. He came back to the WEA in April 1946 as director of research. Later that year he made the mistake of running an article in *Labour News* that bore a striking similarity to an article by Tim Buck that had appeared in the LPP's *Canadian Tribune* a few days earlier. Eugene Forsey, the ever-vigilant CCL research director and CCF partisan, spotted the parallels between the two articles and certain inaccuracies in both. He alerted his CCF comrades in the labour movement, notably Charlie Millard, to this

Communist teachings alleged
by WEA staff
66   CHAPTER 3 / FROM A MOVEMENT TO A SYSTEM: 1947-1955

apparent communist content in WEA publications. This followed an earlier incident in which Forsey reviewed for the CCL a WEA analysis of the federal Speech from the Throne, which had been written by lawyer Irving Himel for the association's Labour Legislative Service. Forsey dismissed the analysis by saying, first, that "Himel is a pompous Communist fool" and, second, that this and previous bulletins from the same service missed important bills, particularly those favoured or supported by CCF legislators. Beveridge resigned as a result of his indiscretion, and both incidents forced the WEA further on to the defensive against charges of communist sympathies.

At about the same time, another staff member was causing additional political problems for the association. In the summer of 1944, the association rented its Port Hope facility to the LPP-affiliated Labour Youth Federation for a summer school. (It was not uncommon for labour organizations to rent their facilities to communist organizations during this time.) Ed Joseph, who was briefly a member of the LPP, attended this school, and later became Ontario organizer for the WEA. While he was employed by the association, Joseph told the Conservative Member of Parliament for Port Hope that, at the 1944 school, communism had been taught by Tim Buck and others. The WEA reviewed Joseph's performance, found him to be incompetent, and dismissed him. These charges provided further fuel for people such as Forsey and Millard in their efforts to paint the association a deeper shade of red.[4]

 These events, and the deepening anti-communist sentiment in the labour movement, played a role in Wren's dismissal from the UAW staff. After Walter Reuther became international president of the UAW in 1946 and gained control of the union's executive board in 1947, he set about to remove all alleged communists and their sympathizers from paid positions within the union. Wren was on his list. Victor Reuther, director of education for the union, wrote to Wren at the end of 1947 to inform him that he was being terminated because the UAW constitution stated that staff should be appointed from the membership and Wren was not a UAW member. Six days later, however, Victor wrote to his brother Walter with a different and fuller account of why Wren was being fired. There were four broad reasons, according to Victor. First, Wren had not produced an educational programme in Canada to justify the expenditure there. Summer schools never exceeded thirty participants and locals in Oshawa, Brantford and Windsor complained about the lack of UAW educational activity. Second, Wren was incompetent in his duties as an educational representative. When asked for articles on Canada for union publications, he sent either no material or material from the WEA that was inaccurate or out of date. The republished Buck article, for example, contained "naïve references" to the Marxist theory of surplus value. Furthermore, Wren antagonized other Congress of Industrial Organizations (CIO) unions in Canada, thereby bringing disrepute on the UAW. Third, Victor alleged, Wren was a member of the LPP and, probably, a member of the party's political bureau. He employed communists such as Harold Beveridge and invited well-known communists such as Tim Buck to attend the Port Hope summer

Wren dismissed

school. Finally, Wren's close association with the LPP meant that the Steelworkers, the United Rubber Workers of America (URWA), the United Packinghouse Workers of America (UPWA) and many members of the UAW refused to work with him. This anti-communist ascendancy in the UAW also produced an internal union investigation of the WEA, undertaken by a committee dominated by non-communist members, which concluded that the association was non-partisan, was doing good work and was worthy of the UAW's continued support.[5]

George Burt, who had been Wren's supporter and comrade since 1938, was a political pragmatist who ensured his own survival under Reuther's leadership by shifting to the right and accepting that Wren had to be sacrificed as part of this significant transition in the UAW's history. In contrast to Victor Reuther's scathing attack on Wren's ability and competence, Burt told Wren early in 1948 that it "has always been my opinion that you were capable and at all times had the interests of the UAW-CIO, and the labour movement in general, as your first consideration." (Indeed, the understanding with Burt when Wren was hired had been that Wren would divide his educational work between the UAW and the broader labour movement in the interests of labour unity; Wren spent about 40 percent of his time exclusively on UAW activities during his years with the auto union.) In 1951, however, Burt argued that Wren had made mistakes as general secretary by, for example, hiring Harold Beveridge and not adapting to political changes in the labour movement. Since Wren did not change, "we [the UAW] changed our educational director," Burt said matter of factly.[6]

The WEA's financial state, shaky at the best of times, was fundamentally threatened between 1947 and 1950 by these events and by the labour movement's apparent unwillingness to support the association. In 1947 the Ontario provincial grant was held up because of charges of communism against the association emanating from the CCL's Ontario Federation of Labour (OFL-CCL). The OFL-CCL leadership, including Millard and others, told the provincial department of education that the labour movement did not support the WEA and hence it should not receive government grants. Responding to a challenge from the department to disprove this charge, Wren and the association solicited letters of support from unions representing the vast majority of organized workers in Ontario. Although the OFL-CCL tried to ensure that its affiliates did not send these letters, the province agreed to reinstate the association's $4,000 grant. This money arrived in April 1948, but no grant was received for 1948-49; the 1949 grant arrived as usual, but there were no funds from the Ontario government in 1950.

While the difficulties the association faced in 1947-48 originated with the CCL and its affiliates, in 1950 the TLC used the communist issue to question its relationship with the WEA. As a condition of further cooperation with the association, the OFL-TLC requested that Wren issue a public statement indicating that he was opposed to "communism and any form of socialism." Other labour leaders, including TLC president Percy Bengough, were making similar

WEA's financial stability at risk

Wren resigned to save WEA

statements. Wren issued a statement saying that he did not belong to any political party, that he had not been approached by the Communist Party for the purpose of influencing WEA policy and that he would oppose the invasion of Canada by any country, communist or otherwise. Although the TLC initially accepted this statement, it was later deemed to be unacceptable and Wren's refusal to amend it was used as evidence of his communist leanings. Russell Harvey, a TLC representative on the association's national board, led the movement within his congress to have the labour movement gain more direct control over the WEA. As part of this process, he told the Ontario government, when the association was accused of communist sympathies, that the association did not have the confidence of the OFL-TLC.[7]

By 1950-51 it was clear to Wren and the national board that there was a concerted attempt on the part of individuals in both the CCL and the TLC to discredit the WEA and to either marginalize the association or bring it directly under the control of union leaders. It was also clear that Wren was the lightning rod for much of the anti-WEA sentiment and that, if the association had any chance of surviving, he would have to resign. On 31 March 1951 Wren resigned formally as general secretary of the WEA after serving in that position for twenty-two years. He did not go quietly, however. As he departed, he delivered a long speech surveying the history of the WEA and offering his analysis of why the association, and he in particular, had been targeted by a significant section of the labour leadership.

Wren believed that the association was a victim of its own success and independence. During the 1940s, it had been the only independent organization in Canada that enjoyed the confidence of labour in such large measure. Union locals across the country were willing and anxious to work with and use the services of the association. And this grassroots support persisted until 1951, Wren claimed, despite the seeds of distrust that were being planted by individual labour leaders. Indeed, the fact that the association was so successful in serving the needs of union locals and rank-and-file members was perceived as a threat by these leaders. As long as the WEA confined its activities to evening classes dealing with general subjects, albeit from a labour point of view, union leaders gave the association token support, but once it began teaching trade unionists about trade unionism, collective bargaining and labour law, its independence and autonomy became a threat to the labour leadership. As an "outside" organization, it could not be trusted to teach union members about trade unionism. The WEA either had to be controlled by the trade union leadership or, failing that, had to be marginalized. In Wren's view, this illustrated that the Canadian labour movement was adopting the business-unionist philosophy of the United States, in which labour education became mere training and indoctrination, and was abandoning the British outlook characterized by a broader critical and social perspective. A non-sectarian, militant, autonomous and critical educational programme that catered to all parts of the labour movement was being abandoned in favour of narrow, union-based training that was under the control of union leaders. There was no room in this view of labour education for independent organizations.[8]

With Wren's departure, the WEA attempted to recreate itself in a way that might appeal to the union leadership. Charlie Millard told the association that the Steelworkers and the CCL were very happy with the internal educational programmes they were developing, and had no reason to use outside agencies, although he did suggest that perhaps the association could work with the CAAE to become a co-ordinating educational service for the labour movement. Nonetheless, the national board devoted considerable time to developing various scenarios and canvassing the labour movement for input and response. With Wren out of the picture, labour leaders such as George Burt from the CCL and Russell Harvey from the TLC were open to suggestions. The CCL established a committee (including Burt, Harry Waisglass [who would found McMaster University's labour studies programme in the 1970s] and others) to explore cooperation with the WEA, while association leaders met with TLC leaders, including president Percy Bengough. Publicly, leaders from both labour centrals voiced support for the WEA and maintained that it had an important role to play as an independent organization in the labour education field. But what would that role be? There was agreement on what it would not be: a teacher of "trade unionism." In other words, unions and their creatures (congresses, councils, federations) would teach their members the various topics that have come to be known as union tools training (steward and related training, leadership training and so forth). Beyond that, the WEA might have some role to play in continuing to teach the more general social and economic courses that dealt with issues spanning the whole labour movement.

In these discussions during 1951 and 1952, despite apparent good will all around, the association's role became limited to evening courses on general topics. But a clear vision of how the association's programme would articulate with the union programmes never developed. The most logical role for the new WEA was providing upper-level labour education for those trade unionists who wanted to take further education after completing some internal union training. Ideally, union educators would have sat down with the WEA to plan a progression from union through WEA courses, but this never happened. Moreover, the union leadership, despite their rhetoric, did not work with the WEA to ensure that the association's government grants were reinstated. In fact, union educators had other things on their minds during this time. For one thing, they were busy developing their own internal educational programmes, and WEA-type general courses were not a priority. Furthermore, to the extent that they did think about external educational activity, they were more likely to turn directly to universities or the CAAE than to the WEA.[9]

The Development of Unions' Internal Educational Capacity

As noted in Chapter 2, the CCL began charting its own educational programme in 1943 with Pat Conroy's memorandum on workers' education, which was followed by other activities throughout 1945 and 1946. In 1947, the congress formally established an education committee composed initially of the education directors from the major congress affiliates and later expanded to include other unions that did not have staff dedicated to education. Andy Andras, who had been informally responsible for education since 1945 as assistant director of research, chaired the new committee until 1950, when he was succeeded by Jim McGuire of the Canadian Brotherhood of Railway, Employees and Other Transport Workers (CBRE). Howard Conquergood, director of education and welfare for the Steelworkers, served as the de facto director of CCL education from 1947 to 1950 while working full time for his home union. When the CCL sorted out some funding problems with the CIO in 1951, and was able to dedicate at least $25,000 annually for education (compared to $6,400 in 1949), Conquergood was hired as the CCL's full-time director of education and welfare. Bert Hepworth from CBRE, who had been agitating for a CCL education programme since 1944, became part-time assistant director of education in 1952. By the 1952-53 fiscal year, the congress was spending $35,000 on education, with $11,500 on administrative staff salaries and $6,000 on production staff salaries.[10]

Conquergood was a product of the Toronto middle class. A graduate of the private and prestigious University of Toronto Schools, who attended Queen's University and the University of Toronto, he combined his scholastic activity with football (including winning the Grey Cup one year), playing in a jazz band and working with troubled youth while he was a post-secondary student. Active in the CCF youth movement (CCYM) in the thirties, he was director of Community Work at the Hamilton YMCA when Charlie Millard recruited him in 1943 to set up the Steelworkers' education and welfare department. He made his mark with steelworkers during the 1946 steel strike, when he set up a fund-raising and welfare distribution system in Hamilton, assisted members who were arrested and was even arrested himself. When the magistrate asked him for a reference after his arrest, he named the officers of the court, whom he had worked with during his YMCA days.[11]

While Conquergood's 1951 appointment as full-time CCL education director was made possible by the stable funding the congress was able to provide, a clarification of the relationship between the education committee and the director was precipitated by conflicts between Conquergood and education committee chair Andy Andras. Andras, it will be recalled, investigated workers' education and had proposed an initial programme in 1945. He had more than a passing interest in the subject, then, and was the first staff member at the congress to have any responsibility for education, although this was never reflected in his job title. Conquergood complained to Pat Conroy in 1950 that he was unable to work with Andras. One source of the problem was that Conquergood worked for the

Canadian Congress of Labour Education Committee members in 1954. Standing, left to right: Andy Andras, CCL Research Department; John Lenglet, United Packinghouse Workers of America; Milton Montgomery, United Steelworkers of America; Gordon Milling, Ontario Federation of Labour; Alan Thomas, Canadian Association for Adult Education; Jack Larette, United Rubber Workers of America; William MacDonald, United Autoworkers; Henry Weisbach, CCL. Seated, left to right: Don Sleven, United Autoworkers; Mary Kehoe, CCL Publicity; unidentified; Bert Hepworth, Canadian Brotherhood of Railway Employees; Howard Conquergood, CCL Education Director. *Jim Yardley. National Archives of Canada, PA-120611.*

Steelworkers, but had his CCL-related expenses covered by the congress. Andras, as a CCL staff member, approved the expenses, and was apparently questioning some of Conquergood's expenditures. Conquergood suggested to Conroy that either Andras should have responsibility for education or the education committee should be chaired by an elected member of the executive rather than a staff member. As a result, Jim McGuire replaced Andras as committee chair and Conquergood was formally appointed as education director. Andras's formal connection with education ceased as a result, and he concentrated his energies in the research department.[12]

Under Conquergood's direction, the CCL established the foundation of the Canadian system of union education that would persist throughout the second half of the twentieth century. The three elements of this system in the CCL years were the weekend institutes, staff-training seminars and the week-long summer or winter schools. In 1948 Conquergood toured the country to establish institutes in conjunction with local labour councils, which were officially in charge of the institutes and responsible for planning and publicity. The following year there were twenty institutes across the country with a total attendance of about two thousand. By the mid-1950s, approximately five thousand trade unionists were taking courses in about forty institutes. The core of the institute was short courses totalling about nine hours of training over two days. A typical institute would have courses on the job of the steward, grievance handling, making the local more effective, labour legislation and how to conduct a local meeting. Other courses/ subjects included credit unions and cooperatives, education leadership, local papers and radio and the history of trade unionism. The course work was supplemented by plenary sessions where union leaders or outside speakers spoke on topics such as labour's role in the community, the university in the community or the Canadian labour movement and world affairs.

Staff-training seminars, meanwhile, began in 1949 for employees of the CCL and unions affiliated to the congress. By 1955, four- to five-day seminars were being held in all five regions of the country, dealing with topics such as trends in collective bargaining, preparing and presenting a case before a labour relations board, CCL education, political action, organizing techniques and techniques in leading an educational course. A staff book service was initiated in 1953 that allowed congress and affiliated-union staff to borrow general interest books by post.

The week-long schools commenced in the summer of 1947 and the winter of 1948. The first CCL summer school was held at Geneva Park, north of Toronto. Subsequent central Canadian schools were held at the Port Huron, Michigan, camp owned by the UAW and operated in conjunction with the Michigan CIO. The first western Canadian summer school was held in 1954 at the Winnipeg YMCA's summer camp. Winter schools began at the University of Toronto in 1948 and were organized jointly with the university's Institute of Industrial Relations. At the Toronto winter school, participants took major (twenty-one-hour) and minor (ten-hour) courses. The curriculum was a mix of tools and issues courses. Tools courses included job evaluation, time study, the union contract, corporation finance and labour law, while the issues courses included economic and political trends, the union in modern society and the government of Canada.

The summer schools at Port Huron, meanwhile, offered only tools courses, and reflected the influence of the international offices of the UAW and CIO. Besides the standard tools courses, participants could study education leadership, time study, labour journalism, effective political action techniques and radio broadcasting. Evening sessions dealt with broader issues, including labour in world affairs and farmer-labour relations. Amicable cross-border tensions developed after the first year of Canadian participation in the CIO school. Being forced to drink American beer for a week at Port Huron in 1948 was too much for the Canadian trade unionists, and they successfully insisted that the organizers import a substantial supply of the stronger and fuller-bodied northern brew for the 1949 session.[13]

While the CCL had developed a substantial educational programme by the mid-1950s, the TLC was relatively inactive. An education committee was formed in the late 1940s, composed of members chosen to give geographic representation, and limited its activities in its early years to preparing course materials in public

Delegates attending a weekend school on compensation for unionists at Timmins, Ontario, in 1955. Left to right: Mrs. MacInnes, Mrs. Degurse, Mrs. Behie. *Photographer unknown. National Archives of Canada, PA-124471.*

speaking and basic economics. The western federations of labour, some district trades and labour councils, and several of the larger TLC affiliates had education committees that organized weekend schools in the late 1940s and early 1950s. Max Swerdlow was appointed director of Organization and Education in 1952, with the understanding that he would devote some time to education when there was no organizing to do. When Swerdlow began to think about what it meant to organize a national educational programme for the TLC he turned first to American labour educators, such as Mark Starr at the International Ladies Garment Workers' Union (ILGWU), and then to Roby Kidd at the CAAE.

By 1954, Swerdlow was reporting that all of the federations of labour and many of the labour councils had established educational committees and were conducting programmes. The TLC role was primarily advisory, however, as Swerdlow did not have an education budget. Most programmes were weekend schools, but the British Columbia and Alberta federations of labour held week-long schools at Parkdale, British Columbia, and at the Banff School of Fine Arts. The weekend schools offered basic tools courses, while the week-long schools ventured into elementary economics, labour law and international affairs. Instruction was provided by leaders and staff in affiliated unions, who knew very little about teaching. As a result, Swerdlow worked with the CAAE to develop several instructor training courses.

In individual unions, meanwhile, provision varied from relatively developed programmes in the Steelworkers, UAW, CBRE, and the ILGWU to more rudimentary, but ideologically distinct, activity in UE, UFAW, Mine-Mill and the CSU. With Conquergood running the CCL education programme from 1947, the Steelworkers' programme became integrated to some degree with CCL activities. Steelworkers made up a substantial number of the participants in congress institutes and schools, at least in the Toronto and Hamilton areas. Besides participation in congress programmes, Conquergood and Gower Markle, his successor at the Steelworkers after 1951, concentrated on workshops, education kits and developing an extensive local programme in Hamilton. A series of one-day workshops were held each year for Steelworker locals on topics such as health and safety, unemployment insurance and workers' compensation. Furthermore, information and work kits were assembled and distributed. The information kits were sent once a month to about two thousand officers, committee members and stewards. The kit contained pamphlets, leaflets and background material on issues such as unemployment, grievance reports, racial discrimination, pensions and life insurance. Work kits were distributed on an occasional basis to serve specific committees.

The Hamilton area council of the Steelworkers, which represented about ten thousand members in twenty-three locals in 1950, had a number of active committees, including one devoted to education. The education committee formed a film council in the early 1950s to train operators and to organize monthly film nights in the locals. The committee also organized classes for stewards and on public speaking and parliamentary procedure. Plant education committees were responsible for generating class participants and distributing literature in the plants. The area-council education committee established a library in the union hall as well and published regular book reviews in the union paper to encourage members to use the library.[14]

After Wren's departure from the UAW at the end of 1947, William Macdonald, a Reuther loyalist and CCF partisan, was appointed education director for the union in Canada. Under Macdonald's direction, the Canadian programme became more integrated into the broader programme of the international, and concentration shifted from Wren's emphasis on general labour education to a narrower union education designed primarily to train stewards, committeemen and the local leadership and to ensure the stability of Reuther's regime. A substantial programme of workshops, classes and special projects developed in this period. One-day workshops and weekend institutes were held in the major UAW centres (Oshawa, Toronto, St. Catharines, Windsor) on topics such as health and safety, bargaining committees, local union publicity, credit unions and the union in national and international affairs. Weekly classes of eight-week's duration were held in some centres, organized and paid for by the Area Education Council, on steward training, advanced collective bargaining and economics. In newly organized plants, a short series of three initiation classes were held for new members covering the objectives of the union, where the due dollar goes and the economics of full employment.

The international UAW was committed to improving race relations in the post-war period, and this was reflected in special courses in the Canadian region designed to fight and eliminate discrimination based on colour and race. Special educational conferences were also held from about 1950 onward on the problems facing women workers, notably equal pay for equal work. Finally, Canadian UAW members made up the bulk of the participants at the CCL summer schools in Port Huron, Michigan, from 1948 onward. Seventy-eight autoworkers attended the 1951 school.[15]

While the Steelworkers and UAW, as major CIO unions, had substantial educational programmes organized and administered by their international offices, the CBRE, the major Canadian-based union in the CCL, had a significant programme of its own. CBRE secretary-treasurer Jim McGuire was the main force behind this activity. He was active in the CAAE, serving on its executive during this period, and chaired the CCL education committee from 1950. Under McGuire the brotherhood's programme stressed the development of well-informed members and competent officers on the one hand, and the cultivation of a responsible, democratic citizenship among the membership on the other. To this end weekend institutes and short evening courses, using audio-visual materials and conducted on a workshop basis, trained officers and stewards in topics such as the job of the president or the job of the financial officer. Following on from these short courses, leadership training courses were held on human relations, group discussion methods and educational methods. In some district councils, such as Manitoba in 1947 for example, film-forum evenings and a six-week course covering the history and current state of the CBRE were held. As a result of McGuire's broader labour and adult education interests, the CBRE cooperated with the CCL education programme, the CAAE, the Canadian Forum book service and other similar organizations.

In TLC-affiliated unions, meanwhile, the ILGWU continued to have the most developed educational programme. This union was also unique in Canadian and American labour education because of the breadth of its programme, offering language and vocational education as well as the more traditional tools and issues courses. In Montreal the union offered courses in both English and French. Furthermore, in the late 1940s "displaced persons" (post-war European refugees) were offered English classes and once-a-week evening forums featuring, for example, lectures and discussions on the history and geography of Canada. The Montreal forums had an average attendance of about two hundred, and often included banquets and socials. In the vocational area, the union organized and conducted its own courses for garment cutters, allowing members to qualify for promotion within the industry. Beyond this, the ILGWU conducted union education programmes with the standard curricula of steward and local leadership training, including films and filmstrips from the international union and other sources.[16]

Communist-led unions in both labour congresses, and as unaffiliated organizations after the expulsions of the late 1940s and early 1950s, did not have formal educational programmes to match the Steelworkers, UAW, ILGWU or even the CBRE. Nonetheless, they did undertake significant educational activity. This was in part a result of an approach to union education, also present in the UAW but relegated to a subordinate current after the Reuther ascendancy, that education should be intimately associated with action and grow out of day-to-day struggles and practice. In the UE, for example, steward meetings were held once a week, and the steward's role, in addition to handling grievances, was to distribute material and discuss it with the members on a regular basis. Membership meetings had an educational element and, during negotiations, extra meetings were held. UE also used radio to reach its membership and the broader community, with at least two locals conducting weekly broadcasts during this period. Beyond this, UE used the WEA's Port Hope facility for summer schools until 1950 and, beginning in 1951, held its own one-week district leadership school. And once a year, special meetings were held with officers and stewards to discuss the policy and activities of the union, including conferences on women in the labour movement. The UFAW, meanwhile, expelled from the TLC in 1954, had its own educational programme throughout this period, stressing union history and tools courses related to the union's particular circumstances. It cooperated with the Trade Union Research Bureau in Vancouver in the preparation of course materials. And the CSU cooperated with the WEA in the 1940s and used material from the National Maritime Union of America's education department, which was under the direction of noted worker-educator Leo Huberman.[17]

But what was being taught in these various courses and programmes? What methods were being used? And what educational philosophies, if any, guided the activities? The stewards' course was the basic component in all union education programmes. While all courses taught the basic elements of grievance handling, the broader role of the steward varied depending on the individual union. In the UAW, for example, stewards were taught the history of shop steward organizing through the lens of industrial unionism. In the standard UAW stewards' manual, which went through a number of editions in the 1940s and 1950s, shop steward history was traced from the First World War in England, with the UAW arguing that, after the war, English workers turned to stewards to handle their grievances because the latter were much more militant and aggressive than was the leadership.

When unions were formed in the mass production industries in the United States, their whole organization was based on the shop steward system. These unions were organized by the workers in the shops, who were determined to control their union. Hence, from the beginning, CIO unions stressed the need for a steward system, writing it into the contract and recognizing the necessity of training shop stewards. This contrasted with traditional craft unions, the UAW claimed, which relied on a top-level committee or business agents to handle grievances. The steward system expressed the industrial workers' desire for democracy. It was a self-conscious "American" democracy, however. While UAW stewards and committeemen were trained to build a more active and united membership through, for example, cooperating with the local education committee to organize and promote events, forums and classes, the resulting activist membership worked within the constraints of stable collective bargaining in workplaces controlled by owners and managers. Indeed, one of the challenges facing stewards in newly organized plants was teaching supervisors how to work with and within the collective agreement. Workplace democracy in this context meant knowing "how to approach foremen and other supervisory employees with a reasonable and businesslike attitude."

The CCL's basic steward course in the 1940s and 1950s was limited solely to training in the processing of grievances. Divided into four parts, the course included an overview of unions, the CCL, labour councils and federations; an overview of the steward's job; grievances; and arbitration. Two aspects of the steward's job were outlined: making the contract work and strengthening the union in the shop. The steward was taught to know the contract, the department and the nature of the work the members performed. The steps in handling a grievance included determining if a grievance existed, not making any rash promises to the grievors, discussing the grievance with all involved, getting it in writing, having all parties sign the settlement and making a report. Stewards in the course were told to remember that companies have rights in the process and in the agreement and that prompt settlement of grievances was essential to good workplace relations.[18]

In Mine-Mill, by comparison, the "good steward" was someone who handled grievances, enforced the contract and defended workers' rights. The Mine-Mill steward defended the democratic wishes of the membership and was attentive to his or her own education in order to help his or her union and the working class make democracy work for the many rather than for the powerful few. This union activist helped the workers stand on their own feet, independent of the boss, in the shop and outside of the shop. Finally, the Mine-Mill steward knew that the workers were the majority in the country and the world, and that by united effort they could grow to have complete control of their lives and their future.[19]

Leo Huberman pushed this theme of workers' control even further in the courses he taught for the Canadian Seamen's Union. CSU ship delegates' (steward) training took place within a broader course that also covered collective bargaining, the double standard of morality in industry, why unions exist, company unions, strikes, employers' anti-union weapons and the corporation. In discussing why unions existed, Huberman began by describing the current capitalist system as one governed by the pursuit of profit and consisting of two groups: capitalists and workers. He then went on to suggest that the job facing workers in capitalist society was, first, to restrict the power that capitalists have and, second, to abolish it. Workers organized unions, he maintained, in order to substitute democratic workers' power for the dictatorial power exercised by employers. As for the ship delegate's immediate responsibilities in the workplace, they were two-fold: to act as a spokesperson for the crew in enforcing the agreement and to act as a spark plug in carrying out CSU policy aboard the ship. Huberman's course examinations, which were used to determine if course participants had understood the course material rather than to test them, contained true-or-false statements such as the following: in the capitalist system, everybody is equal; the interests of employers and workers are the same; modern agreements are so complicated that they require the attention of experts; and union officials who do not work in the mill are more likely to get a better agreement than workers in the mill.[20]

Besides steward training, other tools courses included union administration, education leadership and radio broadcasting. Union administration taught the relationship of the local to the various levels of the union structure, how to organize union committees, the role of the union in the community, public relations and how to handle member problems during strikes and other emergencies. Education leadership was described as a practical course for members of local education committees. Participants were taught how to plan and organize education programmes, develop lines of communication with the membership, improve existing programmes and use film and audio-visual aids. Radio broadcasting, meanwhile, dealt with how to air the union viewpoint and included microphone techniques, speech analysis and script and features writing.

Some institutes and summer schools included spousal courses for women. One summer school, for example, offered Union Wife or Union Widow?, designed to acquaint male activists' wives with union objectives, labour history and community programmes during morning sessions. In the afternoon, millinery, needlework and other arts and crafts were offered. At a Winnipeg weekend institute, meanwhile, two female staff persons from the Communication Workers of America (CWA) and the Amalgamated Clothing Workers of America (ACWA) taught a course called Union Wives in the Community for the wives of male union members.[21]

Standard issues courses in the CCL programme and in the programmes of major unions included understanding our economy, political action (PAC) courses and labour history. One version of the first, taught at the Port Huron summer school, spoke to the individual trade unionist as a consumer, suggesting that, in the course, "we'll talk directly to your pocket book, brother." Designed to develop a better understanding of the factors affecting general living standards, the course addressed the issues of pay cheques and prices and profits; public ownership and subsidies; unemployment, international tension and armaments; and the national tax burden. Eugene Forsey and others taught a variation of this course at CCL institutes. PAC courses reflected the CCL's support for the CCF and were designed to solidify that relationship. A CCL labour history course, which was prepared "under CCF auspices" in 1947 and may have been written by Forsey, was sympathetic to industrial unions and critical of craft-union practice while completely ignoring the historical contributions of communist-led unions. Neither of these interpretative tendencies are surprising given the tenor of the times.

What is noteworthy about the labour history course, however, is the extent to which a social democratic rendering of trade union action in the 1940s is presented in traditional class-conflict terms and is not contained within the constraints of the emerging collective bargaining system. Take the case of strikes, for example. Course participants are asked: "Why is the strike so peculiarly a working-class weapon?" They are told that the strike is the withholding of labour by a group of workers to gain concessions from an employer. Workers are unique in the community because they have only their labour to sell, and since labour is the most perishable commodity, workers must sell it for the highest price possible. This is why workers join unions and it is the main reason for going on strike. Unions and strikes reflect the basic insecurity and social conflict that is part of the capitalist system. Furthermore, the course describes a series of strikes, including economic, union recognition, union security, jurisdictional, sympathetic and general. The course author concedes that strikes could possibly be minimized through adequate labour legislation, but that Canada has yet to develop a body of labour law that would provide avenues for the orderly settling of disputes. Even with such a body of law, however, the course author questions whether the finest legislation could eliminate strikes because "capitalism produces too much friction for that happy state."[22]

A standard PAC course began with the premise that labour had to be involved politically to ensure that past economic gains were protected by legislation from the actions of unfriendly governments financed by "the Boss." The CCF, course participants were told, was the only party pledged to labour's programme, while the Liberals and Conservatives were financed, controlled and owned by the boss. The course acknowledged that some CCF-supporting trade unionists were opposed to PAC because they had seen "the commies" inject politics into trade union affairs, so they concluded that politics meant trouble. But since politics was present anyway, the question was: what kind of politics? It was CCF politics, of course, because the CCL had formally endorsed the social democratic party. The latter half of the course was devoted to the nuts-and-bolts of PAC: raising money, setting up local PAC committees, educating the membership, integrating with the party at the local level, getting wives interested in politics and setting up election machinery.

Another PAC course was designed to counter the resistance among many staff representatives to political-action organizing. The reasons for this resistance, according to course author Henry Weisbach, were that many representatives felt that PAC organizing meant automatically supporting the CCF or telling members to vote CCF. The resistance was met in the course by convincing the representatives that the present trade union position could not be maintained without proper, ongoing legislation and that the representatives should not push the CCF down the throats of members. Rather, the main function of PAC was to educate the membership constantly by keeping the key issues before them.[23]

#6

In communist-led unions, such as UE, by contrast, political education did not mean partisan support for the Communist Party. Rather, UE schools conducted a broad public-policy education on issues such as labour legislation, UE's role in the labour movement and discussion of specific national and international policies such as the Abbott and Marshall plans. The main purposes of this education were to defend working-class living standards against big-business attacks and to consider the practical means of electing a government to represent organized labour, the housewife and the farmer.[24]

How were the courses taught? Generally speaking, labour educators in this period felt that they should conduct their courses and programmes using adult education techniques. Instructors' manuals stressed the importance of combining discussion with the presentation of course material, showing films and film strips and using outside speakers. A Steelworkers guide to shop steward instruction, for example, contained sections on meeting topics and organization, how to set up and lead a good programme and choosing and using materials. A series of five meetings was suggested, with each meeting consisting of three or four topics of approximately fifteen or twenty minutes each. The first meeting, entitled "The Shop Steward: what kind of person he should be; what he should know; what he should do," contained four topics. One topic covered the characteristics of a good shop steward, and instructors were encouraged to start the discussion by having participants brainstorm the characteristics of a good steward and to always ask the participants: "Why is that an important quality?" Once the group's contributions were exhausted, it was suggested that the instructor refer the group to the stewards' manual, which listed the stewards' qualities, and ask the group if they had left anything out. Then the instructor would move to the next topic, such as "How does a shop steward behave?", and repeat the process of facilitating a discussion among the participants using the stewards' manual as a reference point. The instructor was told to summarize the main points made during the meeting at the end. This procedure could then be repeated through the next three meetings, dealing with grievances, grievance machinery and labour legislation, and political action. A different approach was suggested for the last meeting, which was on labour history and union structure. One option here was a panel discussion among union men and women who had helped to make the history they spoke about. Panel members could make short presentations or facilitators could ask questions of the panellists to focus the discussion on specific phases of labour history that were of interest to a particular group.

Instructors were told that there were three key elements to setting up and leading a good discussion programme: setting up the programme, acting as a discussion leader and leading the discussion. The ideal group size for discussion was from twenty to twenty-five participants and an hour and one-half was the ideal length of time. The discussion leader's responsibilities included organizing the necessary information, introducing each topic by telling the group what was to be discussed and why, keeping the discussion going, facilitating maximum participation in the discussion and summarizing the discussion at the end of the meeting. The primary function of the discussion leader was to guide the discussion. And leaders were warned that they should not try to be the expert, but that they should cultivate an atmosphere of educational equality in the group.[25]

While this is what labour educators were being told to do, what was the experience in the classroom? The evidence here is thin, but it appears that the practice varied depending on the skill and temperament of the educator. Leo Huberman, the American labour educator who taught for the CSU and the WEA, seemed to follow democratic and participatory principles. He presented course participants with a body of material to be understood and mastered, even using an examination to determine whether or not he had been successful in conveying his message, but the classes were conducted using questions and discussion designed to maximize participation. For example, Huberman used the following directed questions in one course to guide class discussions to an understanding of the social forces determining workers' lives:

Where do you work?	Students give the names of the companies where they are employed.
Why do you work?	• Have to work in order to live. • Can't eat without working.
Does the man who owns the factory work alongside you?	• (Laughter) That'll be the day. • I've never seen him. • My plant is owned by a big corporation.
Have you ever seen the stockholders of the corporation working in the plant?	• No, they don't work there. • Of course not.
But you all agreed you *had* to work in order to live; now you tell me there are some people who live without working. How come?	• They don't have to work because they own the factory. • They get the profits from the business.
Then there are two groups of people in society. One group to which you belong, lives by....?	• Working.
And the other group to which your employer belongs lives by....?	• Owning
Have you always had to work?	• Yes. • I was laid off for five months once. • My factory was closed during the depression for over a year.
Mary says her plant was closed down for over a year. But she works in a textile mill. Didn't people need the shirts her mill turned out?	• Sure, people needed shirts but they couldn't pay for them because they didn't have any money, so the boss had to shut the mill down. • If I were him I'd have done the same thing. He's gotta make a profit or he must go out of business.

You mean to say that even though people needed shirts, unless the owner made a profit, he closed up?	• Yes, he's in business to make money. • If he doesn't make money, he shuts down the plant. • It doesn't matter if he's a good guy or a bad guy, unless he makes a profit, he has to close up.
What you're saying, then, is that in our system of production, goods will be produced only if there is a profit?	• That's right. • Unless there's a profit, there's no production.
Was that always true?	• Guess so. • No, there was a time when people made what they needed for themselves, when they needed it.
Why don't they make shirts, and washing machines and autos for themselves now?	• Don't have the money. • You need factories and raw materials and expensive equipment to make things people want nowadays.

At this point Huberman summed up the discussion by writing on the blackboard that the workers live by working and the employers live by owning, that the employers own what is necessary to produce goods in society (the means of production), and that this system is called capitalism, the object of which is *not* to produce goods as needed but *to make a profit*. He then continued:

The owners of the means of production, the employers, are also called capitalists. Which of the two groups, workers or capitalists, have more power? Why?	• The bosses have the most power because they have more money. • The capitalists have the most power because if they don't give you a job, you can't pay your bills.
What gives them more power?	• They own the means of production.

Other evidence suggests that many educators were still stuck in lecture mode and did not have the skills or ability to direct discussions. UE area representative Peter Hunter, for example, complained in 1954 that "too many educational evenings contain speakers" and suggested that a successful educational programme must involve as many people as possible in discussions. Similarly, David Smith noted in 1950 that instructors in the CCL institutes did not employ good teaching methods, relying heavily on the lecture method. Nonetheless, Smith remarked that the learning situation in the institutes was excellent, with educators talking a familiar language in an informal and friendly atmosphere.[26]

External Organizations

The labour movement's relationship with external organizations in the area of education changed with the departure of the WEA. This was most noticeable with respect to university-labour relations, but it also affected relations with

government bodies like the NFB and the CBC and voluntary associations like the   # 6
CAAE.

Dalhousie University continued to operate the Maritime Labour Institute under the auspices of its Dalhousie Institute of Public Affairs. With a board of directors composed of an equal number of representatives from TLC and CCL unions, the institute's purpose was to provide trade union members with the best training courses deemed to be useful to organized labour. The institute's main activity was its annual four- or five-day programme for trade unionists. It also ran a radio discussion programme on labour problems during these years. The annual programmes normally contained one topic per day, combining lecture and discussion. Topics included the reasons wages were lower in the Maritimes, the growth of trade unions in Canada and what was taking place in Europe. The 1951 five-day institute also contained a panel discussion with labour and management representatives discussing the industrial potential of the Maritime provinces and workshops on planning a union education programme, union publicity and group discussion methods. Instructors and speakers were drawn from the labour movement as well as from external organizations, including the university, the provincial government and the Canadian Tax Foundation. The Maritime Labour Institute functioned essentially as a tools and issues training programme for the Halifax labour movement. The programme was unique in that both TLC and CCL unions participated in the institute. The University of Toronto's Institute of Industrial Relations, as noted earlier, cooperated with the CCL in organizing winter institutes for the congress in the Toronto region, providing a venue and some of the speakers and instructors. At the University of British Columbia, which had always been lukewarm to overtures from the local WEA, Stuart Jamieson offered extension courses in economics for members of the Vancouver Trades and Labour Council and others provided public speaking instruction for the CBRE and cooperative marking courses for the UFAW.[27]

At the University of Manitoba, meanwhile, the WEA continued to operate until 1950, when the local association dissolved and reconstituted itself as the Manitoba Labor Institute (MLI). The institute operated on the same principles as the WEA, with the University of Manitoba and the provincial department of education paying the instructors, membership open to union members and union locals in the province and low tuition fees for each course. Like the Winnipeg WEA before it, the MLI ran a series of evening courses each year using the university's academic staff as instructors. Course topics included public speaking, human relations in industry, economics, history, everyday chemistry and so forth. It was, then, a continuation of the WEA programme under a different name. The University of Manitoba was unique in that it was the only university in the country to continue to deliver a WEA-style programme after 1950. The University of Manitoba also served as a venue for the CCL's weekend institutes, known as the Manitoba Union Institute in the province, but these were separate and distinct from the Manitoba Labor Institute.[28]

Moses Coady of St. Francis Xavier University speaking to a Canadian Congress of Labour weekend institute in New Glasgow, Nova Scotia, 1950. *Photographer unknown. National Archives of Canada, C-098724.*

St. Francis Xavier University (StFX) continued to have the most extensive labour education programme of any university in the country, which was primarily a result of the Catholic university's ideological commitment to countering the influence of communism among the Nova Scotia working class. The centrepiece of the university's labour education programme was the People's School, which combined radio broadcasts, discussion groups and weekly classroom instruction. The radio portion was a weekly half-hour broadcast every Sunday afternoon for twenty weeks from CJFX, the university's radio station. The broadcast consisted of a panel discussion with panellists from the university, the church and the trade union movement. While every effort was made to control the ideological purity of the trade union participants, unions were allowed to choose their own representatives for the panels. Union executives, such as those of the United Mine Workers of America (UMWA) local in Sydney, which had a communist majority in this period, often sent communist panellists, although the StFX organizers claimed that the unwelcome guests contributed little to the discussions. Groups of school participants gathered to listen to the weekly broadcasts, aided by study bulletins that had been sent to them during the previous week. After the broadcasts, the groups discussed the content of the broadcast. During the following week, the school participant attended an evening lecture and discussion, also based on the broadcast, conducted by a StFX extension worker. In 1950 there were over five hundred participants in the People's School in Cape Breton, Pictou and Inverness.

The explicit purpose of the People's School was to replace the communists in leadership position in the Nova Scotia labour movement with non-communists. The People's School classes were used to teach participants the dangers of communist philosophy and to form underground committees to organize support for non-communist candidates in union elections. The school organizers identified potential leaders among the school participants and groomed them for elections. For example, the school organizers identified and targeted two communist members of the Nova Scotia Federation of Labour for defeat. "Working quietly," it was noted, "the People's School groups were contacted, prepared for the local union election of delegates ... and at the Convention, the list prepared by those delegates [People's School groups for the most part] was elected.... The members of the N.S.F.L executive, as now constituted, are all members of the People's School." School organizers claimed that if it had not been for the People's School in Cape Breton, "the Communists would be so much in control of local unions NOW that there would be continual turmoil in this industrial area."[29]

In the early 1950s, StFX proposed first to the Carnegie Corporation and then to the CCL, the TLC and the federal and provincial departments of labour that an expanded programme of labour-leadership training should be established at the eastern Nova Scotia university. In its 1950 submission to the Carnegie Corporation, the university claimed that its current annual expenditure on labour education was $10,000 and that a further $15,000 per year was required to expand the campus-based and extension work through the addition of two or three staff. There is no record of Carnegie's response, but it was apparently negative. In its submission to the Canadian groups, meanwhile, the university suggested that a labour training school should be established at the Antigonish campus, with an advisory committee consisting of representatives from the university, labour organizations and government departments. The proposed training school would serve three groups: the chief executive members of unions, union staff and minor union officials and rank-and-file members. The course content would include, first, instruction in current social and economic problems and, second, techniques of group relations and leadership and union administration. The CCL was generally supportive of this initiative, but no significant money was forthcoming from any quarter. Nonetheless, the CCL continued to support the People's School during this period, giving a modest annual direct contribution of $100 and, through the James Tompkins Memorial Scholarship, a further $100 per year. More important, the CCL provided moral support by providing a connection between StFX and the Catholic anti-communist forces in the CIO.[30]

With the demise of the trade union film circuits at the end of the war, the NFB ceased for a time to be involved in labour-related filmmaking. Grierson left the board in 1945 and was replaced by Norman McLean, who had the unfortunate task of trying to guide the board through one of its most difficult periods. Staff was cut from 787 to 589 over three years, and the board was under constant attack from the Conservative opposition in Parliament and from the press, who were operating as thinly disguised mouthpieces for the private film industry. After Arthur Irwin was recruited as McLean's replacement in 1950 to reorganize and rehabilitate the board, and a new film act was in place, the board began again to make labour films. In contrast to the wartime labour filmmaking, which had been initiated by the WEA and the labour movement, these new films were initiated and sponsored by the federal Department of Labour as a result of its interest in managing and facilitating orderly collective bargaining. Furthermore, as part of the film board's new mandate to market to an international audience, labour films in the 1950s were made as much for the international as for the Canadian market.

In conjunction with the federal Department of Labour, the board produced a series entitled *Labour in Canada* between 1950 and 1956 that dealt with various aspects of collective bargaining. While this initiative was conceived completely within the civil service, government bureaucrats did recognize the utility of re-establishing a Trade Union Film Committee to provide advice on the project and to assist in distribution. From the time that Pat Conroy wrote to Arthur Irwin in 1950, congratulating him on his appointment as the new government film commissioner and requesting a role for the CCL in choosing subjects for labour films, however, it was clear that the labour movement would have a minor role to play in these endeavours. When the film committee—composed of representatives from the TLC, CCL, Canadian and Catholic Confederation of Labour (CCCL), NFB, CAAE, the Canadian Film Institute, and the federal Department of Labour—was re-established in August 1950, the NFB already had its first film ready for screening. When the committee eventually saw *Strike in Town*, the last film in the series, the labour members expressed frustration that the production of the film had proceeded so far that they were unable to suggest changes to the script. The main purpose of the committee seems to have been to assist with distribution, even though the films were described as having been developed in cooperation with the various congresses.

A version of the trade union film circuits was revived for the 1954-55 season, using a Trade Union Film Library assembled by the federal Department of Labour, but this was mainly a coordinated system of distributing labour films through the respective congresses and their affiliates. In 1955 the committee generated a list of about twenty possible film topics, including automation, international labour, labour history, management rights and the retired worker, and some of the committee members were working with board producers on scripts dealing with labour education and union counselling. None of these were made, it appears, as the board shifted its labour focus from twenty- to thirty-minute features to shorter ten-minute items for *Labour Screen Magazine*, which included more news-related items such as scenes from TLC and CCL conventions. While the labour members of the committee expressed concern about this shift, and the civil servants maintained the development of *Labour Screen Magazine* did not mean less commitment to labour filmmaking on the part of the board and the government, the *Labour in Canada* series marks the most important labour-related film activity during the 1950s.[31]

Labour in Canada was produced by Morten Parker, and included *Local 100*, *Dues and the Union*, *The Shop Steward*, *The Grievance*, *The Research Director*, *The Structure of Unions* and *Strike in Town*. Parker is best known in NFB history for his internationally successful and award-winning *The Stratford Adventure* (1953), an expensive ($83,000) fifty-minute re-creation of the birth of the Shakespeare Festival in Stratford, Ontario. But Parker's primary interest was in work and labour relations. Later in the decade he produced a nine-item, half-hour television series (at from $30,000 to $50,000 each) called *The Nature of Work*, which focused on a range of occupations from manual worker to company vice-president. And in the 1970s he tried unsuccessfully to interest the CLC in using his services when the congress was establishing its audio-visual service with money from Labour Canada (see Chapter 5).[32]

Each of the films in the *Labour in Canada* series, which cost about $30,000 apiece, was didactic and designed to teach the audience about the relevant collective bargaining or trade union functions. Three of them were repackaged for the NFB's television series *Window on Canada* for CBC; host Clyde Gilmour introduced the film and his guest analysts, who discussed the film after it was shown to the viewing audience. Sylvia Wiseman of McGill University and Maurice Wright, Ottawa lawyer for the CCL and the CBRE, viewed *The Grievance* with Gilmour and then discussed with him the operation and merits of the grievance, conciliation and arbitration system; on the eve of the TLC-CCL merger in 1956, Claude Jodoin (TLC) and Aaron Mosher (CCL) joined Gilmour to view the animated *The Structure of Unions* and to discuss the current state of unions in the country.

Five of the seven films in the series were dramatizations. *The Grievance*, for example, depicted a workplace dispute in an Oshawa, Ontario, automotive plant between a member of UAW Local 222 and a General Motors foreman. The UAW member refused a work order because he deemed the work to be unsafe, and the company disciplined him, thereby sparking the grievance. The film follows the grievance through the system, including the decision-making process of the union membership on whether or not to take the grievance to arbitration. *The Grievance* won two honourable mentions at Canadian and American film award ceremonies. *Strike in Town*, meanwhile, told the story of the negotiating process and ultimate strike by IWA members at a furniture-making facility in a small Ontario city. Two films were not dramatizations. *The Research Director* was a documentary-style film about Cleve Kidd, director of research for the Steelworkers, which illustrated the various facets of Kidd's job, and *The Structure of Unions* was an animated introduction to the various components of union organization.

The tone in each of the seven films was that of unions as legitimate and equal players in the collective bargaining system. One has the sense, after watching these films, that unions in the 1950s were an accepted part of Canadian life, with rights and responsibilities towards their members, employers and the society at large. These films were staple parts of Canadian (and some American) labour education programmes until the 1970s.[33]

As for the CBC, there was no systematic labour presence on either its radio network or its emerging television network during these years. And there was no committee for broadcasting that paralleled the Trade Union Film Committee. There were, however, a number of individual programmes and series during the 1950s that contained at least some labour content. Labour leaders appeared regularly on programmes such as *Labour Meets the Press* and *Cross Section*. *Business and Labor Review*, meanwhile, was a weekly roundup of business and labour news that commenced in 1956. Radio dramas occasionally featured labour themes, with *Cross Section* airing "Union Organizer" in 1954 and "Joe Hill" being featured on the national network in 1955, for example.[34]

Labour Education in Canada Report

During the late 1940s and early 1950s, the CAAE tried increasingly to develop a coordinating role of some kind in the area of labour education. Trade unionists were invited to and attended the 1946 CAAE convention, which established the Joint Planning Commission to develop a blueprint for post-war adult education. The two main congresses and individual unions were continuing members of the CAAE. (Indeed, in 1950 CCL president Aaron Mosher told CAAE president James Muir, also president of the Royal Bank of Canada, that the CCL believed that the CAAE should receive the Ontario government grant that had been going to the WEA because, Mosher maintained, the WEA was teaching communism.)

As the WEA was entering its last years as a significant force in Canadian labour education, the CAAE initiated a survey of the field. Following discussions with the labour congresses and the federal Department of Labour, David Smith of Regina was commissioned to undertake the study. Smith collected data in the fall of 1949 and the winter and spring of 1950, issuing a preliminary report in April 1950. A two-day institute was held a month later at the CAAE convention to discuss and respond to the report. After rewriting, a final version of *Labour Education in Canada* appeared in the spring of 1951, at about the same time that Drummond Wren was resigning as General Secretary of the WEA.

Smith's report was the first survey of Canadian labour education ever undertaken. Given his limited resources, it was little more than a partial inventory of what was happening in the field; nonetheless, he appears to have captured most of the significant activity from the CCL through the UAW and the Steelworkers to the ILGWU, UE and the UFAW. Besides internal education programmes, he discussed university provision and Quebec-based Catholic workers' education in institutions such as the School for Labour Action in St. Hyacinthe and the School of Popular Sociology in Hull. The report also included a section on the WEA, which reflected the marginal position it occupied by 1950. The conclusion was the most contentious part of Smith's report, as it included suggestions for the future development of labour education in Canada.

Howard Conquergood took particular exception to this section of the document, and urged the CCL to disassociate itself from the recommendations and, indeed, from the whole report. After its release, Conquergood sent a scathing critique of the final report to Jim McGuire, chair of the CCL education committee, with a copy to Roby Kidd, associate director of the CAAE. Conquergood objected to the superficiality of the study and the fact that the report's purported conclusions were not supported by the data collected and were contrary to Conquergood's own experience as a labour educator. For example, he found Smith's statement that "the practical problems and needs in which labour education develops, provide an excellent learning situation" to be banal and irritating. Yes, of course, said Conquergood, but to suggest, as Smith did in the next sentence, that the need remained for skilful and democratic teachers was objectionable because no one in the labour movement, either as revealed through Smith's data or through Conquergood's experience, was suggesting this need no longer existed. This and other examples suggested to Conquergood that Smith knew little about labour education and the labour movement and that the report did not add anything to what was already known about labour education in the country. He ended his letter to McGuire by rejecting Smith's recommendation to establish national and regional coordinating committees for labour education, which would bring together labour congresses, governments, universities and other organizations, such as the CAAE, the NFB and the CBC. The CCL and other labour organizations were quite capable of establishing their own relationships with external organizations without the help of the CAAE, and there was no need for coordinating committees of any kind in labour education, he concluded.

In his written response, Kidd was clearly mystified by Conquergood's reaction. He systematically reviewed the procedure that was followed in conducting the survey, whereby input was solicited from interested parties at every stage. He noted that Conquergood and other trade unionists had been given numerous opportunities to influence the report's final form, but that responses and suggestions were not made.

Conquergood apparently enjoyed a cordial relationship with Kidd and the CAAE, and it is unclear from the written historical record why he reacted so strongly to the Smith report. This is especially true because, at about the same time, Charlie Millard, his old boss at the Steelworkers and someone who had a history of rigorously guarding union turf, was advocating that the CAAE take a national coordinating role in the area of labour education. Whatever the reason, Conquergood's reaction marked the beginning of a post-WEA position that the Canadian labour movement could and would develop its own education programmes and establish its own independent relationships with external organizations without anyone's help. With the development of a stable internal educational capacity in some unions and in the CCL, there was a new confidence that labour educators had the authority and ability to speak and function as educators outside of their own organizations and movement. Howard

Conquergood and Roby Kidd, for example, could deal directly with each other as equal adult educators with the same status. Nonetheless, the vehemence of Conquergood's reaction to the Smith report may reveal some lingering status anxiety about the extent to which he (and labour educators generally) felt truly equal and confident in the world of Canadian adult education. Throughout the first half of the 1950s, labour educators such as Conquergood, McGuire and Swerdlow continued to have a professional relationship with the CAAE, culminating in the 1956 conference on labour education, which is discussed in the next chapter.[35]

The CCF continued in the late 1940s and early 1950s with its educational programmes directed in part to workers and trade unionists, although the party was focusing more on electoral success and less on movement building in these years, and most of the labour-related political work was left to union political action committees. The Communist Party, in contrast, continued with its ideologically committed system of internal education.

In 1949 there were fifty-eight Communist Party schools across the country with a total attendance of 1237, with women constituting about 40 percent of the total number attending. This included labour colleges in Vancouver, Toronto and Montreal; regional schools for British Columbia seamen and lumberworkers; and weekend schools for trade unionists in Toronto and Vancouver. In the 1950s the course content in the programme shifted to reflect the party's more nationalist stance. At the first session of the Norman Bethune School of Social Science (Toronto) in 1954, for example, Harry Hunter taught a course on the trade union movement in Canada in which he asked: Will Canadian unions always retain their United States affiliation? Hector McArthur's What Is Marxism?, meanwhile, included the questions: Is Canada becoming a U.S. colony?, and Why is parliament a vital instrument for winning Canadian independence and socialism? Finally, at the same school, Victor Hopwood led a course in Canada's artistic heritage and its future, which provided a forum for a discussion of the problems of Canadian culture in the face of United States domination, asking: Is there a Canadian culture and how have our authors portrayed workers, farmers, capitalists, Indians, French Canadians, immigrants and other Canadians?

The party also ran a Scientific Socialism Correspondence Course during the late 1940s and the 1950s. The course was open to anyone living in a district where there were no party classes or schools. It took six months to complete, and consisted of six parts with one part mailed each month. In January 1952 there were about 225 students registered in the distance education course, with Alberta having the largest provincial group (82), including one life-long learner who was taking Athabasca University labour studies courses in the 1990s!

Sources: University of Toronto, Thomas Fisher Rare Book Room, *Robert S. Kenny Collection*, Box 18, File 3, "Communist Party Educational Material. National Educational Material, 1937-1949," National Education Department Activities, 1946-1948, and Box 20, File 8, "Norman Bethune School," The Norman Bethune School of Social Science, winter/spring 1954 brochure, and Box 18, File 6, documents.

Conclusion

By 1956 Canadian labour education had changed from a field in which the WEA played a central role in coordination and provision to one in which unions, congresses and federations managed, developed and taught their own programmes. Senior figures, such as Howard Conquergood and Max Swerdlow, were in the midst of establishing systems to teach trade unionists how to function in the industrial relations system and how to run their unions. They were also redefining the relationship between unions and other organizations involved in or supporting labour education. This shift was partly a result of the organizational growth of unions, as they inevitably provided more of their member services internally and took on more responsibilities, but it also represented an ideological shift that was compounded by the communist purges of the day. Missing in the labour education of 1956, but present a decade earlier, was a commitment to critical, non-sectarian, movement-wide working-class learning. After 1956, Canadian labour education entered a long period of stable and predictable union-based training.

Notes

1. Craig Heron, *The Canadian Labour Movement: A Short History*, 2d ed. (Toronto: James Lorimer & Company, 1996), 75-84; Alvin Finkel, *Our Lives: Canada after 1945* (Toronto: James Lorimer & Company, 1997), 69-76.

2. Gerald Friesen, "Adult Education and Union Education: Aspects of English Canadian Cultural History in the 20th Century," *Labour/Le Travail* 34 (fall 1994): 172-174; Gordon Selman, "The Canadian Association for Adult Education in the Corbett Years: A Re-evaluation," in Gordon Selman, ed., *Adult Education in Canada: Historical Essays* (Toronto: Thompson Educational Publishing, 1995), 119-150.

3. AO, *WEA Papers*, MU 3996, File "Vancouver, BC (4)," Sketch of John Wigdor, and MU 4029, File "WEA National Board Verbatim Minutes, 1944 and following," Board meeting prior to December 1944 and Minutes of a Meeting of the National Executive of the WEA, 1 December 1944.

4. Radforth and Sangster, "'A Link Between Labour and Learning'," 72; NAC, *CLC Papers*, MG 28 I 103, Volume 242, File 7, Eugene Forsey to Norman Dowd, 23 April 1946, Eugene Forsey, "Mr. Buck and the WEA," no date, and Eugene Forsey to Drummond Wren, 16 December 1946.

5. Wayne State University, Reuther Library, *UAW Education Department: Victor Reuther Papers*, Box 3, File "Drummond Wren," Victor Reuther to Drummond Wren, 12 December 1947, and Victor Reuther to Walter Reuther, 18 December 1947; Wren's Address, 1951, 48.

6. AO, *WEA Papers*, MU 4005, File 10.1.2, "United Automobile Workers Regional Office for Canada," George Burt to Drummond Wren, 23 January 1948, and MU 4029, File "WEA National Board Verbatim Minutes, 1944 and following," Minutes of a Meeting of the National Executive of the WEA, 1 December 1944, and MU 4039, File "Proceedings of Annual Conventions of the WEA of Canada," Proceedings of a Meeting of the National Board of Directors, 3 June 1951, 7.

7. Wren's Address, 1951, 43-47.

8. Ibid., 39-44.

9. NAC, *CLC Papers*, MG 28 I 103, Volume 242, File 7, Charles Millard to James Rogers, 24 March 1951; AO, *WEA Papers*, MU 4039, File "Proceedings of Annual Conventions of the WEA of Canada," Proceeding of a Meeting of the National Board of the Workers' Educational Association, 3 June 1951, and Minutes of the Proceedings of the National Convention of the Workers' Educational Association, 2 December 1951.

10. NAC, *CLC Papers*, MG 28 I 103, Volume 217, File 1, Minutes of CCL Committee on Education, 5 November 1947, Volume 122, File 22, J.E. McGuire to Landon Ladd, Eastern Director, IWA, 23 November 1950, Volume 122, File 22, Pat Conroy to A.L. Hepworth, Secretary, Committee on Education, CCL, 7 June 1951, and Volume 123, File 1, CCL Education and Welfare Department, Interim Report for Executive Committee Meeting, 2 February 1953.

11. NAC, *United Steelworkers of America (USWA) Papers*, MG 28 I 268, microfilm reel M-6786, Murray Cotterill, "Pioneer in Union Education," *Information* 6 (5) (1958); "CCL Department Directors," *Canadian Labour* (April 1956).

12. NAC, *CLC Papers*, MG 28 I 103, Volume 122, File 21, Howard Conquergood to Pat Conroy, 12 July 1950, Pat Conroy to Howard Conquergood, 19 October 1950.

13. NAC, *CLC Papers*, MG 28 I 103, Volume 363, File 33, 5th Annual CCL Summer School, Twelve 5 day courses, 22-28 June and 29 June-5 July 1952, at FDR-CIO Labour Centre, Port Huron, Michigan, conducted by CCL in co-operation with Michigan CIO Council, and Volume 123, File 2, Canadian Congress of Labour, Education and Welfare Department Report to Secretary-Treasurer Donald MacDonald, CCL Executive and Council, 31 May 1954, and Volume 343, File "Farmer Labour-Teacher Institute, Annual Meeting (1950)," Donald Smith, "Labour Education in Canada," 1950, 2-4.

14. Max Swerdlow, *Brother Max*, 57, 68-71; Donald Smith, "Labour Education in Canada," 4, 6-7.

15. Thomas E. Linton, *An Historical Examination of the Purposes and Practices of the Education Program of the United Automobile Workers of America, 1936-1959* (Ann Arbor: The University of Michigan School of Education, 1965), part III; Donald Smith, "Labour Education in Canada," 6-9; University of Toronto, Thomas Fisher Rare Book Library, *Robert S. Kenny Collection*, Box 48, File 13, "UAW-CIO. Report to the District Council no. 26," George Burt's Reports June 1951, September 1951, and December 1951.

16. Donald Smith, "Labour Education in Canada," 10-12. Go to http://unionlearning.athabascau.ca_ to see a video clip from *Needles and Pins* (Ottawa: National Film Board, 1955) about the ILGWU educational programme.

17. Donald Smith, "Labour Education in Canada," 9-10, 13; University of British Columbia (UBC) Library, Special Collections, *International Union of Mine, Mill and Smelter Workers (Canada) (Mine-Mill) Papers*, Box 18, Folder 12, "National Office. Shop Stewards," Peter Hunter, Area Representative, "Learning the Union Way," *The Canadian UE Steward* (May 1954); UBC Library, Special Collections, *United Fishermen and Allied Workers Union Papers*, Box 136, Folder 11, "Trade Union History"; NAC, *Clarence Jackson Papers*, MG 31 B 54, Volume 2, File 38, "Canadian Seamen's Union Trade Union School (Montreal, 1947). Teaching Materials (2) c. 1943-1947."

18. NAC, *CLC Papers*, MG 28 I 103, Volume 357, File 39, UAW Manual, "How to Win for the Union: A Discussion for UAW Stewards and Committeemen," various editions, and Volume 268, File 1, Canadian Congress of Labour, Course for Union Stewards, 1949.

19. UBC Library, Special Collections, *Mine-Mill Papers*, Box 22, Folder 11, "National Office. Worker's Compensation. Miscellaneous," What Does a Good Steward Do? no date (but late 1940s or early 1950s).

20. NAC, *Clarence Jackson Papers*, MG 31 B 54, Volume 2, File 38, "Canadian Seamen's Union Trade Union School (Montreal, 1947). Teaching Materials (2) c. 1943-1947"; AO, *WEA Papers*, MU 3996, File "Vancouver BC (2)," CSU Leadership School, The Ship Delegate's Job.

21. NAC, *CLC Papers*, MG 28 I 103, Volume 363, File 33, 5th Annual CCL Summer School, Twelve 5 day courses, 22-28 June and 29 June-5 July 1952, at FDR-CIO Labour Centre, Port Huron, Michigan, conducted by CCL in co-operation with Michigan CIO Council, and Volume 348, File 18, CCL, Manitoba Union Institute, March 15th and 16th, 1952, Education for Union Leadership.

22. NAC, *Lincoln Bishop Papers*, MG 31 B 18, Volume 3, File 18, "History and Function of Trade Unions," no date [prepared in January, 1947].

23. NAC, *CLC Papers*, MG 28 I 103, Volume 363, File 33, 5th Annual CCL Summer School, Twelve 5 day courses, 22-28 June and 29 June-5 July 1952, at FDR-CIO Labour Centre, Port Huron Michigan, conducted by CCL in co-operation with Michigan CIO Council; NAC, *Lincoln Bishop Papers*, MG 31 B 18, Volume 7, File 10, Notes P.A.C. Course, Wawa Institute, 18-20 January, 1953, Discussion Leader—C.C. (Doc) Ames, and Volume 7, File 3, P.A.C. Work and Staff representatives.

24. NAC, *Clarence Jackson Papers*, MG 31 B 54, Volume 2, File 38, UE Summer School, Port Hope, 1948.

25. NAC, *CLC Papers*, MG 28 I 103, Volume 357, File 55, Teacher's Manual for "stewards job in building your union," Department of Education and Welfare, USWA, Toronto, July 1953.

26. Leo Huberman, "How to Spread the Word," *Monthly Review* 19 (7): 44-51 (December 1967); Donald Smith, "Labour Education in Canada," 3; UBC Library, Special Collections, *Mine-Mill Papers*, Box 18, Folder 12, "National Office. Shop Stewards," Peter Hunter, Area Representative, "Learning the Union Way," *The Canadian UE Steward* (May 1954).

27. Donald Smith, "Labour Education in Canada," 14-16; NAC, *CLC Papers*, MG 28 I 103, Volume 348, File 18, Annual Conference for Trade Union Leaders, The Maritime Labour Institute, The Institute of Public Affairs, Dalhousie University, 21-25 May 1951.

28. Donald Smith, "Labour Education in Canada," 15; University of Manitoba, Archives and Special Collections, *University of Manitoba Papers*, Volume 143, File 3, Manitoba Labor Institute Report, 1950-51; StFX University Archives, *Extension Department Papers*, RG 30-3/18/1182, Survey of Labour Education Programs in Canadian Universities; University of Manitoba, Archives and Special Collections, *University of Manitoba Papers*, Volume 105, File 14, W.J. Waines to President A.H.S. Gillson, 16 September 1948.

29. StFX University Archives, *Extension Department Papers*, RG 30-3/18/908-914, Statement of an Educational Program addressed to the Carnegie Corporation of New York by St. Francis Xavier University, Antigonish, Nova Scotia, no date (but March 1950), and RG 30-3/18/921-925, Communists on the Radio (emphases in the original).

30. StFX University Archives, *Extension Department Papers*, RG 30-3/18/908-920, Statement of an Educational Program addressed to the Carnegie Corporation of New York by St. Francis Xavier University, Antigonish, Nova Scotia, no date (but March 1950) and Tentative Proposal for the Establishment of a Labor Training

Programme at St. Francis Xavier University; NAC, *CLC Papers*, MG 28 I 103, Volume 236, File 3, Pat Conroy to Harry Read, c/o James Carey, CIO, 1 April 1950.

31. Gary Evans, *In the National Interest: A Chronicle of the National Film Board of Canada from 1949 to 1989* (Toronto: University of Toronto Press, 1991), chapter 1; NAC, *CLC Papers*, MG 28 I 103, Volume 231, File 7, Pat Conroy to W. Arthur Irwin, Government Film Commissioner, 17 February 1950, and Irwin to Conroy, 20 February 1950, and C.W. Marshall, Co-ordinator of Canadian Non-Theatrical Production, NFB, to Norman Dowd, CCL, 8 May 1950, and Volume 231, File 7, Donald MacDonald, CCL, to D. Mulholland, Director of Production, NFB, 1 June 1953, and Volume 205, File 16, C.W. Marshall, Chief, Canadian Program, NFB, to Howard Conquergood, Education and Welfare Department, CCL, 9 September 1953, and Volume 276, Files 8 and 9, various minutes of the National Trade Union Film Committee, 1953 to 1956; National Film Board of Canada, *Annual Report*, 1950-51, 1951-52, 1954-55; Canada, *Report of the Department of Labour*, 1949-56.

32. Evans, *In the National Interest*, 37, 51; NAC, *CLC Papers*, MG 28 I 103, Accession 92/0293, Volume 71, File "Films and Video-tapes—1975-Dec 1977," Morten Parker to Larry Wagg, 22 June 1977.

33. *The Grievance* (Ottawa: National Film Board, 1954); *Strike in Town* (Ottawa: National Film Board, 1956); *The Research Director* (Ottawa: National Film Board, 1954); *The Structure of Unions* (Ottawa: National Film Board, 1955); *The Shop Steward* (Ottawa: National Film Board, 1953); *Dues and the Union* (Ottawa: National Film Board, 1953); *Local 100* (Ottawa: National Film Board, 1950). Go to http://unionlearning.athabascau.ca to see video clips from films in the *Labour in Canada* series.

34. NAC, *CLC Papers*, MG 28 I 103, Volume 205, File 13, E.S. Hallman, Talks and Public Affairs, CBC, to Aaron Mosher, CCL, 7 November 1950, and Volume 205, File 16, "CBC Press Service," 2 February 1954 and 2 May 1956, and Circular from Howard Conquergood to CCL unions, 22 September 1955.

35. NAC, *CLC Papers*, MG 28 I 103, Volume 204, File 9, Aaron Mosher to James Muir, 3 November 1950; Smith, "Labour Education in Canada," and Volume 204, File "General Correspondence. Canadian Association for Adult Education, 1949-1951," Howard Conquergood to J.E. McGuire, 26 February 1951, and Roby Kidd to Howard Conquergood, 2 March 1951.

CHAPTER 4

Consolidating the System: 1956-1972

The 1950s and 1960s were decades of relative prosperity and stability for organized Canadian workers. Union educators built on the foundation laid in the 1940s and early 1950s, broadening and stabilizing internal educational capacity through the birth of programmes in new unions, the expansion of curricula in older ones and in the Canadian Labour Congress (CLC), and the origin and growth of the Labour College of Canada as a centre of advanced union education. The Canadian Union of Public Employees (CUPE) spawned the first significant public-sector union educational programme, while older American-based unions, such as the International Association of Machinists and Aerospace Workers (IAM), developed their first educational presence in Canada. And the United Automobile Workers (UAW), with an established programme dating from the early 1940s, broadened its efforts to provide peer education with the addition of the Port Elgin residential facility and an initiative using local union activists. CLC educators, for their part, concentrated on maintaining and strengthening the system of weekend and week-long schools inherited from the Canadian Congress of Labour (CCL), with some attention paid to instructor training and the overall direction and organization of union education in Canada.

Outside of the labour movement, meanwhile, universities provided some continued support for labour education. Following the 1956 National University-Labour Conference on Education and Co-operation, a number of local university-labour committees were launched across the country. The University of Manitoba group pioneered its three-year certificate programme with local labour organizations, and St. Francis Xavier University (StFX) continued its People's School and other activities.

While communist-led unions had been successfully purged from the mainstream movement by the time of the 1956 merger creating the CLC, skirmishes continued in places such as Sudbury. Here, a workers' education programme was initiated at the local university as part of efforts by the United Steelworkers of America (Steelworkers) to dislodge the International Union of Mine, Mill and Smelter Workers (Mine-Mill) as the bargaining agent for local miners.

Context

Between the mid-1950s and the early 1970s, Canadian workers faced an economy that was stable relative to earlier periods, with more-or-less low unemployment and a stable collective bargaining system. However, this economy was undergoing changes that would continue to ensure that the world of work was insecure. From the Second World War onwards, the federal government used its power to smooth out booms and busts by using deficit spending when necessary to stimulate the economy and maintain employment levels. Furthermore, governments at various levels became more active participants in the economy by encouraging industrial development and spending new money on educational institutions and hospitals. New social welfare programmes were initiated, including unemployment insurance, health insurance and pensions. At the same time, the overall economic structure was changing with Canada's increased integration into the American economy and an acceleration of the shift from east-west to north-south trading patterns. American-based corporations gained greater control over Canadian manufacturing and resources, while the American-led international capitalist economy expanded and grew at a remarkable speed. Employers in Canada changed the face of workplaces during this period by introducing new technologies, recruiting new workers from the Canadian countryside and abroad, hiring more married women for full-time jobs and requiring higher educational qualifications than previously.

American control ↑

With the merger that formed the CLC, the labour movement outside of Quebec was more unified than it had been for over half a century. The major unions settled into regular patterns of negotiations with employers, gaining increased wages and expanded benefits packages including pensions and medical insurance. Strikes— no longer required to win union recognition—became instruments that negotiators used when necessary to make a point in bargaining. Faced with a legalistic industrial relations system, union leaders and their research, education and other staff focused on the details of grievances and arbitration, collective bargaining and contract enforcement. Unions, as a result, came to parallel the personnel departments of large corporations. Their most important function was to ensure that their members were served as well as possible by the contracts that those departments administered. Workplace activism among members was not encouraged and many rank-and-file members viewed their unions as little more than service organizations to be consulted when a problem with the employer arose.

While workplace relations were relatively stable compared to earlier periods, employers continued to be intransigent and to use whatever opportunity arose to curb union advances or to roll back previous gains. Regional variations in the country and the fragmented nature of bargaining meant that many groups of workers did not fare as well as some others. Furthermore, all workers were affected by dramatic increases in the cost of living during the 1960s and by the pace of automation and technological change beginning in the 1950s. Workers in the manufacturing, resource and transportation sectors faced increasing mechanization, while office workers and others began to find their jobs speeding up or being eliminated by computerization. Finally, new workers were bringing a new dose of militancy to Canadian workplaces. Italian construction workers in Toronto, for example, used the labourer's union to challenge building contractors. More women were becoming permanent members of the workforce and, by the

↑ mechanization; computers intro.

1970s, were making their mark in the labour movement. Finally, the baby boom generation was entering the world of paid employment by the 1960s and, as products of post-war prosperity and the anti-authoritarian youth cultures of the period, often resisted both bureaucratic management practices and bureaucratic and cautious unions. In 1966 there were more strikes than in 1946 and a third of these were wildcat strikes (not authorized by the union leadership), suggesting strains on the industrial relations system and frustration among rank-and-file members. In response, the federal government appointed a task force on labour relations, which reported in 1969. Although some new language on technological change was added to the Canada Labour Code, industrial unrest continued into the 1970s.

Public-sector workers were generally unorganized before the 1960s. Blue-collar municipal employees were covered under private-sector labour legislation, but otherwise civil servants outside of Saskatchewan were excluded from all labour legislation. In the absence of the right to organize, these workers formed associations that, among other things, approached employers from time to time with requests for better wages and working conditions. By the 1960s, however, a combination of declining wages relative to private-sector rates and the increasing use of capitalist management practices designed to reduce public-sector labour costs led these workers to transform their associations into union-like structures demanding collective bargaining rights. In the wake of a 1965 national postal workers strike and with the New Democratic Party (NDP) holding the balance of power, the federal Parliament passed the *Public Service Staff Relations Act* in 1968, granting federal civil servants the right to arbitration or strike action to settle disputes. Following Saskatchewan's pioneering lead in 1944, other provincial governments granted their employees collective bargaining rights between 1965 and 1975, although some jurisdictions denied some or all workers the right to strike. The federal Public Service Alliance of Canada (PSAC) and its provincial counterparts were granted bargaining rights for all workers in their respective jurisdictions, typically with a separate set of negotiations taking place for each occupational group in the union (prison guards or inside postal workers, for example). In contrast to private-sector unions, federal and provincial public-sector workers other than postal workers won collective bargaining rights without having to strike for recognition or even having to go through a certification process.

Beyond those workers employed by federal and provincial governments, municipally employed clerical workers joined their blue-collar brothers and sisters in the Canadian Union of Public Employees (CUPE) during the 1960s and 1970s, where they were joined by non-professional workers from hospitals and schools across the country (although in Quebec many of these workers joined the Confederation of National Trade Unions). With this influx of new workers, CUPE displaced the Steelworkers as the largest union in the country. Professionals such as teachers, nurses, social workers, librarians and professors in the public sector were also propelled into unionization during this period as a result of wage erosion and the impact of capitalist management practices on their jobs. Some of these workers joined CUPE or the relevant provincial employees union, while the rest formed new, occupationally based unions. For the most part, however, nurses, teachers, professors and the like remained aloof from the broader labour movement, afraid to tarnish their professional images by association with the working class, even though they were quite willing to use trade unions—the central working-class institution—to achieve their own objectives.

By the early 1970s the Canadian labour movement had been transformed by the influx of public-sector workers. The percentage of the labour force that was unionized jumped from about 30 percent in 1960 to around 37 percent by the early 1970s, with public-sector workers accounting for about half of all union members in the country. The face of the labour movement changed as well, as it now consisted of significant numbers of clerical workers, women and workers in jobs requiring post-secondary education.

Labour movement politics was characterized almost exclusively by the fate of the Co-operative Commonwealth Federation/New Democratic Party (CCF/NDP). During the late 1950s leading figures in the CCF and the CLC began to discuss the possibility of forming a new social democratic party in Canada that would involve more direct participation by the labour movement. The result was the 1961 New Party, which later became the New Democratic Party. In a bid to broaden its appeal, the NDP played down the CCF's commitment to public ownership (at a time when a significant minority of Canadians supported the concept). Industrial unions such as the Steelworkers and the UAW provided much of the financial support for the new party, while the party's guiding lights consisted of union leaders, professionals and intellectuals. Federally, the NDP was never able to increase its parliamentary representation above the thirty-one seats it captured in 1972, ensuring that it remained a third party throughout the period. It was able, however, to take advantage of minority Liberal governments from 1963 to 1968 and 1972 to 1974 to ensure that several pieces of progressive legislation were passed, including government-funded medical insurance and public-sector collective bargaining rights.[1]

Post-secondary education in this period, meanwhile, was marked by increased government funding that resulted in expanded universities and the development of a community college system across the country. Twelve new universities were built between 1959 and 1966 and full-time university enrolments tripled during the 1960s. While most of the beneficiaries of increased university funding during the 1960s and early 1970s were middle-class Canadians, the resulting expansion did lay the material foundation for the later development of labour studies programmes.

Community colleges, in contrast, were designed to serve a more working-class constituency with an emphasis on technical and vocational training. Through the *Technical and Vocational Training and Assistance Act* of 1960 and the *Occupational Training Act* of 1967, the federal government provided most of the money for the provincially based community college systems to develop. At the end of the 1950s there was one college in Canada, but by 1970 there were 130 of them across the country, with notable concentrations in British Columbia, Alberta, Ontario and Quebec. Under the 1960 Act, the federal government provided 75 percent of the capital costs and 50 percent of the operating costs of college and related vocational training endeavours. And with the 1967 Act, the federal authorities became more deeply involved in training by selecting students for training, purchasing training for them in the provincially run colleges, and providing training allowances. The primary purpose of the colleges was to serve labour-market and employer needs, but liberal educators were able to ensure that college mandates included broader social dimensions. Their designation as "community" colleges suggested that they had a responsibility to serve a variety of purposes and constituencies in their local geographic areas. Labour and other progressive social groups used these designations and mandates to pressure colleges to meet their specific needs.

Adult educators such as Roby Kidd played a role in defining a broader liberal purpose (that is, broader than employer-defined technical training) for community colleges, but they also facilitated the narrowing and professionalization of adult education practice during this period. Kidd was director of the Canadian Association for Adult Education (CAAE) until 1961 and a professor at the Ontario Institute for Studies in Education (OISE) later in the 1960s. He had been the first Canadian to earn a doctorate in adult education, graduating in 1947 from Columbia University where he absorbed the dominant American trends in the field. When he took over the leadership of the CAAE, he drew on his American training to consciously shift the association from its earlier social-action stance, in which adult educators saw themselves as participating in a movement alongside society's disadvantaged, to a neutral body that advocated not for specific social groups or causes but for adult education as a field.

In this view adult education was a broad church that included technical and personnel training in corporations at one extreme and social-movement-based critical education at the other. Moreover, the dominant tone in the field became one in which the techniques of educating adults and training practitioners were emphasized at the expense of its broader social purposes. As a result, the period was marked by increasing emphasis on professional training through the development of credit and non-credit programmes for adult educators in which the common psychological traits of adults were stressed (using educational literature imported from the United States) and the social forces determining their lives and learning were minimized. In some cases, the worst elements of these uncritical and individualized approaches to learning made their way into union education. Furthermore, the dominant tone of adult education practice meant that union educators lacked support in the broader educational community for the type of education that their social reality demanded.[22]

CLC Structures

The various parts of the Trades and Labor Congress of Canada (TLC) and CCL were merged when the two organizations dissolved in 1956 to form the CLC. In the best traditions of the labour movement, the apportioning of educational staff positions in the new organization had more to do with politics than with merit. In the horse trading that transpired as the details of the merger were worked out, Max Swerdlow of the larger TLC won the position of education director while the CCL's Howard Conquergood became political education director. Although Conquergood accepted his new responsibilities with good grace, he was deeply disappointed that he had not received the education appointment. Swerdlow did possess significant educational skills but Conquergood had developed and nourished the successful CCL educational programme, which was more substantial than what the TLC offered and which the CLC inherited, emulated and expanded. Swerdlow remained in his position until 1969, when he left the CLC for a job with the International Labour Organization.

Swerdlow was succeeded by Bert Hepworth, formerly director of the CLC's international department. Born in Montreal, Hepworth became a member of the Canadian Brotherhood of Railway Employees & Other Transport Workers (CBRE) in 1935 when he worked for Canadian National Railway. Ten years later he moved to Ottawa to join the staff of his union as executive assistant and subsequently became education director. He joined the CLC in 1962. Hepworth, it will be recalled, was an early champion of education in the CCL. He remained in the top education job until 1975, when he was replaced by Larry Wagg. Wagg joined the CLC staff as an education representative in 1961 after almost twenty years in the labour movement as a member of the International Typographical Union and, after 1956, as president of the Brantford (Ontario) and District Labour Council. He served as education director in the Prairie (1967 to 1970) and Ontario (1970 to 1974) regions prior to moving to Ottawa to serve as Hepworth's assistant. Wagg left the CLC in 1981 to join the Canadian High Commission in London as a labour counsellor.[3]

In 1956 there were just over one million trade unionists affiliated to the CLC and the budget of the CLC's education department was a little less than $100,000, which represented a per capita expenditure on education of about ten cents. The 1957 education expenditure was 7.5 percent of the congress's total annual expenditure of about 1.3 million dollars. This level of expenditure was generally maintained and enhanced throughout the period with per capita education spending increasing slightly to about twelve cents in 1963 and about fourteen cents in 1971. The education department's percentage of the congress's total annual expenditure, meanwhile, varied from a low of 7.5 percent in 1957 to a high of 11 percent in 1969, and averaged about 10 percent. In the much smaller political education department, by comparison, spending as a percentage of the congress's total annual expenditure ranged from a high of 2.7 percent in 1957 to a low of 1.5 percent in 1972. The per capita spending for political education, meanwhile, was about three-tenths of a cent in the early 1960s and about two-tenths of a cent in the early 1970s. And, finally, spending in political education expressed as a percentage of spending in education ranged from a high of 36.4 percent in 1957 to a low of 16 percent in 1972, with a steady decline from 1957 to 1972. Political education was not only the poor cousin in CLC educational endeavours, then, but its relative fortunes declined over the years.[4]

The mandate of Conquergood's political education department was to provide members with an adequate understanding of the CLC's legislative objectives, pertinent information on current political issues, an awareness of how legislation is enacted and how the various levels of government work, a better understanding of how the economy works and information about the various political parties and electoral procedures. Before his premature death in 1958, Conquergood laid the foundations of the congress's political education programme by offering courses as part of weekend institutes and week-long schools, promoting labour-council and local-union political education committees, establishing a Union Opinion Poll Programme and promoting farm-labour cooperation through a Farm-Labour Coordinating Council.

The opinion poll programme was a creative means to encourage local committee members to talk to regular members about political issues and to obtain rank-and-file opinions about the issues of the day. Each month Conquergood sent local committees a union opinion poll, asking a question about a current political issue. The question was accompanied by a "Facts Bulletin" containing background information on the specific issue. Committee members would then talk to members about the question, record the responses, forward the results to Conquergood and summarize the opinions for the local membership meeting and the labour council political education committee.

The Farm-Labour Coordinating Council, meanwhile, was formed to promote better understanding between the two groups and to explore coordinated political action. The council discussed general farm problems, farm implement prices, joint initiatives such as a farm-union sponsored March on Ottawa and the impact of industrial disputes on farmers. Ontario was home to an annual Farm-Labour Conference, with participation from the Ontario Federation of Agriculture, the Ontario Farmers Union and the CLC and many of its affiliates.

George Home, who became political education director in 1959, devoted much of his efforts to creating and building support for the New Democratic Party, but was able to continue Conquergood's emphasis on broadly based political action to some degree. The department's most significant initiative in the 1960s, besides its partisan political activity, was its annual Citizenship Month. While increased support for the NDP was the ultimate goal of all of the department's activity, this initiative was meant to highlight important issues for the labour movement that unions campaigned on separately from the party. In February of each year a specific issue was highlighted, such as medicare, full employment, housing or public automobile insurance. The department then prepared and distributed promotional information, including booklets, leaflets, car stickers, cards, posters and speakers' kits. Some labour councils were successful in having February declared Citizenship Month in their communities and some unions sponsored radio and television programmes on the issue of the year.

After the CLC's 1958 decision to support the formation of a "New Party" to replace the CCF, Home was busy with meetings across the country—two hundred in 1959—and at staff seminars, weekend institutes, week-long schools, and internal union educationals explaining and discussing the new initiative. From the 1957 federal election forward, political education staff were active in federal and provincial elections, lending support to CCF candidates when they were endorsed by a local labour council or federation and, after 1961, giving general support to the NDP. The department also encouraged local unions to affiliate directly with the NDP. By 1963, 689 local unions representing about 218,000 members had affiliated (representing 20 percent of the total number of members affiliated to the CLC), while in 1969 the comparable numbers were 792 local unions and 266,000 members (17 percent of the total affiliated membership). The NDP amended its constitution in 1969 to allow each of the twelve largest affiliated unions to name a member to the party's executive council. Beyond encouraging affiliations and lending staff support, however, the CLC did little to support the party during the 1960s.[5]

The CLC education department under Swerdlow continued the system that had been pioneered and established by Conquergood in the CCL. At its base were scores of weekend institutes held across the country in conjunction with local labour councils and the occasional day-long workshop on specific topics. Above this were week-long schools organized with provincial federations of labour. Besides these activities designed for local leaders, stewards and rank-and-file members, there were regular seminars for union staff and irregular instructor training programmes. In the late 1950s, there were approximately 150 annual activities of all types (including institutes, week-long schools, staff seminars and so on) with 11,000 to 12,000 participants, about 750 courses and about 150 instructors, which reached about 1 per cent of the total membership. By the late 1960s, there were about 200 activities per year with about 15,000 participants, 900 courses and 180 instructors. Ontario accounted for about 50 percent of this activity. During the 1960s there was an attendance turnover of approximately 90 percent, which meant that the programme was reaching about 10,000 new members each year.

Most of this activity was at the local labour council level, where the weekend institutes were conducted. In 1971, 36 of the 121 labour councils in the country responded to a survey of union educational activity. Of these 36, representing 340,000 members, two-thirds had a committee responsible for education while one-quarter had no one responsible for educational activities. Twenty-six labour councils reported that they had education budgets, with amounts ranging from $50 to $5,000. Thirty labour councils hosted one or more educational events in

1971, with the Toronto and Edmonton councils being particularly active (44 and 38 events respectively).[6]

During the 1960s the CLC and some labour councils developed an innovative programme called "labour education weeks," which were held in conjunction with local weekend schools and were designed to raise the community profile of labour education and the labour movement generally. The first labour education week was organized by the Sault Ste. Marie and District Labour Council in 1960, and included television and radio programmes as well as press releases dealing with labour education. In 1963 the CLC began promoting the concept across the country. The key elements of the weeks included a proclamation by the mayor designating the week immediately preceding the weekend institute as "Labour Education Week," addresses by labour spokespeople to local service clubs and to high school students and displays of labour education material at the local library. In some cases, downtown store windows displayed union-made goods and union services provided in the community; in others, local newspapers published special sections on labour in the community and in Canada. By 1967 about fifty labour councils across the country had conducted labour education weeks.[7]

Some labour councils tried to expand their offerings beyond the traditional tools and issues courses for activists to provide general adult education for rank-and-file union members and their families. The Vancouver and District Labour Council (VDLC), for example, began in the late 1950s to offer evening seminars to supplement the weekend institutes that were held in conjunction with the CLC. In 1960 the education committee proposed a programme of evening meetings for members, their spouses and families on a variety of topics, including automation and full employment ("Will you, your husband or father be working next year?") and automation and recreation ("How will you spend your leisure time—moonlighting?"; "BC, the camper's paradise"; "BC, the hunter's best bet").

The committee had only limited success in attracting participants, however, and its members spent many meetings in the early to mid-1960s analyzing why they were unable to attract participants while thousands of trade unionists attended adult education classes sponsored by the Vancouver School Board. They were especially perplexed when a questionnaire circulated to weekend institute students in 1965 indicated participants wanted a continuous programme of seminars. While the committee elicited a slightly more positive response when it co-sponsored evening courses with the school board, it was never able to fulfil its desire to offer a range of educational offerings to the average union member.[8]

The VDLC education committee's energy and enthusiasm made it successful in establishing and maintaining a human rights educational programme. A Labour Institute on Race Relations was held annually from 1950, organized by the council's human rights committee. The 1957 institute, attended by over one hundred delegates from fifty-three local unions, focused on the recently enacted provincial Fair Employment Practices Act. Besides speeches and discussion groups, this institute featured a series of short skits to illustrate problems typically faced by people seeking employment in British Columbia.

Human rights and racial tolerance made their way onto the Canadian labour education agenda from two sources. One was the Jewish Labour Committee (JLC), which was established in 1935 to fight against dictatorship and to alert the Canadian labour movement to the dangers of Nazism and fascism. Active during the Second World War in aiding refugees and other victims of fascism, the JLC was successful during the 1950s in persuading governments to legislate the abolition of discrimination and to adopt and promote human rights in their jurisdictions. In cooperation with the CLC, the JLC established labour human rights committees in cities across the country. The other source was the international offices of industrial unions such as the UAW and the URWA, which had large numbers of African Americans among their United States memberships. As the JLC raised awareness of racial discrimination and human rights issues, these unions were developing programmes and departments to battle racism in the workplace and the community. Instructors were recruited from the human rights departments of these industrial unions to teach courses such as Fair Practices in Your Local and JLC members such as Kalem Kaplansky— who was CLC Director of International Affairs from 1957 to 1966—helped to shape the programmes and courses in this area.

The 1959 NFB production *A Day in the Night of Jonathan Mole* was often shown in these courses. Written and directed by Donald Brittain, and produced by the federal Department of Labour, this inventive film portrayed the fantasy world of Jonathan Mole, a white office clerk, who blamed immigrants, Jewish people and Aboriginals for his woes. The centrepiece of the film is a dream that Mole has about the country of "Adanac," in which there are laws ensuring that the best jobs are open only to Christian Caucasians. Mole is the judge in a tribunal in which a Jewish man, an Aboriginal man and a recent immigrant are charged with trying to gain entry to jobs reserved for others. Prosecution witnesses provide the racist arguments of the day, while defence witnesses refute the racists. In the end Mole finds the three defendants guilty, but protects their "rights and privileges" by directing them to employment they might find more appropriate (such as trapping and hunting for the Aboriginal person).[9]

The most important educational activities conducted by the various federations of labour across the country were the annual week-long schools held in conjunction with the CLC. Ontario's summer schools were the largest. In 1958, for example, two weeks of courses were held in Nipigon for participants from north-western Ontario, four weeks were held at the International Chemical Workers Union's Club Whitesands facility near Peterborough and a special week-long programme was offered at the UAW's new facility in Port Elgin. By the mid-1960s, five weeks of union education were offered at Port Elgin with a week at Club Whitesands. Annual attendance at the Ontario schools ranged from 400 in the 1950s to an average of from 300 to 350 in the late 1960s and early 1970s.

Survey results from 190 participants in the 1958 schools reveal that 60 were between twenty and thirty years of age, 72 were between thirty and forty, 42 were between forty and fifty, and 12 were over the age of fifty. Fifty-two participants, meanwhile, had been union members for one to five years, 67 from five to ten years, 42 from ten to fifteen years, and twenty-four for over fifteen years. One-hundred and fifty of the 190 held offices in local unions, of which 54 were stewards or chief stewards with the rest holding offices such as local president, vice-president and secretary.[10]

Most federations were involved in other activities in addition to the summer or winter schools. The Alberta Federation of Labour, for example, with 55,000 members in 215 affiliates in 1971, sponsored ten courses, fourteen seminars, and three conferences for 920 participants, which was more activity than any other federation in Canada. In the same year the Saskatchewan Federation of Labour, despite having only 29,000 members in 180 affiliated unions, sponsored sixteen courses, seminars and conferences for 250 participants. These included its annual Farmer-Labour Institute, which began in 1947, and attracted about 60 participants in 1971; ten area conferences of farm, labour and teacher representatives; a jointly sponsored seminar on pollution with Regina Pollution Probe; and radio and television broadcasts on labour and general social issues. The Ontario Federation of Labour, which was Canada's largest with 700,000 members in 2,000 affiliated organizations in 1971, meanwhile, had both an education committee and a staff person devoted full-time to education. That year it held conferences and seminars for 1,000 participants on worker compensation, women's rights, pollution, mass media and regional government.[11]

Besides membership education at various levels, the CLC programme devoted some attention to staff development and instructor training. Bert Hepworth, writing in 1957, envisaged a system of staff and instructor training that would produce a cadre of organizers and educators across the country. As coaches for those who wanted to learn union skills and as purveyors of union information and knowledge, they would parallel or emulate the agricultural representatives available to Canadian farmers. Annual conferences for CLC and affiliate staff were held in the Ontario, Prairie and Pacific regions from 1956. These conferences provided an opportunity for staff to ponder and discuss broader issues that affected their day-to-day work. At the 1958 Pacific conference, for example, Professor Stuart Jamieson spoke on economic trends as they affected collective bargaining, CLC international affairs director Kalem Kaplansky addressed the issue of disarmament and Joe Morris from the International Woodworkers of America (IWA) discussed how to conduct an effective strike. The 1961 Ontario staff conference, meanwhile, included a panel discussion on management's public responsibility with a vice-president of Westinghouse, the editor of *Saturday Night* magazine and the president of Encyclopedia Britannica participating. Another panel, containing a mix of labour and non-labour participants, discussed the extent to which labour's responsibility to its members conflicted with its general responsibility to the public.[12]

Union education programmes were always woefully short of good instructors and the issue of instructor training was a constant concern in the department and at the CLC's National Education Advisory Committee (NEAC). Training was conducted sporadically during the first fifteen years of the congress's history. One course in 1957 was followed by a two-week Ontario course for forty instructors in 1960, conducted in cooperation with the CAAE. Plans were made to hold two- to three-week courses in other regions during 1961, but there was only one course that year. A course in Banff during 1965 was meant to be the first in a new series training fifty instructors per year, but it appears that only two further courses were offered in 1966-67. The Banff conference was able to draw only twelve participants because of more pressing commitments on the part of many potential attendees, prompting one conference planner to suggest that training courses should be given a higher priority by union leaders.

A 1966 conference on instructor training, co-sponsored by the CLC and the CAAE, concluded that the CLC had to make long-range plans for the recruitment and training of competent instructors. Three years later, and with CAAE assistance, the CLC launched a three-year series of instructor training programmes across the country. The main objective of programme courses was for participants to "acquire a knowledge of the fundamentals of training and cultivate skills in the use of basic training methods," and courses covered speaking, reporting, discussion, leadership, visual aids, role playing, case studies, simulated exercises, course planning, evaluation and theories of adult learning. NEAC members noted in 1970 that the programme was beginning to narrow the gap between the demand for trained instructors and the supply, but conceded that there was still a need for additional instructors.[13]

Film continued to be an important resource for union educators. However, after the *Labour in Canada* series, which released its last film in 1955, the NFB's interest in labour filmmaking receded. The CLC's NEAC and the Trade Union Film Committee noted the need for new labour films on a variety of subjects, but it wasn't until the mid-1960s that the public filmmaker again expressed interest in the area. In 1964 it released *The Inheritance*, which is a recounting of the rise of the labour movement in North America through the use of archival footage, still photographs, union songs and commentary. The following year a group of NFB production staff met with some fifteen to twenty union educators to work out story ideas for two or three labour films that the board was planning to make. Two explicitly labour films were made and a third contained significant union content.

The first film was entitled *Do Not Fold, Staple, Spindle or Mutilate*, and it is a remarkable interpretation of the generational conflict in a union local between an ageing leader whose activism dates from the struggles of the 1930s and 1940s and a younger membership who believe the old fellow is being manipulated by management. With a cast including Bruno Gerussi, Ed Begley and Al Waxman, and a musical score by Dave Brubeck, the film explores the relationship between inherited union structures and traditions on the one hand, and a rebellious, hedonistic and jazz-loving male working-class youth culture on the other. Directed by John Howe in a style that mirrors the bebop jazz of the score, *Do Not Fold* won grand prize at the first Western Hemisphere labour film festival held in Montreal in 1967. The other explicitly labour film was *The Labour College*, which portrays the 1965 session of the Labour College of Canada through the eyes of a participant from a UAW local. And *Steeltown*, the third labour-oriented film from the NFB in the mid-1960s, is a portrait of Hamilton, showing how the work performed in its steel production complex affected the city and its rural surroundings. *Steeltown* won the NFB a special prize at the 1967 labour film festival in Montreal for the board's efforts to produce films dealing with union matters.[14]

By the mid-1960s union educators were reflecting systematically on the CLC's programme and its articulation with the affiliates' educational activities.[15] In 1969, responding to calls from various quarters that the country's union educational system had to be revitalized, the congress's executive officers authorized a study and evaluation of the CLC educational structure and programme. A NEAC subcommittee was formed and met with outside experts to determine the contours of such a survey. Eventually Coolie Verner and Gary Dickinson of the University of British Columbia's Adult Education Research Centre (AERC) were given $10,700 by the CLC to conduct a two-year survey of the congress's education programme.[16]

When Harry Waisglass of the federal Department of Labour (and formerly research director for the Steelworkers) learned about the CLC's contract with Verner and Dickinson, he conceived a broader, federally funded plan to survey labour education in unions outside the CLC and in colleges and universities. In 1971 Verner and Dickinson agreed to expand the scope of their study to describe and analyze educational activities in unions, to evaluate the role of the Labour College of Canada in providing advanced union education for Canadian workers and to identify needs and priorities for the future development of union education in Canada. The contractors were expected to draw conclusions regarding the types of assistance required to extend and upgrade Canadian union education, the potential roles of governments and labour organizations, methods for integrating union and government efforts in the area and priority areas for further research. When the separate studies were completed in 1973, Verner and Dickinson were given a further contract to consolidate the various reports into one.[17]

Verner and Dickinson's AERC produced five studies as a result of these contracts. In addition, two masters theses and two research reports were written at the University of British Columbia (UBC) on labour education topics as part of Verner and Dickinson's research programme, and a review of Quebec labour education was prepared at the University of Montreal. As various labour observers complained, these studies relied primarily on statistical analysis. The main research instruments in the general research programme were questionnaires mailed to relevant staff in labour organizations and to participants and instructors in education programmes. The results of these surveys were then analyzed statistically to determine such things as frequency of courses, participation rates, profiles of participants, staffing and finance and so forth. The only interviews that were conducted in the whole research programme were in the Quebec study, in which about thirty to fifty individual interviews were held, and in Maria Brown's case study of a Vancouver local union, where 103 of the 873 local members were interviewed. Even in those cases where structured interviews were held, however, the data collected were primarily quantitative in nature (i.e., numbers and types of courses taken, what factors affected participation in union and adult education and so on). Claire Maynard's UBC thesis on the history of union education was the only study in the project to make significant use of documentary evidence. Nonetheless, the resulting statistical material and analyses do provide a substantial snapshot of the state of union education in Canada at the beginning of the 1970s, and various data and conclusions from these studies are reported in this chapter.[18]

Verner and Dickinson made a number of recommendations for the future of union education in their reports. They observed that, while union education programmes were offered by a variety of sponsors in many areas, there was no systematic approach to education for union members, resulting in a waste of scarce resources and inefficient educational activities. For the most part, they argued, union education in Canada lacked policies regarding the status of education in the labour movement, clearly defined objectives for programmes, unified planning, educationally efficient instruction and sufficient personnel adequately trained in education.

They suggested that union education should be coordinated at all levels in order to rectify these shortcomings. Local labour councils and provincial federations were urged to promote union education actively by providing administrative and support services to plan, develop and conduct educational activities. These included encouraging local unions to designate an education officer or committee, arranging training programmes for local education officers and maintaining constant data records of union educational events held in the area. At the national level, meanwhile, the academic investigators suggested that the CLC "should concentrate its resources on the initiation and improvement of union education but avoid those services and activities that are basically the responsibility of its affiliated bodies." In other words, the congress would concentrate on "education for and about union education rather than with services or programs that do not contribute directly to the development of educational activities and programs." Regional educational representatives, in this vision, would not offer courses directly for unions, but would offer training and assistance to affiliates in such matters as determining learning needs, planning programmes and improving instruction. Those unions that had been relying completely on the congress for their education needs would have to begin to develop their own internal capacity. The CLC, therefore, would confine its activities to periodic national conferences on the role of education in the labour movement, occasional training programmes for union educators, experimental programmes to find new ways to make union learning more efficient and the continual evaluation of union education in the country.[19]

William Dodge, the executive officer in charge of education at the time, and the NEAC had some significant criticisms of the report on CLC activity when they saw the first draft in 1973. NEAC members complained that the authors did not understand union structure, that they relied too much on quantitative surveys and not enough on qualitative interviews, that their academic approach distorted the true functions of workers' education and that the report reiterated what union educators already knew. Nonetheless, they concluded that the report was worthwhile. Dodge, for his part, had nothing good to say about the professors' work. He agreed with NEAC that the results simply restated what was already known to union educators and leaders through observation. He went on to complain that there were no suggestions in the report concerning how scarce resources could be used more efficiently through a coordinated programme with the affiliates, and he rejected the authors' claim that there was a lack of policy with respect to Canadian union education. Dodge also rejected the report's suggestion that the CLC programme should be decentralized, arguing that, if implemented, the recommendations would effectively eliminate the current educational activities of the CLC and relegate the congress to coordinating what the affiliates were doing. Moreover, he claimed that this aspect of the report would fortify the efforts of certain affiliates—notably the Quebec Federation of Labour—to get the CLC out of education.[20]

Internal Union Structures

While the CLC programme and activities were the most visible examples of union education in Canada, individual unions provided a range of services for their own members depending on their size and resources. In 1971, 18 of the 112 national and international unions affiliated to the CLC had Canadian-based education departments. Of these, 13 were in international unions and 5 were in national unions. Among the 88 affiliated international unions, meanwhile, a further 20 had education departments in their American headquarters that may have provided service to Canadians. Larger unions such as the Steelworkers, the UAW and CUPE, not surprisingly, were more likely than smaller unions to have their own education departments to serve and train members.[21]

CUPE, the largest public-sector union in Canada, developed a systematic educational programme in the years following its 1963 founding convention, which brought together the National Union of Public Employees and the National Union of Public Service Employees. It was clear to James Dowell, the union's first education director, that his most important priority was to develop a local union leadership programme. "A well-informed local union leader," he insisted, "is an absolute necessity if we hope to build our union into the strong military force that it should be."

Dowell had found work in the auto industry after service in the Second World War and soon became an elected official in UAW Local 195 in Windsor. During the early 1950s he took a variety of courses in the UAW educational programme.

While he was grateful for the training he received, he was frustrated by the UAW's haphazard approach to education and by a teaching style that emphasized lecturing at the expense of discussion and debate. When he joined CUPE in 1963, he was committed to building a system of union education that made trade unionists out of a diverse range of public-sector workers, included an orderly system of progression from one course to the other, and made use of a variety of teaching techniques.

Dowell's early efforts included the standard preparation of tools-training materials and organizing weekend and week-long schools. But it was evident from the beginning that, with members from one end of the country to the other, it was difficult if not impossible for CUPE to provide access to face-to-face educational opportunities for everyone in the organization. Locally based staff representatives were conscripted to act as course leaders, to encourage the formation of local union education committees and generally to promote education. In addition, educational representatives were established in each of CUPE's five regions in 1967. Even so, many local union officers and stewards who required education were not receiving it.[22]

As a result, Dowell began investigating how distance education could be used as part of the CUPE programme. In 1964 he arranged for the International Correspondence School to offer two courses—Labour Relations in Canada and Human Relations at Work—to CUPE members. These were academic courses, with written papers marked by the correspondence school, and were best suited for the member who had some academic preparation. A few more members were reached by this means, but the problem remained of increasing access to basic steward training.

Dowell saw a possible solution to this problem in a new educational technique called programmed instruction (PI). In 1965 a group of union education departments, coordinated by the CLC, contracted with a Montreal-based company called Personnel Systems to produce a course entitled Union Training Program for Shop Stewards and Committeemen: A Programmed Instruction Course. PI courses consisted of a number of booklets, each containing about seventy questions laid out in a planned sequence, designed so that each question built on the information that preceded it. The questions were on the right side of the page; the answers, which were revealed after each question was answered, were concealed on the left side of the page. For example, one question was: "The steward's role as an educator includes many tasks which help the membership to understand the union's program. Which four of the following eight tasks fall into the category of education?"

PI's promoters claimed that the technique was designed to actively involve the student in the learning process and to provide the student with meaningful and immediate feedback, and it was to be tested and revised until it taught at a predictable level. It was different than a standard instructional manual, its developers argued, in that a PI booklet interacted and communicated with the student while a manual simply presented facts: "An instructional manual may ask questions to highlight points, but, if the questions are not scientifically developed to ensure that learning takes place, it is not programmed instruction." Detractors, who apparently were a minority among Canadian labour educators at the time, believed that the technique resulted in mechanical learning, while those in unions who employed the system viewed it as just another teaching aid to be used either in the classroom or for distance teaching.

Summary of a discussion about programmed instruction at a 1968 meeting of the CLC's National Education Advisory Committee:

Brother Dowell reported on the steps taken by his union and others joined with him in saying that there had been a sufficiently good experience to justify further action. There was a good deal of discussion about past developments involving opinions of the Executive Council, the "sales approach" of the person selling the materials and emphasis on the value of coordinated purchasing and utilization of such material. Brother Morris [CLC Executive Vice-President in charge of education] thought the method was good and that further recommendations should be made. There was some feeling that while programmed learning had many advantages it also had disadvantages including a relatively high expense, individuals working in isolation rather than in a group, and the fact that it might supplant already established and successful programmes of some of the unions affiliated to the Congress. It was agreed that one advantage is that the employment of programmed learning materials helps make up for a chronic shortage of course leaders.

Source: University of British Columbia (UBC) Library, Special Collections, *CLC Education Office (British Columbia) Records*, Box 1, File 1, "Minutes of the National Education Advisory Committee," 17 December 1968.

Dowell first used a PI steward training course in 1965 and later supplemented it with PI courses in other subjects. Initially he used them solely for home study purposes, but after a couple of years he began using them in the classroom as well. He felt that the PI student became actively involved as he progressed from one question to the next. "It involves all students in the class, and eliminates the passive participation which is so prevalent at union schools," he claimed. Furthermore, he continued, "it acts as a tutor, because the questions are skillfully programmed, so there is interaction and communication with the student." PI did not replace other educational approaches, according to Dowell, but was combined with lectures, discussions, role playing and film. CUPE, CBRT (formerly the CBRE), the Steelworkers and some other unions bought substantial numbers of PI courses at two to three dollars a copy in the late 1960s and used them for a number of years thereafter.

By the mid-1970s, however, supplies were dwindling and the course content was becoming dated. As a result, in 1976 the CLC contracted with Lee Daws, the author of the original PI courses, to prepare an updated course on "Problem

Solving for Local Union Officers." The Steelworkers ordered six thousand copies of the course, with CUPE and the Canadian Paperworkers' Union taking four thousand more.[23] CUPE also developed more traditional home study courses in economics and political science for its members.[24]

 # 7

John Fryer, General Secretary, British Columbia Government Employees Union, to Lee Daws, criticizing programmed instruction:

The purpose of all union education, insofar as this organization is concerned, is to develop skills within the rank and file leadership that allow them to make independent judgment, that give them confidence to stand toe-to-toe with supervisors, to overcome the immense socialization that has taken place prior to their entering the work force which has created an almost knee-jerk obedience response to authority, and to develop an understanding of the social and economic climate in which trade unions function in this country.

It is inconceivable that this purpose can be gained by programming leadership to give another set of knee-jerk responses or by teaching union leadership made to relate to another form.

The leadership involved in our education program ask—no, in fact, demand—the right to challenge and question not only the instructor but also the instructional material, and react very negatively to any attempt to program them into a role that they feel, and I must agree, they have a right to define for themselves.

Source: NAC, *CLC Papers*, MG 28 I 103, Accession 86/0112, Volume 18, File "Programmed Instruction," John Fryer to Lee Daws, 14 November 1977.

 # 9

By the end of the 1960s, classroom, home study and programmed instruction courses were combined to form CUPE's six-level certificate programme. The first level consisted of programmed instruction in human relations (steward training), parliamentary procedure and union administration, while collective bargaining was studied at the second level. After taking arbitration at the third level, programme participants took specialized courses in economics, sociology and political science at the fourth level (available through home study). Levels five and six, finally, were the two elements of the Labour College of Canada programme (distance education and residential).

While this programme provided more systematic progression than any other internal union education programme in Canada, it was criticized as being too rigid and academic by some in CUPE. The British Columbia and Alberta divisions, in particular, felt that the programme constrained rather than facilitated union learning. Leslie Hewson, Alberta regional vice-president, told national Secretary-Treasurer Grace Hartman in 1972 that Dowell was "trying to force down the throats of the divisions and district councils" a programme that was ill-suited to serving a variety of age groups and educational backgrounds. The six-level programme, while of some use according to Hewson, did not cover all of the needs of the local union and membership. For example, the Alberta division chief stated that, in order to get older members to develop a taste for education, it was necessary to find courses they were interested in and to show them they had the ability to learn. Hartman and CUPE president Stan Little, while noting that the two western divisions seemed more interested in complaining than in doing the actual work of establishing education programmes, did suggest to Dowell that the education department should become more relevant in the areas of youth, women and community leadership.[25]

Among private-sector affiliates of the CLC, meanwhile, unions with established education programmes deepened their provision, with some moving in new directions and others putting new structures in place. Before 1956, CCL unions were more likely than TLC unions to develop education programmes (with notable exceptions, such as the TLC-affiliated ILGWU). But by the mid-1950s most major unions were developing some internal educational capacity. The IAM, for example, was an old TLC-affiliated union (dating from the nineteenth century) that developed a Canadian educational presence during the 1950s and 1960s. And unions such as the CBRT, the Steelworkers and the UAW continued to expand their existing programmes.

While there is evidence that an IAM educational seminar was held in Vancouver in 1949, Tom Tippett, the union's international educational director, claimed that the first training institute at the local lodge level in Canada was held in Toronto during 1952. By 1954 institutes were being held for lodges in both Montreal and Toronto, covering topics such as the function of the local lodge, planning a local lodge education programme and the history of the IAM in Canada. Tippett reported that the educational outcomes in Toronto differed between the disappointing results in District 78, a new district combining a number of established lodges composed of older skilled men, and the excellent programme in the various lodges at Avro Industries. The Avro lodges had established a local training programme in cooperation with the University of Toronto, with classes held weekly that covered a variety of subjects and weekend institutes at the university's rural campus. This activity ceased when the Canadian government cancelled the Avro Arrow in 1959, resulting not only in the loss of Canadian aerospace capacity but also, apparently, in the death of a vibrant labour education programme.[26]

In 1956, Mike Rygus, an IAM staff representative, was appointed educational representative for Canada as part of a pan-union initiative to establish education representatives in each of the union's "territories," of which Canada was one. But George Schollie, the IAM's general vice-president for Canada, insisted that "to broadcast that we have a *full-time* Educational Director would be to invite trouble" because of Rygus's limited resources and the incredible distances involved in serving a territory the size of Canada. Nonetheless, Rygus set out to service the local lodges and districts as best he could. He began by asking lodge chairs and business representatives for their views on what subjects and approaches should be included in a "training program for the rank and file membership." One business representative replied that an educational programme should never be identified as educational and that, to succeed, "any such campaign must be aimed at our housewives and the children with no direct approach to the dues payer." Another noted that the average mental age of the Canadian adult was twelve years and that most union members would "enjoy a movie cartoon" conveying course materials. And a Grand Lodge representative in Toronto insisted that education, to be of any benefit to IAM members, must be continuous in nature and use a system such as the WEA's weekly study groups.

With this survey in hand, the Canadian region proceeded slowly to establish a programme that encouraged local lodges to appoint an education representative and an education committee, and then provided the necessary information and assistance to the lodges as membership interest in education grew. By the early 1960s, however, when Harold Thayer replaced Mike Rygus as Canadian education director, the region was offering a summer school, short-term (less than a week) full-time staff training, weekend conferences and multi-week educational programmes in French and English. The union was also cooperating with Queen's University in Kingston and the University of British Columbia in Vancouver in organizing its summer schools and weekend conferences.[27]

The CBRT, for its part, had established an education department with a full-time education director in 1955. Bert Hepworth fulfilled this role until 1962, when he was replaced by Harry Jacks. Following a review in 1968, the programme was modified to emphasize three areas: officer training, leadership training and mass information. In the early 1970s the CBRT had two hundred locals with up to eight officers in each local, and the goal of the officer training component was to provide training for all of these officers. Between 1969 and 1972, about fourteen hundred officers participated in three-day seminars across the country. Leadership training, meanwhile, was accomplished primarily through a home-study course that participants could complete at their own pace and according to their own schedule. Three hundred were enrolled in this course in 1972. Those who successfully completed the home-study course could take one- or two-week advanced seminars designed to prepare them for the Labour College of Canada. And, finally, mass information for the general membership included the periodical *Canadian Transport*, published twice a month and sent to all members, and occasional *Current Affairs* leaflets sent in bulk to local education committees for general distribution.[28]

The Steelworkers, by comparison, had an extensive Canadian education programme that had been established by Howard Conquergood in 1943 and was under the direction of Gower Markle from 1951 until 1978. In 1970 the union's Department of Education and Welfare employed four full-time education officers, and about one hundred other people worked with the department each year as they were needed. The department produced a range of educational materials, including a bi-monthly magazine, to service its annual programme of institutes and week-long schools. The Steelworkers conducted all of their basic tools courses in-house, but cooperated with the CLC, provincial federations and labour councils in the provision of more general courses such as history, economics, international affairs and political action. The central bodies were expected to consult with the union about any educational programme or course offered in an area where it had members. A key feature of the Steelworkers' programme was its National Education Fund, a voluntary cooperative fund that was supported in 1970 by two-thirds of the union's locals representing about 85 percent of the membership. Locals contributed five cents per member to the fund and, in return, they were eligible for instruction, materials, films and scholarships from the national office.

Steelworker Local 1005 in Hamilton, Ontario, the biggest union local in the country during the 1960s, was the site of a range of programming from basic tools training to general interest courses. With an annual education budget in 1962 of $15,000, education activists in 1005 tried to ensure that all new stewards received a course in basic stewardship and that new members of the health and safety committee were comparably trained. The educational progress of stewards was tracked through a filing system that recorded all of the courses they took. In addition, the general membership had access to a course explaining the local's medical plan, a course providing an overview of the Workmen's Compensation Board for members who did not speak English as their first language and a wide range of general interest courses, such as photography, conversational French and labour history, offered in conjunction with the local Workers' Educational Association. And, during the winter, the local offered evening forums on specific topics, with attendance open to any member of a CLC- or OFL-affiliated union.[29]

In the UAW, meanwhile, Alan Schroeder succeeded William MacDonald in 1961 as education director of the union's Canadian region. Schroeder had been a UAW staff representative since 1951 and was a veteran of the political wars of the late 1940s and early 1950s as leader of the pro-CCF Reuther caucus in Local 199. During the 1960s, Schroeder presided over the Canadian section of one of the most substantial union education programmes in North America. At mid-decade the international union was involved in a range of activities. Each new UAW member received a kit with materials explaining the history, aims and goals of the union. There were classes for newly established local unions. Monthly discussion outlines were produced for local union executive boards and general membership meetings. A range of institutes, conferences, classes and summer schools were offered to provide leadership training, steward training and skills upgrading for local union officers and committee members. Graduates of the summer schools could deepen their understanding of trade unionism through a distance education course offered in conjunction with the Institute of Labor and Industrial Relations at Wayne State University in Detroit. And various print, audio and video materials were available for union educators to use, including a departmental newsletter, two UAW record albums, and a range of National Film Board of Canada (NFB) and other films.[30]

The most notable elements of this activity in the Canadian region were the New Local Union Basic Education programme, the origin and growth of the Port Elgin residential facility and new courses and programmes for and about women. The New Local Union Basic Education, or New Union Leader (NUL), programme originated as a directive from the 1966 international convention and was designed to provide basic education for elected representatives in newly organized locals by using specially trained discussion leaders (Local Union Discussion Leaders or LUDLs) from among the union's activist membership. It consisted of six or seven weekly two-hour classes.

The first NUL classes were held during 1967 in Windsor, Toronto, Brampton and a number of other centres in Ontario with Gordon Wilson, Bob Nickerson, Vic Cameron and three others providing the discussion leadership. According to Wilson, reporting on his first series of classes in Kitchener, the average attendance per class was ten, the participants' ages ranged from seventeen to twenty-one and bewilderment was the initial reaction to union history and to the union's contemporary role. By the end of the six weeks, however, participants were identifying with the content and suggesting follow-up seminars. Cameron, reflecting on his experience at Oakville, felt that he was more prepared than some of the other discussion leaders for this type of education because he had received his instructor training from members of the UAW education department rather than from Wayne State University faculty. He asked provocative questions, encouraged informality and used visual aids such as the blackboard. While he generally liked the course content, he recommended that it be Canadianized. By 1974 there were fifteen LUDLs teaching in the Canadian region, including one woman (Edith Welch from Local 27 in London, Ontario).[31]

The UAW's Canadian region thought seriously about establishing its own residential facility immediately after it stopped using the WEA's summer school at Port Hope in 1947. The following year it decided to purchase a piece of property at Kingsville, near Windsor, but stopped the transaction as a result of fears that the vendor was not able to sell the property. Nonetheless, the dream of a permanent home for the Canadian region's summer school was kept alive during the 1950s and, over the fall and winter of 1956-57, a summer camp at Port Elgin, Ontario, on the shore of Lake Huron was purchased for $37,500. By 1967, when the Canadian region asked the international union for financial assistance for a major expansion, the Port Elgin facility was valued at $300,000 as a result of steady improvements over the previous decade.

During the 1960s, Port Elgin was busy from May to October with a range of educational activities. The UAW claimed about ten weeks for courses, the CLC was there for five weeks each year for residential schools, and a four-week vacation period was available in July and August for UAW members and their families. A range of other labour, farm, co-operative and NDP groups completed the balance of the schedule. The UAW's "Leadership Education Week" was the highlight of the 1969 season because Walter Reuther visited the facility during the conference for the first and only time. He was joined by a range of other speakers including Tommy Douglas, leader of the federal New Democratic Party, and Howard McCurdy, chair of Canada's National Black Coalition. In 1972 the UAW added a Family Education programme to the Port Elgin schedule in which the spouses and children of members could learn about the union and the labour movement.[32]

The UAW was one of the earliest unions to recognize the importance of providing separate space in its educational programme for women members and for gender-specific subject matter. In 1955 it established a women's department, which advocated stronger female representation in the union, monitored female membership and employment and held an annual women's conference. The Canadian region's first women's conference was held at Port Elgin in 1964. In introducing the event, Cecelia Carrigan from the international union women's department noted that the purpose of the conference was not to separate women's and men's efforts, but to discuss problems that might be of special interest to women, to help them fit into shops and offices with the men and to work towards equal pay for equal work.

Dorothy Meehan, another staff person from the international women's department, spoke about the importance of establishing local union women's committees, stressing that they were necessary to bring women's problems to the attention of shop committees and that, when formed, they should survey the women members to better understand their concerns. When asked to discuss why women sometimes did not take an active part in local union affairs, the sisters suggested that men in the labour movement did not want women to participate on the one hand, and that participation might increase if meetings were followed by parties or fashion shows on the other. Women's conferences were held annually after 1964 and continued to address issues such as forming local women's committees, integrating male and female seniority lists, pursuing equal pay for equal work through human rights legislation and collective bargaining and increasing the number of women on local union executive boards.[33]

The UAW also made a special effort to become more relevant to youth and to link education to the increased strike activity that was a feature of the late 1960s. After Dennis McDermott became Canadian region director in 1968, he began to offer educationals during strikes (with echoes of the British Columbia WEA activity in the 1946 IWA strike). In order to collect strike pay, workers on strike had either to do picket duty or attend classes dealing with union structure, union history and related topics.[34]

What Was Taught, and How

By the 1960s, labour education was seen by its practitioners as a mature, stable and legitimate part of trade union and adult education practice. According to early CLC educators, the first purpose of union education was to stimulate and create a fundamental understanding of society, analyzing the dynamics of industrial society and the labour movement in particular. Its second purpose was to instruct and train union members to carry out their union responsibilities and to help them to play a more important role in the labour movement. The generally accepted view among practitioners in the late 1950s and into the 1960s was that union education had come of age as a practice inside the labour movement and as part of the broader field of adult education. Prior to the widespread industrial organizing of the 1940s, they argued, activists learned organizing, bargaining and leadership skills through experience and by informal contact with more seasoned comrades. Then, during the 1940s and early 1950s, a rudimentary system of union education was established, notably in the CCL, which concentrated on teaching the nuts-and-bolts of union organization and administration. But, the argument continued, the increased staffing, greater resources and substantial labour unity that accompanied the CLC's formation in 1956 allowed educators to broaden the programme and deepen the course and workshop offerings that were made available to members.[35]

Basic tools courses were the most popular offerings in weekend institutes and week-long schools during this period. In 1971, for example, 26 percent of all courses offered in the CLC programme were steward training courses, while next in order of frequency were union administration (10.4 percent) and collective bargaining (9.7 percent). Leadership training (6 percent) and grievance procedure (5.1 percent) were the only other content areas accounting for more than 5 percent of the total courses offered. Other regularly offered tools courses over the years were labour legislation, worker compensation, parliamentary procedure, and communications and public speaking.

A weekend institute, week-long school or staff conference in the late 1950s or early 1960s would include some combination of the following course offerings for staff representatives, local union officers, rank-and-file members and instructors. Staff representatives would have chosen from such topics as collective bargaining, trends in collective bargaining, economics, the analysis of contract clauses, labour law and social legislation, pensions and health insurance, the preparation of briefs and submissions, automation, political education or international affairs. Local union officers, for their part, might have enrolled in local union administration, parliamentary procedure, steward training, grievance procedure, preparation for collective bargaining, community affairs, political education, labour history or fair employment practices. The rank-and-file member, meanwhile, might have chosen interpreting the collective agreement, labour history, the structure and activities of the labour movement, community relations, public speaking or social legislation. And, finally, course instructors might have studied programming, teaching techniques, preparing materials or communications.[36]

Course offerings changed slightly in the 1960s to reflect different priorities and new constituencies. Many schools during the decade included courses such as unionism in the public sector, collective bargaining in the federal public service, unemployment insurance, time study and wage incentive systems and the problems of office workers. The Saskatchewan Federation of Labour summer school in 1964 offered courses on community health clinics and alcoholism in industry, while the Alberta Federation of Labour offered, in 1967, a course entitled How to Influence Workers and Win Union Members, taught by an American university professor. The Ontario programme, which was the largest in the country, listed fifty different weekend institute courses in the mid-1960s, organized around the themes of collective bargaining, steward and local-officer training, the social and political aspects of the labour movement, labour law, courses for special groups such as women or public-sector workers and general courses.[37]

By the early 1970s, environmental concerns were reflected in union education programming through the introduction of courses on pollution and occupational health and safety. However, the most significant change in this period was the increasing number and different focus of women's courses. While women's courses had always been a minor part of union schools, the subject matter had always reflected traditional gender roles. In 1958, for example, a course for the wives of trade unionists was held at the Fort William-Port Arthur (Ontario) Labour Council weekend institute. Conducted by Margot Thompson, editor of *Steel Labour*, the course attracted fifteen participants who learned about "all phases of women's participation in the work of the trade union," including the form and function of Ladies Auxiliaries. And, during the 1960s, the Ontario region of the CLC occasionally offered The Union Widow, which promised to explore solutions to the problem of the highly active trade union member whose family sees him less than they would like.

By the early 1970s, however, courses and educational programming for women were beginning to reflect the influence of the emerging feminist movement. In 1971 the Quebec Federation of Labour and the CLC sponsored a women-only week-long school, which organizers hoped would lead to greater female involvement in union education and the labour movement. Besides two special sessions investigating women's subjugation in North American society and the problems of working women, the cirriculum was devoted to regular courses such as grievance procedure, collective bargaining and political action. Early indications suggested that the experiment was successful as female participation in Quebec union educational events jumped from 4 percent before the school to 13 percent after it.[38]

The basic tools courses taught in this period followed the general pattern established in the 1940s and early 1950s. Courses in steward training, grievance procedures, collective bargaining and so forth offered by the CLC and its major affiliates normally covered some labour history, the steward's role in the union, meetings, dues and the membership, interpreting the contract, grievances and political education. The series of NFB labour films made in the mid-1950s was a staple of union educational programmes until the 1970s, when educators were forced to retire them because they had become outdated. These films, however, besides being well-produced treatments of their subjects, fit the tenor of the times in that they cast unions and the collective bargaining system as legitimate institutions in Canadian workplaces. In *The Grievance, The Shop Steward, Strike in Town* and the others, union activists were presented as responsible workplace actors who represented their members fairly and made the system work efficiently for all concerned, including employers. Unions that had been expelled from the CLC and its predecessors because of alleged communist sympathies also stressed the nuts-and-bolts of contract administration in their courses. But leaders and educators in the International Union of Mine, Mill, and Smelter Workers (Mine-Mill), the United Fishermen and Allied Workers (UFAW), the ILGWU and other like-minded unions placed more stress on rank-and-file control, workplace organizing, and the links between industrial, economic and political democracy than did their sisters and brothers in the mainstream labour movement.

Communist-led unions may also have allowed more participant control over course content within the constraints of their broader political objectives. A Mine-Mill course in 1956, for example, began by asking the participants to list the "Ten Things I Would Like to Learn." Responses included trade union economics and history, labour unity (world, national and within Mine-Mill), collective agreements and bargaining, how to instruct shop stewards, how to carry on work in the community, the relationship of autonomous unions to the international labour movement, how to analyze a company financial statement, strike organization, organizing the unorganized, the relationship between the Canadian and American sections of the union, establishing good morale in a local and many, many more. The instructors then grouped the responses into labour history, Canadian autonomy and union problems (bargaining, organizing and so on), and organized the rest of the school so that Canadian autonomy (an important issue for the union at the time) was highlighted.[39]

The dynamics of human psychology was a dominant theme in CLC and affiliate leadership training courses during the 1960s. The UAW's Applying Psychology to Local Union Leadership, for example, was aimed at developing strategies for working with people and strengthening the union by understanding the factors that influenced people's behaviour. Beginning with the principle that adults must participate in discussions in order for them really to learn what leaders want to communicate, the course explored a number of individual cases to develop participants' abilities to manage the disruption, dissension and opposition that were said to exist in local unions. After viewing the NFB film *Strike in Town*, the class probed the attitudes of various characters. Why were the attitudes of management and labour so inflexible until a strike was called (possibly neither wanted to appear to be weakening)? Why did the wife of a husband-member want him to get a job during the strike? Why did people outside of the union blame the union for the crisis?

In another case study, Jack Wilmot, a quiet fellow who is tormented by his fellow workers, blows up and throws a wrench at someone. In this case, the steward or other local union leader is encouraged to tell the others to lay off and treat him like everyone else. The problem for Wilmot, the course author explains, is that he has no one to talk to: "If he were a woman he could weep when the pressure was more than he could bear. But, in our society, we don't permit a man this healthy release." In the case of "Joe Grimble—the Chronic Complainer," the course author reviews why some members complain about the union. They may not be interested in being in the union, they may be anti-union, they may be negative about most things or they may chafe at any kind of authority. The author then advises that, when the criticism gets you down, remember that criticism often serves the function of draining off frustrations: "These same frustrations might have been channelled into more destructive patterns, such as men quitting the union or going on wildcat strikes." The course concludes by noting that workers do have mental problems, that leaders must go beyond the obvious to get at why the problems exist and that the union has a responsibility to help solve workers' problems.[40]

In the broader issues courses, the subject matter varied across unions and over time. Social science instruction ranged from the UFAW's historical materialism to CUPE's mainstream neo-classical economics. Ben Swankey of Vancouver's Trade Union Research Bureau produced and taught courses for the UFAW at various points in British Columbia. His "Economics for Workers," prepared in 1961, contained six lectures covering the characteristic features of capitalism, the production of surplus value, economic crises, monopoly capitalism, American domination of the Canadian economy, and monopoly capitalist control of the state. The political science course that was part of the CUPE six-level programme, in contrast, used R. Macgregor Dawson's standard introductory university text, entitled *Democratic Government in Canada*, which was a study of Canada's parliamentary institutions divorced from any understanding of underlying economic forces such as the relationship between social classes. CUPE economics students, meanwhile, read a booklet based on a Canadian Broadcasting Corporation (CBC) lecture series by D.E. Armstrong of McGill University in which the "free enterprise" system was accepted uncritically. The course consisted of a series of questions about the readings, which formed the basis for written assignments that were sent to the CUPE education department for marking and comment. As a result of criticism in the early 1970s, the economics course was rewritten to reflect more accurately an economic system in which workers and trade unions played a significant role.[41]

In the 1950s and 1960s, in courses dealing with international affairs and the international labour movement, participants in CLC courses were taught that the Canadian labour movement supported trade union freedoms through organizations such as the International Confederation of Free Trade Unions (ICFTU) and was critical of the Soviet-dominated World Federation of Trade Unions. Participants in a 1968 CLC course learned that ORIT—the ICFTU regional organization in the Americas—worked closely with the American Institute for Free Labor Development (AIFLD) to counter communist influence among Latin American trade unionists in order "to prevent Castro-like revolts which would help the Iron Curtain [i.e., the Soviet Union and its allies]." (The AIFLD was funded in large part by the Central Intelligence Agency and other U.S.-government bodies; it played a key role in U.S. covert operations in Latin America.) Furthermore, the course noted, Canadian trade unionists supported and worked through the United Nations and the International Labour Organization in pursuit of peace and international trade.

A course from the early 1960s began from the premise that "the world's business is our business," and went on to argue that the economic prosperity of Canadian trade unionists depended on the welfare of consumers and wage earners in other parts of the world. Illiteracy in other parts of the world had an impact on Canada's lumber and newsprint industries, while world hunger affected Canada's agriculture and fishing products. A stable international order allowing for orderly trade and the extension of free trade unions would benefit all workers, the course concluded.

In 1960s-era courses dealing with international relations in communist-led unions, meanwhile, domestic prosperity was also tied to international stability and prosperity; in these courses, however, peaceful coexistence between communist and non-communist countries was emphasized. By the 1970s there was a more radical edge to international affairs courses. Participants in a 1975 CLC "International Affairs" course, for example, learned about the global political influence of the ITT corporation, the influence multinational corporations exerted in the international economy and what New Democratic Party governments were doing to control multinational corporations.[42]

Instructor training courses taught such things as approaches to adult learning, communication styles, teaching methods, teaching aids and using resources. Participants in a 1961 course, for example, discussed the meaning of communications in modern society and analyzed case studies illustrating the breakdown of communication in unions. The advantages and disadvantages of lectures, group discussion (and its variations including buzz groups, panels, films as discussion starters), role playing and the case-study method were also considered. At a 1972 instructor conference, union educators shared information on how they presented materials or made use of literature and audio-visual aids. Harry Jacks, CBRT education director, told the group that the instructor was the key to the success of any union educational programme, yet this could sometimes be a sensitive area because programme planners were often reluctant to criticize the performance of voluntary instructors. Some educators wrote their own course outlines while others relied on outlines prepared by colleagues. And those who prepared their own material often followed the accepted practice in union education of "borrowing" material from other outlines. Regardless of how the outlines were put together, Jacks said, they should be adapted to the instructor's own style, follow a step-by-step approach and allow for as much discussion as possible. He concluded that, when teaching a course covering a number of areas, union educators should ask the students what they anticipated would be covered in the course, list these on the blackboard, offer to cover as many as possible in the time available, and always make sure to cover the areas you believe are important.[43]

Comments from Alan Schroeder, Education Director, Canadian Region, UAW, on the 1972 CLC Ontario Region instructor training conference:

Perhaps these don't apply to the session we held this year; however, if another session were planned, I would suggest that we should not try to cover as much ground in such a short time. We might have one session when we demonstrate specific techniques. For example, in the field of participation we might have different groups demonstrate the various discussion techniques such as buzz groups, question and answer, overhead question, reverse question, etc.

When we deal with steward training as in Brother Len Bruder's part of the program, we might have participants in the class demonstrate the questioning of a grievant to get the facts and perhaps one or two other role playing examples. Since we are trying to improve our techniques, we might also demonstrate the more effective use of such films as "The Grievance" by showing it in several sections with a brief discussion after each section. This might also have been done with the film "A Case of Insubordination." Even if our instructors do not need to have this practice, it might remind us that we must be on our toes to get the most out of the use of visual aids.

Source: UBC Library, Special Collections, *CLC Education Office (British Columbia) Records*, Box 1, Folder 1, Alan Schroeder, Education Director, Canadian Region, UAW to Larry Wagg, Education Director, Ontario Region, Canadian Labour Congress, 7 April 1972.

When Dickinson and Verner surveyed union education in 1971 they discovered that, of the 703 courses surveyed, 35 percent were taught by staff from affiliated unions, 32 percent of the instructors were local union officers and 19 percent were CLC or labour federation staff. Seven (1 percent) of the courses were taught by university professors, while the remaining 13 percent were handled by instructors from a variety of institutions. These instructors used lectures for 34 percent of the class time, with 21 percent of the time devoted to questions and answers. Since questions and answers often resulted in mini-lectures, Dickinson and Verner calculated that 55 percent of instructional time involved passive learning. Group discussion occupied 16 percent of instructional time, and other techniques involving active participation by participants (role playing, student projects and so on) accounted for 13 percent of class time. Film was used in 41 percent of the courses. Printed materials were used extensively, with 59 percent of such materials drawn from national and international unions and with 59 percent of instructors using materials they had prepared for the course in addition to those they gathered from other sources. Some union educators admitted that they found it difficult to break out of the lecture mode because it was an efficient means to convey information.[44]

Two years later, Dickinson and a research team conducted a systematic evaluation of CLC instructor training activities. In Ontario they assessed a two-and-one-half-day conference attended mostly by experienced union educators, of whom two were women. Conference events were organized around speakers, question-and-answer sessions and general discussion. The only opportunity for small-group discussion was at coffee breaks and at other informal times. Dickinson and his colleagues noted that, once, while waiting for a film to begin, "the two female participants organized buzz groups to discuss male chauvinist attitudes that they had observed among the other participants. The discussion was heated and was terminated abruptly by the conference manager in order to begin the film program, but it resumed in periods between the films." The researchers concluded that the Ontario programme suffered from poor instructional design and management: there were no opportunities for participants to practice the material being taught, the activities did not involve learner participation to any significant extent and the material presented was not reinforced. They recommended that "future programs should be structured to reflect sound adult education principles so that the participants may learn from what is done as well as what is said."

A seven-day instructor training programme in the Pacific region taught by Dickinson and a colleague, in contrast, was presented as a model of instructional design. This event was divided into a beginning group, which studied the preparation and presentation of brief lessons in a larger programme, and an advanced group, which concentrated on the planning of union education programmes. Each group had clearly defined objectives to achieve by the end of the week. Lectures, reference books and duplicated materials were used to present information about adult learning, instructional techniques, programme planning, lesson preparation and learning evaluation. Participants then worked either individually, in pairs or in small groups to prepare material for class presentation. The evaluators concluded that participant knowledge about instructional design increased significantly during the week, participants were satisfied with the programme and the programme presented a model of instructional design and management that participants could use to conduct their own education programmes.[45]

The Promise and Problems of University-Labour Cooperation

While union educators' energies were directed primarily towards building internal capacity in the 1950s and 1960s, there were some attempts early in the period to rekindle relations between the labour movement and universities. The National University-Labour Conference on Education and Co-operation, held 15 to 17 December 1956, was the first major pan-Canadian labour education event after the end of the WEA era. Co-sponsored by the CLC and the CAAE, it brought together in Ottawa over one hundred delegates from labour, universities, government, media and other organizations. The focus of the conference was the relationship between union education on the one hand, and the mass media, government departments and universities on the other. There was general agreement that with the new CLC education programme and with significant internal programmes in unions such as the Steelworkers and the CBRE, Canadian union education had a basic institutional structure that could provide a foundation for future growth. But labour spokespersons such as Gordon Cushing and Max Swerdlow acknowledged that the typical union member in the mid-1950s was relatively new to the labour movement, and the movement had to invest a significant amount of time and resources in educating this membership. While the labour movement of the 1950s was more stable and established than it had been in the past, including in the educational area, the leadership recognized that, perhaps more than ever, the movement required strategic alliances with external partners. Swerdlow suggested that universities could help the labour movement train more qualified instructors, devise a defined programme of progression from one level of labour education to another, spark interest in education among the general membership and produce more instructional materials. And, while conceding that antagonism had existed between labour and academia in the past, he insisted that the congress was sincerely interested in establishing a practical working relationship with universities.

The CAAE's Gordon Hawkins, in the most thoughtful address to the conference, alerted both university and union educators to the key features that each group had to understand about the other. Unions, he argued, should appreciate that universities had to maintain their own integrity, objectivity and academic standards (including concepts such as academic freedom), and they could work only in fields that were legitimate according to their principles. Universities, for their part, had to accept the legitimacy of collective bargaining and labour's role in society, that unions created educational programmes as clear responses to organizational or membership needs, and that social context—where and with whom one worked, for example—was an important feature of union education.[46]

There were two practical outcomes of the 1956 conference. First, a national and several local labour-university education committees were formed to allow union educational staff and sympathetic or interested university faculty and administrators to meet and coordinate activities. The national committee was to act as a clearinghouse, to assist universities in sponsoring union education, to stimulate the preparation of materials for union education and to facilitate the formation of local committees. Second, the National University-Labour Committee undertook a survey to establish an inventory of labour education in Canadian universities and to determine the status of university-based industrial relations and labour programmes.

Fernand Jolicoeuer (Canadian and Catholic Confederation of Labour), Napoleon LeBlanc (Laval University), Max Swerdlow (CLC) and Gower Markle (Steelworkers) met in January of 1957, immediately following the 1956 conference, to begin putting in place a national committee to continue the work suggested by the conference participants. They contemplated, among other things, a history of the Canadian labour movement and a survey of Canadian labour education. Settling on the latter as a first step, seventeen universities were surveyed between

April 1957 and September 1958, of which fifteen responded. Of these fifteen, eight sent full reports and the remaining seven expressed interest in the committee's work while admitting that they were not involved in labour education.

Seven universities were involved in some kind of labour education through their extension departments, although the level of activity varied from the occasional seminar to more structured courses. St. Francis Xavier University and the University of Manitoba, for example, had ongoing programmes dating from the 1930s. The University of Western Ontario, too, claimed that its relevant educational activities could be traced back to the WEA days, and that it was offering labour-oriented evening classes during the 1950s. The universities of Alberta and British Columbia noted that they conducted occasional conferences and seminars for unions, and that these normally resulted from labour representatives approaching the university for support. Similarly, the University of Montreal and Laval University did not have dedicated labour education programmes, but did respond to union requests for assistance. In addition, Laval had organized a Department of Industrial Relations in 1946, which conducted evening classes and conferences for working people over the years.

The main method of delivery in all cases was the evening course of from ten to twenty-six weeks duration, normally meeting for one class per week, and lasting from one and one-half to two hours per session. This was followed by joint university-labour day-long or weekend conferences and seminars. The courses offered—including economics, sociology, psychology, history, political science and public speaking—covered the issues-type subjects of a liberal education. Very rarely did universities stray beyond these. If on occasion they taught collective bargaining, for example, they emphasized its social, economic, political or psychological context rather than the nuts-and-bolts of negotiations. No universities organized their own institutes, although a number of them took part in weekend institutes organized by unions themselves.

All universities—or, more specifically, the extension directors at those institutions— responding noted that the lack of adequate financial support had hampered the development and expansion of their programmes. In part this was a result of generally inadequate financing for universities, resulting in understaffing. Extension departments did not have staff or funds for labour education but, instead, had to rely on regular faculty who, while committed to labour education in principle, were already overworked. Normally, extension labour courses were expected to be self-supporting while, in practice, the fees did not cover all of the expenses incurred by participating in these programmes.

There was general agreement in the survey responses that universities had a role to play in labour education. At the University of Manitoba this involvement was guided by adult education professional principles of the time. The extension department provided the same service to labour organizations as it provided to any other group in the community. It provided a source of instructors and a source of guidance and counsel in the organization and administration of adult education projects. It was recognized in Manitoba, however, that, in comparison with other groups in the community, labour was well organized and competent in providing leadership and taking the initiative with respect to educational provision. Laval, Montreal and UBC agreed that universities could make a contribution to labour education in two areas. First, universities could provide technical courses to give the rudimentary elements of professional training to union leaders (in the sense of providing specialized knowledge not readily available to the layperson). Second, they could counter the narrowing of perspective that often accompanied technical training and assist union leaders and rank-and-file members to appreciate the wider social milieu of which they were a part.[47]

As it turned out, the labour education survey was the only significant outcome of the National University-Labour Committee. The national committee continued to meet sporadically until 1963, but by that time the labour movement's energies in the area of advanced union education were directed towards the Labour College of Canada (LCC). In 1971 the committee was formally dissolved with its remaining funds transferred to the CAAE. Local union-university committees were formed at St. Francis Xavier, Dalhousie, Laval, Toronto, McMaster, Manitoba, Saskatchewan, Alberta and British Columbia. Some committees, such as the one at UBC, acted as little more than structures to facilitate communication between university personnel and the local labour movement with little of substance resulting. Others, such as the one at Dalhousie, organized occasional seminars or schools for trade unionists using university facilities and instructors drawn from university and union staffs.[48]

At the University of Manitoba, officials acted quickly after the 1956 conference to appoint to a union-university committee four sympathetic faculty members, who, in turn, invited the Winnipeg and District Labour Council to appoint four representatives to join them. The labour council delayed acting as a result of a lingering mistrust of academics, but eventually appointed the representatives. The Manitoba committee formed what turned out to be the most enduring outcome of the various local joint committees across the country. In the fall of 1962, fifty-five students enrolled in the first intake of The University-Labour Three-Year Certificate Programme and three years later twenty-four graduates emerged. Initially, the first year of the programme covered Canadian history and economics, the second year, Canadian government and the history of trade unionism, and the third year, labour law. This curriculum stayed more or less the same over the years, except that the history courses were eventually reorganized and offered in one year as two semesters of Canadian labour history. Instruction was at a university level, with instructors drawn from the community as well as from the ranks of university faculty. The committee, however, was sensitive to the fact that it was dealing with adult learners; as a result, no prior credentials were necessary, students could begin their studies at any point in the programme and those who failed examinations were given the chance to rewrite them. The Manitoba model was observed and considered by other universities: Lakehead, collaborating with the OFL and the Lakehead and District Labour Council, established its own three-year certificate programme in 1969, while Laurentian considered starting one in 1964.[49]

The most successful example of a local joint committee was at St. Francis Xavier, and this was largely because of the previous ongoing relationship between the university and the local labour movement. Nonetheless, there were tensions within the StFX committee, which illustrate the general difficulties that plagued these structures across the country. Formed in 1958, the StFX committee consisted of seven StFX and three labour representatives. While committee discussion in the first few years ranged across the field of labour education, including StFX's People's Schools and a possible basic education programme for the Cape Breton unemployed, by the early 1960s the main activity of the committee was the sponsorship and organization of an annual summer school at Antigonish. The first Trade Union Summer School was held in 1960. Participants attended this and subsequent summer schools from across Atlantic Canada, even though the original mandate of the StFX committee was limited to eastern Nova Scotia and there were turf wars with the less established Dalhousie committee. The number of summer school delegates per year was around seventy early in the 1960s and about fifty later in the decade.

The 1962 school included sessions on Collective Bargaining in the Sixties with McGill University's H.D. Woods, Canada's Atlantic Provinces with W.J. Woodfine of StFX's economics department, and Knowledge, Skills and Communications in the Labour Movement with A.L. Hepworth from CBRT, which was the only labour-led session in the school. The 1966 school, by comparison, had a more balanced labour-non-labour representation with CUPE's Gilbert Levine, the Steelworkers' James Norton and the CLC's John Fryer making up the labour contingent. There was no difference between the subject of the labour and non-labour talks at the latter school, however, with topics ranging from automation to contracting out.

The discussions in the local joint committee reveal that tensions sometimes existed between the academic instructors and the trade union participants. In reviewing the first school in 1960, for example, W.J. Woodfine, an academic, complained that there was too much political talk at the school, particularly with respect to the New Party movement. Furthermore, Woodfine argued that the academic's role was to make an objective analysis of a given situation regardless of the conclusions that flowed from that assessment. Tom Mombourquette from labour countered that Woodfine was viewed by many trade unionists as a mouthpiece for big business because he had argued publicly in favour of mine closures, and many school participants had formed an opinion about him before they came to the school. Other academics supported Woodfine, complaining that, if they objectively presented facts that trade unionists did not want to hear, they were viewed as being anti-labour. Their role, they reiterated, was to go where their analysis led them and to be unconcerned as to whether or not their conclusions were popular with a particular audience. Harold Stafford, CLC Atlantic education director, complained the following year that the original intent of the joint committees—to coordinate ideas between labour and university representatives—had been forgotten as labour was being told rather than asked what education was best for them. Stafford acknowledged that labour did not have high academic standards, but that it had a basic idea of what it required.

StFX's other major labour education initiative during the 1950s and 1960s was the continuation of its People's School. In 1955 the People's School shifted from radio to television. The format previously used in radio was continued on television, with an annual series of from twenty to twenty-five weekly broadcasts designed to supplement local discussion groups at various locations in Cape Breton. The broadcasts were funded primarily by the labour movement, but organized and conducted by the StFX extension department with the assistance of a labour advisory board. In 1958 unions contributed $4,500 of the $6,000 cost of the broadcasts. Father Hogan of StFX, the university figure credited with maintaining good relations with the labour movement during this period, argued that the main purpose of the broadcasts and the discussions was to instruct industrial workers about the legitimate aims of the labour movement through, for example, instruction in parliamentary procedure, the history and influence of labour legislation and the elements of union leadership. Although the perceived threat of communism to Catholic trade unionists had receded in Cape Breton by the mid-1960s, Hogan noted in 1966 that a "good guy/bad guy" approach to union-management relations still persisted among some union leaders and that this attitude had to disappear through education if a "realistic" trade unionism was to emerge. Part of the strategy, it appears, was to dilute the union influence over the People's School broadcasts by, first, enlisting the advisory assistance of selected business owners in 1965 and, second, establishing a formal business advisory committee the following year to counter the labour advisory group. In 1967, for the first time in the People's School's history, there were no specifically labour topics or speakers listed in the broadcast programme.[50]

While the anti-communist crusade that had defined StFX's labour education in the 1930s and 1940s was replaced in the following two decades with instruction in responsible trade unionism, the main front in the Catholic Church's educational war against union-based communism outside of Quebec shifted to Sudbury in 1958. A.J. Boudreau, a graduate of StFX and a practitioner of the Antigonish Movement approach to adult education, was hired that year as the first director of the University of Sudbury's extension department. Boudreau's main task was to establish and conduct an educational programme to aid Steelworkers' raids against Mine-Mill Local 598, which were ongoing at the time.

Boudreau's first task was to offer anti-communist education through a leadership training course to a select group of Local 598 members. In close consultation with Jim Kidd, the CLC representative in Sudbury, he arrived at a class list of 142 participants and began teaching the course in January 1959. With Kidd as an intermediary, Gower Markle (the Steelworkers' education director) provided Boudreau with Steelworkers, CLC and CCF materials, which they trusted would show the workers how a "proper" international union worked and thereby make clear the comparison with Mine-Mill "without actually mentioning Mine Mill." Eighty-eight course participants, of whom eight were Steelworkers-supporting members of the new 598 executive, graduated in June 1959 and received a University Certificate in Leadership. Boudreau invited CLC president Claude Jodoin to attend the graduation ceremonies as an implicit means of showing the congress's support for the Steelworkers' and University of Sudbury's efforts to influence the internal affairs of Local 598. The graduation exercises were designed as a piece of ideological theatre in the political struggle for 598: one thousand people attended and the event was covered by the press, radio and television.

Graduates of the leadership course founded the Northern Workers' Adult Education Association later in 1959. The formal objectives of the incorporated association were to promote and organize adult education among workers through a variety of means (study clubs, various media, lectures, discussion groups), to propagate cooperative ideals and Christian social doctrines, to foster a better understanding of the duties of citizenship and to work closely with the University of Sudbury's extension department. Until at least 1963, the association organized study clubs, trained study-club leaders, provided the study clubs with materials, held regular meetings and developed enthusiasm and legitimacy for the association and its objectives through films, dances and outside speakers. Alan Thomas of the CAAE, for example, spoke about communication and adult education to the association's 1962 annual meeting.[51]

The leadership training course and the subsequent association were designed to deliver Catholic teaching about the place of workers in society using adult education principles such as those developed at StFX. Moses Coady's *Masters of Their Own Destiny* was a guiding text, and association members formed discussion groups consisting of from four to twelve members to carry on their educational activities. Boudreau and the association members studied the worker as a producer, a consumer and a citizen through an assessment of capitalism, communism and the cooperative movement. Capitalism was presented as a system with promise that was debased by the abuses of greedy capitalists. A good capitalism was possible, and the abuses that began with the Industrial Revolution—notably the exploitation of labour and the glorification of the individual—engendered two reactions: communism and cooperation. The first, based on the hatred of the class struggle and leading to dictatorship, was an extreme reaction leading to its own abuses, notably the loss of individual and religious freedom. But the second, based on the love of God and on brotherly unity, provided the basis for a more equitable distribution of resources within a reformed capitalism.

Workers, for their part, were presented as producers of human labour who were interested in strengthening their collective bargaining position through their unions. There was a limit to what could be accomplished at the bargaining table, however. Therefore, the worker had to organize cooperatively as a consumer in order to exercise some control over his economic life (the democratic control of production was out of the question in this approach). But workers were not merely economic units, and they had educational, cultural, political and religious responsibilities as citizens.[52]

University-labour cooperation in this period was limited, then, despite a flurry of activity associated with the 1956 conference. The most concerted efforts were linked to the Catholic Church's attempts to influence the labour movement's internal affairs. By the early 1960s, however, Canadian union educators were preoccupied with building their own institution of higher learning.

The Labour College of Canada

The Labour College of Canada opened its doors in 1963 for its first intake of students, but it had been in gestation for at least six years prior to that. Since at least 1957, union educators had been discussing the need to supplement the basic tools-training programmes with university-level instruction in the humanities and social sciences in order to equip labour leaders with the skills it was believed they required in a modern world. The 1958 CLC convention directed the CLC officers to explore the establishment of a labour college in collaboration with a university. Carleton University in Ottawa was approached first to see if it was interested in working with the Canadian labour movement in this pioneering venture. Carleton president Davidson Dunton expressed guarded interest in the scheme initially. Eventually, however, a Carleton committee produced an unacceptable proposal whereby the college would consist of two separate programmes, one to be taught by Carleton academic staff on the university campus and the other to be offered by the CLC somewhere else. The academics were willing to dirty their hands with labour types, but only a little. Enraged CLC officers terminated the discussions.

After a similar fruitless encounter with the University of Western Ontario, the CLC found a more congenial audience at McGill University and the University of Montreal. The three organizations developed a proposal for a college chartered as an independent academic body and governed by a board appointed by the sponsoring bodies. The college staff would consist of a full-time academic principal, who would be the academic administrator and do some teaching, and part-time instructors from among the academic staff of the sponsoring universities. A CLC staff person would serve as college registrar. There would be two programmes of study each year, corresponding to the two terms of the regular university academic year, available in both French and English, and covering economics, political science, history, sociology and trade unionism. After the proposal was modified to limit the annual programme to one seven-week session, it was approved by all of the sponsoring bodies, including the Confederation of National Trade Unions (CNTU), which had been invited to join the group.[53]

The inaugural board contained nineteen seats, with five each from McGill University and the University of Montreal, six from the CLC and three from the CNTU. R.E. Powell, McGill's chancellor and retired president of the aluminium mining and processing corporation Alcan, was the first board chair. Powell was one of three corporate capitalists on the board, and he hoped that the college "would lead to a meeting of minds between management and labor, and that men trained in the college would have a greater understanding of the problems of management." The CNTU's participation in the college did not last long. It withdrew after three years because it had developed its own labour college and it felt that the Labour College of Canada had been of little use to its members.

At their first meeting in 1961, board members decided, first, to operate the college for an initial three-year experimental period to determine if it had long-term viability and, second, that $240,000 was required to cover operating costs and scholarships for that period of time. As college registrar, Max Swerdlow took responsibility for fund raising and approached the various CLC affiliates and the federal and provincial governments. The labour movement provided about $150,000 of the college's operating and scholarship budget for the first three years with, for example, the CBRT pledging $15,000, the UAW giving $4500, and three hundred locals across the country making contributions ranging from $10 to $1,000 each. Individual unions were also responsible for covering the lost time, tuition and room and board for their members who were chosen as students. The federal government provided $15,000 and the provinces gave about $75,000 for the three-year budget.[54]

The college's first session opened on 3 June 1963 at the University of Montreal for a seven-week programme. Thirty-one men and one woman registered for the French-language section and fifty-three men enrolled in the English-language section, studying economics, history, sociology, political science and trade unionism. All of these students, before arriving in Montreal, had been nominated by their union and had been interviewed in their home region by university-based Labour College "representatives" who determined whether or not the candidates had the academic ability to succeed in the programme and then forwarded their recommendations to Montreal. Most of the students were between the ages of twenty-five and forty and most were from Ontario and Quebec. Only half of the French-language students had completed secondary education, while 85 percent of the English-language students had their high-school certificates. Four English-language students and two French-language students had some post-secondary education. Reg Basken, later president of the Energy and Chemical Workers Union (now part of the Communication, Energy and Paperworkers Union), and Kealey Cummings, who would become a vice-president of CUPE, were among the 1963 graduates.[55]

An excerpt from a 1965 magazine article about that year's Labour College of Canada session:

Last May 24 weekend, four trade-union workers, driving from Montreal to Burlington, Ont., unintentionally set a scholarly record of sorts. They not only took turns at the wheel but also in reading aloud from a history textbook titled: "Between the Wars—America 1919-41." By the end of the day they had covered 600 miles and 195 pages. This was no stunt. As students at the fledgling Labor College of Canada in Montreal, they've got to do the equivalent of half a university year in eight weeks. What makes it even harder, most of the 147 students are in their 30's and 40's and haven't finished high school.

'We wanted to see our families,' says Nick van der Hoeven, a 48-year old Leamington packing-house worker. 'But with a reading list of over 40 books, besides attending lectures and seminars and writing essays, we just couldn't afford to waste any time.' His companions, Dave Pretty, 36, John Kane, 37, and Duncan Longwill, 27, members of the Chemical Workers Union who live in the Sarnia area, also spent their weekends studying.

...the college makes sure that the lack of education [of students] is compensated by intelligence, drive and proven ability for self-improvement, when it comes to screening applicants for the course. To begin with the union locals, which foot the bill, nominate only the go-getters in their ranks. The candidate is then interviewed by a labor-college representative, usually a university professor located in the area (about 30 of these are available across the country) who makes the necessary assessment. He then sends his report to the college which disqualifies those it feels can't weather the course.... To help ease the leap into the academic world, the college arranges, where possible, an indoctrination course of six two-hour lectures at a nearby university. Its main purpose: to introduce the prospective student to the special jargon of the social sciences. The initial classes in 1963, it seems, got lost in the fog of misunderstanding over the lecturers' vocabulary.

...Professor H.D. Woods, a McGill professor and co-principal of the college during its first two years, has stated: 'We have sometimes been asked if we gave the instruction a pro-labor slant. We did not. We behaved as university instructors should. Objectively. We did select the topics in relation to the interest of the student body. History, for example, emphasized the economic rather than the political or constitutional.'

While the college's board of governors has nine labor-union representatives, it also has ten from the two universities. And they include well-known industrialists...: R.E. Powell (Aluminium Co., of Canada and Royal Trust), T.R. McLagan (Canada Steamship Lines and Royal Bank), J.G. Notman (Canadair Ltd. and Canadian Imperial Bank of Commerce).

...Most of the students attend the college 'to become better trade unionists.' Burly 29-year-old Bernie Christophe of Winnipeg, Paris-born chief-executive officer of a retail-clerks union with a 1,800 membership, says: 'I've had to learn by trial and error. Many a time I'd be sitting in on negotiations with management and they seemed to be talking a different language. I'm getting a lot of the answers here. While people are my stock-in-trade and I've learned how they act, I didn't know why.'

His ambition is to become a national vice-president of his union. 'But that's a long way off. I wouldn't dare compete for it now. But maybe one day....'

...Railway carman Alf Walker, 31, of St. Boniface, Man., president of his local, wants to get into union work on a full-time basis. With a Grade 10 education, he's been attending weekend seminars for the past eight years but claims they are not enough, a statement echoed by Max Swerdlow, the CLC's education director, who emphasizes that union educational courses and the labor college operate at different levels.

...One of the two Canadian women trade unionists on the course this year, Alma Faulds of Oliver, B.C. is secretary of the fruit-and-vegetable-packers union (3,000 membership).... She sits on the B.C. labor council, the only woman among 20 men. She claims she has a "tempering effect" on the language and admits to losing her temper only when she gets mail from CLC headquarters addressed to 'Dear Sir and Brother....'

...To management, incidentally, the labor college has extended a standing invitation to send its representatives to take the course, mix with trade unionists, and find out how labor thinks. (2 attended last year and 2 this year.)

Source: NAC, *International Association of Machinists and Aerospace Workers Papers*, MG 28, I 191, Volume 86, File 5, N.R. Dreskin, "Canadian Labor Gets Its Own College," Canadian Weekly 4 September 1965 (supplement to Toronto Star).

The principal provided the overall academic direction for the college. Swerdlow doubled as college registrar and principal until March 1963, when H.D. Woods of McGill and Gilles Beausoleil of the University of Montreal agreed to act as co-principals until a permanent academic head could be found. After offering the job to someone at Ruskin College in the United Kingdom and then to Pierre Trudeau, a University of Montreal law professor and later Canadian Prime Minister, the Board of Governors chose Fernand Martin for the post. Martin, a professor of economics at the University of Montreal, assumed his duties at the beginning of the third term in 1965 and continued in the job until 1969 when he resigned to join the federal government's task force on industrial relations. Lincoln Bishop, the CLC's Ontario education director, served as acting principal until Luc Martin, a sociologist from the University of Montreal, was hired to the post in 1971 and made permanent in 1972.

The principal was joined by the registrar as the other senior administrator at the college. The registrar was responsible for student recruitment, processing applications, fund raising, college finances and other similar duties. Swerdlow handled this job in addition to his duties as CLC education director from 1963 until 1967, when Bert Hepworth took over. By 1970 Hepworth was complaining to the board that his duties at the college were too onerous and that the time had come to appoint a full-time registrar. His concerns were partly addressed with the appointment of Lincoln Bishop, recently retired Ontario education director, as college executive director in 1971. Hepworth continued as registrar with formal

Jean Bezusky, Associate Registrar, talks to two students at the 1972 Labour College of Canada residential session. *Canadian Labour Congress Collection.*

responsibility for the post, but Bishop took over the actual duties in the registrar's office. Bishop was aided by Jean Bezusky, a 1966 college graduate, who became assistant registrar at the same time, replacing Jean-Jacques Jauniaux. Bezusky had been active in her CBRT local in Montreal before joining the college staff in 1968 as secretary to the registrar. When Bishop left in 1972, Bezusky moved into the new position of associate registrar to assist Hepworth. Larry Wagg succeeded Hepworth in 1975 as both college registrar and CLC education director, with Bezusky continuing as associate registrar.[56]

The registrar's most important tasks were to raise money and balance the books. The initial flurry of fund-raising efforts raised more money than expected and the college's income exceeded expenditures in the early years. After the first two years of operation, for example, Swerdlow had built up a surplus of nearly $60,000 on total receipts of about $220,000. By the end of the decade, however, the college was running a deficit. In 1969, expenditures exceeded receipts by about $40,000. Staff costs accounted for a significant portion of the expenditure increase over the intervening years, with higher fees for faculty members and increased salaries and benefits for the support staff as a result of a new contract with the Office and Professional Employees International Union. In 1970, however, Hepworth recorded a surplus of just less than $20,000 on the annual account. In the early 1970s governments were contributing about 40 percent of the college's annual budget, the labour movement was contributing another 40 percent, and the balance came from tuition fees, individuals, foundations and other sources.[57]

The general structure of the annual residential sessions at the University of Montreal, covering economics, sociology, political science, history and trade unionism, remained virtually unchanged during the college's first decade. However, programmes to prepare prospective students for the residential component were introduced and a variety of post-residential seminars were explored. The dream in the earliest discussions about advanced labour education in 1957-58 was that the college would operate year-round. This proved not to be feasible and, after a seven-week session in 1963, the college operated for eight weeks each spring and summer.

It was clear from early in the first session that a large number of the students were overwhelmed by the university-level course materials. During that initial year the academic staff held additional sessions with students and they decided to forgo formal examinations in favour of a written paper in each course. Based on this experience, the co-principals decided to extend the session by a week in subsequent years (although they reintroduced examinations) and to ensure that students received their course materials and textbooks by post prior to their arrival in Montreal. They also explored other means by which students could prepare for the demanding schedule. One option, which was tried for a couple of years, was to offer university-based lectures at various points across the country in order to introduce prospective students to the relevant course content. Another option, which proved to be more substantial and enduring, was to develop a distance education programme that trade unionists from anywhere in the country could take at their own pace. This programme, which began in 1966, contained sections on economics, political science and sociology to provide subject-matter background for most of the courses covered in the residential session. These three units were supplemented by a basic-skills component covering how to read a textbook, how to take notes and write assignments, how to read graphs and basic accounting.[58]

There were limited options for those students who graduated from the LCC and wanted to pursue further labour-related education, especially before some colleges and universities began to develop labour studies programmes in the 1970s. The college attempted to make some provision for these learners by organizing advanced seminars on specific subjects. For example, a 1966 weekend institute was held in Toronto on The Automation Challenge, in cooperation with the WEA, which had become a general adult education provider in the city. The institute consisted of six lectures by six different academics and attracted twenty-eight participants. Another seminar, Devaluation, Gold and Separatism, was held at McMaster University in 1968 and dealt with the relationship between international trade and the threat of Quebec separation. It was attended by thirty college graduates from a variety of unions.[59]

The college student body contained a mix of francophone, anglophone and non-Canadian participants during this period. Eight hundred and twenty-eight students graduated from the residential programme by the end of the tenth term in 1972, of whom 54 percent were anglophone Canadians, 30 percent were

A student reads Ramsay Cook's *Canada and the French Canadian Question* during the 1972 Labour College of Canada residential session. *Canadian Labour Congress Collection.*

francophone Canadians and 16 percent were from other countries. The non-Canadian participants enrolled in the college as a result of a Canadian International Development Agency (CIDA) and CLC initiative that sponsored trade unionists from Commonwealth countries in attending the college for two months and then tour Canadian industrial centres for another month. The international participation ended in 1971 when CIDA discontinued its funding.[60]

The overwhelming majority of the participants were male. Of the 688 Canadian graduates through 1972, only 20 or 3 percent were female. This figure is especially low since women accounted for about 30 percent of the broader labour force during the 1960s, and is no doubt attributable to the facts that unions were still predominantly male at the time and women were less likely to become union activists because of domestic responsibilities and sexism in the movement. However, there were no special efforts made to ensure that more women enrolled in the college, other than encouraging as many women as possible to apply for admission. Five of the 64 participants in 1974 were women, which was three more than the previous average annual female enrolment; 11 women applied for admission that year, however, and the same criteria were applied to them as were applied to the men. Most of the participants (81 percent) were between twenty-five and forty-four years of age, with 8 percent younger and 11 percent older. These numbers, like those for women, are skewed when compared to the broader labour force, where those under twenty-four and over forty-four accounted for about half of all workers in the 1960s.

About three-fifths of the students were from union locals with five hundred or more members, and the average length of union membership for all students was ten years. Almost all of the participants (92 percent) held local union office when they attended the college, while 12 percent of students were employed full-time by their unions. Thirty-six percent had less than two years experience as union officers, while 52 percent had been in office from two to five years and 12 percent had six or more years of experience as elected officers. With respect to previous educational experience, 62 percent of participants had taken two or more union education courses and 15 percent had completed six or more courses, with an average of three union education courses per student between 1963 and 1972. Participants averaged about two general adult education courses per student over the same period, which was slightly higher than the average for the total Canadian adult population.

In 1972 all of the Canadian graduates since 1963 were surveyed to determine their participation in union and educational activities, their mobility in the labour movement and their satisfaction with various aspects of the college programme. More than one-third of graduates reported increased participation in their own union while one-quarter said that they were more active in other labour bodies since attending the college. Only 11 of the 332 graduates who returned questionnaires had received university credit for their college attendance, but over a quarter of respondents reported that they had gone on to take other union education and other adult education courses. Furthermore, 40 percent to 50 percent indicated that their reading of union publications, general publications and books had increased after they left the college.

About 20 percent of respondents left the labour movement after attending the college, with five graduates indicating that college attendance influenced their decision to leave while ten said it had not. Of the 235 graduates who indicated their current and former positions in the labour movement, 70 percent stayed at the same position while 14 percent moved to a higher level and 16 percent to a lower level. This lack of mobility may have influenced those who left the labour movement, but there is no direct evidence of that. The graduates were generally satisfied with their college experience, with francophone graduates slightly more satisfied than their anglophone counterparts (even though the CNTU contended that the college was of no use to its members). Rank-and-file members were more satisfied than were elected officers and staff representatives that the objectives for each course were clearly stated and that the objectives suited their personal interests. Graduates who had left the labour movement were more likely than others to credit the college with helping them advance to a better job.[61]

The distance education programme, meanwhile, was very successful in attracting students if not in graduating them. A total of 1,585 participants enrolled in the programme from its inception in 1966 through to March 1971. Of these, 1,116 took the English-language course and 469 took the French-language course, 269 were active students in 1971 (with 28 nearing completion) and 130 had completed the programme by the same year. While some enrolled in the distance education programme in order to prepare for the residential session, as was its original purpose, many took it as a stand-alone programme because they were unable to go to Montreal for eight weeks. But the low completion rates (50 percent to 60 percent is more typical in distance education) suggest that participants were not getting adequate support or that their commitment to the programme was limited. While students did submit assignments and receive written feedback from instructors, there was no means for them to speak to or otherwise contact a tutor or other students in the programme. And those students who did go on to the residential programme may have abandoned the distance education course without completing it since it was not a prerequisite for Montreal. Furthermore, students had as long as they wanted to complete the course, which no doubt meant that, for some, their studies were quietly abandoned along the way. Nonetheless, simply because adult students do not complete course requirements does not mean they do not benefit from the course materials, and undoubtedly all of the students derived some benefit from whatever limited engagement they had with them. Joe Morris, CLC president, maintained that "one of the best things we ever did was set up the correspondence course program" because it enabled rank-and-file activists, who criticize the leadership and keep alive the movement's democratic principles, to have access to advanced education.[62]

The students in both the residential and distance education programmes were taught by instructors drawn from the faculty of McGill University, the University of Montreal, and some other institutions. The university-based instructors, who taught the purely academic courses, were joined by guest lecturers from the labour movement and other organizations who handled the trade unionism classes. Classroom instruction in the residential programme took place each morning, with one day a week devoted to trade unionism. Afternoons and evenings were reserved for reading and studying, with the occasional evening guest lecture to break the routine. The classes were taught at a first-year university level and the entire session was equivalent to about half a year of post-secondary work. The programme—with an 80-hour work week and a 40-book reading list—was demanding for trade unionists who had been away from formal schooling for many years. This was compounded by the fact that, especially in the early years, instructors used the traditional university lecture format as their primary pedagogical approach. While some instructors, such as Fernand Martin, were lively and engaging enough to maintain the interest of students, others droned on in a style destined to make any topic uninteresting. Even the trade unionism class, which often featured speeches by labour leaders, did not normally use adult education principles. Moreover, many instructors apparently had a limited ability to translate obscure social science jargon into plain language that could be understood by someone other than a fellow sociologist or economist. During the late 1960s, some steps were taken to limit the number of talking heads and increase the amount of discussion, including using role-playing games in the economics class. In addition, a "labour counsellor" system was introduced whereby students were assigned to one of four or five CLC staff who were available to help students with study and essay-writing problems and to organize group discussions.[63]

The residential courses used traditional, liberal social science textbooks (claiming objectivity, but containing a pro-employer perspective), such as Paul Samuelson's *Economics: An Introductory Analysis*. Kari Levitt, who taught for only one year at the college and later wrote the influential *Silent Surrender* in which she analyzes and criticizes the role of multinational corporations in the Canadian economy, objected to Samuelson's "free-enterprise bias" and vowed never to use his book again in her courses.[64] Distance education students, meanwhile, received three books in their course package: *Economics for Canadians* by Helen Buckley, *Politics and Government* by Alfred de Grazia and *Sociological Perspective* by Ely Chinoy. These authors viewed North American society (two of the texts were authored by Americans) as consisting of a variety of interest groups—including labour and capital—that were more or less equal in status; this, of course, was at odds with the experience of those workers who took Labour College courses. To study Chinoy, participants were provided with a two-page introduction followed by about thirteen true-or-false or multiple-choice questions per chapter. They were told to try to think through the implications of what Chinoy was saying and were informed that the "assignments are designed in such a way as to reinforce the approach to concepts as tools to be used" and that "we are not trying to get you to regurgitate the text, but rather to apply the material to areas in your own experience."[65]

As early as 1966, school leaders were wondering if the college should be broader and larger than an eight-week social science programme. While he was academic principal, Fernand Martin produced two documents for the Board of Governors that mapped out a more extensive system of advanced Canadian labour education. He argued, first, that a shorter three-week residential programme should be developed, primarily for reasons of cost and accessibility. The shorter session would be limited to a brief introduction to the content of the various disciplines without providing enough time to teach participants how to think critically about society, but it would expose more trade unionists to university-level material. Furthermore, to make the college programme more accessible across the country, he suggested that the labour movement should encourage Canadian universities to establish programmes duplicating the eight-week residential programme. A second academic level should be added to the college curriculum, he continued, for students who had completed the eight-week residential programme or one of the university-based duplicate programmes. This would be an advanced course teaching the application of social science to labour problems and would be held in residence as part of the LCC and possibly at other locations across the country. In addition, an internship programme should be instituted in which an upper-level undergraduate student at one of the two sponsoring universities would work part-time at the college or a young labour educator could work part-time at the college and study at a university part-time.

Finally, Martin proposed that the college revisit its original dream of a longer-term programme. The eight-week programme, he reminded the college governors, was originally intended as an intermediate step to a programme of one or two years in the tradition of Ruskin College in the United Kingdom or the Institut Superieur de Travail in France. The LCC could work with universities to establish one- or two-year programmes of semi-professional training for research assistants and other staff positions. Students would register as partial students in the universities, follow a curriculum established by the college, receive guidance from the college and eventually obtain a certificate from the college. There is no evidence that any of Martin's suggestions were considered seriously by the Board of Governors; they were discussed at one of their meetings, but were probably forgotten after he left the college in 1969.[66]

Conclusion

By the 1960s, the transition in Canadian labour education from a movement interested in developing critical skills among trade unionists to a system providing training for prescribed roles in the post-war industrial relations regime was complete. And with the New Party process that began in 1958 and culminated in the formation of the New Democratic Party in 1961, this emphasis on orderly collective bargaining at the workplace was complemented by labour's formal endorsement of the party and a corresponding political activism that focused exclusively on seeing it elected. The prevailing ideology that guided this activity saw organized workers as legitimate partners with employers in the workplace and considered the labour movement to be one of a number of interest groups in society. While communist-led unions continued to educate their members about the conflict between workers and capitalists, they were very much a marginal presence in the Canadian labour movement during these deepest years of the Cold War.

The mainstream Canadian labour movement consolidated an educational system between 1956 and 1972, the first purpose of which was training the fewer than 5 percent of organized workers who became active in their unions as stewards, committee persons and local officers. This was an ongoing process, as the new members who entered these positions each year required training. Some efforts were made to provide educational opportunities to the general membership—through Steelworkers Local 1005's and the VDLC's evening courses, for example—but the main focus was on training those people who would represent their fellow members in the collective bargaining system. After the 1956 merger, educators were able to concentrate on expanding the number of institutes and schools, adding new courses in emerging areas, such as automation or public-sector workers, and attending to the persistent problems of staff and instructor training. Tools courses concentrated on the technical—and in some cases, the psychological—aspects of representation, bargaining and local leadership, while issues courses placed labour in its broader social context by, for example, stressing how international trade or fair employment practices benefited Canadian workers. Meanwhile, political education courses taught trade unionists why it was in their interest to support the NDP and trained activists to work on party election campaigns. And the intermittent instructor training courses that were offered from the late 1950s onward stressed the importance of using a variety of adult education principles, but Verner and Dickinson concluded in the early 1970s that the dominant educational style continued to be lecture and question and answer.

The Labour College of Canada represented a further consolidation of this system as union educators identified a need for more sustained leadership training than was possible in the weekend and week-long schools. While acknowledging past tensions with post-secondary institutions, they turned to universities as potential collaborators in this venture in the wake of the 1956 conference. These educators felt that labour leaders had to have university-level instruction in order to possess the requisite skills to meet university-trained employer representatives across bargaining tables. Hence they accepted without question the authoritarian pedagogical style that university-based instructors used in the classroom. Furthermore, since they viewed labour as being merely one of many legitimate social groups in a pluralistic society and a capitalist economy, they accepted the mainstream social science that was taught at the college.

The local committees that were spawned by the 1956 conference renewed the tradition of labour-university cooperation that had been a feature of the 1930s and 1940s. With the WEA absent as a mediator in the 1950s and 1960s, however, both university-based and union educators viewed the relationship in professional-service terms. While the Catholic mission to purge the labour movement of communist voices shifted from StFX to Sudbury in the late 1950s, this was essentially attending to some unfinished business from an earlier, more "ideological" period. Universities continued to be minor players, however, in a field in which labour had developed its own significant capacity.

By the early 1970s the Canadian labour movement had a mature education system that did a reasonably adequate job of training leaders and activists to take their place in an industrial relations system and a capitalist economy that most labour leaders accepted. As Verner and Dickinson concluded, there was some room for rationalization and reform of this system. While labour educators paid little heed to these conclusions, new challenges later in the 1970s would force them to begin to change the way they had done things for the previous thirty or so years.

Notes

1. Craig Heron, *The Canadian Labour Movement: A Short History*, 2d ed. (Toronto: James Lorimer and Company, 1996), 85-103.

2. Gordon Selman, "Roby Kidd and the Canadian Association for Adult Education, 1951-1961," and "Alan Thomas and the Canadian Association for Adult Education, 1971-1970," in *Adult Education in Canada: Historical Essays* (Toronto: Thompson Educational Publishing, 1995), 151-262.

3. Max Swerdlow, *Brother Max: Labour Organizer and Educator* (St. John's, Nfld.: Canadian Committee on Labour History, 1990), 66-67; Interview with Alan Thomas, 14 February 1997; "CLC education directory," *Canadian Labour* (January 1969): 35; "CLC staff changes education dept," *Canadian Labour* (September 1970): 37; NAC, *Larry Wagg Papers*, MG 31 B 36, "Finding Aid"; Interview with Larry Wagg, 11 April 2000.

4. Annual CLC financial reports reprinted in *Canadian Labour*, normally in the April or May issue; Gary Dickinson and Coolie Verner, *Education within the Canadian Labour Congress* (Vancouver: Adult Education Research Centre, University of British Columbia, 1973), 45-47; Coolie Verner and Gary Dickinson, *Union Education in Canada: Educational Activities of Labour Organizations* (Vancouver: Adult Education Research Centre, University of British Columbia, 1974), 36-38.

5. "Political Education," *Canadian Labour* (June 1957): 63-65; Howard Conquergood, "The CLC Political Education Programme," *Canadian Labour* (August 1957): 32-33, 38; "Political Education," *Canadian Labour* (April 1958): 90-91; "Ontario Farmer Labour Conference," *Canadian Labour* (July-August 1961): 31-33; "Political Education," *Canadian Labour* (April 1960): 88-91; "Political Education," *Canadian Labour* (May 1962): 37; "Political Education," *Canadian Labour* (May 1964): 41-42; "Political Education," *Canadian Labour* (May 1966): 56-57; "Political Education," *Canadian Labour* (May 1968): 66-67; "Political Education," *Canadian Labour* (June 1970): 51; Stephen Foster Purdy, *Organized Labour and the New Democratic Party in the 1960's*, Bachelor of Arts Research Essay, Carleton University, 1972.

6. "Education," *Canadian Labour* (April 1960): 66-67; "Education," *Canadian Labour* (May 1962): 29; "Education," *Canadian Labour* (May 1968): 62-63; "Education," *Canadian Labour* (June 1970): 49; Dickinson and Verner, *Education within the Canadian Labour Congress*, 34-36.

7. "A First in Labour Education," *Canadian Labour* (December, 1960): 45; "Labour Education Weeks," *Canadian Labour* (April 1964): 31-33; "Labour Education Week," *Canadian Labour* (May 1967): 6-7.

8. UBC Library, Special Collections, *Vancouver and District Labour Council (VDLC) Records*, Box 2, Folder 33, "Education Committee Correspondence, minutes, etc., 1958-1967," Minutes of Education Committee meetings, 8 March 1960, 1 December 1960, 25 September 1962 and 23 March 1964, and Box 2, Folder 34, "Education Committee. 1964-1965," Minutes of Education Committee meeting, 2 March 1965.

9. "Seventh Annual Labour Institute on Race Relations," *Canadian Labour* (May 1957): 53; NAC, *Jewish Labour Committee of Canada Papers*, MG 28 V75 , "Finding Aid"; NAC, *Kalem Kaplansky Papers*, MG 30 A53, "Finding Aid"; "Human Rights Education Conference," *Canadian Labour* (January 1957): 28; *A Day in the Night of Jonathan Mole* (Montreal: National Film Board of Canada, 1959). Go to http://unionlearning.athabascau.ca to see a video clip from *A Day in the Night of Jonathan Mole.*

10. NAC, *International Association of Machinists and Aerospace Workers (IAM) Papers*, MG 28 I 191, Volume 84, File "Education—Correspondence, General, 1958," Henry Weisbach, Ontario Regional Director of Education, CLC, "Report of the Ontario Canadian Labour Congress Summer School Program 1958"; NAC, *Lincoln Bishop Papers*, MG 31 B 18, Volume 2, File 16, "Canadian Labour Congress, Report, 1966 Ontario Summer School"; "360 at Ontario Summer School," *Canadian Labour* (September 1964): 57; "Family Week at CLC Summer School," *Canadian Labour* (September 1965): 39; "CLC Education Program," *Canadian Labour* (July-August 1971): 4-5, 16.

11. Dickinson and Verner, *Education within the Canadian Labour Congress*, 36-44.

12. Hepworth, "Where is Labour Education Heading," *Food for Thought* (March 1957): 272; NAC, *CLC Papers*, MG 28 I 103, Volume 268, File 2, "Second Annual CLC Staff Seminar, British Columbia, Pinewoods Lodge, Manning Park, BC, 13-17 January 1958"; "CLC 1961 Ontario Staff Conference, Niagara Falls," *Canadian Labour* (April 1961): 14-15.

13. UBC Library, Special Collections, *CLC Education Office (British Columbia) Records*, Box 1, Folder 1, "Circular Letters from A.L. Hepworth—1956-1972," Minutes of the National Education Advisory Committee, 3 November 1961 and Minutes of the National Education Advisory Committee, 4 April 1967; NAC, *CLC Papers*, MG 28 I 103, Accession 86/0112, Volume 21, File "Survey of CLC Education Program, 1971-1972—File 1," Alan Thomas, Director, CAAE, to Joe Morris, Vice-president, CLC, 25 March 1967; NAC, *Lincoln Bishop Papers*, MG 31 B 18, Volume 3, File 1, Prairie Region Education Department, Canadian Labour Congress, "Manual for Course Leaders on Basic Trade Union Subjects," 1970, and Volume 5, File 6, Report of National Education Advisory Committee, CLC, May 1970.

14. NAC, *Amalgamated Clothing and Textile Workers Union (ACTWU) Papers*, MG 28 I 219, File 16, "Education. John Whitehouse Correspondence. 1963-1967," Roy Little, Secretary, Canadian Labour Film Committee to John Whitehouse, 21 January 1966; NAC, *CLC Papers*, MG 28 I 103, Volume 477, File 10, "International Film Festival"; *The Inheritance* (Montreal: National Film Board, 1964); *Do Not Fold, Staple, Spindle or Mutilate* (Montreal: National Film Board of Canada, 1967); *The Labour College* (Montreal: National Film Board of Canada, 1966); *Steeltown* (Montreal: National Film Board of Canada, 1966). Go to http://unionlearning.athabascau.ca to see video clips from *Do Not Fold, Staple, Spindle or Mutilate* and *The Labour College.*

15. NAC, *ACTWU Papers*, MG 28 I 219, File 16, "Education. John Whitehouse Correspondence. 1963-1967," A.L. Hepworth, chairman, CAAE Committee on Labour and Adult Education, to members of the Committee on Labour and Adult Education, CAAE, 3 February 1965; NAC, *CLC Papers*, MG 28 I 103, Accession 86/0112, Volume 21, File "Survey of CLC Education Program, 1971-1972—File 1," Alan Thomas, Director, CAAE, to Joe Morris, Vice-president, CLC, 25 May 1967, and Andy Andras to Joe Morris, 28 December 1967.

16. UBC Library, Special Collections, *CLC Education Office (British Columbia) Records*, Box 1, Folder 1, "Minutes of the National Education Advisory Committee," 4 April 1967, 17 December 1968, and Box 1, Folder 2, "Correspondence—A.L. Hepworth, 1969-1972," Bert Hepworth to Joe Morris, 11 September 1969; UBC Library, Special Collections, *Coolie Verner Records*, Box 18, Folder 7, A.L. Hepworth to Coolie Verner, 2 December 1969, and memorandum from A.L. Hepworth, Secretary, NEAC, to

Fernand Martin, Alan Thomas, George Topshee and Coolie Verner, 13 March 1970; NAC, *CLC Papers*, MG 28 I 103, Volume 392, File U7, Bert Hepworth to Joe Morris, 26 August 1970, re. survey and evaluation of Congress education programs.

17. NAC, *CLC Papers*, MG 28 I 103, Accession 86/0112, Volume 21, File "Survey of Union Education in Canada—Other than CLC," Bert Hepworth to Joe Morris, 29 December 1970, and Agreement between the federal Department of Labour and AERC, UBC, September 1971, and Volume 21, File "Survey of CLC Education Program, 1971-1972—File 3," Gary Dickinson to Fred Lennarson, Economics and Research Branch, Federal Department of Labour, 15 November 1973.

18. Dickinson and Verner, *Education within the Canadian Labour Congress*; Gary Dickinson, James Thornton, and Nicholas Rubige, *Evaluation of Union Instructor Training* (Vancouver: Adult Education and Research Centre, University of British Columbia, 1973); Gary Dickinson, *Education in Unaffiliated Unions* (Vancouver: Adult Education and Research Centre, University of British Columbia, 1973); Gary Dickinson and Marvin Lamoureux, *Labour College of Canada: The First Decade* (Vancouver: Adult Education and Research Centre, University of British Columbia, 1973); Verner and Dickinson, *Union Education in Canada: a Report of the Educational Activities of Labour Organizations*; Kenneth Kerr, Jacynthe Deault, and Pierre Amyot, *Enquete Sur L'Education Syndicale au Quebec* (Montreal: Service d'Education Permanente, University of Montreal, 1973); Maria Brown, *Adult Education Among Members of a North Vancouver Labour Union*, M.A. Thesis, University of British Columbia, 1972; Claire Maynard, *The Development of Education in the Canadian Labour Congress*, M.A. Thesis, University of British Columbia, 1972; Jean McAllister, "Education Programs Sponsored by National and International Unions in Canada," unpublished research report for the Adult Education and Research Centre, University of British Columbia, 1973; and Khatun H. Remtulla, "Canadian Labour Congress Education Program Evaluation," unpublished research report for the Adult Education and Research Centre, University of British Columbia, 1973.

19. Verner and Dickinson, *Union Education in Canada*, 203.

20. NAC, *CLC Papers*, MG I 103, Volume 477, File 11, Minutes of a meeting of the National Education Advisory Committee, 25-26 July 1973, and Volume 392, File U7, William Dodge, Secretary-Treasurer, CLC, to Joe Morris, President, CLC, 3 December 1973.

21. Verner and Dickinson, *Union Education in Canada*, 60-65.

22. NAC, *Canadian Union of Public Employees (CUPE) Papers*, MG 28 I 234, Volume 32, File 1, "Circulars—Education Department, 1963-1970," 29 October 1963 circular from Jim Dowell, 21 April 1966 letter to CUPE field representatives from Jim Dowell, and 23 January 1967 circular from Jim Dowell; Interview with James Dowell, 27 April 2000.

23. NAC, *CUPE Papers*, MG 28 I 234, Volume 32, File 1, "Circulars—Education Department, 1963-1970," 8 May 1964 circular from Jim Dowell; NAC, *Lincoln Bishop Papers*, MG 31 B 18, Volume 4, File 19, Union Training Program for Shop Stewards and Committeemen: A Programmed Instruction Course, by Personnel Systems, division of NML, Montreal, 1965, and Volume 3, File 6, Lee Daws, "What is Programmed Instruction?", *Labor Education Viewpoints* (fall 1968), and James Dowell, "Programmed Instruction," no date; NAC, *ACTWU Papers*, MG 28 I 219, File 16, "Education. John Whitehouse Correspondence, 1963—1967," John Whitehouse to Hank Skinner, Regional Representative, IWA, 26 November 1965; NAC, *CLC Papers*, MG 28 I 103, Volume 477, File 8, Larry Wagg, Director, Education Department, to NEAC, 6 April 1976, and Volume 479, File 14, various letters and documents on programmed instruction from 1976, including Lee Daws, "Problem Solving for Local Union Officers." The Canadian Brotherhood of Railway Employees and Other Transport Workers (CBRE) changed their name to the Canadian Brotherhood of Railway, Transport and General Workers (CBRT) in 1958.

24. NAC, *Lincoln Bishop Papers*, MG 31 B18, Volume 3, File 5, CUPE, "Home Study Course, Democratic Government in Canada"; NAC, *CUPE Papers*, MG 28 I 234, Volume 32, File 1, "Circulars—Education Department, 1963-1970," 27 April 1967 circular from James Dowell.

25. UBC Library, Special Collections, *Coolie Verner Records*, Box 18, File 7, "Canadian Labour Congress Survey, 1969—1974," notes from a meeting about the CLC survey; NAC, *CUPE Papers*, MG 28 I 234, Volume 24, File 4, "Education Department, May 1970—September 1975," Leslie Hewson, Regional Vice-President, Alberta Division to Grace Hartman, National Secretary-Treasurer, 17 January 1972, and Volume 24, File 5, "Education Department Meetings, August 1970—November 1974," Summary of Departmental Meeting with J. Dowell, 25 April 1972.

26. NAC, *IAM Papers*, MG 28 I 191, Volume 87, File "Seminars—Canadian IAM, 1949, 1952, 1961," various documents.

27. NAC, *IAM Papers*, MG 28 I 191, Volume 87, File "Territorial Education Representatives—Correspondence 1956-62," various documents, Volume 84, File "Education—Correspondence, General, 1947, 1956," various documents, Volume 84, File "Education—Correspondence, General, 1957," IAM Education Program by General Vice-President Schollie, no date, and Volume 84, File "Education—Correspondence, General, May-Dec., 1962," Report to the CLC dated October 1962 on survey of labour education activities in IAM.

28. UBC Library, Special Collections, *CLC Education Office (British Columbia) Records*, Box 1, Folder 1, Harry Jacks, "Planning the Education Program," Prepared for the CLC Conference for Instructors, Toronto, Ontario, March 28-20, 1972; "New Post for Hepworth," *Canadian Labour* (October 1962): 28.

29. Dickinson and Verner, *Education within the Canadian Labour Congress*, 91-95; James Brechin, "Education in Canada's Largest Local," *Information* (July 1962): 32-34.

30. NAC, *Allen Schroeder Papers*, MG 31 B 43, Schroeder autobiography; Wayne State University (WSU), Reuther Library, *United Autoworkers (UAW) Region 7, Canadian Regional Office Papers*, Box 19, "2. Summer School Delegates' Basic Fact Book, 1966."

31. WSU, Reuther Library, *UAW Region 7, Canadian Regional Office Papers*, Box 56, "4. Allen Schroeder, Education Director, 1967," various memoranda from and to Allen Schroeder, January to April 1967; NAC, *International Union, United Automobile , Aerospace and Agriculture Implement Workers of America (UAW) Papers*, MG 28 I 119, Volume 282, File 23, "Education Department—General Correspondence, Part 2 of 3. 1973-1979," Gordon Wilson to Dale Parkins, International Representative, Education Department, re. Canadian region LUDLs, 18 December 1974.

32. WSU, Reuther Library, *UAW Region 7, Canadian Regional Office Papers*, Box 51, "3. George Burt, Director, 1948," various correspondence, February to June 1948, re. purchase of Kingsville property, Box 19, "1. Summer School Site, 1956-57," Box 19, "5. Education and Summer School, 1966-67," UAW Canadian Council Executive Board to Emil Mazey, Secretary-Treasurer, UAW, circa July 1966, and Box 56, "1. Allen Schroeder, Education Director, 1964," Allen Schroeder to Members, Camp Management Committee, UAW Education Centre, 6 May 1964; NAC, *Lincoln Bishop Papers*, MG 31 B 18, Volume 12, File 10, Brochure, "One Week in the Life of the Canadian UAW Education Centre"; NAC, *UAW Papers*, MG 28 I 119, Volume 282, File 15, "Correspondence: Gordon F. Wilson, Director of Education for Canada—International Metalworkers' Federation," Gordon Wilson, Education Report, Spring 1977.

33. WSU, Reuther Library, *UAW Region 7, Canadian Regional Office Papers*, Box 56, "1. Allen Schroeder, Education Director, 1964," Summary, Canadian Region, UAW Women's Conference at Port Elgin, Ontario, 12 and 13 September 1964, and Box 19, "7. Education and Summer School Program, 1969," Fifth Annual UAW Women Workers

Conference, 7-8 September 1968, Port Elgin, Ontario; Pamela Sugiman, *Labour's Dilemma: The Gender Politics of Auto Workers in Canada, 1937-1979* (Toronto: University of Toronto Press, 1994), 156-158.

34. NAC, *Alan Schroeder Papers*, MG 31 B 43, "Autobiography of Alan Schroeder"; Sam Gindin, *The Canadian Autoworkers: The Birth and Transformation of a Union* (Toronto: James Lorimer and Company, 1995), 161.

35. Max Swerdlow, "Education and the Canadian Labour Congress," *Canadian Labour* (August 1957): 25-28; A.L. Hepworth, "Where is Labour Education Heading?", 269-273; Max Swerdlow, "The Education Programme of the Congress," *Canadian Labour* (November 1960): 6-10; J.H. Craigs, "Labour's Role in Adult Education," *Canadian Labour* (March 1965): 23; Max Swerdlow, "Liberal Education in Canadian Labour Education," in Freda H. Goldman, ed., *Reorientation in Labor Education: A Symposium on Liberal Education for Labor in the University* (Chicago: Center for the Study of Liberal Education for Adults, 1962).

36. Dickinson and Verner, *Education within the Canadian Labour Congress*, 57-58; Max Swerdlow, "Education and the Canadian Labour Congress," *Canadian Labour* (August 1957): 25-26.

37. "Seventh SFL Summer School," *Canadian Labour* (July-August 1964): 35; "100 attend two Alberta Federation winter schools," *Canadian Labour* (April 1967): 45; NAC, *Lincoln Bishop Papers*, MG 31 B 18, Volume 2, File 16, Canadian Labour Congress, Ontario Region, List of Courses for Week-end Institutes, 20 January 1966.

38. "Women's Role in the Trade Union Movement," *Canadian Labour* (January 1959): 50; NAC, *Lincoln Bishop Papers*, MG 31 B 18, Volume 2, File 16, Canadian Labour Congress, Ontario Region, List of Courses for Week-end Institutes, 20 January 1966; "Women's school," *Canadian Labour* (May 1971): 12.

39. NAC, *Lincoln Bishop Papers*, MG 31 B 18, Volume 4, File 15, Canadian Labour Congress— Lakehead Labour Institute Stewards' Training (Basic Course), 24-25 November 1956; UBC Library, Special Collections, *International Longshoremen's and Warehousemen's Union (ILWU) Records*, Box 10, Folder 8, "ILWU Workshops. 1950-1970," ILWU Canadian Area Shop Steward Training Course, 1964; UBC Library, Special Collections, *International Union of Mine, Mill and Smelter Workers (Canada) (Mine-Mill) Records*, Box 8, Folder 7, "National Office. Shop Stewards," Discussion guide, and "National Office. Education Department," Questions and Answers.

40. NAC, *Lincoln Bishop Papers*, MG 31 B 18, Volume 5, File 6, Psychology for Union Leaders, 30 July 1962, and Volume 4, File 4, United Autoworkers, Applying Psychology to Local Union Leadership, April 1966.

41. NAC, *Lincoln Bishop Papers*, MG 31 B18, Volume 3, File 5, CUPE, "Home Study Course, Democratic Government in Canada"; NAC, *CUPE Papers*, MG 28 I 234, Volume 32, File 1, "Circulars—Education Department, 1963-1970," 27 April 1967 circular from James Dowell, and Volume 24, File 5, "Education Department Meetings, August 1970—November 1974," Summary of Departmental Meeting with J. Dowell, 15 December 1972.

42. NAC, *IAM Papers*, MG 28 I 191, Volume 84, File "Education—Correspondence, General, 1958": Kalem Kaplansky, Director, Department of International Affairs, CLC, "Outline for a Course on International Affairs," no date (but late 1950s or early 1960s); "The World Labour Movement," no date (but 1967-68); "International Affairs Class Discussion Sheet," CLC Summer School, Port Elgin, Ontario, 1975; UBC Library, Special Collections, *ILWU Papers*, Box 10, Folder 9, "Area Education Course. 1950-1963."; Paul Buhle, *Taking Care of Business: Samuel Gompers, George Meany, Lane Kirkland and the Tragedy of American Labor* (New York: Monthly Review Press, 1999), 147-158.

43. NAC, *Lincoln Bishop Papers*, MG 31 B 18, Volume 5, File 6, Selection, Induction, and Training of New Instructors, St. Agathe Educational Seminar, November 30-December 3, 1961, CLC; UBC Library, Special Collections, *CLC Education Office (British Columbia) Records*, Box 1, Folder 1, Conference of Instructors Involved in the CLC Education Program, 28-30 March 1972, and Harry Jacks, "Planning the Education Program."

44. Dickinson and Verner, *Education within the Canadian Labour Congress*, 57-62; UBC Library, Special Collections, *ILWU Records*, Box 10, Folder 9, "Area Education Course. 1950-1963," Dave Thompson, Educational Director, ILWU Local 142, Hawaii, to Leo Labinsky, President, Canadian Area ILWU, 31 May 1963.

45. UBC Library, Special Collections, *CLC Education Office (British Columbia) Records*, Box 2, Folder 28, Gary Dickinson, James E. Thornton, and Nicholas Rubige, "Evaluation of Union Instructor Training II. Ontario Region Program," Adult Education Research Centre, University of British Columbia, June 1973, 12, 17, and Gary Dickinson, James E. Thornton, Nicholas A. Rubige, and Michael Mann, "Evaluation of Union Instructor Training III. Pacific Region Program," Adult Education Research Centre, University of British Columbia, July 1973.

46. *Labour-University Cooperation on Education: A report on the National Conference on Labour Education sponsored by the Canadian Labour Congress and the Canadian Association for Adult Education held in Ottawa December 15th to 17th, 1956* (Ottawa: Canadian Labour Congress, 1956).

47. NAC, *CLC Papers*, MG 28 I 103, Volume 477, File "Labour Education, 1963-1977," "Report on a Survey of Labour Education in Canadian Universities," and Volume 477, File "Labour Education, Universities and Colleges Programs, Part 3," Max Swerdlow, "Labour-University Interaction," The Faculty-Extension Seminar, 1963, The University of Western Ontario; StFX University Archives, *Extension Department Records*, RG 30-3/18, "Survey of Labour Education Programs in Canadian Universities."

48. UBC Library, Special Collections, *VDLC Records*, Box 2, Folder 17, "Regional Committee on University Education—Labour Education, 1957-1958"; Dalhousie University Archives, *Guy Henson Papers*, MS 2 373, File E67.

49. ASR Tweedie, "Manitoba's University-Labour Course," *Information* (November 1966): 34-35; Gerald Friesen, "H.C. Pentland and Continuing Education at the University of Manitoba: Teaching Labour History to Trade Unionists," *Labour/Le Travail* 31 (spring 1993): 305-306; AO, *Mike Solski Collection*, MU 8276, File 4 "Laurentian University Extension Dept. Workers Educational Association. Sudbury Labour Council 1960-66," J.O. Robertson, Representative, Education and Welfare, USWA, Toronto, to A.F. Mckee, Assistant Director, Extension, Laurentian University, 3 February 1964; NAC, *CLC Papers*, MG 28 I 103, vol. 477, File 2, "Lakehead University—Labor Three-Year Certificate Course" 1969.

50. StFX University Archives, *Extension Department Records*, RG 30-3, various Extension Department annual reports, especially 1960, 1961, 1962, 1966, 1967, and 1968.

51. Hogan, Brian F., "Hard Rock and Hard Decisions: Catholics, Communists and the IUMMSW—Sudbury Confrontation," paper presented at the Canadian Historical Association conference, 1985; AO, *Mike Solski Collection*, MU 8276, File 3, "Laurentian University Extension Dept. Workers Educational Association Canadian Labour Congress 50/67," James Kidd to A.J. Boudreau, 6 January 1959, Jim Kidd to Gower Markle, 14 January 1959, A.J. Boudreau to Gower Markle, 18 February 1959, A.J. Boudreau to Claude Jodoin, 5 June 1959, File 5, "Laurentian University Extension Dept. Workers Educational Association. 1960-63," Bylaws of the Northern Workers' Adult Education Association, incorporated in 1959, and Northern Workers' Adult Education Association, no date (but early 1960), Tentative Program. Northern Workers' Adult Education Association, no date, and File 6, "Laurentian University Extension Dept. Workers Educational Association. 1960-63."

52. UBC Library, Special Collections, *Mine-Mill Records*, Box 8, Folder 7, "Leadership Course for Miners, From January 13th to May 10th, Lecturer: Professor A.J. Boudreau"; AO, *Mike Solski Collection*, MU 8276, File 5, "Laurentian University Extension Dept. Workers Educational Association. 1960-63," "Tentative Program. Northern Workers' Adult Education Association," no date, and File 7, "Laurentian University Extension Dept. Workers Educational Association. Discussion Groups 1960-61," "Study Clubs. January 1960."

53. Swerdlow, *Brother Max*, 90-100; NAC, *Labour College of Canada Papers*, MG 28 I 287, Volume 6, "Report of preliminary discussions of a committee of representatives of the Canadian Labour Congress, the University of Montreal and McGill University Submitted as a basis for further discussion," 30 September 1960.

54. NAC, *IAM Papers*, MG 28 I 191, Volume 86, File 5, clipping, "Open Labor College First in North America," *Globe and Mail*, 3 June 1963; NAC, *Labour College of Canada Papers*, MG 28 I 287, Volume 4, Robert Sauve, General Secretary, CSN, to Max Swerdlow and Fernand Martin, Labour College of Canada, 24 May 1966; NAC, *IAM Papers*, Volume 86, File 4, Labour College of Canada, "Ontario Campaign Committee," minutes, 13 December 1962, and Volume 86, File 4, Report of the first session of the Labour College of Canada, 3-19 July 1963.

55. NAC, *IAM Papers*, MG 28 I 191, Volume 86, File 4, Report of the first session of the Labour College of Canada, 3-19 July 1963.

56. Swerdlow, *Brother Max*, 104; NAC, *IAM Papers*, MG 28 I 191, Volume 86, File 5, Labour College of Canada Press Release, 2 May 1971; NAC, *CLC Papers*, MG 28 I 103, Volume 392, File U3, part I, CLC press release, 24 January 1972; UBC Library, Special Collections, *CLC Education Office (British Columbia) Records*, Box 1, Folder 3, "Correspondence—A.L. Hepworth, December 1968-December 1972," Bert Hepworth to Regional Educational Representatives, 2 December 1969; "Names in the News," *Canadian Labour* (September 1970): 13; NAC, *CLC Papers*, MG 28 I 103, Volume 392, File U2, part II, Labour College of Canada press release, 1 February 1971 and A.L. Hepworth to Bill Dodge, Secretary-Treasurer, CLC, 16 November 1970; NAC, *Labour College of Canada Papers*, MG 28 I 287, Volume 4, The Report of the Labour College of Canada, January 1-June 30, 1975.

57. NAC, *IAM Papers*, MG 28 I 191, Volume 86, File 5, Report of the second term of the Labour College of Canada, 8 May to 31 July 1964; NAC, *Labour College of Canada Papers*, MG 28 I 287, Volume 7, Labour College of Canada, Proposed Budget—1969; UBC Library, Special Collections, *CLC Education Office (British Columbia) Records*, Box 1, Folder 11, Report to the Ninth General Meeting of the Members of the Board of Governors, Labour College of Canada, 30 March 1971.

58. NAC, *IAM Papers*, MG 28 I 191, Volume 86, File 5, Labour College of Canada, "Principal's Report—1963" and Max Swerdlow, Circular letter, re. 1965 Labour College of Canada session, 1 October 1965; NAC, *Lincoln Bishop Papers*, MG 31 B 18, Volume 4, File 19, Correspondence Course in the Social Sciences.

59. NAC, *Labour College of Canada Papers*, MG 28 I 287, Volume 7, Notes of a meeting to discuss cooperation between the Labour College of Canada and the Workers' Educational Association in holding weekend seminars for labour college graduates; NAC, *Lincoln Bishop Papers*, MG 31 B 18, Volume 4, File 9, Post-graduate Labour College Seminar, 6-7 April 1968, McMaster University, Hamilton.

60. Coolie Verner and Gary Dickinson, *Union Education in Canada: Educational Activities of Labour Organizations* (Ottawa: Labour Canada, 1974), 168; "Canada Needs the Labour College," *Canadian Labour* (May 1970): 11; NAC, *Lincoln Bishop Papers*, MG 31 B 18, Volume 4, File 10, Sidney H. Ingerman and A.L. Hepworth, "The Labour College of Canada," reprint from *Civil Service Review* (PSAC) (March 1972).

61. Verner and Dickinson, *Union Education in Canada*, part 5; NAC, *CLC Papers*, MG 28 I 103, Accession 84/0293, Volume 71, File "Labour College of Canada—Current Correspondence, October 1975-December 1977," Circular letter from J. Morris, Chair, Labour College of Canada Board of Governors, 28 September 1977; NAC, *Labour College of Canada Papers*, MG 28 I 287, Volume 4, Jean Bezusky, Assistant Registrar, "Address to Women's Rights Conference, 11 May 1974, Vancouver, B.C."

62. UBC Library, Special Collections, *CLC Education Office (British Columbia) Records*, Box 1, Folder 11, Report to the Ninth General Meeting of the Members of the Board of Governors, Labour College of Canada, 30 March 1971; NAC, *Lincoln Bishop Papers*, MG 31 B 18, Volume 4, File 10, Sidney H. Ingerman and A.L. Hepworth, "The Labour College of Canada," reprint from *Civil Service Review* (PSAC) (March 1972); NAC, *Labour College of Canada Papers*, MG 28 I 287, Volume 6, Wilf McDonald, Edmonton, to A.L. Hepworth, Registrar, Labour College of Canada, 1 January 1973; NAC, *CLC Papers*, MG 28, I 103, Accession 84/0293, Volume 71, File "Labour College of Canada—Current Correspondence, October 1975-December 1977," Report of the Registrar and Secretary Treasurer to Meeting of the Board of Governors, 2 December 1976, by Larry Wagg; NAC, *Lincoln Bishop Papers*, MG 31 B 18, Volume 4, File 9, "Minutes of the Annual General Meeting of Members and a Meeting of the Board of Governors," Labour College of Canada, 17 April 1969.

63. "Labour College of Canada," *Canadian Labour* (July-August 1971): 2-3, 16; NAC, *Lincoln Bishop Papers*, MG 31 B 18, Volume 4, File "Education and Training, 1968-1969," Labour College of Canada, Evaluation of the 1969 Session; student comments and classroom scenes in *Labour College* (Montreal: National Film Board of Canada, 1966). Go to http://unionlearning.athabascau.ca to see a video clip of college classroom scenes from *Labour College*.

64 NAC, *IAM Papers*, MG 28 I 191, Volume 86, File 4, Report of the first session of the Labour College of Canada, 3-19 (July) 1963, and Volume 86, File 5, Labour College of Canada, "Principals' Report, 1963"; NAC, *Labour College of Canada Papers*, MG 28 I 287, Volume 4, Kari Levitt, McGill University, to Mr. Chapados, undated, summer/fall 1963; Paul Samuelson, *Economics: An Introductory Analysis*, 2d ed. (New York: McGraw-Hill, 1961); Kari Levitt, *Silent Surrender: the Multinational Corporation in Canada* (Toronto: Macmillan of Canada, 1970).

65. Helen Buckley, *Economics for Canadians* (Toronto: Macmillan of Canada, 1960); Alfred de Grazia, *Politics and Government: the Elements of Political Science* (New York: Collier, 1962); Ely Chinoy, *Sociological Perspective* (New York: Random, 1954); NAC, *Lincoln Bishop Papers*, MG 31 B 18, Volume 4, File 19, Correspondence Course in the Social Sciences, and Volume 3, File 14, Labour College of Canada, Sociology Correspondence Course, 1960s.

66. NAC, *Labour College of Canada Papers*, MG 28 I 287, Volume 4, File "Montreal Oiste," Suggestions to modify the academic program, March 1966, 7; UBC Library, Special Collections, *Coolie Verner Records*, Box 18, Folder 7, Fernand Martin, "Some Thoughts on the Future of the Labour College of Canada," Position paper presented to the Board of Governors at their meeting of April 17, 1969, by the Principal; NAC, *Lincoln Bishop Papers*, MG 31 B 18, Volume 4, File 9, "Minutes of the Annual General Meeting of Members and a Meeting of the Board of Governors," Labour College of Canada, 17 April 1969.

CHAPTER 5

New Issues and Old Structures: 1973-1985

The 1970s and 1980s marked a significant shift in the general history of the Canadian labour movement and the beginnings of an important shift in the history of labour education. By the mid-1970s governments and employers had begun to renege on the informal compromise between capital and labour that had ensured the relative prosperity and growth of the 1950s and 1960s. As a result, labour could no longer rely on a relatively stable industrial relations system to deliver increasing wages and benefits, but had to begin to learn new ways of representing their members. In addition, new feminist and other voices inside the labour movement challenged what some viewed as the complacency of the existing leadership and senior staff. The inherited approaches to traditional labour education themes were questioned and modified, while new themes and programmes were introduced. The most significant development during this period for the Canadian Labour Congress (CLC) education programme was a substantial infusion of public money that was part of a federal government strategy to soften the blow of its anti-worker policies. The congress used the money to establish and operate its new Labour Education and Studies Centre (LESC) to deliver advanced union education, to produce print and audio-visual resources and to sustain and enhance the Labour College of Canada's (LCC) offerings.

For labour education outside of unions, meanwhile, the expansion of post-secondary education that took place in the 1960s and early 1970s provided the material foundation for colleges and universities to develop labour studies programmes to teach labour-related material both to regular post-secondary students and to trade unionists. Ironically, this renewed interest in labour-related programming on the part of higher-education institutions occurred at precisely the time that the labour movement was feeling educationally self-sufficient because of its government grant. As a result, and combined with the historical tension that existed between trade unionists and academics, the labour movement made it clear that it would work with colleges and universities on its own terms or not at all.

Context

By the early 1970s, the North American economy was suffering from a combination of unemployment and inflation brought about by the United States' conduct of the Vietnam War, higher oil prices and the decline of American economic influence in the face of competition from Europe, Japan and a number of newly industrializing countries. As prices rose steadily, and with the uncertainties in global markets having a negative effect on corporate profit margins, Canadian governments and employers blamed workers' wage and salary demands for the economy's ills and agreed that the solution to the inflationary scourge lay in curbing these demands.

The federal government led the way by first using traditional government intervention. After a fruitless attempt to persuade employers and workers to curb prices and incomes voluntarily, Pierre Trudeau and his Liberals introduced wage and price controls in 1975. As Trudeau had noted in campaigning against controls during the 1974 federal election, it was impossible to control prices but relatively easy to control wages; hence, this was really a wage control programme with the promise of price controls included to create the illusion of even-handedness.

By the third year of the programme, wage increases had dropped dramatically but prices continued to rise. Trade unionists were justifiably outraged by this attack and showed their displeasure in a one-day general strike in 1976. Trudeau tried to soften the blow by talking about a post-controls environment in which government, business and labour would work together to manage the economy. With business vigorously opposed to any suggestion of workers or governments having a hand in managing their affairs, this idea went nowhere, although it did appeal to some labour leaders. With inflation continuing to plague Canadians in the late 1970s, the federal government moved away from active intervention in the economy to embrace the tight-money policy called monetarism. The Bank of Canada attempted to slow down the economy using high interest rates, causing a recession in the early 1980s that resulted in plant closings, layoffs and an official unemployment rate of 12 percent. This was accompanied by significantly tightened unemployment insurance eligibility criteria that made it difficult for those unable to find work to collect the benefits to which they were entitled. The labour movement responded to the new monetarist policies in 1981 with a demonstration on Parliament Hill that attracted 100,000 people.

Governments at all levels supplemented these economic policies with harsher labour laws. Provincial and federal governments resorted increasingly to back-to-work legislation, unilaterally eliminating the right to collective bargaining for various groups of public-sector workers. In one of the more authoritarian actions of this kind, Jean-Claude Parrot of the Canadian Union of Postal Workers (CUPW) was jailed in 1978 for not ordering his members to return to work after they had been legislated back. Furthermore, between 1982 and 1984 the federal and most provincial governments reintroduced wage controls for their own employees, conveniently bypassing the collective bargaining process. And in an audacious general attack on collective bargaining rights, the British Columbia government in 1983 introduced a range of legislation designed to weaken if not cripple the province's labour movement.

Private-sector employers, who were encouraging governments to get tough on workers, became more aggressive towards their employees. In a change from previous practice, employers started coming to bargaining tables with demands for wage and benefit rollbacks and increased managerial "flexibility" in such things as scheduling, layoff and recall, and hiring. Increasingly they turned to part-time and temporary employment and contracting out as a means of lowering their labour costs and circumventing collective agreement obligations. Employers also regrouped as a class in the 1970s and 1980s to coordinate their efforts to turn back labour's gains of the previous thirty years. Organizations such as the Canadian Federation of Independent Business, the National Citizen's Coalition, and especially the Business Council on National Issues, aided and abetted by right-wing research bodies such as the Fraser Institute and the C.D. Howe Institute, prepared the ideological ground for the rightward shift of successive federal and provincial governments.

The labour movement continued to support the New Democratic Party (NDP) in this harsh climate, although that support was tested as the party gained power in some provinces. Federally, the party remained in third place, although it did hold the balance of power between 1972 and 1974. At the provincial level, meanwhile, the party formed governments in Manitoba (1969), Saskatchewan (1971) and British Columbia (1972), where they addressed part of labour's agenda by introducing new workplace legislation covering occupational health and safety and technological change. Workers learned a new and bitter lesson about social democracy, however, when the Manitoba and British Columbia administrations legislated striking workers back to work during their terms in office, contributing in part to their subsequent electoral defeats.

Just when the NDP was beginning to enjoy some success at the ballot box, the New Left was challenging the assumptions of electoral politics and parliamentary democracy. Fuelled by a youth culture that rejected inherited forms of authority including those practiced by the old-line left parties, participants in a range of social justice campaigns including disarmament, anti-poverty and opposition to the Vietnam War championed extra-parliamentary means of politics including demonstrations and sit-ins. By the 1970s, various forms of Marxism were providing the intellectual guidance for this activity in a range of new socialist organizations that rejected both the social democracy of the NDP and the old-line Marxism of the Communist Party. They accepted, however, that trade unions and organized workers were crucial ingredients in resisting capitalism. Hence, many members took jobs in unionized workplaces and became activists who pushed a militant agenda.

A substantial number of these new activists were women, who were feminists as well as socialists. Modern feminism emerged among New Left women who rejected the secondary status they were accorded in the movement by New Left men. They began to hold separate meetings, or "consciousness-raising groups," to explore their common experiences of sexual oppression in their relationships with men, in their families and in society at large. From this kernel grew a new social movement that demanded such things as reproductive choice, acceptable day care, equal rights at work and generally an end to the sexism that was a feature of twentieth-century Canadian life.

In the 1970s this politics began to permeate the labour movement (which, as a result of public-sector unionism, contained substantially more women than in the past) through the explicit efforts of New Left activists, who were often from non-working-class backgrounds, and by the general influence of the movement on working-class women. Women began demanding that their issues—such as day care—be taken up in bargaining and that space be made available in union structures for women. Through hard work and perseverance, some women made their way into elected positions and had their voices heard. Trade union women began to form their own caucuses and women's committees and, through sisterly solidarity and old-fashioned organizing, changed the face of the labour movement.

Included in the New Left arsenal was an analysis of imperialism, or the domination of one country by another. In the era of the Vietnam War and increasing U.S. domination of the North American economy, this had a special resonance for Canadians. As part of a larger critique of Canada's subordination to U.S. interests, some nationalists began to question the role and presence of "international" unions in Canada. A number of locals across the country broke away from their parent unions and formed the nucleus of the Confederation of Canadian Unions (CCU), which became a beacon for those trade unionists and others who supported a labour movement that was free of American influence. While the CCU remained a small organization, the idea of Canadian union autonomy took hold and reverberated throughout the labour movement in the 1970s and later. (One unexpected result of this was that in 1973 the CLC agreed to readmit the old communist-led unions in an attempt to keep them from joining the CCU.) Canadian communications workers split from their American parent in 1972 and were followed by paperworkers in 1974, energy and chemical workers in 1980, autoworkers in 1985 and woodworkers in 1986. In all cases Canadian workers were seeking greater control over internal union affairs and often the pleas for Canadian autonomy signalled a more significant gulf between an American labour leadership that was willing to cooperate with employers by accepting concessions, for example, and a Canadian membership that was more likely to resist employer demands.

Not all Canadian trade unionists were happy with the nationalist trend, however. Craft unions, mostly in construction, chafed at the CLC's "autonomy guidelines" issued in the 1970s to encourage greater independence for Canadian members within international unions. They also resented the congress's willingness to tolerate increased autonomy for the Quebec Federation of Labour and its stepped-up support for the NDP. As a result, twelve of these unions were expelled from the congress in 1981 for not paying their dues. A year later nine of them formed their own Canadian Federation of Labour and three others remained independent.[1]

Adult education in the 1970s was marked by renewed interest in social-purpose education that gave rise to conflict between those who supported an older professionalism and those who advocated an even older commitment to social change. Educational approaches from Europe and developing countries joined with new social forces emanating from the women's and other movements to shift debate in the field. Sixties-era European literature that emphasized recurrent education (interspersing work and education) and lifelong learning began to have an influence in Canada by the early 1970s. Leading Canadian adult educators such as Alan Thomas used these approaches to argue that learning, which he considered to be more important than education, occurred in a variety of social sites of which the formal education system was but one. Various groups and organizations were influenced by these developments, with the federal government, for example, appointing a commission in the mid-1970s to study paid educational leave. Equally important for the future of labour education, community and development educators (for whom education was linked to social change) drew their influence from popular educators such as Brazilian Paulo Friere, who advocated a "pedagogy of the oppressed" in which education was part of a broader programme of political and economic struggle.

The field of adult education became more fractured and fractious as a result. The Canadian Association for Adult Education (CAAE) moved closer to its roots in social-purpose education and thereby alienated many of those practitioners in governments, educational institutions and businesses for whom adult education was a neutral profession followed in pursuit of benign institutional goals. Many of these self-styled professionals formed their own organizations concentrating on their particular subfield. Community educators, too, created their own organizational structures either to give voice to specific groups (as in the case of the Canadian Congress for Learning Opportunities for Women, formed in 1979) or to address specific social problems (the Movement for Canadian Literacy, formed in 1977, for example). Labour educators, who faced an adult education profession in the 1950s and 1960s that was little interested in social-purpose education, now had a broader community of educational activists with whom to mix and work.[2]

Union Education

The basic structure of Canadian union education had been established between the 1940s and the 1960s. In the 1970s the CLC continued to offer its programme of weekend and week-long schools, larger affiliates maintained their extensive systems and smaller ones took advantage of what the congress had to offer. Courses teaching the skills required to participate in the various aspects of the industrial relations system remained the most important and most extensive offerings, but with broader forces at play, changes occurred in certain areas of union education. For example, new approaches to member-centred teaching were explored in a number of unions, political education was expanded in the CLC, courses for and about women changed, visual media were used in different ways and the CLC's regional school in British Columbia emerged as an important testing ground for new ideas.

The Public Service Alliance of Canada (PSAC) and some of the provincial civil service associations followed the Canadian Union of Public Employees (CUPE) in using programmed instruction and other forms of automated learning in their stewardship and other tools training during the late 1960s and early 1970s. In the mid-1970s, however, PSAC shifted gears to develop a "Union Development Program" that was a break with previous public-sector union education and was noticed by educators across the labour movement. This was a five-level course designed to provide the union with a core of knowledgeable and active members. In contrast to earlier public-sector union education, this programme used participatory educational approaches and was taught in a semi-structured seminar-type setting.

The original Union Development Program was conceived and developed by Fritz Bauer. Bauer was working as a teacher in Ottawa when he was hired by the Union of National Defense Employees (a PSAC component) to put together their education programme. PSAC president Claude Edwards noticed Bauer's work and offered him a job developing a similar programme for the Alliance. At the time, the various components of the Alliance system were controlled by executive secretaries who were appointed rather than elected. Bauer designed the programme to build up a cadre of grassroots activists who collectively would change the PSAC from an association of civil servants into a union. Participants were drawn from the general membership, were given basic union education, and then, it was hoped, would move into elected positions in their components.

The programme was four weeks long at first and was later reduced to three weeks. Participants attended each level in the programme for four or five days, returned to their workplace for a couple of weeks and then came back for the next level. Level One in the initial programme introduced participants to the union local and outlined the reasons for a union local's existence, its method of operation and the essential role of the Component-Alliance system (the Alliance's internal structure) in representing members' interests. Level Two increased the capacity of participants to take an active part in their locals by teaching problem-solving skills at the local level, creating confidence in the participants and in the Alliance and systematically exploring members' rights and obligations. Level Three moved from the local to the broader union to explore how members related to and could influence the larger organization. Level Four focused on the general labour movement by asking what influence Alliance members had on labour councils, federations and other labour bodies on the one hand, and what influence these bodies had on the union's membership on the other. And Level Five, the last level, brought the various parts of the programme together by exploring, first, how union needs could be met by membership participation and, second, how class participants would facilitate this participation when they went back to their union locals and workplaces.

Bauer and his education officers used a variety of participatory techniques in their programme, including role-play, group discussion, simulated bargaining sessions and video-taping participant speeches. The instructors played facilitating rather than didactic roles, only intervening to supply specific information or when the class was totally unable to come up with their own ideas and experiences. They provided a brief introduction for each topic covered in the programme. Following questions and answers involving the whole group, participants were divided into various smaller groups for further discussion. Group leaders, appointed by the instructors, recorded the discussion and reported to the whole class, where a consensus was developed. In the case of Level One, the programme designers believed that "the discussion should lead to the conclusion that locals are useful and effective forms of organizations for serving the needs of our membership—if the necessary knowledgeable leadership exists."[3]

While PSAC was establishing its new approach, the Steelworkers union was reassessing its thirty-five-year programme with a view to making it more responsive to member needs in their locals and workplaces. Gerard Docquier became Canadian national director of the union in 1978 on the strength of his support in Quebec. Prior to his election he had overseen the development of a new approach to labour education in Quebec, which had been designed and implemented by Michel Blondin beginning in 1975. Rank-and-file activists were trained as worker-educators in order to reduce the reliance on staff; courses, in turn, were shortened to two or three days and were held on-the-spot in locals rather than in central locations. Gower Markle, who had been Steelworkers education director in the Steelworkers' Canadian region since 1951, did not agree with this approach to union education and, more importantly, had worked for Docquier's opponent in the 1978 election. As a result, he resigned from his position after the election and went on to manage the labour education programme at Labour Canada.

Docquier moved to the union's national office in Toronto as a complete outsider. No one in the office had supported his candidacy and his previous contact with the office had been acrimonious at best as he had struggled for more autonomy for Quebec programmes. As a result, he decided to hire Markle's replacement from outside of the labour movement rather than promoting from within. He chose a young adult and popular educator named D'Arcy Martin, who was working on international development issues at Toronto's Development Education Centre at the time. Martin brought to union education what he had learned as a solidarity activist—and from radical educators such as Paulo Friere—about developing and maintaining a democratic learning culture when working with oppressed peoples. In addition, Martin maintained a continuing relationship with the academic world through his connection with the adult education department at the Ontario Institute for Studies in Education (OISE), allowing him to keep abreast of new developments in areas such as critical pedagogy and feminist theory.

When Martin took over from Markle, the Steelworkers was going through a period of dynamism and militancy, marked by revived member participation, recruiting the unorganized and activity in new areas such as health and equity. It was, Martin recalls, a time when the "openings for conscious, radically democratic education work seemed legion." One of Martin's first tasks was to prepare a report based on consultations conducted during 1977 and 1978 with local union leaders in Ontario regarding the future of the union's education programme. This report then formed the basis for the Steelworkers' "back to the locals" campaign launched in 1979 to guide its internal education outside of Quebec. Before he joined the Steelworkers, Martin had been aware of Blondin's work in labour and adult education, and with Docquier's urging and backing, he set about to translate Blondin's model to English Canada.

During the consultations, local union leaders identified stewards as the "kingpins" and the "backbone" of the union, yet there was a lack of imaginative and up-to-date materials for their education. It was a priority, therefore, to revise, improve and standardize the steward-training course materials, making sure to offer stewards a broad knowledge of the union and the labour movement as well as a technical understanding of grievance handling. While steward training was identified as the priority, local union leaders also needed updated materials as part of a coordinated programme to target locals with new leaders and where officer turnover was high. Local officers needed help in particular with financial administration and leadership (communications, human relations and conducting meetings). In the past most courses had been taught by union staff members, and this would continue, especially with respect to more advanced courses. In order to expand the programme and tap the latent knowledge and skills available among activists, however, the national office began "train-the-trainer" courses to prepare peer instructors to teach and assist staff representatives in developing their teaching skills.

Local leaders also suggested that the union's scholarship fund, which supported attendance at week-long schools, should be made more flexible to allow financing of shorter courses. In addition, they proposed that locals increase their contributions to the national education fund to something greater than the then-current five cents per member per month, that government grants be sought to supplement the union's resources and that a major drive be started to negotiate paid educational leave.

The leaders further indicated that they wanted courses closer to the workplace to ease travel costs and minimize the impact on members' domestic responsibilities. In some cases this meant using the local union hall, though the facilities were often less than ideal in that the halls had not been designed for educational use. In others, it meant renting space in a hotel or in an educational institution. Many courses were reorganized so that they could be offered on a Friday and a Saturday. This lessened the financial burden on locals, which covered the lost wages of participants, because the participant would be compensated for only one work day and was expected to volunteer his or her time on Saturday.

Finally, local leaders reasserted the traditional Steelworkers view that the union should be responsible for its own basic tools courses, but should send members to labour-council weekend schools or CLC week-long schools for more advanced courses. A more fundamental but related problem that affected internal as well as external union courses, however, was how to plan a programme that contained a variety of courses at different levels of complexity and how to ensure that members who participated in the programme were able to combine courses to attain the maximum benefit possible. Participants in the consultations recognized that there was a need for basic and advanced study in most subject areas but that there was overlap and unevenness in the courses currently available. As a result, experienced unionists often found the available courses in their area to be too basic, some members attended the same course a number of times and some classes were attended by a mix of highly experienced activists and relative novices. Therefore, the education programme was organized into introductory, overview and specialized courses, and the distinction among these types was explained clearly in course brochures. Martin and others in the union decided not to establish prerequisites for the overview and advanced courses, however, on the understanding that some members who had not taken union courses might otherwise have the background to take overview and advanced courses as a result of knowledge and experience gained elsewhere. Once established, the "back to the locals" campaign provided the basis for the Steelworkers' education programme throughout the 1980s and 1990s.[4]

Besides implementing the back to the locals campaign, D'Arcy Martin also developed a "Facing Management" course while working for the Steelworkers during the late 1970s and early 1980s. Sparked by management initiatives to "humanize" the workplace following the 1978-79 strike at Inco in Sudbury, this course was designed to help workers respond to employer attempts to create the illusion that capitalist workplaces were caring, participatory or democratic places. As a kind of "management relations" (as opposed to "labour relations") course, Facing Management exposed workers to the new human-relations literature that managers were being taught in business schools and as part of their in-house training. This material was designed to promote bonding between managers and workers, divide workers and, in its worst incarnations, promote a union-free workplace. In Martin's course, participants interrogated the material to expose its anti-union and anti-worker agendas and then devised strategies to resist these overtures and maintain solidarity. In the section on the "politics of furniture," for example, the power relations involved in meeting rooms were explored and discussion included various ways of drawing managers out from behind their desks.

Source: D'Arcy Martin, *Thinking Union: Activism and Education in Canada's Labour Movement* (Toronto: Between the Lines, 1995), 47-55.

Book to use for research

Martin, Bauer, Gordon Wilson at the United Automobile Workers (UAW), Ed Seymour at the Textile Workers Union of America (TWUA) and Elisabeth Plettenberg at CUPE were part of a new wave of union educators in the 1970s who were placing more emphasis on rank-and-file activist learning than had been the case in the past. Wilson was one of the first Local Union Discussion Leaders in the UAW, while Seymour was essentially a "street-smart" organizer in the tradition of union organizers who travelled from workplace to workplace talking union and signing up members. Best known outside of the labour movement for his *An Illustrated History of Canadian Labour,* Seymour had a catch-as-catch-can approach to education: he seldom used manuals, but was always collecting material to be used to mobilize and educate members.

Plettenberg, meanwhile, was trained as a school teacher and joined the CUPE research department in 1965. Nine years later she moved over to education as James Dowell's assistant, eventually replacing him as director when he retired in 1987. When she joined the department, Plettenberg was struck by the authoritarian nature of classroom practice: courses were taught by staff representatives who most often lectured to a passive group. With Dowell's support, she reorganized courses over the following years—by introducing more discussion, role-play and the like—to draw on the underutilized learning resources that were present among class participants. Furthermore, she developed new-member courses to provide educational opportunities for those who were not yet ready to take on leadership or steward responsibilities. In addition, she spearheaded CUPE's instructor training programme in the early 1980s after assessing Germany's public-sector union education during a 1977 study tour. With the support of new CUPE president Jeff Rose, she overcame internal staff opposition and eventually established a system of one- and two-week courses that had prepared three hundred member instructors by the mid-1980s. Working in teams of two, these member-educators used binders of teaching aids prepared by Plettenberg as a teaching framework that was then infused with their own workplace and other experiences.

During the late 1970s and early 1980s, Martin, Wilson and others used the CLC's Harrison Hot Springs week-long school as a testing ground for new ideas. Known in the labour movement as the "Cannes Festival of labour education" or the "Workers' Republic of Harrison," the school had been revitalized by Art Kube after he became the CLC's Pacific region education director in 1974. Union educators from across the country would go to Harrison each year to teach something—anything—and soak up new ideas as well as the labour culture that was part of the week's activities. Harrison was one of the first places where Martin's successful and influential Facing Management course was offered.[5]

One of the undersides of the Harrison week-long school and other educational activities in the labour movement during the 1970s was the sexism and good-old-boys atmosphere that pervaded them. Challenges to this and other aspects of union education emerged from newly formed women's committees that were giving form to an incipient trade-union feminism in some unions and federations. In British Columbia, for example, a Women's Rights Committee was formed in 1969 as an offshoot of the B.C. Federation of Labour's Human Rights Committee. Beginning in 1970, it organized annual women's conferences addressing such issues as child care, equal opportunities on the job and in the union, parliamentary procedure, public speaking and contract analysis. The committee developed a "Women in the Workforce" course for the 1975 Harrison school (subsequently condensed for weekend offerings) designed to develop basic skills such as public speaking, parliamentary procedure and labour movement structure among rank-and-file female trade unionists.

International Women's Year in 1975 provided a focus for increasing female involvement in labour education and highlighting gender issues in its programmes. CUPE, with a relatively large female membership, launched a major campaign to fight sexual discrimination in the workplace. The campaign, including films, pamphlets, slide-shows, conferences and schools, was designed to show working women that collective bargaining was the most powerful tool they had for fighting against discrimination. At the heart of the campaign was an affirmative-action programme, meant to develop strategies at the workplace to remove barriers restricting employment and promotional opportunities for women. Joint union-management committees were established, and workplaces were evaluated to identify inequities in the status of male and female employees. Week-long workshops were held to train women to identify discriminatory practices in their workplaces and to develop tools to rectify them. Margot Trevelyan, a CUPE member employed at the Canadian Broadcasting Corporation, worked at the union on a short-term contract as part of the campaign to write an affirmative-action handbook and to produce a film on women in the union called *Don't Call Me Baby*.[6]

Plettenberg, with the support and encouragement of Grace Hartman (who became CUPE president during 1975), oversaw this campaign and worked to ensure that woman-friendly content was a part of all educational activities in the union. Her view, not shared by some of her union sisters, was that women's issues were union issues and that "women's" content should form part of all courses rather than being offered in separate, sometimes women-only, events. Modules on maternity leave, therefore, became part of all stewards courses, for example. In addition, she ensured that as many women as men participated in the instructor training programme and, from the early 1980s, made special efforts to train people of colour as occasional instructors.

By the early 1980s even traditionally male-dominated unions such as the Steelworkers (with a 15 percent female membership in Canada) were feeling the winds of feminist change. Laura Sky's union-backed production of *Moving Mountains,* about women in the mining industry, was used in union educationals, while women's rights courses and Arlene Mantle's militant songs became features of the union's week-long schools. These changes did not take place without a struggle, however, as men often protested that things were moving too quickly and women countered that the pace of reform was too slow.[7]

Political education also changed during the 1970s to respond more effectively to the social and economic restructuring that was beginning to take place. While the CLC formally endorsed the NDP as the political arm of labour, in practice this amounted to little more than encouraging locals to affiliate to the party, lending some staff support during election campaigns and confirming the movement's ongoing support for social democracy at convention time. During the 1960s the movement had been content to attempt to influence government policy through efforts such as the congress's ineffectual annual Memorandum to the Government of Canada. By the 1970s, however, some were beginning to wonder whether or not the old ways were delivering the goods. Activists who gathered at Port Elgin in 1973 for the annual Ontario Federation of Labour (OFL)-CLC political education conference, for example, questioned whether or not labour was on the right track politically and whether the liaison with the New Democratic Party was still worthwhile. They concluded that activists had to do more basic educational work about unionism in general in their own locals before political consciousness would develop and that the NDP's social and economic analysis had to be deepened to deal with issues such as plant relocations, the ownership or regulation of corporate property and assistance to underdeveloped countries and to Aboriginal peoples.[8] Throughout most of the 1970s, unions such as the Steelworkers and the UAW actively supported the NDP, but the CLC continued its policy of passive endorsement while flirting with tripartism (participating in formal structures with government and employers) in the wake of the wage control policy of 1975-76.

With increasing attacks on the labour movement by the end of the 1970s, however, it was becoming imperative to find new ways to mobilize workers politically and to try to make the relationship between unions and the NDP work. Ed Broadbent became federal leader of the NDP in 1975 with a pledge to build a more solid foundation with the labour movement and, three years later, Dennis McDermott was elected president of the CLC committed to defeating the federal Liberal government through more active labour support for the New Democrats. This new relationship was cemented during the 1979 and 1980 federal elections, when the CLC spearheaded a labour "parallel campaign" designed to mobilize as many trade unionists as possible to work for and elect NDP candidates by operating outside of the normal party campaign through union-only channels.

Organized by new Political Education Director Pat Kerwin, who replaced George Home in 1977 (Home had retired in 1975), this initiative trained activists in campaign skills, established phone banks across the country, produced materials and organized visits by labour leaders to priority ridings for the 1979 campaign. A year later it was expanded to include face-to-face contact with fellow trade unionists at the worksite. Local stewards and executive members were given training in how to conduct on-the-job canvasses, instructors were taught how to train the canvassers and short programmes were developed for staff representatives and business agents to use at membership meetings. The CLC provided overall direction and support for this campaign, but it was up to the affiliates to do the actual work on the ground. Oshawa, Windsor and Brantford were deemed to be in UAW territory, for example, and it was left to that union to coordinate efforts there. While only a few affiliates joined the campaign in 1979, there was fuller participation in 1980. The campaigns proved difficult for the PSAC, however, because its members were forbidden by legislation from participating in partisan political activity. The union did get involved on a non-partisan basis, though, forming political action committees across the country in 1979 to call for a "fair deal" for public-sector employees and, in 1980, conducting on-the-job canvasses to determine what issues members were most concerned about.

While hard to gauge, the impact of the parallel campaigns was modest at best. The NDP did increase its representation by ten seats in 1979 and a further six seats in 1980, with an increase from seven (1974) to ten (1979) to fourteen (1980) seats in the areas covered by the 1979 phone banks. Still there was no significant increase in the trade union vote for the NDP. Since the birth of the party, approximately one-quarter of voting trade unionists cast ballots for the New Democrats, and that figure did not change substantially in 1979 and 1980. Nonetheless the campaigns were deemed to be qualified successes, in part because they brought various parts of the labour movement together (although they alienated some of the building trades, who did not agree with supporting a political party).

Following the 1980 election, the on-the-job canvasses were continued, political education was increasingly integrated into the CLC's regular tools courses and more political education courses were added to the regular weekend and week-long schools. In addition, the on-the-job canvasses were used for general union-building purposes. United Food and Commercial Workers' (UFCW) Local 832 in Manitoba, for example, participated in the canvass as part of the 1981 provincial election campaign and subsequently adopted the technique as part of its collective bargaining strategy.[9]

Videotapes, including one about the on-the-job canvass, were increasingly used in political and other educational courses by the end of this period. Film was still important to labour educators in the 1970s, but video replaced film as their medium of choice during the decade because the new technology was cheaper and it allowed unions to do their own production. The advent of video programming at the National Film Board (NFB) brought new opportunities for collaboration with publicly funded professional videomakers, but with the money and ability to produce video on their own, labour educators were less interested in these opportunities than they had been in the past.

The Trade Union Film Committee, which had brought together labour educators and professional filmmakers in the 1940s and 1950s, ceased to function some time during the 1960s, but in 1973 an effort was made to re-establish a formal relationship between the labour movement and the NFB. Frances Bairstow, director of industrial relations at McGill University and consultant to the NFB on labour films, initiated a meeting between the NFB, the federal Department of Labour and the CLC. Union educators took this opportunity to rehearse their wish-list of labour films, which was updated to reflect some new concerns of the 1970s (the environment, women's rights, paid educational leave, white-collar work and the non-union worker). The CLC representatives also restated their position, which the NFB seemed to accept when the mood struck them, that labour films should be undertaken only after consultation with the labour movement.[10]

Either as a result of these consultations or for other reasons, the federal government agreed to provide the funds for a remake of *The Grievance*, which was part of the 1950s *Labour in Canada* series. *The Grievance* was a staple film of Canadian (and American) labour education programmes, but by the early 1970s, it and the other films in the series were out of date. In 1974 the federal Department of Labour commissioned Morten Parker, the original producer of the series, to make a new film on the grievance procedure. Parker met with members of the CLC's National Education Advisory Committee (NEAC) to discuss how a 1970s version of the film should include white-collar and women workers. He began work and made substantial progress on the project, but had to interrupt production when Labour Canada (the federal Department of Labour after 1975) would not provide completions funds. In 1977 the CLC was given the rights to the Parker script. Eventually, however, Labour Canada coughed up the necessary money and *The Case of Barbara Parsons* premiered in 1979.

The grievance in this film, shot on location at Canadian Admiral Corporation in Mississauga, Ontario, and eventually costing $185,000, concerns a competition for a technician's position. Barbara Parsons, an external candidate, is hired on the strength of her academic qualifications and her previous experience. But Michael Blais, an internal candidate who lacks Parsons' formal qualifications, possesses the stated qualifications for the job and has taken continuing education over the years in the relevant academic area. Blais grieves the fact that he did not win the job competition, and the film follows the various players through the grievance procedure to an eventual arbitration. Blais wins the grievance and the film ends with Parsons and Blais becoming romantically involved. While Parker had made some effort to include female and white-collar workers in the film (though the grievance did not deal with an issue of sexual discrimination), female trade unionists found the final scene to be distasteful and a decision was made by the CLC's Women's Committee to splice it out of their copies.[11]

While *The Case of Barbara Parsons* was being completed, American and Canadian labour educators were in discussions with Morten Parker regarding a new film series to replace the 1950s *Labour in Canada* series. Deliberations began with correspondence between Larry Wagg and Carroll Hutton, Education Director of the UAW, regarding a remake of *The Shop Steward*. Hutton told Wagg that this was "a film classic" and "we are indebted to the Canadians for making it," but it was out of date in the 1970s. In separate conversations, Hutton and Parker agreed that a number of new labour films should be produced at the rate of about one a year, at a cost of from $120,000 to $130,000 per 30-minute film, and to be paid for with monies raised from six to ten American and Canadian labour organizations. Apparently nothing came of this venture. Parker also approached the LESC separately with an offer to help them plan and produce labour films, but no interest was shown in his gesture.

Source: NAC, *CLC Papers*, MG 28 I 103, Accession 86/0112, Volume 12, File "Films and Video Tape, 1978-79," Carroll Hutton to Larry Wagg, 4 May 1978, Larry Wagg to Carroll Hutton, 15 May 1978, and Morten Parker to Larry Wagg, 8 November 1978; NAC, CLC Papers, MG 28 I 103, Accession 92/0293, Volume 71, File "Films and Video-tapes—1975-Dec 1977," Morten Parker to Larry Wagg, 22 June 1977, and Larry Wagg to an unidentified person in the United Nations, 28 January 1976.

In the early 1970s the CLC commissioned two films from a private producer. *Festival of Communication* (1974) merely chronicled a meeting of the thirty-person CLC Executive Council and the annual CLC presentation to the federal government. But *What If Nobody Came?* (1974), which received an award at the New York International Film and Television Festival, was a pioneering investigation of workers' concerns with industrial pollution.

In the early 1970s the NFB introduced an innovative programme called Challenge for Change, which provided the board's resources and expertise to community groups and social organizations interested in using the new medium of video. Laura Sky, a regional project coordinator for the NFB, explained to the CLC in 1975 that the board was planning to dedicate two years of studio time for this programme and was interested in producing videotapes for the labour movement. As an example, Sky explained that if the CLC education department wanted a specific point illustrated in a pre-retirement class, they could send the NFB an outline and eight to nine weeks later a complete tape would arrive. Unions could borrow the tapes and reproduce them for the cost of the blank cassette. Sky was also willing to teach trade unionists how to use the equipment.

By 1975 the Challenge for Change programme had already produced documentaries on the Artistic Woodworking strike (involving a CCU union) and on lead pollution in Toronto, and was in the process of doing a tape on occupational health and safety. The latter project developed into an Industrial Hygiene Educational Programme two years later, bringing together the Labour

Council of Metropolitan Toronto, Humber College's labour studies programme and Challenge for Change. The labour council provided office space and administrative support, while the NFB provided salary costs and technical support. The project collected, copied and catalogued existing audio-visual material in occupational health and safety for use and distribution by the labour council and produced tapes modelled on Humber College's Industrial Hygiene course.[12]

Challenge for Change was one of those windows of opportunity for government support that often accompany the development of new communications technologies in Canada. In the early 1970s, when public resources were more available than they often are and with a group of generally progressive producers anxious to do community-based work, the NFB was willing to offer public assistance to various social groups to assist them to use video technology for their own educational purposes. While the labour movement took some advantage of this opportunity, it was increasingly looking inward during the 1970s in order to increase its own capacity in a number of areas including media and learning technologies.

Paid Educational Leave

Paid educational leave (PEL) became a significant issue among Canadian labour educators after the International Labour Organization adopted a policy supporting the concept in 1974. At its eleventh convention two years later, the CLC passed a resolution demanding that "a national system of paid educational leave must be implemented." Furthermore, the Canadian government supported the concept as part of its attempts to improve the rocky industrial relations climate during the mid-1970s. In 1977, federal Labour Minister John Munro considered "the right to paid educational leave one of the most important principles in his 14-point program" to soothe relations between workers and employers in Canada. Munro's department issued far-reaching recommendations that federal and provincial governments enact employment standards to protect workers on educational leave, that they establish a fund to enable workers to take educational leave, that federal and provincial Workers' Education Councils be formed, that a national Open Community College based on distance and open learning be established, that employers and unions make educational leave a priority and that provincial governments devote more of their budgets to adult education to cope with the increased demands resulting from the development of paid educational leave.

In the wake of the CLC resolution and the federal government's apparent support, many affiliates passed their own resolutions supporting PEL and urged governments and employers to implement the concept. In a working paper endorsed by its National Education Advisory Committee, the congress insisted that a number of standards must apply in negotiating PEL. While leave should be available to all employees for all levels of education, labour must ensure that leave is available for labour education programmes operated by the congress and its affiliates. Furthermore, funds collected through a PEL clause should go into a separate fund from the union and the employer, and should be administered by the union. And, finally, decisions on the use of the money and by whom must remain those of the union.[13]

In 1978 the federal government appointed a Commission on Educational Leave and Productivity, chaired by Professor Roy Adams of McMaster University, to review national and international practice in the area, to elicit opinions on the matter and to make public-policy recommendations. Various labour organizations made presentations to the commission, restating labour's position that the federal government should ratify ILO Convention 140 and legislate PEL for workers under its jurisdiction, that PEL-funded labour education should be administered by unions alone and that all other PEL-funded education should be administered jointly by labour, management and government.

When the commission's final report was issued, the CLC welcomed its call for more attention to trade-union training and its recognition that labour education was as important to the national welfare as many other forms of education then financed by government. The congress was disappointed, however, that the commission did not recommend leave for general, social and civic education as well as vocational education and that there was no recommendation ensuring that educational leave would be available to all workers. And it was particularly distressed that the commission viewed educational leave as merely a tool to achieve identifiable objectives rather than as a general social entitlement. Four years later the federal government appointed a task force on educational leave and again labour made the same arguments supporting the concept as a general right of citizenship. Nothing was done at the legislative level, however, and paid educational leave disappeared from the public-policy agenda in the mid-1980s.[14]

By 1976 it was clear to union educators such as Gordon Wilson, who had succeeded Alan Schroeder four years earlier as education director of the UAW's Canadian region, that Canada was not about to legislate a PEL system and that they would have to try to win the provision through collective bargaining. The UAW proved to be the only union that was able to establish a permanent PEL presence in this way, although other unions, such as the International Union of Electrical Workers (IUE), the International Association of Machinists and Aerospace Workers (IAM) and the Steelworkers, did negotiate some PEL provisions in individual contracts. Wilson was successful in having PEL accepted as part of the UAW Canadian region's bargaining priorities in 1976, although there was some apprehension in the union leadership that members would prefer money in their own pockets rather than cents-per-hour in a union-controlled educational fund. The following spring the union and Rockwell International signed the first contract in Canada giving workers paid educational leave to take union education in a programme controlled entirely by the union. The contract covered 1,100 members in three Ontario cities, and the company agreed to contribute one cent per hour for each member of the bargaining unit. By the end of 1977 there were PEL clauses in thirty-five collective agreements covering 15,480 members. All of the funds collected under the provisions of PEL clauses were paid directly into a PEL fund administered by the UAW's Canadian regional office.[15]

UAW sample contract language on paid educational leave:

The Company agrees to pay into a special fund one cent per hour per employee for all hours worked for the purpose of providing paid education leave. Said paid education leave will be for the purpose of upgrading the employee's skills in all aspects of Trade Union functions. Such monies to be paid on a quarterly basis into a trust fund established by the union.

The Company further agrees that members of the bargaining unit, selected by the Union to attend such courses, will be granted a leave of absence without pay for twenty days of class time, plus travel time where necessary, said leave of absence to be intermittent over a twelve month period from the first day of leave. Employees on such leave of absence will continue to accrue seniority and benefits during such leave.

Source: NAC, *UAW Papers*, MG 28 I 119, Volume 286, File 20, "Paid Education Leave. List of Paid Education Leave (PEL) Negotiated Agreements, Bankbook, Statements. 1976-1979," Gordon Wilson, "Paid Education Leave," no date (but 1976 or 1977).

Bob White, director of the UAW Canadian region from 1978 to 1985 and president of the Canadian Auto Workers from 1985 to 1992, reflecting on the reluctance of rank-and-file members to accept PEL in the early days of the scheme:

I knew the membership couldn't care less about paid education leave. I could picture a picket being asked what the strike was about and having to answer, "We want a penny an hour for paid education leave." The membership would have killed us for holding out on that issue.

Source: Bob White, *My Life on the Line* (Toronto: McClelland and Stewart, 1987), 150.

Some UAW staff representatives were reluctant to push PEL as a bargaining priority, and after the initial flurry of agreements in 1977, the negotiation of PEL provisions stalled in 1978. These staff and some local union leaders were concerned that PEL graduates would compete for their jobs. However, the issue disappeared when Canadian Region Director Dennis McDermott told a staff meeting that no staff person was allowed to take PEL off the negotiating table without his approval. Unless an employer was particularly intransigent, it was easier to get the item in the negotiated agreement than to have to call McDermott. American Motors accepted PEL in 1978, but the big breakthrough with the Big Four automakers came when General Motors accepted the provision a year later. By the end of 1979 over 110,000 UAW members were covered by PEL in 250 collective agreements, and the concept was firmly established in the union.[16]

Dan Benedict, a seasoned trade unionist with a long history in the international labour movement, was hired in the spring of 1978 to develop the first PEL programme. Originally a latheman in a General Electric shop where he had been a shop steward in the United Electrical, Radio and Machine Workers (UE) and the IUE, he was later associate director of international affairs in the Congress of Industrial Organizations (CIO) working for Victor Reuther. Prior to his move to McMaster University in 1977 to work in its new labour studies programme, he had been assistant general secretary of the International Metalworkers Federation for twelve years. Benedict brought to the UAW extensive experience with the global workers' education movement. He was particularly influenced by the socialist workers' education that was practiced in the French CFDT union and by the Danish "Folk High Schools" that promised a general, broadly based lifelong education rooted in participants' local cultures.[17]

The first UAW PEL session opened in the fall of 1978 with 93 participants, each of whom had been selected by their local union. The per-student cost of approximately $2,200 (lost wages, travel, room and board) was covered by the PEL trust fund. The participants, who were divided into three equal groups, met for five four-day sessions at Port Elgin, with a two-week break between each session. They therefore spent a total of twenty days in class over the course of three to four months. From the beginning, Benedict and Wilson were committed to adult education approaches by, for example, using Local Union Discussion Leaders (peer educators) to facilitate discussions and starting from participants' experiences when they explored issues in the programme.

The programme was divided into five sections to correspond to the five four-day periods. The first section started with tips on how to study and then proceeded to investigate the roots of the UAW through a brief history of the union, the place of the UAW in the Canadian labour movement and reports by participants on how their local started (which they had prepared before travelling to Port Elgin). Participants then looked more closely at the UAW local in the second section, studying how it worked in the shop and in the community. In the third section they developed their skills in "communications, learning and action" by practising public speaking and making reports. They then turned their attention to "practical economics for trade unionists," where the nature of capitalist profit and power was revealed through an analysis of an individual worker's household budget in the context of company, industry, national and international economies. Finally, in the fifth section, participants investigated, first, the global suffering and inequality that resulted from international capitalism and, second, the political efforts of national and international labour bodies to challenge these phenomena.[18]

By the early 1980s, paid educational leave was an integral part of the UAW's educational system. At the same time that the autoworkers union was establishing this programme as a negotiated benefit, the CLC was using the very different route of government funding to build its new labour education and studies centre.

The Labour Education and Studies Centre

Following the Verner and Dickinson surveys of the early 1970s, union educators continued to monitor their programmes with a view to making them more efficient and more responsive to members' needs. A 1975 NEAC retreat, for example, concluded that there should be a clearer division of responsibility between the CLC and its affiliates, with the latter developing their own programmes and training their own course leaders while the former concentrated on offering courses in broad social, economic and political issues.[19] More significantly, however, the 1974 CLC convention directed the congress to explore the formation of a national labour studies centre for advanced union education. The recently retired Bert Hepworth was chosen to head a study committee, which, after conducting an international study tour, produced a report that was accepted with some modifications by the 1976 CLC convention.

The committee recommended, first, that the CLC and its affiliates establish a national Labour Education and Studies Centre to initiate, encourage and stimulate the provision of education and training for union members and their families. While based in Ottawa, the centre would operate regionally through a type of extension service (with regional centres envisaged for the future). The Labour College of Canada would come under the umbrella of the new centre and its mandate would be broadened to include negotiating accreditation and other arrangements with colleges and universities. Second, it recommended that the centre acquire permanent facilities including study, recreational and cultural facilities, residential accommodation, student common rooms, and a library and documentation centre. Furthermore, it would assemble a core staff combining skills in research, the preparation of print and audio-visual materials, residential and extension programming and the supervision of library and documentation units.

Third, the committee suggested that a per-capita tax of two cents per month per member be established to assist with the operational requirements of the centre. In addition, affiliates and local unions would be asked to contribute one dollar per member per year for a three-year period to provide capital funding. Fourth, and finally, it recommended that the centre's programme include advanced tools courses such as union accounting or pensions and academic courses such as economics or sociology. Course offerings would be supplemented by instructor training programmes, assistance to affiliates in establishing and expanding their own programmes and research about labour education methodology and techniques. The committee hoped that the new centre would finally allow the Canadian labour movement to follow a progression model in labour education, with participants in CLC and affiliate schools given credits that would allow them to progress from one level of learning to the next.[20]

While the CLC was exploring the possibility of establishing its new centre, the federal government was looking for ways to funnel some money to the labour movement to soften the blow it had administered to workers with its wage control policy of the mid-1970s. A 1975 national conference on labour education sponsored by the federal Department of Labour (the first since 1956 and the last in the century to bring together trade unionists, post-secondary educators and others around this topic) recommended that federal and provincial governments increase their financial support for labour education. Labour minister John Munro endorsed this proposal and saw increased support for union-centred industrial relations training as a key element in his strategy to achieve labour-management peace in the country. Labour Canada officials initially offered the CLC an extraordinary grant of $5 million over five years, which was subsequently increased to $10 million over the same time period. The minister found a further $600,000 to support labour education in unions outside of the CLC and in post-secondary institutions.

The agreement between the federal government and the CLC envisioned the establishment of a national labour studies centre and five regional centres "to enable officers, officials and potential labour leaders of the Congress and its affiliates to acquire a comprehensive knowledge and understanding of the goals, policies and responsibilities of the Canadian Labour Movement and of the Congress, ... [and to acquire] the skills and knowledge necessary for the discharge of their duties in the Canadian labour movement." In practice, the CLC intended to use the money to implement the recommendations of the feasibility report and to establish a broadly based, upper-level labour education programme in Canada. Furthermore, it accepted the money on the understanding that it was free to spend it without government interference.[21]

The Labour Education and Studies Centre, which operated separately from the congress's education department, consisted of the national centre in Ottawa and four regional centres in the Atlantic, Ontario, Prairie and Pacific regions. (Funds from the grant to support labour education in Quebec were transferred from the CLC to the Quebec Federation of Labour [QFL] according to a 1974 agreement that granted the QFL complete control over labour education in that province. There was also a separate Labour Canada grant to the Confederation of National Trade Unions [CNTU].) A National Coordinating Committee (NCC) met bi-monthly and a national Board of Directors convened twice a year to review and ratify NCC decisions. The NCC appointed regional boards and advisory committees, authorized national and regional expenditures, supervised national and regional employees and developed and executed national policy.

The annual budget of $2 million was divided equally between the regions and Ottawa. The QFL received a lump-sum transfer, but operations in the rest of Canada were funded directly from Ottawa. Staff were paid centrally, programmes were funded on a project-by-project basis and scholarships for individuals to attend regional courses were paid directly to the participant's home union. Crucially, however, no project or scholarship funds were given directly to affiliates. As a result, the CLC's NEAC—as the mediating committee between affiliate education departments and the LESC—became a more important body: committee members felt compelled to attend in order to monitor what courses were being offered and who was receiving scholarships.

The first national director was the Canadian Brotherhood of Railway, Transport and General Workers' (CBRT) Harry Jacks, who took up his duties on 1 July 1977. Other key staff in the first few years of operation included an administrative and finance officer, a research and programme officer, an audio-visual production officer, a health and safety programme development officer and the regional directors. In the first five years of funding, the national and regional centres concentrated on developing print and audio-visual instructional materials and offering courses, conferences and seminars on topics not normally taught in regular union courses. The first priorities were to train union staff and local union leaders in organizing, leadership and instructional skills; to teach health and safety officers and committee members how to protect and enhance workers' rights under the new provincial occupational and health and safety acts; and to provide advanced courses for staff in areas such as arbitration and contract clauses, socio-economic planning, public and corporate finance, and new issues in servicing (paid educational leave, union counselling, affirmative action and the like). In addition, the centre responded to requests from other departments in the CLC and from affiliates for course materials. For example, the centre funded the development of a number of courses and audio-visual productions for the congress's Women's Bureau. By the early 1980s a rudimentary division of labour had developed, with the national centre responsible for developing, testing and distributing programmes and materials and the regional centres responsible for programme implementation.

Course packages normally consisted of an instructor's manual, a participant's manual and, perhaps, a handbook for participants to use once they were back in the field. Many course packages were also enhanced by audio-visual materials such as slide presentations, audiotapes or videotapes. Materials were developed both in-house and with the assistance of other congress staff or outside consultants. George Nakitsas, a CLC economist, assisted with the course Economics and Full Employment, while labour lawyers Jeffrey Sack and Howard Goldblatt wrote Arbitration and Contract Clauses.

The various courses developed by or with the assistance of the national or regional centres were offered across the country as part of weekend schools or in special weekend or week-long sessions. Centre monies were used to pay course-related expenses and, most importantly, to cover the travel and lost-wages

Rodney Brown (left), a union folk singer, and Damon Dowbak entertain at a 1982 Labour Education and Studies Centre-sponsored school in Thunder Bay, Ontario. *Canadian Labour Congress Collection.*

costs for the course participants. In the 1980 Pacific region week-long school, for example, the following subjects were offered under the auspices of the LESC: arbitration, union counselling, labour economics, occupational health and safety, women in the workforce, labour journalism, labour advocacy, advanced arbitration, time management and instructor training. In addition, the LESC sponsored an annual conference on the British Columbia economy.

In a number of subject areas, notably health and safety but also women in the workforce and some others, emphasis shifted from large conferences disseminating information in the first couple of years to small-group activities aimed at developing skills and strategies. Instructor training, too, changed over the years from its initial focus on training instructors for specific programmes to training instructors who could, in turn, train other instructors. Leadership education, however, never made the shift from teaching local activists to training senior leaders in affiliates and the CLC, despite the difficult problems the latter faced in managing complex organizations and confronting employers and governments.[22]

The national and regional centres also funded a number of special projects during their first five years. For example, Max Swerdlow was given a consultant's fee and expenses to produce a book on his work and experiences in labour education. Although Swerdlow originally offered to produce a broader history of labour education as well, Secretary-Treasurer Julien Major was emphatic that Swerdlow be contracted to produce only his autobiography. The result was Swerdlow's *Brother Max: Labour Organizer and Educator*, published in 1990 by the Committee on Canadian Labour History. In British Columbia, meanwhile, centre monies were used to fund two labour education positions in Simon Fraser University's continuing education department.[23]

The most innovative and high-profile part of the LESC was its audio-visual department. It was also its most disappointing contribution, especially given Canada's relatively rich labour-media history. A significant portion of the centre's budget (perhaps one-third or more annually) was devoted to the production and reproduction of audiotapes, videotapes, slides and transparencies. However, the department produced very little that was of enduring quality, and in retrospect, the decision to equip a full-scale television production facility may have been a mistake. Some of the department's capacity was devoted to producing multi-media components for the course materials that the centre was developing. For example, slides were produced to accompany the CLC's basic stewards course and the centre's health and safety course, while videos were shot for its two organizing courses.

A large part of the department's time was consumed by special projects and requests from affiliates. By 1979 Frank Swartz, the audio-visual coordinator, was complaining that the department was overburdened, and that 70 percent of its time was spent responding to outside requests while 30 percent was spent on centre business. The output ranged from the simple recording of speeches and other activities at conferences or meetings, which seemed to consume most of the department's time, to more highly produced features dealing with specific issues or campaigns. One of the first video projects was a series of interviews with labour leaders and retired staffers, such as Dennis McDermott, Joe Morris, Bert Hepworth, Kalem Kaplansky and Eileen Surfin, who talked about their experiences in the labour movement. In another project, in which video was used to support an organizing drive, fishers in the Maritime provinces were featured discussing their problems and why they were supporting the Maritime Fishermen's Union.

One crucial element that was lacking in the LESC, according to one union educator, was skilful and imaginative staff who understood both video production and the labour movement. Technology that was soon out of date consumed a large portion of the audio-visual department's budget, while staff did not have the ability to anticipate and respond to the labour movement's needs. A culture developed in the centre that militated against cooperative relationships with independent, labour-friendly video producers.

An educational media specialist was hired to review some of the audio-visual department's output as part of an evaluation of Labour Canada's Labour Education Program and was highly critical of what he saw. He was impressed with only one of the five videos and one of the three slide programmes he reviewed. He maintained that, in general, little understanding was shown of the

Jane Burton, production assistant in the CLC's Labour Education and Studies Centre, works on a slide show in 1983. *Canadian Labour Congress Collection.*

role or power of media as instructional tools and there was little evidence of an awareness of the basic characteristics of adult learning or the elements of a systematic approach to instructional development. He added that the LESC would benefit from an in-house staff training programme designed to develop educational skills in distance education techniques, multi-media applications and general instructional development. The video *National Boycott of Iceberg Lettuce*, for example, which featured United Farmworkers of America leader Cesar Chavez, suffered from being a two-camera studio interview which did not capture Chavez's dynamism. Furthermore, having Dennis McDermott conduct the interview with Chavez was dangerous because "'personalities' want to stress their own interpretations or otherwise talk too much." The slide presentation produced to accompany the CLC's Manual for Stewards, meanwhile, was dismissed as being merely illustrations of the main points made in the manual and of little use as an aid to learning.

The one video that received high marks in this evaluation was, in fact, a film produced on contract by Crawley Films. *The (Blankety Blank) Unions*, which gave a brief history of unions and discussed the problems and views of people towards unions, was praised for its good mix of live action film interviews, stills, newsreel footage, audio and photographs and its learning effectiveness. *Right to Survive*, a slide, audio and script presentation on health and safety was praised as an outstanding example of an educational programme in that it had a clear set of instructional goals, which were set out clearly in a well-written and narrated script accompanied by compelling graphics.[24]

Others criticized the lack of coordination between the audio-visual and print materials in specific courses. Collective Bargaining, for example, contained a set of videotapes from the University of Toronto that focused on the technical aspects of bargaining and were obviously designed to be used in both labour education and management training. Moreover, as one labour critic charged, both the externally produced videos and the internally produced print materials treated bargaining as a specialized task requiring highly skilled participants when, in fact, bargaining was a political activity that should rely on the direct involvement of local members. While the print materials made some reference to the power of workers, and could be revised to emphasize the mobilizing potential of the bargaining process, the critic claimed, the video materials were hopelessly flawed by their use of examples that served management's interests and by their inherent sexism.

Overall, the print resources received favourable reviews. One adult educator did claim that, while an early version of the instructor training course was successful at training robots to reproduce techniques, it failed to develop "thinking leaders who can change horses in mid-stream if necessary." But Alan Thomas and David Abbey, who reviewed the LESC programme for Labour Canada, argued that the print materials were of generally high quality. The centre staff, they claimed, had learned to develop print resources "through the systematic and sensitive evaluation of need, use of the expertise of the labour movement, and the careful testing and revising of materials." They concluded that the original decision of the LESC to develop its own programmes and resources rather than buying them from external sources had been a wise one. Their only caveat was that the staff had to learn to use audio-visual media as successfully as they used print.[25]

The Labour College of Canada

The feasibility study that provided the blueprint for the LESC contained a proposal that the Labour College of Canada be integrated into the centre's operations. While this did not happen, the college did benefit from the services provided by the new centre and, more importantly, from a share of the Labour Canada money.

By the late 1970s the college was once again faced with declining enrolments, and questions were being raised about its future and its place in Canadian union education. Nineteen seventy-seven marked the last time that residential sessions were held in Montreal, and the 1978 session was cancelled to give the college time to conduct an internal review of its current state and future prospects. Those conducting the review reaffirmed that Canadian labour education needed an academically oriented residential programme addressing the social, economic, political and historical aspects of labour. They suggested, however, that labour law replace trade unionism as the fifth subject of study.

They also reaffirmed that eight weeks provided enough time to give minimum treatment to the programme of study, while noting that a longer session might be possible in the future if paid educational leave became more widespread. The reviewers noted that there had been a decline in the number of participants in the French-language sessions, partly because the QFL was taking over control of labour education in Quebec. They felt, nonetheless, that the college should continue to offer sessions in both English and French. Furthermore, they acknowledged that there had been calls by some, particularly in western Canada, either to alternate the location of the residential programme or to establish a satellite campus in the west. These calls were rejected, but the reviewers did recommend that the residential programme move from Montreal to Ottawa.

During the 1970s the composition of the college student body changed as more students came with previous post-secondary education and as the proportion of students with less than ten years of trade union experience increased. The reviewers wondered if separate streams of study should be established to accommodate these differences or if applicants with post-secondary experience should be denied entry to the programme. They rejected these options, arguing instead that heterogeneity could be a benefit if teaching methods were used that promoted worker solidarity and included all participants in the learning process. In order to accomplish this, they recommended that an annual orientation seminar be held exposing teaching staff to adult education approaches and to current trends and preoccupations in the labour movement. And with an eye to the resources available through the Labour Canada grant and the LESC, they suggested that seminars be held across the country for college graduates. Finally, the reviewers recommended that the Board of Governors be enlarged to broaden the base of union representation and to involve a larger number of post-secondary institutions.[26]

The Board of Governors accepted most of these recommendations. The eight-week residential programme was moved to Ottawa beginning in 1979, with a slight modification in the course structure to include a session in labour law. French-language classes had to be dropped because of low enrolments and because attempts to cooperate with the QFL to ensure their continuation proved fruitless. The organizational structure was left largely unchanged, with the University of Montreal and McGill University continuing to be represented on the board. The original Quebec charter incorporating the college was dissolved, however, and a federal charter was obtained to reflect the fact that the college's administrative offices and residential programme were now in Ottawa. In 1979 Robert Bisson, who had been working on a temporary contract at the college, was appointed permanent coordinator of studies to oversee the academic programme. Jean Bezusky continued as associate registrar, assisting Larry Wagg who became registrar in 1975 when Bert Hepworth retired.

The internal review had suggested that instructors make more use of student experiences in their teaching. As a result, a workshop on adult education principles was held in early 1979 with Ian Morrison of the CAAE and Anne

Harley of Simon Fraser University taking the sometimes sceptical teaching staff through various experiential practise exercises. In a July post-session evaluation, the instructors reviewed the extent to which it had been possible to use adult education methods to teach academic subjects. Graham Lowe, a sociology instructor, argued that the method was difficult to use when dealing with theoretical material. The purpose of his course was to provide participants with a framework for analysis, but it was difficult for them to conceptualize broad problems in general terms. They were often interested in discussing only immediate solutions to specific problems in their workplaces. History instructor David Millar claimed some success in using buzz groups to interpret specific historical events and adapting individual written assignments to a student's local union or personal experience.[27]

Students, however, often expected a "university atmosphere" when they attended the college and resisted attempts by instructors to use participatory techniques that they believed were not normally part of university courses. Bob Hatfield, for example, a PSAC education officer who taught public-sector labour relations at the college during the 1980s, used small-group discussion, group presentations and a variety of writing exercises in his classes. Still, he was unable to use the full range of adult education approaches that he normally employed in his regular union education sessions, partly because of student resistance and partly because of the large body of material he had to cover in a short period of time.[28]

The Labour Canada grant provided the college with its first period of real financial stability. In the years immediately prior to 1978, the annual budget of the college was approximately $68,000, with revenue coming from the following sources: $25,000 from the federal government, $10,000 from provincial governments, $12,000 from the CLC, $15,000 from other labour organizations and the balance from miscellaneous sources including distance education registrations. This budget covered the staff and administrative costs of maintaining the office and running the residential and distance education programmes; it did not include the lost wages, travel and room-and-board costs of residential-programme participants, which were covered by scholarships that individual unions offered to their members. The annual budget in 1978 was $144,000, with the federal government providing $100,000 through the LESC and the balance coming from provincial governments ($10,000), the CLC ($12,000), other labour organizations ($15,000) and miscellaneous sources ($7,000). A year later the annual budget was $195,000 (or almost three times as much as two years earlier), with the federal government contributing $128,000 through the LESC. The new money allowed the college to offer an advanced programme for graduates, including specific courses designed for the college as well as places for college graduates in LESC courses such as Instructor Training. Socio-Economic Planning was originally developed for college graduates and was offered across the country. This was later supplemented by a course in union-management strategies.[29]

With the shift from Montreal to Ottawa, the primary composition of the college instructional staff changed from full-time university-based professors to part-time teachers, researchers or consultants for progressive causes who taught at the college as one of a variety of part-time jobs. Part-time instructors in community colleges and universities began unionizing during the 1970s, setting the stage for a similar bid among the Labour College of Canada staff in 1982. Since the Board of Governors—the college employer—was dominated by trade unionists, the eleven instructors thought that their request to it for voluntary recognition of their bargaining unit would be granted quickly and quietly. They were astounded when, after much delay, the board responded by saying that it was unable to grant voluntary recognition because the instructors did not constitute a permanent workforce: they were on short-term contracts and had other employment elsewhere, the reasoning went, so they were not entitled to the benefits of unionization. Particularly disturbing to these educational workers was the later revelation that the board's trade union members unanimously supported this decision.

The board did agree, however, to meet informally with instructor representatives to discuss conditions of employment for the 1983 session. Finding these deliberations unsatisfying, the staff decided in March of that year to apply to the Ontario Labour Relations Board for formal certification. When classes commenced in May, students began asking questions about the Board of Governors' actions. After learning that the Board of Governors was going to oppose the bid for certification, the students confronted the college management and then met with CLC President Dennis McDermott to determine for themselves why the board was acting as it was. With McDermott dismissing the college workers as irrelevant academics "who study the underbellies of ants," the students decided that all avenues of protest had been exhausted and they organized a boycott of classes. They and their instructors arranged to continue discussing the course materials, but they met in the students' residence rather than in the regular classrooms. Over the next few days the students organized a strike committee and issued a press release accusing the board of contravening the right to free collective bargaining. As a result, some students were ordered by their sponsoring unions to return to class or to return home.

In press interviews, McDermott continued to dismiss the college workers as "high-priced academics playing at being Joe and Jane Worker" (though earning less per hour than many members of McDermott's own UAW). By this time, however, some locals and labour councils across the country were beginning to question the board's actions, and a meeting was arranged between McDermott and representatives of the instructional staff. It was agreed that the board would approve voluntary recognition if the instructors joined the Canadian Union of Labour Specialists, the union representing CLC staff. A first contract was negotiated and approved in 1984 without incident. In the process, however, the college teaching staff learned some unpleasant truths about the attitudes of Canada's labour leadership towards them and, perhaps, towards educational and part-time workers in general.[30]

Community Colleges, Universities and the Labour Movement

labour education
connection to
colleges

While the Labour College of Canada was firmly established as the labour movement's institution of advanced education in Canada by the 1970s, the expansion of post-secondary education across the country, in the form of new community colleges to provide applied education and new public spending on universities, furnished a foundation for the origin and growth of labour studies programmes. These programmes were designed to provide trade unionists and other interested students with the opportunity to learn about the place of the labour movement in the broader society. Union educators, however, were apprehensive about these new overtures.

Niagara College in Welland, Ontario, was the first college or university in the country to establish a labour studies programme, which it began in 1969. With thirteen union members participating, it was viewed by the labour movement as an appropriate model for other colleges to follow because it was planned in close consultation with the labour councils and major unions in the area. Furthermore, programme staff included John Whitehouse, with twenty years' experience as Canadian education and publicity director of the TWUA, and Cleve Kidd, former research director for the Steelworkers (and subject of the 1954 NFB film *The Research Director*). The key person here was Whitehouse, who, besides his union background, held a bachelor and master's degrees from the University of Oxford in the United Kingdom. When he was hired by Niagara College in 1968, Whitehouse was enrolled in a master's programme under Roby Kidd at OISE and was a member of that institution's Board of Governors. He subsequently started a doctorate with Kidd with the intention of writing a dissertation on the history of Canadian labour education.[31]

At OISE Whitehouse produced a series of papers making the case for a community-college role in labour education, and this research provided the rationale for his work at Niagara. He started from Kidd's argument that the community college, located as it was where people live and work, could be an intellectual bank for people of any age to use for their various educational, training and cultural needs and aspirations. As a truly community-based educational institution, Kidd maintained, colleges were well-suited to the tasks of broad-based continuous (lifelong) learning. Whitehouse applied this view to labour education in suggesting that trade unionists, since they represented a significant portion of the tax-paying public, should have access to community-college services in the subject areas that interested them. Echoing the sentiments that had been voiced in 1956 to justify closer labour-university relations, he argued that rapid changes in collective bargaining, coupled with the increasingly sophisticated social, economic and technological processes facing workers, required formal leadership training for trade unionists. College-based labour education programmes, developed and administered in collaboration with the labour movement, Whitehouse claimed, would allow union students "to advance from one learning level to another in pursuit of meaningful objectives in a systematic, disciplined manner, through an accessible educational institution that has the material and appropriate instructional resources to do the job."

Whitehouse rejected the distinction between tools training and liberal workers' education, arguing that Canadian trade unionists blended elements of the more pragmatic American and the more liberally oriented British labour education traditions to create their own mix that was relevant to their history, culture and objectives. And he contended that, because Canadian labour education combined industrial pragmatism and social idealism, a college-based labour education programme was particularly relevant. A successful college-union collaboration required that a number of conditions be met, however. First, the college had to accept the legitimacy of collective bargaining and labour's role in society. Second, the labour movement had to recognize the college's need for objectivity, intellectual integrity and teaching standards. Third, the college programme had to be based on the concrete needs of the labour movement as determined by full and meaningful consultation with labour representatives. Fourth, there had to be ongoing liaison between the college and the labour movement regarding the development and administration of the programme. And, finally, college instructors had to be prepared to relate to the needs of adult learners and to involve the learners in the learning process.[32]

Niagara College's programme was well established and serving trade unionists and other learners in the Niagara peninsula area of Ontario by the time Whitehouse left the college in 1974 to direct the International Labour Organization's (ILO) Workers' Education Branch. A year later Humber College in suburban Toronto opened its Centre for Labour Studies as a joint venture with the Labour Council of Metropolitan Toronto. While teaching a range of courses, including Labour History and Politics, Labour Leadership, Instructional Techniques for Labour Educators, and Challenges and Perspectives for Women in the 1970s, the Humber centre concentrated in its early years on the emerging area of occupational health and safety training. The Humber programme flourished until the labour council severed its connection with the institution in the mid-1980s and established a link with George Brown College in downtown Toronto.[33]

In British Columbia, meanwhile, colleges such as Capilano in North Vancouver, Cariboo in Kamloops, and the British Columbia Institute of Technology in Vancouver attempted to build links to the labour movement with mixed results. Capilano and Cariboo approached the CLC with separate proposals to establish a formal link with the Labour College of Canada. Both were rebuffed. As Capilano began to offer labour courses in 1970, the coordinator of community services asked the CLC if it were interested in working out an arrangement whereby Capilano courses could be accredited as equivalent to the college's correspondence course, to part or all of the residential programme or to both. Bert Hepworth, LCC registrar at the time, replied that the college was not interested in a formal arrangement, but he had "no doubt that any trade unionist doing [your] course would be in a better position to attend" the college. Cariboo, meanwhile, suggested that it was interested in becoming the western Canadian arm of the LCC. In a letter to CLC Pacific education director Ron Tweedie rejecting the idea, Hepworth wrote that it was already difficult to find students for the current programme in Montreal and that the college and the congress had already concluded that, while a college in the east and the west might be a good idea, the labour movement could not sustain it at the moment. Furthermore, he expressed concern that if labour studies programmes such as the one at Cariboo continued to develop across the country, they could have a detrimental affect on recruitment for the LCC.[34]

While its proposal for a collaboration with the LCC was rejected, Capilano College did go on to establish a labour studies programme in cooperation with the local labour movement. Capilano proposed in 1974 that it establish a labour education programme funded by the British Columbia government. The prospective programme was designed for a worker constituency, including union officers, activists, other interested trade unionists, school leavers and unorganized workers. It was anticipated that labour would be involved in the planning and administration of the programme, which would include tools-type courses such as steward training, collective bargaining, media skills and labour rights for unorganized workers as well as issues courses exploring the broader context in which labour operates. While provincial funding was not forthcoming (as a result of the defeat of the NDP government), the programme was launched with the endorsement and participation of the CLC.

In 1976, a series of tools courses was offered, although the labour advisory committee expressed concern about the abstract nature of some of them. The programme was promoted through the CLC Pacific office and Art Kube, CLC Pacific education director, taught the collective bargaining course.[35] In the latter part of 1976, however, the CLC withdrew its endorsement of the Capilano programme and refused to participate in it. According to Kube, the college had presented the labour advisory committee with "a program which was a fait accompli, which was not based on any recognized needs within the trade union movement, [and] which was solely originated on the basis of some political romanticism by a few inexperienced well-meaning instructors." Furthermore, said Kube, the programme persisted only because of political divisions in the British Columbia labour movement, by which he meant that unions with communist leadership continued to work with Capilano. Northwest Community College in Prince Rupert was also refused a CLC endorsement for its labour education programme, even though Kube conceded that the college was in a region with a lot of trade unionists who were members of unions not affiliated to the CLC and perhaps it filled a need.

Kube cultivated relationships with Simon Fraser University (SFU) beginning in 1975 and, following the rupture with Capilano, these relations were strengthened and deepened. Joint conferences, seminars and workshops were offered on a variety of topics, and Kube promoted the CLC-SFU connection as a model other post-secondary institutions could follow in establishing labour studies programmes. What made SFU desirable, according to Kube, was that the university was willing to let labour determine the content and nature of its programme offerings. The University of British Columbia, which has shown only sporadic and limited interest in labour education throughout its history, proposed a Labour Studies Certificate Program in the early 1970s to be governed by a labour advisory committee similar to those operating at Manitoba, McMaster, StFX and Dalhousie. The programme, to be offered through the university's continuing education centre, was described as being part-time for current and aspiring union leaders and designed to assist them to function in leadership roles and to perform social and civic responsibilities. The proposal appears to have been an attempt to capture some of the money that the NDP provincial government of the day was promising for labour education, and nothing came of it after Social Credit came to power.[36]

Art Kube, CLC Pacific education director in 1978, on the Labour Education and Studies Centre and on labour's relationship with colleges and universities:

Everyone has heard about the funding of labour education by the federal government and everyone is having high expectations that there is just oodles of monies around to be spent. Well, I am sorry to disappoint some people. In the first instance, the grant given to the Canadian Labour Congress for labour education consists of two million dollars a year, one million of which is set aside for the national clc labour education and studies center and the other one million dollars per year is split up on the basis of five regions, of which BC and the Yukon are one, so, therefore, in this region here, we have a total of two hundred thousand dollars to spend in addition to what we are spending now on labour education.... Simon Fraser University obtained $25,000 to hire an assistant labour studies coordinator; Capilano College received $13,000 for their so-called labour studies program and Northwest Community College received $9,000 for their so-called labour studies program.

I think, in the case of Simon Fraser University, it was a wise decision because Simon Fraser University has, in the first instance, met all the aims of labour education and also the criteria of the labour education program in BC. Since 1975, Simon Fraser University's Continuing Studies has, with CLC and BC Federation of Labour joint sponsorship, held twelve conferences, workshops, seminars, week-end schools and week-long schools which are attended by well over one thousand union representatives, local union officers, stewards and committee members. The topics at these functions ranged from pre-retirement, union counselling, consumer protection, citizen and the law, instructors' training and labour economics.

> *Now, let's take a look at Capilano College, which also wanted to do things for labour. Capilano College presented to a Labour Advisory Committee a program which was a fait accompli, which was not based on any recognized needs within the trade union movement, which was solely originated on the basis of some political romanticism by a few inexperienced well-meaning instructors, which in the beginning spent a considerable amount of monies from regular college budgets with very small enrolment and questionable results, and presently maintains its existence because of a political feud present in the trade union movement in the province.*
>
> *Source:* NAC, *UAW Papers*, MG 28, I 119, Volume 286, File 15, "Paid Educational Leave Conference, Vancouver 1978. Correspondence, Speeches, Report. Part 1 of 2. 1975-1978," Address by Art Kube, Regional Director of Education, Canadian Labour Congress to Delegates Attending the B.C. Association of Continuing Education Administrators Annual Meeting and Conference, 28 April 1978.

The NDP government in Manitoba made a similar commitment to labour education at about this same time. The Manitoba Labour Education Centre that was announced in June 1977 was to be a cooperative venture between the province's universities, community colleges and labour movement. With a projected annual budget of $300,000 in 1977-78 and $500,000 in subsequent years, the centre was to organize and coordinate credit courses and programmes offered by universities and colleges; set up non-credit courses, seminars and conferences; and provide a focus for research and study in labour history, labour relations and labour law. While these extensive plans died when the Conservatives took power later that year, the labour education centre continued to exist with limited government support as a part of the Manitoba Federation of Labour, offering internal union education services. The University of Manitoba, for its part, began a for-credit labour studies programme in 1979 to supplement its long-standing non-credit University-Labour Three-Year Certificate Programme.[37]

In Atlantic Canada, meanwhile, Dalhousie resuscitated its labour-university committee in 1969 to produce a vision of a workers' education programme in Nova Scotia. The committee suggested that the problems of labour education in Nova Scotia at the end of the 1960s consisted of a lack of continuity in programmes, difficulty in formulating effective goals, a failure to structure programmes with respect to needs and to short-term and long-term goals, a lack of effective coordination among the various programmes then in operation and the difficulty of funding programmes and finding suitable educational resources. The committee concluded, referring to the 1956 national labour education conference recommendation that university-based labour studies centres be established across the country, that a labour-university workers' education programme was required in Nova Scotia. They called for an endorsement by the provincial labour movement, a province-wide Nova Scotia Federation of Labour

(NSFL) committee that would form the labour side of a NSFL-Dalhousie Education Committee, a clear statement of educational goals that would form the basis of a programme and coordination with the CLC and the LCC. While nothing came of this initiative, the committee was reactivated again following the 1975 national conference on labour education. Its efforts in the late 1970s were directed primarily at securing some of the Labour Canada monies that were offered briefly in 1978-79 to support labour education initiatives in college and universities, although a Dalhousie Labour Institute was held in 1979.[38]

Despite Dalhousie's activities, St. Francis Xavier continued to be the main centre of university labour education in Nova Scotia and the Atlantic region in the 1970s. While Dalhousie was producing its vision of workers' education, StFX was initiating a certificate course in unionism at its Sydney campus. In 1969-70, twenty unionists enrolled in the first year of the programme, which consisted of five courses over three years, with each course consisting of twenty lectures and an assignment. StFX was also cooperating with the local labour movement to offer short courses, conduct a summer institute and assemble a labour education tool box.[39] The most significant development in this period, however, was the launch of the Atlantic Region Labour Education Centre (ARLEC) in 1972.

The origins of ARLEC lay in the formation of the Atlantic Development Council (ADC) in 1969. Paul LePage and John Lynk, presidents of the New Brunswick and Nova Scotia federations of labour respectively, and ADC members, argued that an education programme for trade unionists should be a component of the council's work. In 1970 representatives of StFX and the CLC crafted a proposal for a labour education centre based at StFX and governed by a board representing StFX and the labour movement. The ADC approved the proposal as part of its development strategy and it became part of a submission made to the federal Department of Regional Economic Expansion (DREE). DREE accepted the proposal, and in 1972 the federal department entered into a formal agreement with StFX to establish and fund the centre. This agreement expired in 1978, at which time ARLEC became the Atlantic-region arm of the CLC's LESC, with funding from Labour Canada. The relationship with StFX continued after 1978, and the Atlantic region was unique in the LESC structure in that it was the only region that worked with a formal university partner.

ARLEC was governed by a board of directors with representation from the ADC, the CLC, the four Atlantic federations of labour and the extension department of StFX. The centre's general purpose was to provide a broader education than was possible in the weekend and week-long schools that were the heart of the CLC's educational system. In the language of the Antigonish Movement, which permeates the archive of the early ARLEC, the purpose was "to sharpen the social consciousness of the unionist rather than their (sic) negotiating and contract administration skills." The hope was that, after returning home, ARLEC students would become active in community, provincial and national affairs. The more specific objectives of the centre's

goals of ARLEC

programme included making union members aware of the role of their union in the community, improving members' ability to analyze social problems and provide alternative solutions, enhancing members' analytical, communication and research skills, and developing personal leadership skills.

From 1972 to 1975 the programme consisted of one two-week module available in English or French. This was supplemented in 1976 by a second two-week module (also in French and English) called ARLEC II, while the first module became ARLEC I. ARLEC II was available only to ARLEC I graduates. The objective of the first module was to develop individual leadership skills in participants, while the objective of the second was to develop team leadership skills. Or, as expressed by a 1976 participant, "ARLEC I builds you up to the point that you leave here full of vim and vigor, ready to conquer the world *on your own.* ARLEC II breaks you down so you realize that you *need other people* to conquer the world, and then shows you how to work with those other people." Participants in the first module were taught media techniques, communications, the Antigonish Movement, political education, poverty in Canada, and social reform and business unionism. Instruction in communications and media techniques continued in the second module and was supplemented by economics and political science.[40]

courses taught

The labour leadership, educational staff and programme participants appear to have greeted ARLEC's birth with enthusiasm. There were some dissenting voices, however. At the launch of the first session in the spring of 1972, a scathing critique of the perceived class-collaborationist nature of the centre's programme appeared in the region's alternative press. Larry Katz (who would later become research director at CUPE) argued that ARLEC "was basically an attempt to instill trade unionists with the ideological biases of management and their labor accomplices." As partial proof, Katz noted that employer-produced materials were used in the programme and that certain individuals affiliated with ARLEC were guilty of anti-labour practices. He concluded that an acceptable alternative to ARLEC had to be economically and politically controlled by working people, and he cited Vancouver's Trade Union Research Bureau (which was anathema to the labour leadership of the early 1970s because of its Communist Party connections) as an exemplary model.[41]

Katz's warnings notwithstanding, a 1981 evaluation of ARLEC's first decade revealed that former participants and instructors felt that their time at the centre was worthwhile and positive, but that there was some room for improvement in the programme. ARLEC I participants were almost unanimous in praising the programme as an excellent learning experience. A minority of respondents commented that there was too much lecturing and not enough time for class discussion in the courses other than Public Speaking, while about half commented that two weeks was too short a time to cover all of the topics adequately. Virtually all ARLEC I graduates went on to other educational activities in the labour movement (Labour College, weekend and week-long schools and so on), and about half pursued more academic training and became

Charles Bauer (second from left), CLC public relations director, talks with Phyllis Margetti (Sydney, Nova Scotia), Derek Ball (Pasadena, Newfoundland), and Bill Carroll (Tantallon, Nova Scotia) at the 1974 session of the Atlantic Region Labour Education Centre. *Canadian Labour Congress Collection.*

more involved in their communities. Slightly less than 100 percent said they had become more active in their union and labour council, the NDP, town council or a similar venue after participating in ARLEC. Some of the participants in the French-language sessions complained that there were not enough materials available in French.

ARLEC II was less favourably received by participants than ARLEC I. They wanted more functional courses and they complained that the existing courses in the second level were not sufficiently labour-oriented, lending credence to Katz's criticism of the inaugural session. One graduate complained, "This school is for the 'lieutenants' of the labour movement and should make us better leaders. But so much emphasis is placed on seeing the other side and sympathizing with management, government and politicians it is little wonder that people leave here confused and uncertain.... This course takes the 'fire' out of good people in the labour movement." Despite these criticisms, which could be extended to earlier StFX labour education endeavours, some ARLEC II graduates suggested there should be an ARLEC III.

Instructors, meanwhile, tended to be more positive in their assessment, although there was general criticism of the overall design and planning of the school. Class instruction was a mix of lectures, questions and answers, and group discussions, and a substantial majority of instructors expressed satisfaction with the level of student participation in the courses. Most instructors felt that ARLEC provided a new beginning for students and a springboard for them to play a new and vital part in their unions and communities. At least one, though, felt there was insufficient labour content in the curriculum and a lack of participation in the programme by ex-students.

Many instructors noted that they had not been given a clear indication of what the organizers of the school expected the participants to receive from their courses. An occupational health and safety instructor, for example, complained that "no concept was expressed in advance as to the goals or content of the session." Furthermore, he did not have enough time in his session to cover the subject adequately, which for him raised basic questions about ARLEC's concerns about occupational health and safety: were students to be given an overview, or introduced in some depth to organizational methods, hazards, legislation and so on? Others suggested that ARLEC should be more closely integrated into the CLC's longer-term objectives and that there was a desperate need for educational opportunities for ARLEC graduates.[42]

ARLEC represented a unique collaboration between a university and labour, and grew out of the long-standing cordial relationship that StFX enjoyed with a significant section of the Atlantic labour movement. The other major university-based labour studies initiative in this period was at McMaster University in Hamilton, Ontario. Here, too, there was promise of a firm university-labour collaboration—largely because the first director at McMaster had a long history in the labour movement—but tension seemed to permeate the relationship from the start.

In 1974 Harry Waisglass, former research director for the Steelworkers, was seconded from the federal Department of Labour to establish a labour studies programme at McMaster University. Over the following two years Waisglass began running weekend and week-long seminars for CUPE and Steelworkers staff and, in collaboration with the Hamilton and District Labour Council, established a certificate programme consisting initially of six thirteen-week courses. In anticipation of the formal opening of the labour studies programme in July 1976, Waisglass told the *Hamilton Spectator* that the purpose of the three-year experimental programme at McMaster was to train the potential leaders of unions who were responsible for administering millions of dollars annually in members' dues. Sounding more like a labour-department bureaucrat than a former union staffer, he added that "[s]ome of the most costly and longest strikes recently have been in the public sector where union leaders and negotiators, who have newly acquired the right to strike, have not fully picked up all the skills required."[43]

Waisglass was successful in securing $200,000 in Ontario government money to help finance his programme over the course of the 1976-77 and 1977-78 fiscal years. He hired Dan Benedict as an assistant to organize joint educational initiatives with the labour movement. Benedict's most significant activity, before moving on to the UAW's Canadian region in 1978 to organize its new paid educational leave programme, was to organize a 1977 conference at McMaster exploring the elusive relationship between union educators and post-secondary institutions.[44]

This was an especially important issue for the McMaster programme because, despite Waisglass's union background, his relations with the labour movement were frosty at times. The OFL noted in 1976, for example, that a CLC advisory committee to the programme had not met for a year and that it appeared that Waisglass was happy to work without it. Furthermore, his objectives for the programme were obscure and he talked in general terms about training trade union representatives as instructors "which would create problems for us." Rather, said the OFL, it was necessary for the labour movement to assert its vision in this area, "otherwise labour education in Ontario [would] fall into the hands of academic empire builders."[45]

Nonetheless, the CLC and McMaster agreed in January 1977 to endorse a set of objectives for a labour studies programme at the university. This included expanding and improving continuous and progressive learning opportunities for workers as individuals and as community leaders; facilitating the use of McMaster's education and research resources to develop the knowledge and skills of the leaders and staff of labour organizations; and encouraging improvements and expansion in labour research and education aimed at strengthening certificate, undergraduate and graduate programmes in the labour field. In the fall of that year, however, CLC Executive Vice-President Julien Major sent a letter to Waisglass indicating that he was asking all labour members of the McMaster advisory committee to withdraw their participation because Waisglass was displaying bad faith with respect to the wishes of the labour members.

By this time, however, the OFL had named McMaster University as a cooperating institution in a $360,000 grant application to the Ontario government to support the training of occupational health and safety officers. Their plan was to teach occupational health and safety instructors to train health and safety committee members to work on job sites. The money would pay for ten three-hour modules and a resource data bank. The CLC letter to McMaster was delicate for the OFL, therefore, because the federation needed the university partnership in order to receive the grant. This problem was resolved, however, when the OFL replaced McMaster with the Ontario region Labour Education and Studies Centre as the cooperating "institution" for purposes of the grant application.[46]

Throughout the 1970s, the CLC and the labour movement generally had been trying to establish some general operating principles to guide their relations with colleges and universities in order to ensure that their interests were protected and promoted. In 1971, the CLC and the OFL offered the following direction for Ontario trade unionists forced to deal with a community college-based programme: labour councils should determine what courses colleges could offer trade unionists, a labour advisory committee should be established, the college should be discouraged from offering tools courses, economics and industrial relations were appropriate academic subjects for colleges to offer, and instructors should be selected with care to ensure they are sympathetic to and understand the labour movement.[47]

In 1977 the CLC redrafted and expanded these guidelines to govern the relationship between the LESC and colleges and universities. Under the new rules, college and university programmes would operate under the "umbrella" of the national and regional LESCs and would come under the control of the labour movement. More specifically, post-secondary labour studies programmes were to be managed by a committee appointed by the relevant labour council or federation, with responsibility for all aspects of the programme including instructor selection, the establishment of fees and course content and materials. In addition, if a full-time administrator was required, that person would be appointed by the union committee following consultation with the institution involved. While the CLC recognized that some institutions offered labour-related courses or programmes for a general audience, and it supported public awareness of the labour movement, it was concerned that trade unionists might confuse these programmes with CLC-sanctioned ones. Hence the congress endeavoured to ensure that no labour organization was associated by name with courses that did not follow the general guidelines, that such courses were monitored to determine whether or not they met with the CLC's approval and that suggestions for curriculum content were established and distributed to colleges and universities.[48]

The CLC sent these guidelines to every college and university president in Canada. In addition, labour leaders and staff took various opportunities to communicate their position to post-secondary educators. At the 1977 McMaster conference on labour-university relations, for example, the CLC's Julien Major made it clear to all assembled that the LESC would be a labour-controlled enterprise: most instructors would come from the labour movement, and all course content would be controlled by the central administration and, ultimately, by the CLC executive council. It was possible for university and college programmes to collaborate with the LESC, he allowed, but programmes outside the labour movement would have to adhere to the CLC's ground rules.

Further, at a 1978 labour-university consultation in Toronto, attended by twenty-five post-secondary and union educators, labour spokespeople such as Larry Wagg of the CLC, James Dowell of CUPE and Greg Murtagh of the OFL made it clear to the college and university folks that the labour movement would set the labour education agenda. There was a role for colleges and universities in assisting with new areas such as occupational health and safety or doing relevant research, they conceded. The labour movement, however, "resented" notions such as that of academic freedom, which they claimed provided too much autonomy for post-secondary educators but which educational workers had struggled for decades to achieve and were finally beginning to enshrine in collective agreements during the 1970s.

Post-secondary educators such as Alan Thomas of the Ontario Institute for Studies in Education and Walter Pitman of Ryerson Polytechnical Institute, for their part, cautioned the trade unionists against being too confrontational in insisting on complete control of all aspects of college- and university-based labour studies programmes. Indeed, Pitman argued that it was illegal in Ontario for outside groups to have the degree of control over post-secondary programmes that the union educators were demanding.[49]

Post-secondary educators, meanwhile, were renewing their interest in labour education during the late 1970s, not only because of the perceived opportunities associated with the LESC, but also because Labour Canada announced in 1977 that it would begin providing direct support for labour education initiatives in colleges and universities. Although this programme was terminated after only one year, it did spark a flurry of projects across the country that strengthened existing provision in some cases and sparked new programmes in others. Niagara and Humber colleges in Ontario and Capilano College in British Columbia, for example, used their grants to develop new courses and materials to augment their established programmes, while Confederation College in Thunder Bay developed courses as part of a process to establish a Labour Studies Centre for Northern Ontario. The University of Saskatchewan, too, applied for and received funds for course development to begin to build a labour studies programme. And Athabasca University undertook a provincial labour education needs assessment for the Alberta Federation of Labour, which laid part of the groundwork for the subsequent development of that university's labour studies programme.[50]

Conclusion

By the mid-1980s labour education had the outward appearance of stability and prosperity, while its practice was beginning to change in response to the increasingly hostile environment workers and their unions were facing. The heightened government and employer attacks on workers were creating conditions that required changes in the way union education was conducted while, at the same time, a significant infusion of government money designed to soften the blows from these attacks was reinforcing inherited union educational structures. The changed conditions for workers meant that a system of union education that focused almost exclusively on training local leaders and stewards to perform their roles in the industrial relations system was no longer adequate. Furthermore, new voices in the movement were demanding to be heard. In some areas, such as women's programming and political education, shifts were evident. And in new initiatives, such as the Steelworkers' "back to the locals" campaign, PSAC's Union Development Program and the UAW's

PEL programme, a renewed emphasis on member-centred mobilizing was apparent. The LESC, meanwhile, built a significant bank of labour educational resources, but failed in the area of audio-visual production where it attempted to build its own capacity and rely less on external resources.

The LESC's grant did allow the Labour College of Canada to continue to teach its residential and distance education courses, and to offer advanced courses and seminars for graduates of the residential programme. And, despite the misgivings of some of the instructors, the college did make a concerted effort in the early 1980s to temper the university-level instruction with adult education methods. The dispute over collective bargaining rights, however, suggests that the labour leaders on the Board of Governors felt that the principles that were being taught in the college classrooms did not extend to those doing the teaching.

Labour studies programmes, meanwhile, were established in colleges and universities across Canada during this period as a result of the expansion of colleges and universities since the 1960s, the presence of progressive and union-friendly academic staff in these institutions, provincial government money for such things as occupational health and safety training and the short-lived federal government funding for post-secondary labour education. Yet despite decades of complaints about how publicly funded post-secondary educational institutions ignored them, trade unionists responded to these developments with scepticism and suspicion. Bolstered by the government funding they were receiving, the labour movement told college- and university-based labour educators that it was no longer interested in their services unless it could control the relationship completely.

Notes

1. Craig Heron, *The Canadian Labour Movement: A Short History,* 2d ed. (Toronto: James Lorimer and Company, 1996), chapter 5; Alvin Finkel, *Our Lives: Canada Since 1945* (Toronto: James Lorimer and Company, 1997), 145-152, 268-271, 284-287.

2. Gordon Selman, "Alan Thomas and the Canadian Association for Adult Education, 1961-1970," and "Specialization or Balkanization: Organizations of Adult Educators," and "Between Social Movement and Profession: A Historical Perspective on Canadian Adult Education," in Selman, *Adult Education in Canada: Historical Essays* (Toronto: Thompson Educational Publishing, 1995), 201-262, 103-116, 29-36.

3. NAC, *UAW Papers,* MG 28 I 119, Volume 286, File 18, "Paid Education Leave. Correspondence, Printed material, Holograph notes. Part 1 of 2. 1974-1976," Fritz Bauer, Assistant Director, Education, PSAC, to Gord Wilson, 26 March 1975; NAC, *CLC Papers,* MG 28 I 103, Volume 478, File 1, "National Education Advisory Committee Meeting, 19-20 November 1975," [Public Service Alliance of Canada,] "Union Development Program"; Interview with Bob Hatfield, 12 May 2000.

4. D'Arcy Martin, *Thinking Union: Activism and Education in Canada's Labour Movement* (Toronto: Between the Lines, 1995), 16-20; Interview with D'Arcy Martin, 13 April 2000; NAC, *CLC Papers,* MG 28 I 103, Accession 86/0112, Volume 13, File "Labour Education—General 1978-1979," *Worker Education, Real Power: A Report and Proposals on the Education Program in District 6, Based on Consultations with Local Unions held between October 1977 and May 1978, Prepared by the Education Office, National Office [United Steelworkers of America]*, November 1978. Go to www.thompsonbooks.com/unionlearning to hear an audio clip of D'Arcy Martin discussing his approach to labour education.

5. Interview with D'Arcy Martin, 13 April 2000; Edward E. Seymour, *An Illustrated History of Canadian Labour* (Ottawa: Canadian Labour Congress, 1976); Interview with Elisabeth Plettenberg, May Day 2000; interview with Art Kube, June 1, 2000.

6. Joy Langan, "Trade union women's committees," *Canadian Labour* (September 1976): 12-13, 21; NAC, *Canadian Union of Public Employees (CUPE) Papers,* MG 28 I 234, Volume 24, File 5, "Education Department Meetings, August 1970—November 1974," 19 November 1974 circular from James Dowell, and Volume 32, File 5, "Equal Opportunity at Work—A CUPE Affirmative Action Manual (CUPE Education Department)"; "CUPE programme for women's year," *Canadian Labour* (June 1975): 16-18; Margot Trevelyan, *Don't Call Me Baby* (Ottawa/Montreal: National Film Board and the Canadian Union of Public Employees, 1976).

7. Interview with Elisabeth Plettenberg, May Day 2000; D'Arcy Martin, *Thinking Union,* 56.

8. *Democratic Socialism in the '70's: Past, Present and Future* (Political Education Departments of the Ontario Federation of Labour and the Canadian Labour Congress, 1973).

9. NAC, *CLC Papers,* MG 28 I 103, Accession 86/0112, Volume 16, File "National Political Education Committee Meeting, July 31, 1978," Pat Kerwin to NPEC members 30 June 1978, and Volume 18, File "Political Education Committee Program, 1979-1980," various documents; Cynthia Law-Butler, *The Canadian Labour Congress's Parallel Campaigns for the New Democratic Party, 1979 and 1980,* Master of Arts Research Essay, Carleton University, 1980; Interview with Pat Kerwin, 17 April 2000.

10. UBC Library, Special Collections, *CLC Education Office (British Columbia) Records*, Box 2, Folder 32, "National Education Advisory Committee, 1973," Bert Hepworth to NEAC, 11 May 1973; NAC, *CLC Papers*, MG 28 I 103, Volume 477, File 11, Minutes of Meeting of NEAC, 25-26 July 1973.

11. *The Case of Barbara Parsons* (Montreal: National Film Board, 1978); NAC, *CLC Papers*, MG 28 I 103, Volume 477, File 12, Resume of discussions with Morten Parker and Sub-committee of National Education Advisory Committee and others, February 1975, and Minutes of a meeting of NEAC, 19-20 November 1975; NAC, *CLC Papers*, MG 28 I 103, Accession 84/0293, Volume 71, File "Audio-Visual: Production of new film on grievances (1975)," Julien Major to Thomas Eberlee, Deputy Minister of Labour, 11 January 1977, and Volume 71, File "Films and Video-tapes—1975-Dec 1977," Julien Major to Thomas Eberlee, 2 March 1977, and Morten Parker to Larry Wagg, 22 June 1977; NAC, *CLC Papers*, MG 28 I 103, Accession 86/0112, Volume 12, File "Films and Video Tapes, 1978-1979," Julien Major to Thomas Eberlee, 26 March 1979 and Clare Booker to Larry Wagg, 29 March 1979. Go to http://unionlearning.athabascau.ca to see a video clip from *The Case of Barbara Parsons*.

12. NAC, *CLC Papers*, MG 28 I103, Accession 92/0293, Volume 71, File "Films and Video-tapes—1975-Dec 1977," Clare Booker to Larry Wagg, 9 October 1975, re. Challenge for Change program, NFB, and Jim Gill, Executive Secretary, Labour Council of Metropolitan Toronto, to Larry Wagg, 14 January 1977. Go tohttp://unionlearning.athabascau.ca to see a video clip from *Our Health Is Not for Sale* (Montreal: National Film Board, 1978), a Challenge for Change production on occupational health and safety.

13. "Ottawa wants educational leaves," *The Globe and Mail*, 14 June 1977; NAC, *UAW Papers*, MG 28 I 119, Volume 286, File 14, "Paid Educational Leave Conference, Windsor 1977. Leaflets, Discussion paper, Notes. 1977," J.K Eaton, Labour Canada, "Paid Educational Leave," September 1977, and Volume 282, File 2, "Canadian Labour Congress and other Unions on Paid Educational Leave. Correspondence, Policy, printed material. Part 1 of 2, 1975-1979," CLC policy statement on Paid Educational Leave, Paid Educational Leave—Working Paper, recommended by the [CLC] National Education Advisory Committee, June 1977, and C.A. Edwards, President, PSAC, to PSAC Board of Directors, 29 March 1976.

14. NAC, *UAW Papers*, MG 28 I 119, Volume 282, File 3, "Canadian Labour Congress and other Unions on Paid Educational Leave. Correspondence, Policy, printed material. Part 2 of 2, 1975-1979," Response of the Canadian Labour Congress to *Education and Working Canadians*, Report of the Commission of Inquiry on Educational Leave and Productivity, November 1979; Skill Development Leave Task Force, *Learning a Living in Canada*, Report to the Minister of Employment and Immigration Canada (Ottawa: Employment and Immigration Canada, 1984); D'Arcy Martin and Ian Curtin, "The School of Hard Knocks: Labour Market Planning and Educational Leave," Background Paper 19, Skill Development Leave Task Force (Ottawa: Employment and Immigration Canada, 1983).

15. Reuben Roth, *"Kitchen Economics for the Family": Paid-Education Leave and the Canadian Autoworkers Union*, Master of Arts thesis, Ontario Institute for Studies in Education, University of Toronto, 1997, chapters 2 and 3; NAC, *UAW Papers*, MG 28 I 119, Volume 286, File 18, "Paid Education Leave. Correspondence, Printed material, Holograph notes. Part 1 of 2. 1974-1976," Paid Education Leave, and Volume 286, File 20, "Paid Education Leave. List of Paid Education Leave Negotiated Agreements, Bankbook, Statements. 1976-1979," Gordon Wilson, "Paid Education Leave," and Volume 282, File 14, "Correspondence: Gordon F. Wilson, Director of Education for Canada—Other Trade Unions," Bruce Davidson, Assistant Education Director, to Cyril McGuire, 6 December 1977.

16. Interview with Gordon Wilson conducted by Nicholas Saul, August 1993, and quoted in Nicholas J. Saul, "'Organizing the Organized': The Canadian Auto Workers' Paid Educational Leave (PEL) Programme," Master of Arts dissertation (University of Warwick, 1994), 19; NAC, *UAW Papers*, MG 28 I 119, Volume 282, File 3, "Canadian Labour Congress and other unions on Paid Educational Leave. Correspondence, Policy, printed material. Part 2 of 2, 1975-1979," "Paid Education Leave is underway," *UAW Solidarity*

(October 1978), and Volume 282, File 16, "Correspondence: Gordon F. Wilson, Director of Education for Canada—Local union Presidents," Circular letter, 3 January 1979.

17. NAC, *UAW Papers*, MG 28 I 119, Volume 282, File 20, "Correspondence: Gordon F. Wilson, Director of Education for Canada—Robert White, Director for Canada and International Vice-President," Robert White to Doug Fraser, 4 May 1978; Roth, *Kitchen Economics*, 71-73.

18. NAC, *UAW Papers*, MG 28 I 119, Volume 282, File 14, "Correspondence: Gordon F. Wilson, Director of Education for Canada—Len Hope, Administrative Director UAW," Len Hope to presidents and financial secretaries at locals 397, 1325 and 1474, 7 July 1978, and Volume 284, File 28, "Federal Commission of Inquiry on 'Educational Leave and Productivity'. Correspondence, Briefs to the Commission. Part 2 of 3. 1978-1979," UAW-Paid Education Leave Program September 19 through December 21, 1978, Report to Canadian Region UAW District Council, January 26 1979.

19. NAC, *CLC Papers*, MG 28 I 103, Volume 477, File 13, Notes on NEAC Think Tank, UAW Education Centre, Black Lake, Michigan, 29-30 May 1975; Gary Dickinson and Coolie Verner, *Education within the Canadian Labour Congress* (Vancouver: Adult Education Research Centre, University of British Columbia, 1973), 93.

20. NAC, *UAW Papers*, MG 28 I 119, Volume 287, File 9, "Paid Educational Leave Trust Fund. Correspondence, Agreement, Reports. Part 4 or 4. 1976-1979," A Labour Education and Studies Centre for Canada, Report of the Feasibility Study, Committee of the Canadian Labour Congress, Ottawa, Canada, February 1976; Larry Wagg, "Towards a Labour Studies Centre," *Canadian Labour* (December 1976): 2-3, 30.

21. Brian Pearl, ed., *Labour in Canada: Report of the National Conference on Labour Education* (Ottawa: Information Canada, 1975), 73-83; "Ottawa to give CLC $10 million for labour education," *The Globe and Mail*, 20 May 1977, A1; NAC, *CLC Papers*, MG 28 I 103, Volume 71, File "NEAC Meeting June 15, 1977, Toronto," Agreement between the Government of Canada and the Canadian Labour Congress, 20 May 1977; Larry Wagg, "CLC Labour Education and Studies Centre," *Canadian Labour* (December 1977): 25-27, 31; Interview with Larry Wagg, 11 April 2000.

22. NAC, *CLC Papers*, MG 28 I 103, Accession 86/0112, Volume 13, File "Labour Education and Studies Centre, General—1978," Larry Wagg to Gower Markle, 21 September 1978, and Volume 16, File "National Education and Studies Centre, National Coordinating Committee," Toward the 1979-80 Programme Year, and Volume 9, File "B.C. Winter School—1980," Art Kube to Larry Wagg, 20 June 1980; Interview with Larry Wagg, 11 April 2000; Interview with D'Arcy Martin, 13 April 2000; Alan M. Thomas and David S. Abbey, *Evaluation of Labour Canada's Labour Education Program (1977-1981)* (Toronto: Ontario Institute for Studies in Education, 1982), 240-288.

23. NAC, *CLC Papers*, MG 28 I 103, Accession 86/0112, Volume 13, File "Labour Education and Studies Centre, General—1978," Julien Major to Larry Wagg, 11 September 1978, and Volume 13, File "Labour Education and Studies Centre—Pacific Regional Board, 1977-78," Minutes of meeting of CLC-LESC, Pacific Region, 28 November 1978.

24. NAC, *CLC Papers*, MG 28 I 103, Accession 86/0112, Volume 20, File "VTR Equipment," Larry Wagg to Don Montgomery, 30 March 1976, and Volume 16, File "National Education and Studies Centre, National Coordinating Committee," Toward the 1979-80 Programme Year; Interview with D'Arcy Martin, 13 April 2000; Alan M. Thomas and David S. Abbey, *Labour Canada's Labour Education Program. Preliminary Evaluation: The First Two Years (1977-78; 1978-79)* (Toronto: Ontario Institute for Studies in Education, 1980), 282-290.

25. Thomas and Abbey, *Labour Canada's Labour Education Program, Preliminary Evaluation*, 297-309; Thomas and Abbey, *Labour Canada's Labour Education Program (1977-1981)*, 357-360, 275-278.

26. NAC, *CLC Papers*, MG 28 I 103, Accession 86/0112, Volume 13, File "Labour College of Canada, General—1979," Interim Report on the Future Role of the Labour College of Canada, August 1978.

27. NAC, *CLC Papers*, MG 28 I 103, Accession 86/0112, Volume 13, File "Labour College of Canada, General. 1979," Report of the Registrar and Secretary-Treasurer to the Meeting of the Board of Governors, Labour College of Canada, 17 April 1979 and Labour College of Canada, Report of the 1979 Session by Robert Bisson, Coordinator of Studies.

28. Interview with Bob Hatfield, 12 May 2000.

29. NAC, *CLC Papers*, MG 28 I 103, Accession 84/0293, Volume 71, File "Labour College of Canada—Current Correspondence, October 1975-December 1977," Report of the Registrar and Secretary-Treasurer to Meeting of the Board of Governors, 2 December 1976; NAC, *CLC Papers*, MG 28 I 103, Accession 86/0112, Volume 13, File "Labour College of Canada, General, 1979," Statement of Revenue for the year ended 31 December 1978, and Statement of Revenue for the year ended 31 December 1979, and Volume 16, File "National Education and Studies Centre, National Coordinating Committee," Toward the 1979-80 Programme Year.

30. John Bullen, "'Rewarding Your Enemies, Punishing Your Friends': The Labour College Strike of 1983," *Labour/Le Travail* 27 (Spring 1991): 163-174.

31. NAC, *ACTWU Papers*, MG 28 I 219, File 16, "Education. John Whitehouse Correspondence. 1963-1967," various letters and clippings; NAC, *CLC Papers*, MG 28 I 103, Accession 86/0112, Volume 21, File "Survey of Union Education in Canada—CCL and TLC period (Mrs. Maynard, UBC)," John Whitehouse to Coolie Verner, 2 November 1971; "Labour Program at Niagara College," *Canadian Labour* (December, 1971): 11-12; NAC, *John R.W. Whitehouse fonds*, MG 31 B 35, "Finding Aid."

32. University of Toronto, Industrial Relations Library, *Education and Labour File, 1951-1971*, John R.W. Whitehouse, "College-Centred Labour Education: A Trade Union Approach" (March 1968), 5-6, and J.R.W. Whitehouse, "The Implications of College-Centred Labour Education" (17 February 1969), Social Foundations of Adult Education, Ontario Institute for Studies in Education; J.R.W. Whitehouse, "Toward a College-Centred Labour Studies Program," *Continuous Learning* 7 (6) (November-December 1968): 265-272; J.R. Kidd, *The Implications of Continuous Learning* (Toronto: W.T. Gage, 1966). Whitehouse also wrote the following while at OISE: "The Labour College of Canada" (October 1965); "Workers' Education in Canada: Some Social, Political and Economic Influences Affecting its Historical Development," (April 1967); "University-Centred Labour Education: The United States Model with Particular Reference to the Labor Education Program at Rutgers, The State University" (November 1967); and "The International Agencies and Workers' Education with particular reference to the Role of the ICFTU" (April 1968). He later self-published J.R.W. Whitehouse, *From Union Hall to Labour College of Canada: An Historical Perspective* (Port Credit, Ontario, 1971).

33. NAC, *CLC Papers*, MG 28 I 103, Volume 477, File 1, "Centre for Labour Studies, Humber College."

34. UBC Library, Special Collections, *CLC Education Office (British Columbia) Records*, Box 2, Folder 12, "Capilano College, 1974," Garth Edge to Lincoln Bishop, 16 August 1970, and A.L. Hepworth to Garth Edge, 25 August 1970, and Box 2, Folder 13, "Cariboo College, 1973," Bert Hepworth to Ron Tweedie, 19 June 1973.

35. UBC Library, Special Collections, *CLC Education Office (British Columbia) Records*, Box 2, Folder 12, "Capilano College, 1974," P.J. Spratt, Principal, Capilano College to Art Kube, CLC Regional Education Director, 20 November 1974; UBC Library, Special Collections, *VDLC Records*, Box 12, Folder 24, "Labour Studies Program Advisory Committee," Minutes Capilano Labour Studies Programme Advisory Committee meeting, 2 March 1976.

36. NAC, *CLC Papers*, MG 28 I 103, Accession 86/0112, Volume 19, File "Report of the Department of Education, Jan 1 to Dec 31, 1976"; NAC, *UAW Papers*, MG 28, I 119, Volume 286, File 15, "Paid Educational Leave Conference, Vancouver 1978. Correspondence, Speeches, Report. Part 1 of 2. 1975-1978," Address by Art Kube, Regional Director of Education, Canadian Labour Congress to Delegates Attending the BC Association of

Continuing Education Administrators Annual Meeting and Conference, 28 April 1978; UBC Library, Special Collections, *CLC Education Office (British Columbia) Records*, Box 3, Folder 19, "Adult Education," A Proposal Submitted by The Centre for Continuing Education," UBC, no date (but early 1970s).

37. NAC, *CLC Papers*, MG 28 I 103, Accession 92/0195, Volume 236, File "Labour Studies Centre—Manitoba," Manitoba Government Press Release, 17 June 1977; NAC, *CLC Papers*, MG 28 I 103, Accession 86/0112, Volume 12, File "Grants Committee, Labour Canada," Art Coulter, Executive Secretary, Manitoba Federation of Labour to Larry Wagg, 14 July 1978, and Volume 11, File "Conference on Labour Education, Winnipeg, November 5-6, 1979," Report.

38. NAC, *CLC Papers*, MG 28 I 103, Volume 477, File 1, Dalhousie Labor-University Committee, Toward a Labor-University Worker's Education Program in Nova Scotia, no date (but 1969); NAC, *CLC Papers*, MG 28 I 103, Accession 86/0112, Volume 11, File "Dalhousie Labour-University Education Committee—1978-79," various minutes of meetings.

39. StFX University Archives, *Extension Department Records*, RG 30-3, Review of the work of the extension department of St. Francis Xavier University, May 1968-June 1969 and June 1969-June 1970.

40. StFX University Archives, *Extension Department Records*, RG 30-3, Review of the work of the extension department of St. Francis Xavier University, June 1971-1972, and "Atlantic Region Labour Education Centre," and "24 March 1973 speech by Rev. G.E. Topshee to Grand Falls and District Labour Council"; Mark Alexander, "ARLEC is helping things happen in the Maritimes," *Labour Gazette* (December 1976): 644 (emphasis in the original).

41. StFX University Archives, *Extension Department Records*, RG 30-3, clipping, Larry Katz, "ARLEC isn't the Answer: The Labor Movement Must Train Its Own People," *The 4th Estate* (June 1, 1972).

42. StFX University Archives, *Report of an Evaluation of the Atlantic Region Labour Education Centre (ARLEC), March 1972 to February 1981* (February 1981), 55-56 and *passim*, 64, 64-68.

43. NAC, *CLC Papers*, MG 28 I 103, Accession 92/0195, Volume 236, File "McMaster—General Correspondence 1977—," The McMaster Labour Studies Programme, May 1976; NAC, *Lincoln Bishop Papers*, MG 31 B 18, Volume 13, File 27, Clipping, "Degrees for labor leaders may be a reality in a few years," *The Spectator* [Hamilton], Saturday, 29 May 1976.

44. NAC, *CLC Papers*, MG 28 I 103, Accession 92/0195, Volume 236, File "McMaster—Press Clippings," "Labour Ministry Contributes $50,000 to Labour Studies Program," Ontario Government Press Release, 19 January 1977, and "Labour Course for unionists produces first graduates," *Globe and Mail*, 23 June 1977. Despite Benedict's long history of involvement in the international labour movement, CLC Executive Vice-President Julien Major wrote to Larry Wagg, CLC education director: "If this guy [Benedict] is a labor education specialist then you and I are specialists' specialists in labour education." NAC, *CLC Papers*, MG 28 I 103, Accession 92/0195, Volume 236, File "McMaster—General Correspondence, 1977—," Julien Major to Larry Wagg, 3 February 1977.

45. NAC, *CLC Papers*, MG 28 I 103, Accession 92/0195, Volume 236, File "McMaster—General Correspondence, 1977—-," [Ontario Federation of Labour,] McMaster University Labour Studies Program. Probable subjects for discussion on 20 December, 1976, 17 December 1976.

46. NAC, *CLC Papers*, MG 28 I 103, Accession 92/0195, Volume 236, File "McMaster—General Correspondence, 1977—," Draft joint statement re. Joint Committee on McMaster University Labour Studies Programme, 26 January 1977, and Volume 236, File "National Education Advisory Committee Meeting, Ottawa—Nov. 8-9, 1977," Minutes of NEAC Meeting, 8 November 1977.

47. UBC Library, Special Collections, *CLC Education Office (British Columbia) Records*, Box 2, Folder 8, "CLC Circular Letters—A.L. Hepworth—Jan 1973—May 1974," Larry Wagg and Henry Weisbach to all labour councils in Ontario, 14 October 1971.

48. NAC, *CLC Papers*, MG 28 I 103, Accession 84/0293, Volume 71, File "NEAC Meeting—June 15, 1977, Toronto," The Relationship between the CLC Labour Education and Studies Centre Programmes and Colleges and Universities.

49. NAC, *CLC Papers*, MG 28 I 103, Accession 86/0112, Volume 9, File "Canadian Association for Adult Education Labour Education Committee," Ian Morrison to Participants in the Consultation Meetings on Labour Education, Re: Draft edited transcript of proceedings, 11 July 1978.

50. Thomas and Abbey, *Evaluation of Labour Canada's Labour Education Program (1977-1981)*, 311-316, 329-330; Abram G. Konrad, D. Bruce Baker, and William W. McNairn, *Labour Education in Alberta: An Assessment of Activities, Needs and Preferences* (Edmonton: Centre for the Study of Postsecondary Education, University of Alberta, 1979).

CHAPTER 6

Rebuilding a Movement: 1986-2000

The labour movement continued to be challenged during the final fifteen years of the century by aggressive employers who took advantage of a global environment in which workers' rights and standards of living were under attack. Nothing seemed to be safe as employers reorganized workplaces and reopened collective agreements to extract more profit, and governments sold off public services and reduced spending on social services that workers and other citizens had struggled for decades to achieve. Workers, however, were not passive. While it had taken unions some time to adapt to the changing circumstances that began to develop in earnest during the 1970s, by the 1980s it was clear that they had to defend their rights and interests themselves and in concert with others who shared their values.

In union education, the new approaches that had been introduced in the 1970s and early 1980s were broadened and deepened. A new emphasis on activist education meant that general membership mobilization became at least as important as leadership and activist training. In addition, the scope of union education widened as the labour movement became more directly involved in the delivery of workplace training. Labour studies in colleges and universities, meanwhile, reached a new level of maturity with older programmes expanding and newer ones being formed. Some new alliances with the labour movement developed, such as those involving Athabasca University's new distance education labour studies programme, but a gulf remained between unions and educational institutions for the most part. In the latter half of the period there was an unsuccessful attempt to unite university and college labour educators in a common organization.

Context

In the late 1980s and during the 1990s there was general agreement among members of the employing class and their friends in government about how to ensure the country's economic health. Businesses had to be allowed to operate with as little public regulation as possible; government spending, especially on social programmes, had to be cut; government services had to be sold to private investors or contracted out to private companies; unions, especially those in the public sector, had to be restrained; and taxes had to be cut. In other words, "economic fundamentals" had to be established that would ensure rising corporate profits, stable or declining labour costs, and fewer and less expensive public services.

Successive Conservative and Liberal federal governments—joined by their provincial counterparts—used the alleged threat of a debt crisis to slash social spending, sell off valuable government assets and fire public-sector workers. Furthermore, in order to control inflation and keep unemployment high, the Bank of Canada continued to pursue a high interest-rate policy that was, in fact, the major cause of government debt in the first place. During the 1980s employer groups such as the Business Council on National Issues pressured governments to allow the "market" to operate freely, which really meant allowing privately held corporations to function without public restraints. The pursuit of free trade—or the elimination of various governmental controls on business activity—became the centrepiece of this right-wing programme. The Canada-United States Trade Agreement came into effect in 1989 and was followed by the more far-reaching North American Free Trade Agreement in 1992. Besides lowering a number of tariffs, these agreements had the more profound effect of encouraging Canadian businesses to demand further cuts in public spending and worker protections in order to compete with their United States and Mexican counterparts.

Inside their own firms, meanwhile, employers were closing plants and relocating to areas with lower labour costs, merging with competitors and laying off workers. Those workers who remained on their jobs faced new computer technologies, new forms of work organization and deteriorating terms and conditions of employment. The proportion of workers using computers at work increased from 15 to nearly 50 percent between 1985 and 1994, and this new technology allowed employers to reduce their workforces, monitor workers more closely and organize production among a variety of plants around the world.

The introduction of new technologies was coupled with the rise of a so-called "new human-resource management" that sought to create a new spirit of employer-worker cooperation in workplaces. Schemes such as Total Quality Management, Japanese Production Management and so forth were designed to exploit worker solidarity in order to increase productivity by reorganizing workers into "teams." Employers hoped that workers would force each other to work harder through loyalty to the team and that they would identify more closely with the company and management. The impact of these schemes in Canadian workplaces was limited compared to American ones, but the fervour with which many employers pursued them cost workers and their unions valuable time and energy in responding to human-resource managers' bright ideas. While employers used the jargon of the new human-resource management to try to convince workers that they were all part of one big happy company family, their behaviour at the bargaining table told a different story. The pattern of aggressive employer demands that appeared in the late 1970s and early 1980s continued and many workers—such as those at Gainers in Edmonton in 1986— had to conduct long and bitter strikes simply to maintain contracts. By the 1990s, Canadian workers faced a labour market that offered little job security, fewer well-paying, full-time jobs than there had been previously, and severely reduced government support in the case of unemployment.

Unions, placed on the defensive in this period by the incessant battering at the hands of governments and employers, developed new strategies to defend their members. The movement for Canadian autonomy continued in the late 1980s and reached its most acrimonious level when the Newfoundland Fishermen, Food, and Allied Workers decided to leave the American-based United Food and Commercial Workers' Union (UFCW) to join the Canadian Auto Workers (CAW). The Canadian leaders of international unions charged the CAW with raiding, and Bob White, the autoworkers' leader, countered that many of those unions provided less than democratic representation for their Canadian members. While the issue was never resolved to anyone's satisfaction, the various parties did agree to disagree. Bob White went on to become president of the Canadian Labour Congress (CLC), serving in that capacity for most of the 1990s and symbolizing the fact that, by the middle of that decade, less than 30 percent of organized workers in Canada belonged to international unions. Before he retired in 1999, White succeeded in convincing the construction unions in the Canadian Federation of Labour (CFL) to return to the CLC fold.

One of the results of the various breakaways from American-based international unions, in combination with the generally hostile climate for unions and workers in this period, was a wave of mergers to form a smaller number of larger unions. The CAW, for example, grew from a union of primarily autoworkers in the mid-1980s to a general union by the mid-1990s that included railway workers from the old Canadian Brotherhood of Railway, Transport and General Workers (CBRT), electrical workers from the old United Electrical, Radio and Machine Workers (UE), various workers from a number of Confederation of Canadian Unions (CCU) affiliates and some newly organized workers in the retail sector. Similarly the Steelworkers transformed themselves into a general, multi-purpose union with the addition of retail workers and rubber workers among others. Even the federation of provincial government employees in the country joined the trend by bringing brewery workers into its fold and subsequently changing its name from the National Union of Provincial Government Employees to the National Union of Public and General Employees (NUPGE).

While this organizational transformation was taking place, the face of the labour movement continued to change as women gained more prominent roles in unions and minority groups demanded more attention to issues that they considered important. Grace Hartman became president of the Canadian Union of Public Employees (CUPE)—Canada's largest union—in 1985 and Shirley Carr, also from CUPE, became CLC president the following year. And in 1987 Gwen Wolfe became the first woman to head a provincial federation of labour when she was elected president of the Nova Scotia Federation of Labour. By the mid-1990s it was commonplace to find women in leadership positions in the Canadian labour movement, with, for example, women occupying the presidencies of the federations of labour in the three prairie provinces. In addition, by the end of the century most labour organizations had active women's committees and guaranteed a minimum number of seats for women on their executive boards. While women had made significant strides in improving their wages and working conditions and in combating sexual harassment and discrimination in the workplace and in their unions over the previous thirty years, many issues were still on the table. Women continued to earn substantially less on average than did their male counterparts, and such long-standing demands as affordable day care were still a long way from being achieved. Furthermore, many positive changes that had been won were being eroded or rolled back in a more hostile climate; Ontario's pay-equity legislation, for example, which promised to deliver equal pay for work of equal value, was scrapped by the Conservative government when it assumed power in 1995.

Workers of colour, lesbians and gays, and the disabled began in the 1980s to meet in informal caucuses to discuss their specific issues. Groups such as the Workers of Colour Support Network in Manitoba, formed in 1985, put pressure on the labour movement to address concerns such as workplace discrimination and harassment. By the 1990s anti-racism education and anti-discrimination policies were a feature of many unions and federations, and some unions were demanding anti-discrimination clauses in collective agreements. In 1987 the Ontario Federation of Labour (OFL) became the first labour organization in the country to create a position on its executive for a visible-minority representative; the CLC followed suit in 1992 with two seats (one male, one female) on its executive council. While the labour movement is changing slowly to accommodate these new realities, minority groups—such as women—are finding it difficult to move their workplace agendas forward in the face of hostile employers.

One of the many positive outcomes of the recognition of the labour movement's diversity has been its effect on union politics. In developing their own voices inside unions, women and minorities cultivated connections and drew strength from broader communities. These workers saw themselves as female (or feminist) unionists, workers of colour, or lesbian or gay unionists. They were more than pure-and-simple unionists and, as a result, were open to working with communities and groups outside of the labour movement with whom they shared a common cause. Whereas in the past labour's involvement in politics had meant primarily working to elect New Democratic Party (NDP) candidates or quietly lobbying governments, unionists increasingly worked in broad-based coalitions in this period designed to influence public policy on specific issues by bringing together citizens from a variety of constituencies. The most notable part of this movement was the Action Canada Network, which began life as the Pro-Canada Network fighting against the Canada-United States Free Trade Agreement in the late 1980s. For many unionists and other citizens, the NDP's weak opposition to this trade agreement meant that they had to build their own structures to ensure that their voices would be heard in this defining moment in Canada's political history. While the Conservative government promoting the trade agreement was re-elected in 1988 (though a majority of voters supported parties opposed to the agreement), an alternative left politics was born that weakened labour's automatic commitment to the NDP and, more importantly, created ongoing links between the labour movement and what became known as its coalition partners.

This trend continued and deepened as a result of labour's experience with the first NDP government in Ontario's history and the fiercely reactionary Conservative government that replaced it. The province's labour movement was outraged when Bob Rae—the NDP premier in Ontario, who was a liberal at best but certainly no socialist—reopened public-sector collective agreements to freeze wages. A split developed in the Ontario Federation of Labour between public-sector unions and the CAW, on one side, who severed their connections with the party or withdrew their financial support, and primarily private-sector unions such as the Steelworkers, UFCW and the Communication, Energy and Paperworkers Union (CEP) on the other, who argued that the NDP was the labour movement's long-term friend and there was no other party for it to support. After Mike Harris's Conservatives came to power in 1995, partly because a significant number of unionists refused to work for Rae's re-election, the labour movement bypassed the NDP to organize its own escalating series of "Days of Action" in conjunction with other groups opposed to the government, designed to draw attention to the negative effects of Harris's policies on the province's public services and quality of life. Again, however, there was a split between those unions who wanted to work closely with the NDP to defeat Harris electorally and those who wanted to build a broader movement in which electoral politics was but one part. At the end of the century, the federal NDP was attempting to remake itself as a Tony Blair-style liberal party, and coalition politics had yet to solve the problem of translating its diverse energy and mobilizing capacity into a vehicle to pursue political power.[1]

The lurch to the right by governments and businesses in this period affected the area of adult education, too, as privatization and devolution became features _use_ of the education and training system. The federal government began in the 1980s to spend more of its training dollars on private providers and less in the public education system. This led to a proliferation of private trainers anxious to take advantage of this new access to public monies. As a result, public educational institutions became starved for funds and were forced to focus more closely on those areas that yielded an immediate economic return. Furthermore, the federal government in the 1990s began to abandon its historic commitment to training by transferring responsibility to the provinces, resulting in a series of weak and fractured systems across the country. _still weak systems today_

Adult education practice, meanwhile, continued to be influenced by both the progressive social movements and the dominant commercial ethos of the period. At its fiftieth anniversary celebrations in 1985, the Canadian Association for Adult Education (CAAE) recommitted itself to citizenship education by pledging to strengthen its cooperative working relationship with six social movements—adult literacy, the peace movement, cultural sovereignty, environmental citizenship, local economic development and the women's movement. When its federal government funding was eliminated in the 1990s, however, the association's future became uncertain. As the CAAE languished, progressive adult educators regrouped in the fledgling Canadian Network for Democratic Learning (CANDLE), which was formally incorporated in 2000 and included a significant number of union educators among its membership. Citizenship and "social-purpose" education were minority currents in the field at the end of the century, however. The proliferation of private trainers, the business fascination with new approaches to controlling workers and new fads in management and professional training combined to ensure that adult education was dominated by approaches that focused on competency and skills-based training at the expense of critical and broad-based education.[2]

Union Education

By the 1980s it was clear to most union educators that the more hostile climate that was being fostered by governments and employers required a more systematic approach to membership mobilization. While the 1970s and early 1980s had seen the development of a number of new initiatives that pointed in this direction, activist education became a defining feature of Canadian union education in the 1980s and 1990s. In 1994, the CLC's National Education Advisory Committee (NEAC) produced a consensus on the future development of union education in which it concluded that education should infuse all aspects of the local union and union educators should coordinate their activities more closely with other parts of the labour movement. Furthermore, education activists were urged to share the labour movement's vision for social change, justice and solidarity with young people, equity groups and progressive organizations beyond the workplace. In other words, the days in which union education was first and foremost industrial relations training were long past. In future, while steward and collective bargaining courses would still be offered, these and other courses would be taught in a way that placed priority on mobilizing members to engage in a social movement that encompassed the workplace but extended beyond it. The creation of the CLC's Education and Campaigns department in 1997 was designed to facilitate closer cooperation between union educators and activists engaged in a range of ongoing and specific campaigns, including those organized by the congress's new youth coordinator.

A key feature of this activist education was that workers should teach other workers. The persons best suited to facilitate and lead discussions were workers themselves, and emphasis was placed on training and supporting workers in the objectives and principles of adult and popular education. The twenty thousand CUPE members who attended one or more courses in a given year during the

1990s, for example, were likely taught by one of the 250 occasional facilitators who were trained in popular education techniques and normally taught courses in teams of two. Peer educators in the Public Service Alliance of Canada's (PSAC) Alliance Facilitators' Network, meanwhile, were trained to identify learning needs and to develop and deliver union education modules locally across the country; they met regularly, either locally, regionally or nationally, to exchange ideas, methodology and materials to support one another. And the Steelworkers had a network of 140 trained local members across the country, each equipped to instruct a variety of courses when called upon to do so by the union.

Instructors for the United Steelworkers of America were told in the 1990s to observe the following teaching methods in their stewards training:

- *Be student-centred and not subject-centred.*

- *Deal with whole problems regardless of subject divisions.*

- *Build up the confidence of students.*

- *Train students systematically in the basic skills and the techniques of study.*

- *Make use of the students' personal experiences.*

- *Work from the known to the unknown.*

- *Allow for the fact that students learn at different rates.*

- *Work from the concrete to the abstract.*

- *Allow for the fact that there are "plateaus of learning" which, it is hoped, are periods of subconscious consolidation.*

- *Allow for the need to "over-learn" (to revise and reinforce).*

- *Stress especially the "reproduction" of what has been learned.*

- *Make use of all suitable media, tools and techniques.*

- *Allow for the fact that things that are only heard and seen are forgotten sooner than things done.*

- *Always entail a co-operative partnership between the tutor and students, with active participation by the whole group.*

- *Use every opportunity for practical work, especially work with a clear social value.*

Source: Winston Gereluk, *Labour Education in Canada: A Research Report from the Field* (Athabasca, Alta.: Athabasca University, 2000), 133-134.

The core union education courses remained those designed to train local activists to be effective leaders, stewards and so forth. However, the emphasis was different than in the past. PSAC, for example, taught The Organizing Model and Local Organizing and Administration in its "Union Orientation" stream of courses and Social Change Activism in its "Leadership Development" group, while NUPGE included basic human rights issues, privatization and work reorganization in its Local Officers' Training course. The Union of Needletrades, Industrial and Textile Employees (UNITE) had optional modules on harassment, violence in the workplace and stress management in its Stewards' Training and Collective Bargaining courses. And CUPE completely revamped its six-level steward and leadership training programme during the 1990s to place more emphasis on general activist education, downplay technical training and employ popular-education approaches. The new four-level programme focused on problem solving, communication, education, leadership and organizing, while exploring specific issues such as harassment and racism.

A variety of other courses appeared in the 1980s and 1990s across the movement as a response to the new challenges faced by labour. NUPGE, for example, developed courses to deal with the erosion of public services, including Negotiating Quality Public Services and The Value of Public Services, Fair Taxation and Debt/Deficit Myths. The first sought to ensure that the union's agenda of maintaining strong public services was reflected in the ongoing restructuring of the workplace, while the second examined the economics of public funding and developed arguments to counter the deficit myth. PSAC, for its part, developed a programme stream entitled "The Changing Workplace" that included courses such as The Information Highway, Telework, Globalization and Free Trade, and Total Quality Management.

In private-sector unions, meanwhile, the CAW began offering a new human rights course in the late 1980s, which led to a 1994 constitutional convention resolution affirming a 50/50 funding split between the national union and local unions that allowed the course to be offered to local union leaderships. Initially offered by the education department, the course became the responsibility of the union's newly created human rights department in 1996. And UNITE kept the spirit of the old International Ladies Garment Workers' Union (ILGWU) and Amalgamated Clothing Workers of America (ACWA) educational programmes alive with its general education offerings for members and their families, who were often new Canadians. Local 459's Learning Experience Centre in Winnipeg, for example, offered its members courses in reading, writing, mathematics and attaining Canadian citizenship, and supplemented these with learning activities for children. The centre claimed to pursue a "holistic" approach to learning that took account of the individual as a whole person, providing programmes that affected life in the workplace, the community and the family.[3]

At the end of the 1990s the Saskatchewan Federation of Labour pioneered an Annual Prairie School for Union Women. Women from across the prairies attended the week-long school to learn about and discuss issues such as women and ageing, young women in unions, lesbians in our union, shop-floor militancy and First Nations and Métis women in focus. The following is an excerpt from the 1999 course descriptions:

Young Women Unite: Are you one of the only young women in your workplace or union? Are you tired of being underestimated or ignored because of your age or gender? This workshop will bring together women aged 29 and under to talk about their struggles and to strategize about how to get their concerns front and centre. We'll learn how to get loud, get active and get results!!

Time for Change: This course will focus on issues facing our lesbian sisters and how we, as supportive trade union and community activists, can begin to understand these issues and develop strategies to overcome discrimination on the basis of sexual orientation in everyday life and at the bargaining table.

Aboriginal Women, Dynamics, Issues and Unions: This course will focus on issues facing a diverse working environment, especially the dynamics affecting Aboriginal women. We, as supportive trade unionists, can begin to understand these issues and develop strategies to encourage sisterhood.

Negotiating Family Friendly Workplaces: Tired of balancing family and work? This course will examine a broad range of strategies including collective bargaining to create more flexible workplaces that respond to growing family needs and demands.

Source: Saskatchewan Federation of Labour, Third Prairie School for Union Women, 1999, quoted in Gereluk, *Labour Education in Canada*, 87-88.

Among the more creative courses that appeared in the 1980s and 1990s were two that D'Arcy Martin developed while working for the CEP. Solidarity Skills: Working Together across Social and Political Differences and Union Judo: Strategies for the Changing Workplace were attempts to use the "street smarts" that workers brought to union education to interrogate the professional and academic literature that sought to understand and interpret the workplace. The first course used materials such as John Cleese's video *More Bloody Meetings* and Deborah Tannen's book *You Just Don't Understand: Men and Women in Conversation*, while the second drew on Sun Tzu's *The Art of War* and John Fisher and William Ury's *Getting to Yes*. The two courses addressed contemporary changes taking place in the areas of cultural and sexual oppression on the one hand and work reorganization on the other. In Union Judo, which was a remake of a course he had developed for the Steelworkers, Martin introduced course participants to management literature on workplace reorganization, had them tease out its ideological underpinnings, and helped them devise strategies for using this literature against managers in their workplace interactions (hence the judo analogy).[4]

Union educator D'Arcy Martin on the labour educator's craft:

It takes time in courses to help people learn to listen critically; it takes nerve to argue that it isn't just for quantifiable goals that people are attracted to union life but because it gives them a taste of a better way of being together; it takes imagination to value the creative streak in course participants and the commitment of labour-positive artists by building both into educational events. And it takes stamina to keep seeking common ground with people whose reflexes are different.

Marge Piercy speaks to the beauty of work, including the work of the labour educator in the title poem of her collection "To Be of Use":

> *The work of the world is common as mud.*
>
> *Botched, it smears the hands, crumbles to dust.*
>
> *But the thing worth doing well done*
>
> *has a shape that satisfies, clean and evident.*
>
> *Greek amphoras for wine and oil,*
>
> *Hopi vases that held corn, are put in museums*
>
> *but you know they were made to be used.*
>
> *The pitcher cries for water to carry*
>
> *and a person for work that is real.*

May union courses have a shape that satisfies, and may all Canadians have work that is real.

Source: D'Arcy Martin, "Adult Education in the Labour Movement," in Gordon Selman, Mark Selman, Michael Cooke, and Paul Dampier, *The Foundations of Adult Education in Canada*, 2d ed. (Toronto: Thompson Educational Publishing, 1998), 395.

A number of unions expanded their education around international issues with the support of their newly created solidarity funds. The CEP and the Steelworkers, for example, created Humanity Funds that were financed on a cents-per-hour basis through collective bargaining or by individual members making a direct contribution. These funds supported projects such as a vocational school in Peru or a women's shelter in Canada, but they were also used to develop course materials dealing with global solidarity. In the Steelworkers course entitled Thinking North-South, for example, activists from among the 280 locals that had contributed to the fund gathered together in week-long schools to think about the workings of the global economy. Participants mapped out the pattern of the global economy, starting with their own workplace and eventually creating a complex picture linking structural adjustment in the south with free trade in the north. In 1995 the Steelworkers joined the CAW,

CUPE and CEP in a CLC initiative called the Labour International Development Committee, which used Canadian government money to develop worker-to-worker and union-to-union solidarity across borders. The CLC also produced a "Toolbox for Global Solidarity" to assist affiliates in their solidarity education and actions. This series of factsheets, readings, exercises and instructor notes included modules on globalization, free trade, women in the global economy and getting involved in global solidarity.[5]

The increasing attention to international issues represented a broadening of what was considered political education in the labour movement, while the larger focus on activist education was blurring the distinction between political and union education. Political education departments—renamed "political action" in some cases—continued to concentrate on electing NDP candidates, but the new coalition and community-based politics that was a feature of this period required a slight modification of this approach. In the 1988 election campaign, for example, the labour movement worked with the Pro-Canada Network, a coalition of groups opposed to the Canada-United States free trade agreement. The free trade agreement was the main issue in this campaign, with both the Liberal and New Democratic parties opposed to the Conservative government's attempt to pursue greater integration of the two economies by reducing barriers to trade (not surprisingly, the Liberals completely reversed their position when they regained power in 1993). The CLC once again used its parallel-campaign approach to appeal to trade unionists through telephone canvasses and on-the-job personal contacts. First, it worked with the Pro-Canada Network prior to the election to inform people of the pitfalls of the proposed deal and to attempt to prevent it from being signed. Then, during the election, it tried to deliver the labour vote to the NDP in order to defeat the government and stop the deal. While the Conservative's were re-elected and the deal proceeded, the CLC continued to work with the Action-Canada Network (the Pro-Canada Network's successor) against the North American Free Trade Agreement and other corporate initiatives.[6]

The union education classroom in the 1990s, meanwhile, was much more diversified than had been the case twenty or twenty-five years earlier. In the 1970s, the classes were composed primarily of men, although public-sector unions such as CUPE and PSAC had significant female participation in their courses. Furthermore, course participants had a clear sense of who the boss was in their workplaces and the function of union education was to equip them with the tools to be more effective in confronting management. In the 1990s, by contrast, workplace control was much more diffuse as a result of management initiatives to divide workers. Workers were often stressed, overworked and doing more with less. Although workers often brought a general or abstract class consciousness to the classroom (they resented the increasing wealth disparity in the country, for example), they had a much less clear idea of who the boss was than had been the case in earlier periods. Management-promoted friction and tension among workers meant that union educators were faced with the task of negotiating solidarity among diverse groups of workers. As a result, course participants in the 1990s were more interested in learning how to handle workplace harassment and conflict resolution than in more traditional topics such as parliamentary procedure.[7]

The new spirit of union education was captured in a 1997 conference that the CLC co-sponsored with the American Federation of Labor-Congress of Industrial Organizations (AFL-CIO) and the United States-based University and College Labour Education Association. Four hundred and fifty labour educators gathered in Toronto for "Educ-Action: Union Building for the 21st Century." While about a third of the delegates were from the United States and Latin America, most were Canadian. Keynote speeches by CLC President Bob White on the union educator's role in promoting labour's alternative vision and by AFL-CIO executive vice-president Linda Chavez-Thompson on transforming unions into locals that organize, educate and mobilize set the tone. In workshops such as Health and Safety as a Mobilizing Issue, Popularizing Economics Education, and Labour-Community Links in Anti-Racism Work, activists thought about, debated and planned how education could inform both their workplace and community activity.

In the New Media and Technology for Worker Education workshop, for example, participants informed a seemingly technical subject with a vision of using new technologies to support activist education. Countering ultra-leftist arguments such as those proffered by American academic David Noble about the conservative tendencies of educational technology, rank-and-file and staff educators swapped experiences about the positive uses of new media and suggested possible future strategies that labour could adopt. In a critical and constructive presentation to the group, Rosa Cruz Toledo from the Metro Labour Education Centre in Toronto explained how she and her colleagues sought to demystify computers in the courses they taught. While critically assessing how this technology was often used against workers' interests through deskilling and workplace monitoring, they explored how computer communications might be used to make education accessible to more workers and as an alternative means for activists to connect and share ideas.

adult
union
ed.
+
computer
tech.

In another workshop about thirty-five people exchanged experiences about using popular education in unions. Using popular-theatre techniques and small-group discussion, the participants explored how to link their members' experiences with the experiences of workers in other parts of the world, how to persuade people to respect their own knowledge and experience and how to connect individual workers' concerns to the larger issue of globalization, among other things. In this and other discussions about the relationship between popular and union education at the end of the century, a contrast was often posed between the "democratic," participant-centred and critically engaged practice in popular education and the "top-down," goal-oriented and formal teaching structures at play inside unions. Popular educators, the reasoning went, could change moribund union educational programmes by infusing them with the lessons learned from educational activities in developing countries and in Canadian community-based groups. While it is true that a number of creative popular educators brought new approaches to union education, it is not clear that the contrast between the two traditions was as dramatic as some suggested. Some unions were undoubtedly more democratic than others, but the best union educators throughout the century attempted to ensure that participant needs and experiences were honoured while balancing these against the broader membership's requirement for competent and strong workplace representatives.[8]

The CLC continued to receive Labour Canada financial support for education during this period and the flow of money was made permanent at the end of the second five-year funding period in 1987. Questions raised about the programme that same year by a ministerial task force reviewing government expenditures, though, signalled that there were potential problems down the road. In 1994 the Conservative government announced that the funding would be phased out over the following three years. In the late 1980s and early 1990s, however, the CLC was receiving about five million dollars annually for educational purposes, of which about one million dollars flowed through to the Quebec Federation of Labour and the Atlantic Region Labour Education Centre. The national centre received about half of the balance and the regional centres got the rest.

The grant money continued to be used for programme development and audio-visual production. Dan Mallett was promoted from program developer to national program development coordinator in 1987 and was responsible for the production of training manuals and aids over the following twelve years. In the late 1980s, for example, an organizing manual was developed to supplement existing materials in steward training, collective bargaining and other areas. In addition, a kit was devised to assist labour council activists to go into various levels of the school system to talk to students about unions and the workplace. Instructor training remained a priority, and a newsletter was introduced to assist instructors in the field.

As in the past, the audio-visual department turned out its mix of subject-specific material to complement other CLC materials or campaigns, productions for affiliates and raw footage of CLC and affiliate activities. Short pieces were produced, such as *The CLC National Day of Mourning* and *Women on the Line* for CLC projects, for example, while *The USWA Humanity Fund*, *This is NUPGE*, and *CAW Local 199 New Member Orientation* assisted affiliates. Equipment and videographers were dispensed regularly to record events such as workshops on various topics, rallies and demonstrations.[9]

In advanced union education, meanwhile, CAW's paid educational leave programme (PEL) had sharpened its focus by the late 1980s and early 1990s. The original structure was modified slightly to include a weekend orientation and four sessions of five days each over approximately three months. And the curriculum was reorganized to introduce participants to a coherent theoretical perspective that mapped the various aspects of working-class life. The course began with a critique of the educational system, in which participants shared their unhappy childhood experiences of school, realized their individual histories were not unique and prepared to take part in an educational process designed to serve and advance the interests of working people. Over the following four weeks they were exposed to a survey of human history from early egalitarian to contemporary capitalist societies, a class analysis of Canadian society in order to locate the respective positions of workers and employers, a close inspection of the Canadian state (government and bureaucracy) to reveal its close links with the employing class and the relationship between unions and politics. The presentation of material throughout the four weeks was informed by an explicitly Marxist analysis (though Marx was never mentioned) that employed concepts such as means of production, use and exchange value, surplus value and profit. Analyses of the state, in turn, emphasized its functions of accumulation, legitimation and coercion. By the time they returned to their workplaces, PEL participants in the 1980s and 1990s were equipped with an alternative world-view that challenged the prevailing "common sense."

Ken Luckhardt, the PEL coordinator during these years, continued the practice established by Dan Benedict of using Local Union Discussion Leaders (LUDL) to conduct the classes. At the beginning of the course, participants received a package of notes, readings and other course materials, which were supplemented by other course resources such as videos. The LUDLs, who were PEL graduates and had taken instructor training, took their fellow workers through the material using a variety of union education methods including small-group discussion, buzz groups and public reading (in which participants took turns reading passages from the course materials). Participant experiences were connected as much as possible to the material, but this was not "popular education" in the sense that the participants negotiated the curriculum and their experiences formed the central element of the pedagogy. Rather, the centrepiece was the theoretical and empirical material that participants were expected to read, view, absorb and discuss. Still, they engaged with the material with the assistance of peer educators with whom they could identify.[10]

In 1992 the Canadian Union of Postal Workers (CUPW) followed CAW's example and negotiated an educational leave provision in its collective agreement with Canada Post. The Union Education Fund supports a four-week residential programme similar to PEL (and held at the CAW's Port Elgin facility) and five-day skills-building courses across the country. Like PEL, CUPW's Union Education Program begins from the premise that working-class children are most often taught the values of employers in the school system and that these influences have to be countered. During the four weeks, participants' awareness and pride in trade-union and working-class values are strengthened through interrogations of sexism and racism, analyses of the role and history of the state, and role-playing in mock conventions where their leadership skills are developed. At the end of the four weeks, the participants are prepared to return to their locals to act as peer educators who work with local union officers to build a culture of resistance in their workplaces.[11]

The Labour College of Canada retained its standing as the most important advanced education programme in the country. While keeping its general academic orientation, it shed its formal university connections in the 1980s and, at the end of the 1990s, was reorganized in the wake of the loss of federal government funding. After the instructors' strike of 1983, CLC President Dennis McDermott ignored the college, allowed it to drift and did not even bother to call board meetings. When Shirley Carr took over the leadership of the congress, a number of interested observers asked her to take some action to put the college back on course. Fred Pomeroy, for example, who was president of the Communications and Electrical Workers of Canada, wrote to Carr in the fall of 1986 asking that the board meet as soon as possible, adding, "I did not pursue this matter with Dennis because he seemed to have a rather cavalier attitude to the College and the work it does." Eleven college instructors, including Bob Hatfield and Sid Ingerman, also wrote to the congress president that same year requesting a meeting to discuss a number of issues, including expanding the residence curriculum, updating the distance education programme, reinstituting post-graduate courses and reviewing the board's composition. While Pomeroy's correspondence was received respectfully, CLC Secretary-Treasurer Richard Mercier fumed to Carr that college affairs were "not their [the instructors'] business!"[12]

When Dick Martin assumed responsibility for the college from Mercier in the fall of 1986, he quickly called a board meeting and proceeded to reorganize the college governing and administrative structures. The two boards overseeing the college and educational services were merged, and a Curriculum Development Advisory Committee (CDAC) was established to advise the college on day-to-day affairs and on issues as they arose. In addition, the university representation (McGill and Montreal) on the board was eliminated, with the new representatives including the congress executive committee, three affiliated unions, three federations of labour, the national director of educational services, a representative of the college alumni and Labour Canada officials (because of the government grant).[13]

The political skills of Martin and the CDAC were soon tested when eight women complained about sexist incidents during the 1987 residential session. Writing to Nancy Riche, one of the CLC executive vice-presidents, the eight women observed that seventeen of the sixty-two participants that year were women. They then outlined a number of incidents of sexual harassment and sexist behaviour that had taken place, complaining that there was no systematic programme designed to address issues of this kind at the college. Noting that sexism and related issues were dealt with in courses at the discretion of the individual instructors, they insisted that a systematic commitment to educating students about these matters should be put in place.

Martin, as the officer responsible for the college, wrote to the seventeen women who had been at the 1987 session reporting that a sexual harassment policy had been established to govern the behaviour of students, instructors and staff. He added that in future years students would be asked to select a male and a female representative to serve as stewards and sit on a complaint-resolution committee. Two students—a woman and a man—complained separately to Martin that his letter had been sent only to the female members of the class, with the man claiming that "you have used this slanderous letter to injure the reputation of my name, my union, and the male students of the class of '87."

CDAC subsequently reviewed the women's issues content in the various college courses. Sid Ingerman, the instructor representative on CDAC, reminded his committee colleagues that the tradition at the college was that the instructors developed their own courses. While agreeing that CDAC could look at the general thrust of courses, he hoped that it would not become a body that told instructors what they should teach. Martin, for his part, argued that the committee could ask instructors to incorporate specific material into their courses. "If they do not," he continued, "it will come down to administration and instructor. They have the right and we do too." When CDAC did meet with instructors to discuss the degree of women's content in the courses, committee members were reluctant to criticize instructors directly for perceived inadequacies; instructors, in turn, were able to convince the committee that there was more women's content in their courses than was obvious in the course outlines.[14]

The pattern established in the late 1970s of employing part-time instructional staff for the residential programme continued through the 1980s and 1990s. Sid Ingerman, who had been with the college since the 1960s, still taught economics, and was joined by a range of colleagues over the years. Some, such as Don Wells and Barbara Cameron, went on to establish prominent academic careers; Bob Hatfield and other union educators also taught from time to time. The residential curriculum that had been revised in 1979 remained constant too. Course content in the 1990s was much more critical and labour-friendly than it had been in the 1960s, however. Labour historians such as Peter Campbell and Peter McInnis introduced students to the fruits of the "new working-class history" that placed union history in the broader context of class relations and the complexities of working-class life, while Wells, Cameron and others taught a political science that also focussed on class and explained the power relations present in a capitalist society. And Ingerman continued to use his *Economics for Canadian Trade Unionists*, originally published in 1980, to provide a labour-friendly view of the economy.[15]

By the early 1990s the college's annual budget was well in excess of $300,000, with the Labour Canada grant providing almost two-thirds of it. Some members of the governing board worried that it was not healthy for it to be so dependent on outside funding, while others argued that the money should be used as the basis for a much-expanded college that could operate fifty weeks a year. When the Conservative government announced in the 1995 budget that the CLC's grant for labour education was to be eliminated by 1997, however, the

labour education + gov't dependant

1993 Labour College of Canada Award Recipients. Left to right: Robert White, President, CLC, and Chairperson, Board of Governors, Labour College of Canada; Raymond Smith, Local 503, Canadian Union of Public Employees; Pervaiz Chaudhary, Local 1-405, IWA-Canada; Sharon Binkley, Local 1556, CUPE; John Cunningham, Local 677, United Rubber, Cork, Linoleum and Plastic Workers of America; Donna Finkleman, Local 0206, Manitoba Government Employees Union; Keith Patrick, Local 1860, CUPE; and Nancy Riche, Executive Vice-President, CLC, and Vice-Chairperson, Board of Governors, Labour College of Canada. *Canadian Labour Congress Collection.*

reality of government dependency became clear. Fortuitously, Bob White had appointed a committee in 1994 to review all aspects of the college. The committee reported in the fall of 1995 and recommended a significantly modified residential programme to take account of the reduced revenues.

The report began by recognizing the need for the residential programme to be more closely coordinated with other union education, more accessible to members of affiliated unions across the country, sensitive to potential participants' family and other responsibilities and promote greater gender parity and equity representation. It then recommended a five-year process during which the delivery method in the core programme would change from purely face-to-face classroom instruction to a combination of face-to-face and distance education. By 1998, according to this plan, there would be a three-week residential programme in Ottawa, a week-long school in each of the regions and a weekend session in each of the regional CLC schools. These face-to-face offerings would be linked and enhanced by distance learning using computer-mediated communications such as electronic mail and online conferencing. The old "correspondence" course, meanwhile, would be updated and offered in partnership with Athabasca University as a "home-study" course using print-based materials and a telephone tutor and as an online course using computer conferencing.[16]

changes to labour ed recommended

Eventually, after the 1996 CLC convention accepted the general sentiment of the committee's report, the board agreed to a modified and reduced residential programme consisting of four weeks in Ottawa (covering economics, history, sociology and political science) and one week as part of the week-long regional schools (covering labour law). The recommendations regarding the use of new educational technologies to overcome barriers to participation in the residential programme were rejected or ignored. However, the college did proceed with its arrangement with Athabasca University to replace the old distance education course with a more substantial and current offering.

Members of the instructional staff and the governing board had been complaining for years that the distance education course needed updating, as it had not been revised since 1978. Jean Bezusky, college registrar, turned to the Athabasca University labour studies programme in 1994 for advice on how to proceed with a revision. The initial plan was simply to update the existing material. Eventually, however, Bezusky and her university colleagues decided to change the course entirely. In the end, a team of professors at Athabasca wrote a new university-level course entitled Introduction to Labour Studies: Labour College of Canada that covered the same subject areas that were treated in the residential programme (but in less detail). This three-credit course formed part of the regular Athabasca curriculum, but was open only to members of unions affiliated to the CLC. Students registered for it through the Labour College of Canada and were then treated as regular Athabasca students, with access to the university's services, including a telephone or e-mail tutor and the use of the library. When students completed the course, which took up to six months while working at their own pace, they were awarded three university credits (equivalent to one thirteen-week course at a traditional university) that could be applied to an Athabasca credential (such as the degree in labour studies) or transferred to another university or a college. In the late 1990s, sixty to seventy trade unionists were enrolled in this course annually, but the university had the capacity to teach hundreds more.

A significant transition occurred at the Labour College of Canada in late 1999 and early 2000. Jean Bezusky announced her retirement at a meeting of the college alumni during the 1999 CLC convention. Bezusky had been with the college for over thirty years. A graduate of the 1966 residential programme, she had started working as a secretary in the college's Montreal office in 1968. Noel Stoodley, Bezusky's successor, had had a varied career in union education. Originally a UAW member, he designed that union's Family Education Program in 1972. He then joined the CLC in 1978 as the first Ontario coordinator of the Labour Education and Studies Centre, and subsequently served as congress education director in the Prairie and Pacific regions before being appointed national director of educational services in 1985. When he was chosen as the new college registrar, Stoodley was employed in the CLC's international department.[17]

Workplace Training

[handwritten: Craft union influence on apprenticeships]

[handwritten: use]

The scope of union education expanded in the 1980s and 1990s as the labour movement became more involved with the issue of workplace training. Unions had always been interested in training. The labour movement emerged in the nineteenth century partly in response to employer attempts to wrest control over the education of apprentices from journeyman craftworkers. Craft unions, which were concentrated in the building and construction trades by the end of the twentieth century, never lost this influence completely and continue to play a role in apprenticeship programmes. Most unions, however, lost control of training during the nineteenth and twentieth centuries as employers shifted workplace skills from the heads of workers to machines that they owned, and educational institutions took increasing responsibility for preparing young people for the labour market. The labour movement always supported public education and, as governments increased their funding for post-secondary skills training in the decades after the Second World War, it devoted more of its energies to monitoring public policy in this area and contributing to the relevant debates.

As employers and governments restructured the economy and dismantled public institutions in the 1980s and 1990s, however, the terms of the training debate shifted. First, members were demanding that their unions assist them as they faced the prospect of finding a new line of work when their jobs were relocated to the southern United States, Mexico or somewhere further afield. In some cases, this meant helping them to negotiate their way around the changing and shrinking unemployment insurance system or to gain access to government or employer training-adjustment programmes. In others, it meant becoming actively involved in training delivery by pursuing government grants or bargaining training trust funds with employers to establish union-controlled programmes. Second, trade unionists were represented on the sector councils and labour-force development boards that formed part of the federal government's strategy for managing the economic dislocation of the late 1980s, requiring that they develop their own (hopefully coherent) agenda on training and related issues.

[handwritten: key pt.]

The distinction between labour education and training became blurred as unions became more involved in the direct delivery of training. In the services that the UFCW's National Training Programme provided, for example, or in the various union-based literacy initiatives that developed across the country from the late 1980s, activists used trade union principles to serve the broader educational needs of their fellow members.

In the early 1980s UFCW locals began negotiating training trust funds, and Local 1977 in Ontario opened the first of the union's training centres. The union's Canadian Council decided in 1990 to establish a National Training Programme (NTP) to coordinate activity in the area. Janet Dassinger was hired the following year to run a lay-off and closure programme and subsequently became NTP director. She stayed in that position until she left the union in 1999, although she was seconded for a short period in the 1990s to coordinate the CLC's Workplace Training Strategy. By the time Dassinger moved on, the UFCW had one of the most extensive union-training programmes in Canada.

The centrepiece of the UFCW training system was its network of training centres across the country. In the late 1990s there were seven such centres in six provinces (one each in Nova Scotia and the four western provinces and two in Ontario). Each one was based in a specific local and financed out of the local's negotiated training trust fund. The centres were responsible for sparking an interest in training among the membership and providing the direct delivery of training in areas that the membership deemed to be important. The nature of provision varied from centre to centre. In 1998, for example, the Local 2000 training centre in British Columbia was offering members industry-specific courses such as Sausage Making and Baker/Deli/Cooking, a more general industry-related course called Women in Trades, computer training courses, and general interest courses such as Writing with Confidence, Public Speaking and Self-Defense for Women. All of these courses were funded by the local's training trust fund. In addition, the centre used external federal and provincial government money to offer programmes for the broader community, including one to introduce unemployed youth to the basic tools and techniques of a number of apprenticable trades. Other locals, such as 401 in Alberta and 832 in Manitoba, placed more emphasis on traditional union education such as steward training in their centre's offerings, while 175 in Ontario concentrated a large part of its efforts on computer training in response to member demand.

The seven training centres in operation at the end of the 1990s had the potential to reach less than half of the UFCW's 200,000 members in Canada, leaving more than 100,000 members in 130 locals without direct access to training services. The National Training Programme was designed to serve these members as much as possible and to provide support and coordination to the training centres. Those locals that had negotiated training trust funds contributed one cent per hour to a National Training Fund that was used to support the NTP. The national programme produced materials such as a kit to assist locals in negotiating training trust funds, conducted workshops for training-centre staff and other local staff and activists involved in training issues and provided support to locals negotiating training or labour-adjustment agreements. It also liased with external organizations such as the CLC, the federal government and the relevant sector councils.

There was general agreement inside the union on a number of principles underlying its approach to training. Members should enrol voluntarily, the learning should be portable and contribute to an individual's general development and the programmes should promote critical thinking and avoid propaganda. In addition, programmes should endeavour to promote awareness of labour principles. Furthermore, workers should teach workers, with professionals providing a coaching role, and the training style should encourage collective interaction. Finally, every member should have access to training and education, regardless of previous schooling, age, culture, race, gender or geographic location. The practice varied however. Many training centre offerings looked little different than what might be available through a general continuing education outlet, other than the fact that a substantial portion of the cost was borne by the training trust fund. In others, notably those courses that developed employment-related or labour relations skills, union principles were more prevalent.

One of the casualties of Dassinger's departure in 1999 was a proposal she had been working on to map the future direction of training in the union. Inspired by the education and training programme in Unison, a public-sector union in the United Kingdom, she wanted to integrate the various aspects of the union's activity, employ innovative delivery methods to reach members who did not have access to training services and use the union's leverage to partner with colleges and universities in the development of courses and programmes suited to the membership's needs. Moreover, she was committed to ensuring all facets of the national and local programmes were grounded more securely in the union's training principles. By the end of the twentieth century, then, UFCW had built a significant amount of internal training capacity and was poised to consolidate its growth and enter a new stage.[18]

One of UFCW's most important training initiatives during the 1990s was its National Literacy Programme, which was supplemented by a number of smaller literacy projects conducted by individual training centres. These activities, along with parallel projects in other labour organizations, were funded mostly by the federal government's National Literacy Secretariat (NLS). Announced by the Conservative government in 1986, the NLS began funding a variety of literacy initiatives in unions and elsewhere two years later. The labour movement, which had always supported the expansion of literacy and numeracy through its commitment to public education, became actively involved in specific campaigns to promote literacy in the 1970s through, for example, endorsements for Frontier College (which had become a literacy organization by this time). In the 1980s, however, unions started to become directly involved in the promotion of basic education (literacy, numeracy, English as a Second Language) among their members. The Ontario Federation of Labour's Basic Education Skills Training (BEST) and the Saskatchewan Federation of Labour's Workers' Education for Skills Training (WEST) programmes set the standard for initiatives of this kind.

BEST was conceived as part of the OFL's broader critique of the general direction of public education in the mid-1980s. Arguing that the educational system worked against the interests of working people, the federation concluded that it had to become actively involved itself in providing basic educational opportunities for members of its affiliated unions. With a grant from the Ontario Ministry of Skills Development, supplemented by union contributions to cover lost time for course participation, the first group of BEST participants graduated in the spring of 1989 with basic skills in mathematics, reading and communications. WEST, meanwhile, secured NLS funding in 1989 to establish a parallel programme using the Ontario experience as a model.

The people who developed and administered both BEST and WEST were influenced by Friere's approach to popular education and by Myles Horton and the activities of the Highlander Folk School in the American South. In both these examples, literacy education was viewed as an inherently political activity in which the teaching of basic skills could not be separated from the broader social and economic structures determining the participants' lives. Furthermore, learning and knowledge emanated from the participants rather than from the teachers, who were renamed "course leaders" or "facilitators" to reflect this fact. Using their own experiences as a starting point, course participants came to understand the political nature of literacy and illiteracy as they learned reading, writing and other basic skills.

BEST and WEST activists used popular-education techniques such as those promoted by Friere and Horton to build what they believed to be learner-centred programmes. Course leaders were equal members of the groups in which they participated, encouraging all participants to take an active and critical role in determining subject matter, learning methods and class direction. If a group wanted to learn to fill out an accident form, for example, knowledge and experience in the group would be pooled, questions the group could not answer would be identified and additional information would be found and brought back to class for reading and discussion. While participants learned how to read and write and do mathematics in the courses, these were presented as tools to be used for broader social purposes. In some cases the tools would facilitate individual career enhancement, but in others they would be used in union work or some other collective endeavour. Indeed, a number of WEST participants began the programme with limited commitment to the labour movement and subsequently became actively involved in their unions.[19]

By the mid-1990s the labour movement was involved in a range of training-related initiatives. A 1997 survey of CLC affiliates revealed that at least thirteen affiliates were involved in training, with three having separate training departments. More than fifty union staffers across the country had some responsibility for training. While there was obviously a significant amount of activity taking place, much of it was invisible to people inside and outside the labour movement and there was little sharing of information and strategies among various unions. To help rectify this the CLC hosted a conference in 1997 to bring together labour training activists from across the country to begin to develop a union vision of workplace training.

In his opening speech to the conference, congress President Bob White provided a preliminary sketch of the broad issues involved in "training on union terms." For one thing, there were conflicting views in society about what training should involve. Employers and governments wanted to adapt workers to speedups and work reorganization, while labour was interested in increasing worker control and improving the work environment and economic benefits that workers received. Furthermore, employers and governments wanted the unemployed to accept their situation passively, but labour wanted them to learn how to challenge the system as well as learn the essential skills they needed to survive in the labour market. For another, there were conflicting views in the labour movement regarding labour's involvement in training. Over the previous ten to fifteen years, as the UFCW example illustrates, unions in the industrial, public and service sectors had joined those in the building and construction trades in the direct delivery of training opportunities for their members. In some cases this arose out of frustration with overstretched public education systems that were providing what some believed to be mediocre service. But NUPGE and other unions that represented educational workers in the public sector feared that unions delivering their own training were aiding and abetting the erosion of the public system and the privatization of their jobs. The task of the conference, therefore, was to begin to develop a collective vision by exploring what labour's role in the training system should be and why labour was involved in training in the first place.[20]

> The United Steelworkers of America's Guidelines for Training:
>
> 1. *The content of all workplace training programs provided to union members must be jointly developed and approved by the union and the company. Employee representatives on workplace training committees must be selected and appointed by the union;*
>
> 2. *Training must be an integral part of every job, and must not be done on the employees' own time;*
>
> 3. *Training should be developmental and continually deepen the employees' knowledge;*
>
> 4. *Training should emphasize generic skills which are portable and not limited to specific jobs;*
>
> 5. *Opportunities for training must be offered to all workers on a fair and equitable basis. We must identify and overcome barriers to training for women and other groups traditionally disadvantaged in the labour market;*
>
> 6. *In workplaces where it is apparent that there is a lack of basic literacy and numeracy skills, we must ensure that individual workers are treated positively, and will not have to risk repercus-sions from the employer or co-workers for indicating that they require such training;*
>
> 7. *The identification of training needs must not be undertaken according to narrowly defined performance factors as determined solely by employers, consultants, or government agencies. Skill needs assessments must be jointly developed;*
>
> 8. *In most cases our own members make the best teachers. Instructors should be trained from within the union.*

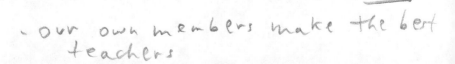

> 9. Where training programs are to be provided away from the work-place, they should be delivered through public educational institutions rather than by profit-oriented private sector trainers.
>
> Source: "Special Conference Statement on Training," Canadian National Policy and Bargaining Conference, Hamilton, Ontario, 1992 (Toronto: United Steelworkers of America, 1992).

The major outcome of the conference was a series of recommendations for action in the areas of apprenticeship, basic skills, employment services, public education programmes for adults and skills training. These recommendations then informed the CLC's Workplace Training Strategy (WTS), which was launched after the conference with funding from the federal government. The purpose of this three-year project was to build union capacity in the area by developing a labour vision of training, better preparing the labour movement to deal with the training system, developing networks to share knowledge and information and providing the necessary tools to be effective in training policies and programmes. A series of provincial and regional conferences were held across the country to bring local activists together, WTS staff worked with affiliates and federations on specific training projects and union-related training resources were gathered and placed on the CLC website and in other locations.[21]

One problem the training strategy had to tackle was the acrimony that existed between some members of NUPGE and other unions, who argued against any union involvement in the direct delivery of training, and those unions that had developed a significant involvement in training provision. One of the features of the 1997 national conference and the subsequent provincial and regional conferences was debate about this issue. NUPGE issued a series of position papers on Post-Secondary Education and Related Topics in 1998, claiming that those unions who became involved in the direct delivery of training were complicit with governments in the erosion and privatization of public education. "It is important that our sister Unions know that they are being used to create chaos within the labour movement," it argued. Training activists in unions such as UFCW, who felt they were responding to the pressing needs of members battered by economic restructuring when they developed their training programmes, were furious about these attacks.[22]

As a result, the CLC developed a protocol to regulate the union delivery of training, education and employment services. With input from all sides, the congress's executive council approved the document in June 1998. The protocol began by recognizing that the Canadian training system was in upheaval as a result of unemployment, lay-offs, cutbacks and the devolution of training services from the federal government to the provinces. And it rehearsed the reasons why some unions had become involved in training and why educational workers in the public sector argued that this provision should be in the public education system. It then noted some general principles that everyone agreed to, including the belief that the primary responsibility for education funding remained with governments and that public institutions should be the primary deliverers of training and education. It continued by stating that all labour-sponsored or joint training programmes must enhance and not duplicate public programmes and services already in place, but that the public education system should become more responsive to the values and needs of working people.

The protocol did recognize that some unions would continue to develop their own training programmes, however. Those unions doing so had a responsibility under the general protocol to inform the relevant public-sector union, the CLC, the provincial federation and the relevant labour councils. A project-specific protocol would then be established to clarify the aim of the project and the respective roles of various unions in the project. In all cases, unions would work to ensure that unionized public-sector institutions were used to deliver labour-sponsored or joint training initiatives. However, education unions recognized under the protocol that peer learning and teaching were important parts of many union training and education programmes and had to be respected; and they agreed to promote labour's involvement in shaping and developing the curricula used in labour-sponsored or joint programmes. The protocol was one of the most tangible outcomes of the CLC's Workplace Training Strategy and its immediate effect was to lessen some of the animosity and tension that had been developing around the issue. Players on both sides continued to maintain firm positions, however, and its long-term impact was uncertain.[23]

Colleges and Universities

College and university labour studies programmes did not expand substantially during this period, but some new ones were born and there were renewed attempts to work more closely with the labour movement. In addition, university-based labour educators tried different strategies to cooperate among themselves.

Athabasca University in Alberta developed a unique labour studies programme in that all of its courses became available through distance education. It was conceived in the late 1970s, subsequently received development money from the Alberta government that was used by university administrators primarily to fund a number of non-labour-studies appointments and eventually developed certificate and degree credentials in the 1990s. With a wide range of labour-related courses, the Athabasca programme staff took advantage of their facility and expertise in distance education to work with labour organizations and sister labour studies programmes to establish partnerships in order to provide post-secondary educational opportunities to trade unionists across the country and, in some cases, in other parts of the world. From 1996, for example, Athabasca cooperated with the Labour College of

Canada to offer the college's distance education course. Trade unionists from across the country took this university-level and -accredited course through traditional distance education (course package and a telephone or e-mail tutor) or via an online workshop on the World Wide Web.

Moreover, in the early 1990s the Athabasca programme began working with Marc Belanger of the Canadian Union of Public Employees to offer credit and non-credit labour education courses for trade unionists using the online Solinet conferencing system that Belanger had pioneered in the mid-1980s. CUPE was the first union in the world to use computer communications in a significant way, and it was arguably the first national organization of any kind to establish its own computer-communications system in Canada. In 1987 Belanger loaded the text-based CoSy e-mail and conferencing system onto a computer at CUPE headquarters in Ottawa and connected the computer to the country's datapac system, which allowed individuals in cities across the country to dial in to a local telephone number using their modem and connect to his computer in Ottawa. In the months and years that followed, a small but significant group of Canadian trade unionists began using Solinet to exchange e-mail among themselves and establish "conferences," or online workshops and meetings. CUPE used Solinet's conferences to facilitate bargaining and carry on subject-specific discussions, but the most interesting parts of Solinet were the conferences that were open to everyone in the Solinet community.

Belanger's philosophy from the beginning was that Solinet should be a service for the whole labour community (first in Canada and later, when the technology permitted, for the whole world). One of the liveliest spaces on the network was the "lounge," where any and all labour-related subjects were discussed. In addition, general subject-specific discussions on topics such as technological change and labour and the NDP were held periodically. In 1992 the formal relationship between Solinet and Athabasca University began with Athabasca labour studies staff organizing and facilitating a month-long workshop on the general subject of labour education. Later, the Athabasca programme used Solinet to conduct its first online offering of a for-credit labour studies course. As innovative and exciting as Solinet was, its impact and reach were limited to a small number of enthusiasts as long as online communication remained the purview of university researchers and those with a particular interest in new technologies. Things changed with the advent of the World Wide Web in 1995—which allowed for the use of graphical images, photographs, and eventually sound and video in online communication—and the explosion of interest in the Internet. Belanger and Solinet made the leap to the Web with a new conferencing system called Virtual-U that, like the older CoSy-based system, allowed participants to conduct online workshops and meetings but, since it was on the World Wide Web, was accessible to anyone in the world with a Web browser and an Internet account.

In 1996 and 1997 the "new" (Web-based) Solinet and the Athabasca labour studies programme collaborated to offer a series of non-credit online labour education workshops. Beginning with a general course called Labour Education and the Internet, designed in part to give potential online facilitators some familiarity with the new medium, the series consisted of twelve month-long workshops covering a range of topics from The Third World and the Internet to Women Organizing. Over one thousand participants from around the (mainly developed and English-speaking) world registered for at least one of these workshops. With the exception of one women-only course, all of the workshops were open to whomever wanted to participate. Facilitators chosen from around the world for their subject-matter expertise contributed their knowledge and guided the discussions. Those participants who responded to online surveys (about 18 percent of the total) indicated that they enjoyed the opportunity to interact with fellow trade unionists from a variety of different countries. Belanger saw this series as a prototype for an international online labour college, but if such an enterprise were to develop, it would not be on the network that he had built.

The union leadership decided in 1998 that Solinet should be accessible only to CUPE members. A year later Belanger moved on to the International Labour Organization to teach computer communications, and, sadly, CUPE disabled Solinet completely. A significant chapter in the Canadian labour movement's innovative use of new educational technologies was closed. But the Athabasca labour studies programme continued to operate its own version of Solinet and, at the turn of the century, was working with the CLC to build online educational capacity among the congress's member organizations. In the fall of 1999, for example, Athabasca and the CLC conducted an online workshop to train activists in the art of online facilitation; early the following year the two organizations held another online workshop for labour council and other activists from across the country to share experiences and mobilize for May Day 2000.[24]

While the Athabasca programme made online education a priority in its work with the labour movement, it was also interested in finding ways to make the connection between union education and post-secondary labour studies programmes as seamless as possible. In practice, this meant working out a mechanism to award university credits for union education. In the early 1990s the university began granting credits to students who had graduated from the Labour College of Canada's residential programme and the CAW's PEL programme. This proved to be straightforward in that the materials and instruction in these courses were clearly at a post-secondary level and a credit equivalent could be determined and defended easily. In the case of the standard weekend and week-long courses on steward training, collective bargaining and so forth, however, the process of determining credit equivalencies proved to be more difficult. At the end of the 1990s, Athabasca programme staff were reviewing a variety of union education programmes to determine their credit equivalencies and building a template to allow them to easily grant credit for specific courses. Capilano College in North Vancouver and George Brown College in Toronto also developed assessment and recognition mechanisms during the 1990s.

These efforts by college and university labour studies programmes to grant credit for union education took place in the context of a broader debate among governments, employers, unions and educational institutions about the uses and abuses of what was generally known in Canada as Prior Learning Assessment and Recognition (PLAR). The purposes of PLAR (or, as the labour movement preferred, Recognition of Prior Learning) were to take account of the learning that an individual had acquired in a variety of settings during his or her lifetime and to formally recognize that learning in an educational institution, a workplace or in some other way. As government and employer enthusiasm for PLAR developed, however, labour observers concluded that the concept, while potentially useful for workers, posed some dangers. Unions were interested in ensuring that the skills and knowledge of their members were properly valued by employers and educational institutions. However, employers were interested primarily in streamlining the training system to avoid duplication and, according to labour, pitting workers against each other based on credentialism and credit inflation. Educational institutions, for their part, saw PLAR as a means of attracting students to their programmes and were more concerned with assessment than recognition. In a PLAR "values" statement prepared as part of the New Approaches to Lifelong Learning research network at the end of the 1990s, labour education and training activists concluded that PLAR should recognize the skills and knowledge that workers had acquired, benefit working people as a whole, be learner-centred and not undermine existing provisions for hiring, promotion, education and training in negotiated collective agreements.[25]

Besides working to bridge the gap between union education and post-secondary labour studies, the Athabasca programme also tried to link the various college and university programmes more closely together to provide labour studies students across the country with a wider range of course options. While labour studies programmes in traditional institutions provided a service to the local geographic area in which they were located, Athabasca was national in scope because of its distance delivery format. Hence it was ideally suited to work with other institutions to coordinate offerings so that, for example, a student in the University of Manitoba programme could take a mix of Athabasca and Manitoba courses for his or her credential. While older university-based programmes showed little interest in using this opportunity to expand options for their students, others were more forthcoming. When Laurentian University launched its new labour and trade union studies programme in 2000, for example, a formal collaboration agreement allowed students to take any Athabasca labour studies course as part of their Laurentian programme. Athabasca staff hoped that similar agreements elsewhere, combined with a national system of PLAR for union education, would eventually create a network of labour studies programmes across the country that would allow each student to build an optimal programme that took full account of his or her previous learning.[26]

Laurentian's new programme brought university-level labour studies to north-eastern Ontario for the first time, although Cambrian College in Sudbury did offer a labour studies programme for a few years in the 1970s. Mercedes Steedman and Peter Suschnigg worked closely with the local labour movement to put together a programme that was sensitive to the needs of working people in the Sudbury basin and promised to be a model of university-union cooperation. Further south in Ontario, the McMaster programme continued to offer a certificate in conjunction with the Hamilton and District Labour Council and a successful undergraduate degree. Furthermore, McMaster negotiated an innovative arrangement with the CAW at the end of the 1990s to offer a certificate specifically for workers employed by the Big Three auto manufacturers. The union's collective agreements with General Motors, Ford and Chrysler allowed for tuition rebates for university courses, but few members took advantage of this provision. The purpose of the CAW-McMaster certificate was to capture some of this potential money in a university programme that benefited the union and its membership. CAW and McMaster staff cooperated to develop a curriculum highlighting CAW history and the economic and political context of autoworkers. Face-to-face classes were held in the communities where the workers lived and were supplemented by Internet-based discussions. In the neighbouring Niagara Peninsula, Niagara College's pioneering programme continued to serve local trade unionists, while Brock University in St. Catharines launched an undergraduate degree as part of its regular Faculty of Arts programming.[27]

McMaster University-Canadian Autoworkers Labour Studies Certificate description:

McMaster University and the CAW have formed a partnership to develop a certificate programme in labour studies that will address the needs of autoworkers who wish to pursue life-long learning at the university level, but who cannot participate in traditional educational formats. The McMaster-CAW Certificate in Labour Studies will offer university-level certificate courses designed specifically for autoworkers that will integrate classroom education and computer mediated education. The certificate courses will be delivered by a combination of face-to-face instruction, computer conferencing, video conferencing and self-directed learning via the Internet and CD ROMs.

Certificate Philosophy

The Certificate will be grounded in principles of adult education.

There must be a connection between education and collective change in our working lives, communities and society.

Education has an important role in building a knowledgeable membership and workplace leadership.

An educational program will develop members capacities for critical thinking.

The learning process is built upon a commitment to participants that translates into respect for prior experience, skills and activism.

The educational program creates a learning culture that continues when classes end.

There is a commitment to weave an inclusive analysis of gender, race and sexual orientation into all educational content and process.

Source: McMaster University Labour Studies Programme Website (http://www.socsci.mcmaster.ca/~labrst/cawindex.htm)

In Toronto, meanwhile, York University developed an interdisciplinary labour studies undergraduate degree designed primarily for regular post-high-school students. It also ran a Centre for Research on Work and Society (CRWS) that worked closely with the labour movement on projects of mutual interest. Among other things, the centre was the home of the Labour Education and Training research network in the late 1990s and in 2000 that brought together academic and labour researchers to investigate a variety of subjects related mostly to union-related training but with some attention to union education. Also in Toronto, George Brown College replaced Humber College in the mid-1980s as the collaborating educational institution with the Labour Council of Metropolitan Toronto and York Region. At the same time the labour council formed its own Metro Labour Education Centre (MLEC) to offer labour education programming to trade unionists in the city. MLEC offered a range of courses from basic tools training to issues courses such as labour history. In the 1990s its curriculum included the fullest complement of union-based computer and Internet training courses in the country. The centre's arrangement with George Brown College was unique in that MLEC delivered its own Certificate in Labour Studies that was accredited by the college: all of the courses were developed and delivered by MLEC, but successful participants received a George Brown certificate and attended a graduation ceremony at the college.[28]

St. Francis Xavier University's long involvement with labour education in Atlantic Canada came to an end with the demise of the Atlantic Region Labour Education Centre (ARLEC) when the federal government withdrew its labour education grant in 1997. While trade unionists across the region protested and lamented the loss of this twenty-five-year-old programme, the adult education and extension departments at the university had lost their commitment to labour education by that time. Rather, the legacy of the Antigonish Movement—as expressed in StFX's Coady International Institute—was directed to popular-education projects in the developing world. Capilano College continued to have the most important programme in British Columbia, despite the CLC's ongoing refusal to cooperate with it. The congress finally ended its boycott in 1998 when it worked with the college to organize a provincial conference on unions and training, signalling the end of the cold war in British Columbia labour education. Simon Fraser University greeted the new century with an announcement that it was developing an undergraduate degree in labour studies to complement its non-credit work in the area. A succession of energetic directors—including Elaine Bernard, Kate Braid and Tom Nesbit—developed a varied continuing education programme in the 1980s and 1990s to serve trade unionists in British Columbia's lower mainland. The Summer Institute for Union Women was especially successful.

In Winnipeg, which had the longest continuing history of labour-university collaboration in the country by century's end, the thirty-five-year-old certificate programme almost closed in the late 1990s when the University of Manitoba threatened to terminate its relationship with the Manitoba Federation of Labour (MFL). While an advisory group of sympathetic academics controlled the content of the programme in consultation with the relevant union educational committees, the certificate was administered by the Faculty of Continuing Education's management education division. These administrators, besides having little sympathy for or understanding of labour education, were under pressure from their bosses to make money—or at least break even—on the courses that they controlled. While teaching managers the latest fad for reengineering the firm might turn a profit, running a programme that helped workers think critically about the world around them was less lucrative. The MFL cast around for other potential partners, but in the end the university granted a reprieve on the understanding that the labour movement would make a greater effort to attract more paying participants.[29]

During the 1990s, university-based labour educators made an unsuccessful attempt to form a national organization in which they could discuss common problems and exchange experiences. In the spring of 1993 a small group met at a session of the annual conference of the Society for Socialist Studies to discuss Labour Education in Canada: Toward a National Network?, and agreed that an effort should be made to build a national association (the idea had also been discussed in the 1992 Solinet computer conference on labour education). Six months later a separate group met informally at a CRWS-organized conference on lean production and arrived at the same conclusion. Discussions between representatives of the two groups led to an organizational meeting in the spring of 1994 at which the Canadian Labour Education and Research Association (CLERA) was born. Capilano College's Ed Lavalle, who convened the 1994 meeting, became secretary-treasurer of the new organization and Larry Haiven, with the University of Saskatchewan's labour studies programme, was named president.

CLERA's founders agreed that the association should be open to labour educators in unions and educational institutions and the initial response was positive. Most college and university labour studies programmes outside of Quebec (and one from Quebec) joined, as did a few union educational departments. Others joined as individuals. A regular newsletter appeared and an e-mail list was established to exchange information. The centrepiece of the association's activities, however, was a conference that was held annually for three years. The first two were held in conjunction with the annual "Learned Societies" meetings that brought together social science and humanities academics from across the country, while the third in 1997 coincided with the CLC/AFL-CIO Educ-Action conference in Toronto. The 1995 conference in Montreal was a great success. Sessions were held on work reorganization, programmes and pedagogy in labour education, women and the labour movement, unions and community economic development, and sovereignty and the labour movement in Quebec. When the association met at Brock University in St. Catharines, Ontario in 1996, however, enthusiasm for the project had apparently waned and attendance was low. The Toronto meeting the following year was more successful, in part because joint sessions were held with the U.S.-based University and College Labor Education Association, which was co-sponsoring the Educ-Action with the CLC and the AFL-CIO.

After the Educ-Action conference, however, CLERA seemed to languish. Part of the reason was that Ed Lavalle, who kept the information flowing, moved on from the Capilano programme to the presidency of his provincial union, the College and Institute Educators Association. But Lavalle needed information and assistance from his colleagues to do his job, and these were not forthcoming. Many were preoccupied with activities in one or more of the federal government's Social Sciences and Humanities Research Council of Canada-funded education and training research networks, which began operation in 1997. The Labour Education and Training and the New Approaches to Lifelong Learning networks, in particular, included many participants who had been active in CLERA. More fundamentally, however, CLERA's founders may have set the association up for failure by being too ambitious from the outset. The 1994 meeting drafted a constitution, established significant membership fees and produced an extensive list of objectives, but perhaps the new edifice was more than its members could sustain. One issue on which the association floundered was its relationship with the labour movement. There were a few union educators involved in CLERA, but it was primarily an organization of university- and college-based people. Yet, many in the association wanted it to be a place where they could exchange ideas with union-based educators, even though union educators were showing little apparent interest in the association. Others felt that, while union involvement was desirable, perhaps the association should concentrate on the concerns and preoccupations of university and college labour studies programmes.

CLERA - poor relationship with labour movement

A CLERA-sponsored meeting at the 1999 CLC convention in Toronto attracted a healthy turnout, including a number of union educators. The group concluded, as had similar groups in 1993, that a national network of labour educators was necessary. A number of those present committed to using the association's e-mail list to share information and discuss issues. While there was a slight increase in online activity, Canadian labour educators outside of unions have yet to solve the problem of how they connect, communicate and discuss common concerns.[30]

Conclusion

Union education in Canada at the end of the century was marked by a new dynamism and flourished in spite of the loss of government funding for CLC programming. Indeed, according to some, there was a contradiction between government support and the increasingly political and activist education that was developing. Employer aggressiveness and governmental retreat from its broader obligations to citizens were creating a climate in which unions had to ensure that their members were fully informed about a variety of issues and, more importantly, that they could be mobilized in support of workplace actions and broader political campaigns. The CAW's and CUPW's paid educational leave programmes, which provided explicit analyses of the relationship between employers, workers and governments in a capitalist society, were the most substantial programmes of this kind. However, shorter sessions designed for weekend and week-long schools, such as NUPGE's courses on defending the public sector or PSAC's organizing courses, revealed a willingness on the part of union educators and their political leaders to infuse their programmes with content that moved beyond industrial relations training.

Peer education and popular education techniques played a large role in the way Canadian union educators delivered their programmes. Yet, as the CAW PEL experience revealed, some material was not conducive to experiential learning. Whether peer or more highly trained instructors were used, a sophisticated understanding of the broader social world in which workers lived required some engagement with textual material (often based on the work of university-based researchers).

College and university labour studies programmes, meanwhile, were thriving across the country at century's end. And, while the CLC's 1970s-era guidelines for collaborating with colleges and universities in the delivery of labour education were still on the books, the specific practice on the ground was determined more by the degree of trust that existed among the key players than by any direction that came from Ottawa. Local initiatives, such as the McMaster-CAW certificate and the Laurentian University labour and trade union studies credential, were promising collaborative examples, while Athabasca University's pan-Canadian programme worked with selected national organizations. And the attention some unions, colleges and universities were paying to prior learning assessment and recognition suggested that one significant barrier from the past might be broken down. Nevertheless, the degree of cooperation between labour educators inside and outside of unions was generally limited in Canada in comparison to other countries, especially the United States. Some union educators felt that Canada's "worker-centred" union education compared favourably with that of the U.S., where unions relied on colleges and universities to deliver part of their basic tools training. As a result, they felt that Canadian union education suffered from too close an association with academics (who, of course, were themselves members of unions). CLERA's inability to sustain itself was partly a result of this suspicion.

Notes

1. Craig Heron, *The Canadian Labour Movement: A Short History*, 2nd ed. (Toronto: James Lorimer and Company, 1996), chapters 5 and 6; Alvin Finkel, *Our Lives: Canada Since 1945* (Toronto: James Lorimer and Company, 1997), 281-304, 381-385; Jeff Taylor, "Labour in the Klein Revolution," in Gordon Laxer and Trevor Harrison, eds., *The Trojan Horse: Alberta and the Future of Canada* (Montreal: Black Rose Books, 1995).

2. Gordon Selman, Mark Selman, Michael Cooke, and Paul Dampier, *The Foundations of Adult Education in Canada*, 2d ed. (Toronto: Thompson Educational Publishing, 1998), 373-403.

3. *Canadian Labour Education at a Glance*. Booklet prepared for Educ-Action: Union Building for the 21st Century, Toronto, April 1997 (Ottawa: Canadian Labour Congress, 1997); Winston Gereluk, *Labour Education in Canada: A Research Report from the Field* (Athabasca, Alta.: Athabasca University, 2000), 50, 121-123.

4. D'Arcy Martin, "Building Capacity, Caring and Craft," keynote speech to the annual conference of the Canadian Association for Adult Education, Winnipeg, June 1996, 9.

5. Bruce Spencer, "Educating Union Canada," *The Canadian Journal for the Study of Adult Education* 8 (2) (November 1994): 56-57; *Toolbox for Global Solidarity* (Ottawa: Canadian Labour Congress, 1996).

6. National Archives of Canada (NAC), *Canadian Labour Congress (CLC) Papers*, MG 28 I 103, Accession 93/0297, Volume 38, file "Political Education," Preliminary Election Review, unsigned, undated (but fall 1988); Interview with Pat Kerwin, 17 April 2000.

7. Interview with D'Arcy Martin, 13 April 2000.

8. *Educ-Action: Union Building for the 21st Century: Report on the Educ-Action Conference, Toronto, Canada, April 10-12, 1997* (Ottawa: Canadian Labour Congress, 1998); Special Labour Education Conference Issue, *Our Times* (September-October 1997); David Noble, "Digital Diploma Mills," http://communication.ucsd.edu/dl ; David Noble, "Comeback of an education racket," *Le Monde diplomatique* (April 2000), 15.

9. NAC, *CLC Papers*, MG 28 I 103, Accession 93/0297, Volume 2, file "D4. Labour Education and Studies Centre," Secretary's Report to CLC Educational Services Board of Directors Meeting, 7 December 1987.

10. Spencer, "Educating Union Canada," 54-56; Nicholas Saul, "'Organizing the Organized': The Canadian Auto Workers' Paid Educational Leave (PEL) Programme," Master of Arts thesis (University of Warwick, 1994), 21-30; Reuben Roth, "'Kitchen Economics for the Family': Paid Education Leave and The Canadian Autoworkers Union," Master of Arts thesis (Ontario Institute for Studies in Education/University of Toronto, 1997), chapter 4. The CAW PEL programme changed again in the late 1990s to include, among other things, more popular education techniques.

11. Gereluk, *Labour Education in Canada*, 127-128; *Canadian Labour Education at a Glance*.

12. NAC, *CLC Papers*, MG 28 I 103, Accession 93/0297, Volume 38, file "Labour College General 1986," Labour College of Canada Instructors to Shirley Carr, Chair, Board of Governors, Labour College of Canada, 14 July 1986, Richard Mercier to Shirley Carr, 24 August 1986, and Fred Pomeroy, President, Communications and Electrical Workers of Canada to Shirley Carr, 23 September 1986.

13. NAC, *CLC Papers*, MG 28 I 103, 93/0297, Volume 38, file "Labour College General 1986," Dick Martin to Shirley Carr, 3 December 1986, and Volume 2, file "D2. Labour College of Canada," Minutes of a special meeting of the Board of Governors, 25 March 1987.

14. NAC, *CLC Papers*, MG 28 I 103, Accession 93/0297, Volume 2, file "D2. Labour College of Canada," eight women students to Nancy Riche, 30 June 1987, Richard Martin, Executive Vice-President, Canadian Labour Congress to the seventeen women students at the 1987 Labour College of Canada residential session, 21 March 1988, male student to Dick Martin, 10 April 1988, and female student to Dick Martin, 28 April 1988; NAC, *CLC Papers*, MG 28 I 103, Accession 93/0297, Volume 38, file "Labour College of Canada 1986," Noel Stoodley to Dick Martin, 30 November 1987, and file "Labour College of Canada 1988-89," Minutes of a meeting of the Curriculum Development Advisory Committee, 8 March 1988 and Report of the Registrar and Secretary-Treasurer to the Meeting of the Board of Governors, 13 September 1988.

15. Sidney Ingerman, *Economics for Canadian Trade Unionists* 2d ed. (Ottawa: Labour College of Canada, 1985).

16. NAC, *CLC Papers*, MG 28 I 103, Accession 93/0297, Volume 2, file "D2. Labour College of Canada," Minutes of a special meeting of the Board of Governors, 25 March 1987; *Interim Report of the Labour College Review Committee*, 18 September 1995 (Ottawa: Labour College of Canada, 1995).

17. Some of the material in this section is based on information in the author's personal files; "Stoodley director of CLC Educational Services," *Canadian Labour* (April 1985).

18. D'Arcy Martin, *Building A Solid Foundation: Next Steps in the UFCW* (Toronto: National Training Programme, United Food and Commercial Workers Union, 1998); various reports from training centre directors to UFCW Training Directors Meeting, Winnipeg, December 1998; Jim Sutherland, "A Trade Union Approach to Learning Strategies in a Global Economy," paper presented to the Canadian Labour Congress/Ontario Federation of Labour Training Conference, Toronto, June 1998.

19. *OFL Focus*, 6 June 1989; Lori A. Stinson O'Gorman, "Popular Education and Working-Class Consciousness: A Critical Examination of the Saskatchewan Federation of Labour's Workers' Education for Skills Training Program," in Thomas Dunk, Stephen McBride, and Randle W. Nelsen, eds., *The Training Trap: Ideology, Training and the Labour Market* (Halifax: Fernwood Publishing, 1996), 167-192; Jean Connon Unda and Sandra Clifford, "Instructor Empowerment in the Ontario Federation of Labour's Best Project," in Maurice C. Taylor, ed., *Workplace Education: The Changing Landscape* (Toronto: Culture Concepts, 1997), 145-162. Go to www.thompsonbooks.com/unionlearning to see a video clip from *BEST for Us*, a film about the BEST project.

20. Bob White, "Training On Union Terms," speech presented to *CLC National Training Conference*, Ottawa, June 1997; "Workshop Reports," *CLC National Training Conference*, Ottawa, June 1997.

21. The "Training" page on the CLC web site at www.clc-ctc.ca (in development at the time of publication) contains a variety of union-related training materials gathered as part of the Workplace Training Strategy, including papers, speeches, conference reports, and databases of union training documents, bargaining language, union-friendly researchers, and training activists (although the last database is not accessible to the public). The page also contains information about the CLC's Workplace Literacy Project, which coordinated and facilitated labour's literacy work.

22. "In Defense of Public Post-Secondary Education," in National Union's Education and Training Working Group, *Position Papers: Post-Secondary Public Education and Related Topics* (Ottawa: National Union of Public and General Employees, 1998), 3. The NUPGE case is also made in Susan Hoddinott and Jim Overton, "Dismantling Public Provision of Adult Basic Education: The Anti-Literacy Politics of Newfoundland's Literacy Campaign," in Dunk, McBride, and Nelsen, eds., *The Training Trap*, 193-222.

23. *CLC Protocol on the Delivery of Training, Education and Employment Services*, prepared by John Anderson (Ottawa: Canadian Labour Congress, 1998).

24. Jeff Taylor "The Continental Classroom: Teaching Labour Studies On-Line," *Labor Studies Journal* 21(1) (Spring 1996); Jeff Taylor, "The Solidarity Network: Universities, Computer-Mediated Communication, and Labor Studies in Canada," in Teresa M. Harrison and Timothy Stephen, eds., *Computer Networking and Scholarly Communication in the Twenty-First-Century University* (Albany: State University of New York Press, 1996); Bruce Spencer and Jeff Taylor, "Labour Education in Canada: A Solinet Conference," *Labour/Le Travail* 34 (fall 1994). Go to http://unionlearning.athabascau.ca to see a video clip of Eric Lee, author of *The Labour Movement and the Internet: The New Internationalism* (London: Pluto Press, 1997), discussing his experience of conducting a 1997 Solinet workshop.

25. Bruce Spencer, "Workplace Learning, PLAR and Learning Labour," in *Researching Work and Learning Conference Proceedings*, University of Leeds, United Kingdom, 10-12 September 1999, 280-290; Peter H. Sawchuk, *Building Learning Capacities in the Community and Workplace Project: Final Report of the Industrial Workplace Skills and Knowledge Profiling Research* (Toronto: Advocates for Community-Based Training and Education for Women, 1998); PLAR-Labour Working Group, "A Labour Perspective on Prior Learning Assessment and Recognition" (Toronto: New Approaches to Lifelong Learning, 1999).

26. "Collaborations," Athabasca University Labour Studies Programme Website, http://www.athabascau.ca/html/depts/workcomm/labourst.htm.

27. "CAW/McMaster Certificate," McMaster University Labour Studies Programme Website, http://www.socsci.mcmaster.ca/~labrst/cawindex.htm.

28. Metro Labour Education Centre Website, www.mlec.org.

29. The material in this section is drawn from information in the author's personal files. See Gerald Friesen, "H.C. Pentland and Continuing Education at the University of Manitoba: Teaching Labour History to Trade Unionists," *Labour/Le Travail* 31 (Spring 1993), for a first-hand account of teaching labour history in this programme, and Dennis Haughey, "From Passion to Passivity: The Decline of University Extension for Social Change," in Sue M. Scott, Bruce Spencer, and Alan M. Thomas, eds., *Learning for Life: Canadian Readings in Adult Education* (Toronto: Thompson Educational Publishing, 1998) for a general critique of the commercialization of continuing education in Canada.

30. The material in this section is based on information in the author's personal files, including CLERA newsletters and correspondence.

CHAPTER 7

Conclusion

Drummond Wren and his fellow activists in the Workers' Educational Association attempted to create a non-sectarian, militant, autonomous and critical educational movement that appealed to all parts of the labour movement and linked workers to available post-secondary educational resources. Their dream was extinguished when the union leadership marginalized the association between 1947 and 1951. For the following thirty years or more, labour organizations developed and expanded their own educational programmes designed primarily to train stewards and local leaders to participate effectively in the country's industrial relations system. As social and economic conditions deteriorated for workers in the 1970s and 1980s, however, and as the composition of the labour movement changed, new voices appeared in union education to challenge the form and content of inherited practices. By the 1990s a new emphasis on broad-based activist education existed throughout the labour movement, promising to rekindle the sense of an educational movement that had been present in the 1930s and 1940s.

The core of the union education curriculum remained constant from the first significant union courses in the late 1930s through to the end of the century. Stewards, committee persons and local union leaders had to be trained to represent their members in the workplace and to use the industrial relations machinery effectively. In the 1940s, when the industrial unions were young and collective bargaining legislation was new, this basic training had an activist edge to it. In the communist-led unions in particular, but also in the United Automobile Workers (UAW) and others, stewards and local leaders were expected to mobilize their members as well as provide them with fair representation under the relevant collective agreements. UAW courses, for example, stressed that stewards were part of a shop-floor movement that dated from the teens, and the union's training was meant to strengthen and maintain that movement. With the stabilization of labour institutions after 1950, however, steward and local-leadership training settled into a pattern in which the techniques of contract interpretation and grievance representation were emphasized, while broader issues of mobilization became less important. However, when governments and employers began to rewrite the rules of labour-capital relations after 1975, many union educators and their political masters realized that the old ways of training local activists were no longer adequate. As a result, organizing and mobilizing themes re-entered steward training, and by the 1990s it was rare to encounter a course that dealt only with the nut-and-bolts of collective agreements.

The broader issues courses covered a wide range from the 1930s to the 1990s. In the Workers' Educational Association (WEA) days, the evening programmes included academic subjects such as literature and psychology or history and economics. Shorter institutes on particular pieces of industrial relations legislation or sector-specific subjects such as the history of the automobile industry were also offered. As the Canadian Labour Congress (CLC) and its larger affiliates developed substantial programmes in the 1950s and 1960s, the academic subjects disappeared for the most part, although labour history, economics for trade unionists and the psychology of union leadership closely paralleled more traditional academic offerings. Most issues courses in these years were concerned with making the industrial relations system work for trade unionists, with supplementary offerings in areas such as international affairs and political action. A minority Marxist current persisted in those communist-led unions that used the services of the Trade Union Research Bureau in Vancouver. In the 1970s, however, issues courses across the movement began to develop a more critical and activist tone. International affairs courses analyzed the role of transnational corporations in the global economy, political education was geared to mobilizing members to become politically active and new courses were offered to equip members with the skills they required to face employers who were reorganizing workplaces. This trend continued through the 1980s and 1990s, with public-sector unions in particular mounting a variety of courses designed to counter governmental efforts to privatize and reduce public services.

Courses for and about women were a feature of union educationals from the 1930s to the 1990s. In the WEA years these courses addressed issues such as the role of women in unions and the experience of women in the workplace. And, as the photographs of WEA Ontario summer schools in this book suggest, a significant number of women attended labour educational events in the 1940s. During the 1950s and 1960s, however, the focus narrowed in the CLC and most affiliate programmes to courses such as The Union Widow, offering advice to the wives of male labour activists, or millinery and needle work. The UAW and some other unions did offer courses and conferences addressing women members as workers and trade unionists, but the dominant tone in this period was that women were homemakers who were not part of the labour market. This attitude began to change in the 1970s under the influence of the women's movement and as a result of the increasing number of trade union women. Women's caucuses and eventually women's committees demanded more space for women and their concerns in educational programming and, by the 1980s, there were even women-only courses in week-long schools. And, as a result of incidents such as those that were reported to have taken place at the 1987 residential session of the Labour College of Canada, sexual harassment policies became a standard feature of union schools.

Many popular educators who entered union education in the 1970s, 1980s and 1990s believed that they were confronting another bastion of traditional, hierarchical and undemocratic educational practices. However, union educators have always struggled with the problem of how to balance the experiences that workers bring to the classroom with the material that is being taught. When Leo Huberman and Gerry Culhane taught their course on trade unionism at the 1945 WEA summer school in British Columbia, for example, workers' experiences were used to test the material that the instructors were conveying. And when workers' theatre troupes showed WEA summer school participants how dramatic techniques could be used in union activities, they anticipated later popular educators' participatory approaches. While some of these worker-centred methods were lost as union education became more focused on industrial relations training after 1950, many union educators stayed abreast of developments in adult education, and small-group discussion, role-playing, audio-visual usage and buzz groups remained features of labour programmes in the 1960s and 1970s. Some union educators did succumb to workplace-training techniques, such as programmed instruction, and others, such as those at St. Francis Xavier University, used learner-centred techniques for conservative purposes.

In order to improve and enhance their teaching, Canadian labour educators have made extensive and, at times, innovative use of educational technologies. From the beginning they were faced with the problem of providing educational opportunities to trade unionists spread from Nova Scotia on the Atlantic coast to British Columbia on the Pacific. The WEA was able to take advantage of publicly owned communications resources that were available during the Second World War to institute labour-related radio programming and a Trade Union Film Circuit that included some union-specific film production. Moreover, the association integrated these media into a mass education strategy that also included film strips, short training institutes, discussion groups, study circles and university-level instruction. The National Film Boards's *Labour in Canada* series of the 1950s was a staple feature of union education courses well into the 1970s, but the labour movement's role in determining the content and scope of these and other productions during this period was limited. The audio-visual capacity that the CLC was able to develop after 1977 with its Labour Canada grant held the promise of re-creating the WEA experience, but the results were disappointing. While a tremendous amount of footage was shot during the audio-visual department's twenty years of operation, and a number of good productions were made to accompany courses and workshops or to benefit affiliates, a strategy was never devised to determine how audio-visual resources were to be used as part of overall educational programming. Such a comprehensive strategy may have been politically impossible. When we look at what the WEA was able to achieve with more limited resources, however, it is hard not to conclude that a significant amount of money was wasted on projects that had little use or appeal.

The Solinet experience with computer communications, meanwhile, paralleled the WEA's use of film in that in both cases a forward-thinking faction of the labour movement experimented with new communications technologies to determine how they could be used for union purposes. Marc Belanger, like Drummond Wren, was faced with building a communications capacity that could serve a large country. Belanger, unlike Wren, ran a union technology department rather than a workers' educational association. He therefore teamed up with labour educators to develop labour-relevant content. While Solinet had a relatively short life at CUPE, it did allow educators to test the technology and develop some capacity in the area. It remains to be seen whether or not the technology becomes incorporated into union educational programmes as part of coherent strategies, or is used only as an occasional technique.

The labour movement's ability to use educational technologies has often relied on its access to government funding or public resources, and its experience in this area has been mixed. The WEA made good use of its wartime access to the Canadian Broadcasting Corporation and the National Film Board. Though the radio and film projects were shortlived and there were limited resources available, Wren and the association were able to incorporate these new media into a broader workers' education strategy. The limits of wartime liberalism were tested, however, when the radio broadcasts contained material about workplace conditions that was deemed to be too critical of the government's war effort. And post-war reaction ensured that the semi-autonomous union film circuits could not be sustained. Thirty years later the CLC received its substantial grant from the federal government to provide internal union education. With the freedom to use the money as it saw fit as long as the education dealt in some way with the collective bargaining system, the congress developed instructional materials, offered advanced programming and established a sophisticated audio-visual production facility. During the twenty years of funding, however, CLC programming and the Labour College of Canada became dependent on the federal government support. When the cheques stopped coming in the late 1970s, union educators had to scramble to ensure that they could continue to mount credible programmes, especially at the college.

Max Swerdlow and other senior union educators emerged from the 1956 university-labour conference determined to forge new alliances with post-secondary educational institutions. They particularly wanted partners to help them realize their dream of building a labour college to provide advanced instruction for future labour leaders. They believed that the best possible advanced training that such students could have was to be taught relevant social science courses at a university standard by regular professors. The eventual arrangement with McGill and Montreal universities meant that trade unionists were plucked from their jobs, dropped into a regular university routine for eight weeks and expected to work at least as hard (if not harder) than regular undergraduate students. They studied course material that was generally relevant to their experiences, but only occasionally union-friendly. Indeed, professors who taught in the college during the 1960s, such as H.D. Woods, believed that students should be taught "objectively," which meant offering a standard economics or industrial relations course in the same way it would be taught to management students or regular undergraduates. The early college, then, was unique to the extent that it was designed for trade unionists (although management students were welcome to attend for a number of years), and future leaders could mingle with their own kind for a couple of months, but the course materials and the pedagogical approach were no different than what was found in non-labour programmes.

This changed somewhat following the late 1970s review and after the college moved from Montreal to Ottawa. The review noted the traditional teaching methods that were being used and suggested that adult education methods be employed. And the move from Montreal to Ottawa coincided with a shift from an instructional staff composed of regular university professors to part-time instructors drawn from the ranks of university graduate programmes or progressive organizations. These people were often immersed in the more critical and labour-friendly approaches that emerged in the social science disciplines from the late 1960s onward. The instructors' "strike" of 1982-83, besides provoking Dennis McDermott to utter some intemperate remarks, revealed a degree of consciousness among the staff and a level of solidarity between students and staff that would have been unthinkable ten to twenty years earlier.

By the 1990s, the course material used in the college was uniformly labour-friendly. With few exceptions, however, the university regime of term papers, examinations, lectures and limited discussion still reigned. The college had been largely bypassed by the shift to worker-centred learning and worker-to-worker teaching that had become a feature of union education generally in Canada. Furthermore, the vision of the college as a comprehensive bridge between the union and post-secondary educational systems, as had been envisioned in the Martin reports in the 1960s and the Hepworth Labour Education and Studies feasibility report of the 1970s, was largely forgotten. While still providing a valuable service to the Canadian labour movement at the end of the century, there was much more that the Labour College of Canada could accomplish.

As the college's early attempts to establish a collaborative arrangement with certain universities illustrate, the relationship between the labour movement and post-secondary educational institutions has been difficult. The original WEA system was based on university cooperation, with the association bridging the gulf between worker-students and the alien culture of academe. While this approach provided some trade unionists with educational opportunities, it had limited appeal. Despite the efforts of sympathetic academic staff to soften the edges of traditional university pedagogy, most workers were either uninterested in or unprepared for university-level instruction. Wren and his colleagues recognized this problem in the inherited WEA model, and hence developed their mass education strategy linking advanced education to visual education, short courses and other delivery media. An incipient model of educational progression was in place in the late 1940s when the association was forced out of its central role in Canadian labour education.

At the same time that the WEA was maturing, St. Francis Xavier University in Nova Scotia was establishing its peculiar brand of labour education designed to support and bolster the more conservative forces in the labour movement. Using the Antigonish Movement's allegedly progressive pedagogical techniques, the university's extension service ran a varied programme in which the central message was that responsible trade unionists should avoid militancy in favour of labour-capital cooperation. The message and techniques remained the same when this Catholic crusade shifted its focus to Sudbury in the late 1950s, and education played an important role in the struggle for control of the International Union of Mine, Mill and Smelter Workers (Mine-Mill) Local 598.

From the early 1950s to the early 1970s, union educators made occasional overtures to universities that were largely uninterested in labour education. The 1956 conference promised to launch a new era of cooperation between the two sectors. While a significant and enduring programme was launched in Winnipeg, little else was accomplished. Individual unions such as the International Association of Machinists and Aerospace Workers (IAM) worked with universities on specific projects, and various sympathetic professors were features of union educational programmes in these decades, but a broad-based cooperative strategy never developed or showed signs of developing. Even when the labour movement went looking for a partner for its labour college proposal, it was rebuffed by two universities that were apparently unwilling to provide a direct service to Canadian workers.

As universities became more responsive in the 1970s, and as community colleges developed with mandates to serve a variety of social constituencies, the labour movement ironically began to erect barriers to cooperation with post-secondary institutions. By this time Canadian unions had developed an extensive and sophisticated system of internal education, and many union educators were apprehensive about the intentions of the new college- and university-based labour studies programmes. They wanted to ensure that the new programmes did not encroach on what was perceived to be the union turf of tools-training courses. In addition, some union educators and labour leaders apparently believed that any labour-related education that was directed at organized workers should be under the control of union leaders and staff people. This position became entrenched when the CLC received its unprecedented grant from the federal government for labour education. Despite the reservations registered by some university-based educators, the congress leadership adopted and publicized a formal policy dictating that labour organizations would control any joint programmes involving unions and colleges or universities. Unfortunately, one of the outcomes of this hard-line approach was that opportunities were lost to develop comprehensive relationships between the labour movement—or even specific labour organizations—and post-secondary institutions to serve the varied educational interests of union members.

By the 1990s, however, there were a number of local, regional and national arrangements among labour educators inside and outside unions suggesting that a new era of cooperation might be possible. McMaster University's work with the Canadian Auto Workers (CAW), Laurentian University's good relationship with the Sudbury and District Labour Council, and the labour-university connections in the various education and training research networks, for example, were fruitful collaborations. However, there were no broad-based, comprehensive initiatives such as the one that Wren and the WEA were building in the 1940s. The Canadian Labour Education and Research Association (CLERA) did approach the CLC during the 1994-95 Labour College of Canada review process to propose that the college programme be coordinated with the various labour studies programmes across the country, but it received no response. It was unlikely that a new model of labour-university collaboration would emerge from traditional union education in any event, if only because the antipathy towards college- and university-based educators was so entrenched. Labour-based training was a different story. Here, as the protocol on programme and course delivery confirmed, the public sector and public-sector educational workers were key players. Indeed, the issue for labour-based trainers was how to ensure that the training needs of their members were met in a system in which public-sector provision remained dominant but suffered from decreasing resources and the growth of competing private trainers.

International Context

Twentieth-century Canadian labour education grew as part of a broader international history. Activists developed their own unique approaches while sharing common traditions with other movements, particularly those in the United States, the United Kingdom, Australia and New Zealand. The Workers' Educational Association was a British institution that was transplanted to Canada as well as to Australia, New Zealand and a number of other former and existing colonies. The WEA and the more radical National Council of Labour Colleges in the United Kingdom conducted a critical and independent workers' education during the 1920s and 1930s, designed to appeal to all trade unionists and to provide them with the skills required to understand and, ideally, resist capitalist society. Australia and New Zealand established their own Workers' Educational Associations on the British model in 1913-14. University-based instructors provided evening classes for a working-class constituency on traditional academic subjects as well as more worker-specific concerns such as industrial law. In neither country, however, was the WEA able to establish a firm and ongoing relationship with the labour movement. Militants in the movement chafed at the association's non-partisanship and, in Australia, a U.K.-inspired Plebs League adopted the mantle of the defenders of independent working-class education. In both countries the WEA had evolved into a general adult education provider by the post-war years. In contrast to North America, however, there is no evidence that unions developed their own significant educational capacity in this period.[1]

Wren and his colleagues were also influenced by American developments such as the labour college movement and by union educators such as Mark Starr. More importantly, however, most organized workers in Canada were members of American-based international unions. Older unions such as the International Ladies Garment Workers' Union (ILGWU) and newer ones such as the Steelworkers and the UAW developed their own substantial internal education programmes to serve all of their dues-paying members, including Canadians. The move away from WEA provision in Canada in the late 1940s was at least in part a shift in orientation from British to American practice. However, a similar process was also taking place south of the border. An older autonomous workers' education tradition present in the labour colleges and in some university programmes that emphasized liberal adult education was displaced by internal union programming that focused on industrial relations training. This corresponded to a broader shift in the American labour movement away from the militancy associated with the industrial organizing period to the relatively prosperous 1950s and 1960s, during which American labour made its peace with capitalism and was content to be a subordinate player in the Democratic Party.

Canadian and American experiences between the early 1950s and the early 1970s were similar in some respects and different in others. Internal programmes in the major unions that had their own educational staff and resources were similar across the continent, with the exception that Canadian political education stressed support for a social democratic party while the American labour movement endorsed one of the two capitalist parties. Differences existed, however, in the degree to which the respective labour movements cooperated with post-secondary institutions. The American post-secondary educational system included publicly funded universities in most states that had a responsibility to provide extension services to a variety of social groups, including organized workers. As a result, many university extension services in the United States taught tools and issues courses for unions throughout this period (and, according to current American Federation of Labor-Congress of Industrial Organizations (AFL-CIO) education director Bill Fletcher, kept the flame of critical labour education alive while the labour movement was dominated by business unionism). Canadian universities, in contrast, were mostly reluctant to cooperate with unions even though the labour movement was willing to work with them. The uniquely Canadian Labour College of Canada, built in collaboration with two universities, was the exception that proved the rule of university intransigence.[2]

In the United Kingdom, meanwhile, the Trades Union Congress (TUC) and affiliated unions expanded their own offerings after the Second World War to provide local leaders and activists with industrial relations training. The TUC's takeover of the NCLC and the WEA's union arm in 1964 signalled a centralization of labour education under the labour movement's exclusive control and a shift away from critical and autonomous liberal education towards more technical industrial relations training. While the TUC offered some courses in its own training centre, most of them were provided in collaboration with educational bodies such as universities, the WEA and, increasingly, technical colleges. In Australia and New Zealand, meanwhile, the respective WEAs had become general adult education providers with no specific commitment to workers' education by the 1950s, although there were scattered attempts to serve a trade union constituency. In 1964, for example, the WEA of South Australia pioneered a distance education course for trade unionists in partnership with the Australian Council of Trade Unions and a number of its affiliates, while the New Zealand WEA instituted a similar programme. Generally, however, union education as practiced in the United Kingdom and North America did not exist in these two countries in the 1950s and 1960s. This no doubt was at least partly because of the compulsory conciliation and arbitration systems in place there, which contrasted with the more adversarial industrial relations systems in the United States, Canada and the United Kingdom.[3]

In the final three decades of the century the various national experiences outside of the United States and the United Kingdom converged in some respects. Australia's Labour government emulated the Labour College of Canada when it established its Clyde Cameron College in 1975 under the authority of the *Trade Union Training Authority Act* of the same year. For the following twenty years the federal government provided direct support for the Australian labour movement to offer industrial relations training for its members. Two years later, the Canadian Liberal government followed the Australian example and provided direct funding to the CLC for its internal union education programmes. In New Zealand, meanwhile, a Labour government established a Trade Union Training Board in 1974, composed of union, employer and government representatives, to develop and coordinate industrial relations courses. More significantly, however, ten years later another Labour government established the Trade Union Education Authority, which was government funded, union controlled and provided a modest but legislated right to paid educational leave. By the end of the 1990s, though, the various experiments in state support for union education had come to an end. Governments in all three countries joined the right-wing crusade to reduce public expenditures, including programmes to facilitate orderly industrial relations.[4]

In the United Kingdom, the TUC's focus on industrial relations training was reinforced and deepened as a result of close collaboration with the 1974-79 Labour government. Paid educational leave was provided for union representatives, and union education was funded directly by the government, but investigations of public policy that might lead to criticisms of the Labour Party were discouraged. In contrast to Canada, Australia and New Zealand, where conservative governments cut public funding for labour education, the Thatcher regime of the 1980s maintained the grant. With government representatives joining TUC officials to monitor course content, however, the curriculum was not allowed to stray beyond the technical aspects of workplace relations. While this was the dominant form of United Kingdom labour education in the latter part of the century, there were pockets of alternative activity in the 1990s associated with individual unions and their educational partners. The Transport and General Workers' Union and the University of Surrey, for example, mounted a programme that combined basic skills training, labour history, economic policy and political education.

The dominant technical-training approach to union education continued in the United States during the 1970s and 1980s as well, with university extension services still offering many tools and issues courses. However, a "service model" of labour education developed alongside this "instrumental model" in the 1970s as a result of the growth of public-sector unionization. Unions began offering a variety of educational programmes to their members, including job upgrading, retraining for computer-based occupations and degree programmes. While this was individually oriented education, it did represent a broadening of educational opportunity for trade unionists, albeit in a broader labour environment in which militancy was discouraged. At the end of the 1990s, however, a change of leadership in the AFL-CIO signalled a new approach in which organizing and membership mobilization were aligned more closely with education campaigns.[5]

Viewed in this broader context, Canadian labour education has developed at the intersection of the American and United Kingdom traditions. Prior to 1950 there were some parallels with the United Kingdom, Australian and New Zealand histories to the degree that the WEA in each country played a role in workers' education. The Canadian association was unique in that it tried to make the transition from a university-connected liberal education provider to a comprehensive and integrated labour education organization. Despite this noble effort, however, the Canadians suffered the same fate as their colleagues elsewhere when the respective labour movements marginalized the autonomous worker education movements. In Australia and New Zealand, little labour education took place during the 1950s and 1960s, while in the United Kingdom, the United States and Canada, the labour movement concentrated on its own industrial relations training. United Kingdom unions worked with the WEA and post-secondary educational institutions in collaborations that the labour movement controlled, while American unions allowed some university extension services to deliver some of their courses. The Canadian labour movement became more insular than any of the other four during this period in that, having destroyed the WEA as a mediating force between it and the universities, it was unable and eventually unwilling to enter into any substantial arrangements with external providers.

In the 1950s, 1960s and 1970s, however, the three movements that were involved in labour education in a significant way concentrated on industrial relations training for leaders and activists at the expense of general education for the broader membership. While the Canadian movement began to break with this tradition in the 1970s, it was reinforced in Australia with TUTA, and continued in the United Kingdom through the TUC's support for Labour governments and in the United States through the AFL-CIO's support for the Democratic Party and its continuing belief in the virtues of the capitalist system. The emerging activist orientation in Canada was echoed in New Zealand during the 1980s as the TUEA provided space for a critical labour education to appear. By the late 1990s, when government monies for labour education were disappearing in the Commonwealth countries and a new leadership was changing the face of education in the American movement, the Canadian model of activist education had been maturing for approximately twenty years and there were signs that educational practice was changing in the other four countries as well.

Looking Forward

Canadian labour education is generally vibrant and healthy in 2000. The substantial system of internal union education that was established in the 1950s and 1960s has been recently revitalized with a new wave of activists and popular educators who are ensuring that new voices are heard and that education is connected to various union campaigns designed to mobilize members around a progressive agenda. This new energy suggests that a labour education movement might be developing for the first time since the WEA-inspired activity in the 1930s and 1940s. The earlier movement was able to combine the energy and enthusiasm that came from broader struggles with a comprehensive strategy that linked various levels of provision together, from university-level evening courses to techniques such as film strips designed to spark an interest in education. Union educators today have succeeded in invigorating their internal programmes through a variety of influences, but they have been less successful in developing overall learning strategies for their organizations. What is needed are new approaches that meet the needs of labour organizations for trained and critically engaged workplace representatives, that provide union members with a thorough understanding of the labour movement and its agenda, and that allow trade unionists to gain access to a range of educational opportunities from basic skills to university-level courses. However, accomplishing this requires revisiting the enduring issue of the labour movement's relationship with external educational allies and providers.

How might this happen? An individual union with a developed education and training programme would begin by reviewing its existing provision. The United Food and Commercial Workers (UFCW), for example, provides traditional tools-type union education for its local leaders and stewards and a range of training opportunities for those members who have access to its network of training centres or to specific labour-adjustment programmes. Members may also attend CLC weekend institutes, week-long schools and the Labour College of Canada. With an understanding of the current state of internal education and training, the union would then develop a long-term education and training strategy. One key feature of this strategy would be to establish principles and a framework for negotiating articulation agreements and brokered arrangements with colleges and universities to allow members to progress in their learning beyond internal union education and training. For example, the union might negotiate an arrangement with a university or group of universities to develop a labour studies credential for union members. The agreement might include recognition of prior learning for members' previous union education, the use of peer educators to offer part or all of the credential in the union's training centres, and the use of new learning technologies to make the programme accessible to all members regardless of geographic location or time constraints. Other arrangements with colleges or universities might include credentials in industry-specific skills, taught according to labour's training values and the CLC's education and training protocol.

A renewed Labour College of Canada that was more closely integrated into the CLC's Education and Campaigns department, meanwhile, would provide national, cross-union coordination of labour's internal education and training programmes as well as its brokered arrangements with external providers. The college would begin by reviewing the relationship between internal union education programmes and its residential and distance education courses to ensure that they were complementary. It would also assist affiliates to integrate learning technologies into their programmes in a way that optimized learning opportunities for their members and to ensure progression from basic to more advanced courses in their own educational programmes. It would then review its own programme to increase the use of popular-education methods, peer educators and learning technologies. Finally, it would play its own brokering role with colleges and universities to ensure further opportunities for its own graduates in labour studies and other areas. It would also assist affiliates to broker their own arrangements either individually or in concert with other unions.

The women and men who built the first workers' educational movement in the 1930s and 1940s had few models to follow for guidance. They learned quickly, however, that the inherited British model of university-based provision was ill-suited to the needs of newly organized industrial workers. They therefore cobbled together an incipient system that provided a potential range of educational opportunities for Canadian trade unionists. However, as unions developed their own internal educational capacity in response to the pressing need to develop networks of trained local leaders and workplace representatives, the range of educational activity was narrowed. As a new educational movement takes shape in the Canadian labour movement today, union educators and leaders have seventy-years of experience to guide them. There is no reason why the members they serve cannot expect the best possible opportunities for union learning.

Notes

1. Brian Simon, "The Struggle for Hegemony," in Brian Simon, ed., *The Search for Enlightenment: The Working Class and Adult Education in the Twentieth Century* (London: Lawrence and Wishart, 1990), 15-70; Derek Whitelock, *The Great Tradition: A History of Adult Education in Australia* (St. Lucia: University of Queensland Press, 1974), chapter 6; E.M. Higgins, *David Stewart and the W.E.A.* (Sydney: The Workers Educational Association of New South Wales, 1957), 46-47, 63-70; Gerald Friesen and Lucy Taksa, "Workers' Education in Australia and Canada: A Comparative Approach to Labour's Cultural History," *Labour/Le Travail* 38 (fall 1996): 181-189; Michael Law, "The TUEA experiment: trade union education in New Zealand 1986-1992," *27th Annual SCUTREA Conference Proceedings* (1997), 275.

2. Stanley Aronowitz, "The New Labor Education: A Return to Ideology," in Steven H. London, Elvira R. Tarr, and Joseph F. Wilson, *The Re-education of the American Working Class* (Westport, Conn.: Greenwood Press, 1990), 26-27; Everette J. Freeman and Dale G. Brickner, "Labor Education: A Growth Sector in a Stagnant Industry," in London, Tarr and Wilson, eds., *The Re-education of the American Working Class*, 6-8; author's notes of Bill Fletcher, Address to the Canadian Labour Congress's National Education Advisory Committee meeting, April 1997.

3. John McIlroy, "The Demise of the National Council of Labour Colleges," and "The Triumph of Technical Training?" in Brian Simon, ed., *The Search for Enlightenment*, 173-243; John McIlroy and Bruce Spencer, "Despatches From a Foreign Front: The Decline of Workers' Education in U.K. Universities," *Labor Studies Journal* 17(3) (Fall 1992): 56-57; Whitelock, *The Great Tradition*, 292; "Trade Union Postal Courses," Workers' Educational Association of South Australia, *Annual Report* (1983), 12; Law, "The TUEA Experiment," 276.

4. Friesen and Taksa, "Workers' Education in Australia and Canada," 195; Law, "The TUEA Experiment"; Michael Law, "Workers' Education and Training in a New Environment," in John Benseman, Brian Findsen, and Miriama Scott, eds., *The Fourth Sector: Adult and Community Education in Aotearoa/New Zealand* (Palmerston North: The Dunmore Press, 1996), 166-172.

5. McIlroy and Spencer, "Despatches From a Foreign Front," 57-59, 68-69; Aronowitz, "The New Labor Education," 27-29; Paul Buhle, *Taking Care of Business: Samuel Gompers, George Meany, Lane Kirkland and the Tragedy of American Labor* (New York: Monthly Review Press, 1999), 249-263.

Index

AGMV Marquis

MEMBER OF THE SCABRINI GROUP

Quebec, Canada
2000